# APL IN PRACTICE

The Practical APL Conference
Washington, D.C.
9-11 April 1980

STSC, Inc.

# APL IN PRACTICE

## What You Need to Know
## To Install and Use
## Successful APL Systems
## And Major Applications

Edited by
**ALLEN J. ROSE**
**BARBARA A. SCHICK**
and
Staff from STSC, Inc.

JOHN WILEY & SONS, INC.
New York, Chichester, Brisbane, Toronto

**Library of Congress Cataloging in Publication Data**

Main entry under title:

APL in practice.

    Includes index.
    1.  APL (Computer program language)
2. Interactive computer systems,  I.  Rose,
Allen J.  II.  Schick, Barbara A., 1951-
QA76.73.A27A18        001.64'2       80-5351
ISBN  0-471-08275-9

Printed in the United States of America.

10  9  8  7  6  5  4  3  2

# Foreword

In the early part of the computer era, the cost of the computer itself overshadowed all other costs associated with computing. Over the years, however, engineering advances (in particular the integrated circuit) have steadily chipped away at the cost of computing hardware, and it is no longer the dominant component of computing costs.

Labor costs, particularly systems analysis and programming, are the largest component of computing activity today. This situation has encouraged many researchers to augment the features and usage conventions of tradition- al computing languages to squeeze more efficiency from them.

This book deals neither with new approaches nor with facelifts of proven concepts. Rather, it reports the state of the technology of *APL*, a method of interactive computing introduced in the late 1960s. *APL* is one of the most concise, consistent, and powerful programming languages ever devised. The simplification and efficiency offered by its rich and powerful handling of work involving multiple data structures have saved a great deal of time and money for the organizations that have used it. Its proven benefits, however, have been largely obscured in the literature by the many incremental improvements made to more traditional programming languages.

This book offers some compelling arguments for considering *APL* for business computing. It also serves as a handbook for those who know *APL*'s advantages, but need help in preparing to use *APL* for a wide range of applications. As with any expanding technology, it would be presumptuous for us to claim we have all the answers, although there are some of us who have worked toward making *APL* applicable to the full range of computer-related tasks required of modern business. What we do offer is the collective experi- ence of over fifty proven *APL* practitioners—approximately 250 people-years' worth—drawn from virtually every area of practical *APL* usage.

The papers in this book were prepared as background for presentations given at "The Practical *APL* Conference", which was sponsored by STSC, Inc., and held in Washington, D.C., on 9-11 April 1980. Three goals dominated the selection and editing of the topics covered:

- To provide general management with sufficient knowledge of *APL* to cut through the mystique that surrounds the data process- ing profession.

- To aid data processing managers and working professionals in bridging the gap between their familiar turf and new fields—such as financial planning and conceptual information management—that are easily mastered with *APL*.

- To broaden the horizons of convinced *APL* users so that they can better relate to the real problems of general management and data processors.

Although we were always aware of these goals while editing, many of the topics (necessarily) contribute to more than one theme. We suggest that you begin in that part of the book with which you most closely identify, but that you sample the wares of the other parts as well. Most importantly, we hope that this volume will encourage you to apply an *APL* solution to some business problem.

Although the book implies that *APL* can be used for the full range of computer activities, we recognize that successful advances in data processing application come by evolution, rather than revolution. In that spirit we suggest that you start with some small project. Only after success with a variety of applications should you begin addressing the main question: Should *APL* be used for all new application development in your organization?

Many of the presentations in this book contain examples illustrating the use of *APL*. To aid you in distinguishing between user entries and system output, user entries are given in *APL* boldface type.

We are grateful to all the contributing authors who shared their experiences and knowledge in this book. So that you can put each author's contribution in perspective, we have included biographies at the end of each article.

We are also grateful to the following people from STSC, Inc., who assisted in the editing and production of this book: Sarah R. Beirn, Shelly L. Dimmick, Connie L. Kiernan, Karen M. Kromas, Laurie A. Russell, Nancy T. Vernon, and James G. Wheeler, editors; and Donna E. Kromas and Jean Medinger, publications assistants.

Allen J. Rose
Yorktown Heights, New York

Barbara A. Schick
Silver Spring, Maryland

10 April 1980

# Contents

Part 3—The Core of *APL*

**Part 1**

# The Data Processing Viewpoint

J. Murray Spencer

# *APL* Concepts
# For Systems Management

"The dogmas of the quiet past are inadequate to the stormy present. The occasion is piled high with difficulty, and we must rise with the occasion. As our case is new, so we must think anew."

—Lincoln, Second Annual
Message to Congress.

Information processing successes have led information processing clients to expect more and better applications. At the same time, pressures of inflated costs and limited budgets require planners to wisely balance human, software, and hardware resources to meet these expectations.

The price of human effort is steadily rising, while the cost of fast hardware is going down. As fast hardware becomes more available and as its speed increases, improved software is needed to make wise use of the new speed. As "people time" costs go up, it becomes increasingly desirable to require less of it to implement and maintain applications. *APL* serves both of these needs by transferring many of the tedious, error-prone tasks in coding from the programmer to the CPU (central processing unit). *APL* also provides many powerful language and system support features with which to design applications. Not only are the tools more powerful, but because *APL* language features more naturally represent data and calculations, the user's initial perception of a problem translates more readily and directly into *APL* than into other programming languages.

In fact, programmers often find that knowledge of *APL* notation improves their ability to represent, and consequently to analyze, problems. *APL* accomplishes this improved representation through a variety of data structures and a large, carefully chosen set of primitive functions. The primitives are written in a concise notation that allows complex algorithms to be represented compactly. The *APL* language subsumes detail through array-oriented primitives that reduce the need for explicit control structures. These features reduce the need for housekeeping to a bare minimum and permit the user to state only the essence of the problem. Programmer productivity is improved by working in a higher-level language; *APL* is as much higher than FORTRAN, COBOL, ALGOL, or PL/1 as these are higher than Assembler language.

It is often agreed that a programmer can work effectively with a page of program code at a time. A page of *APL* code is so concise that it is able to represent five to ten times as much algorithm as a page of FORTRAN, COBOL, ALGOL, or PL/1. Therefore, in *APL* a programmer can work with much more of a problem at one time. This reduces the amount of time the programmer spends switching between blocks of code, because there are fewer blocks. Shorter programs also reduce the work of typing the code. This saves time handling code, and reduces the chance of typing errors.

Most *APL* language processors execute code interpretively. Originally this was dictated by the language requirements and the available development resources. The interpretive approach allowed addition of powerful debugging aids as the workspace concept was employed and strengthened. *APL* language processors come with permanent storage facilities for workspaces (as developed by IBM) and permanent storage for data in files (as first developed by STSC, Inc., in 1970). Regardless of the CPU architecture or operating system, *APL* language processors provide a complete working environment for application developers and users. At the heart of *APL* design philosophy for the language and its use is the premise that the programmer and user should be required to know absolutely as little as possible about computer hardware and system software.

*APL* is a tool for thinking about data and algorithms. How to use *APL* to design algorithms is not the topic of this presentation. Readers who would like to pursue this direction are referred to the paper entitled "Making *APL* Palatable", which appears elsewhere in this book, and to K. E. Iverson's "1979 Turing Lecture", which is to be published in *Communications of the ACM*. The presentation that follows will concentrate on how *APL* accomplishes its wonders via features such as the active workspace, the symbol table, the file system, and the efficiency of the *APL* interpreter.

### The Active Workspace: A Dynamic Execution Area

One of the obstacles to executing a conventional assembled or compiled program in most operating systems is the work involved in linking together the assorted routines from various libraries and loading them into an execution area. In *APL* systems, the user is always "in" a working execution area called the *active workspace*. Linking is done automatically among all programs in the active workspace, so all that is required is to copy or load the programs into the workspace. If they are present in the active workspace, they will run. A main program and all of its subroutines are easily saved as a permanent workspace in the user's workspace library with a single command called )*SAVE*.

In addition to programs, the active workspace contains data stored in variables. The user can enter any *APL* statement from his terminal and the statement will be executed immediately in the context of the active workspace. Such an *immediate execution* statement can reference a variable in the active workspace, and it can call any program in the active workspace as a subroutine. In fact, there is no need for a "run" command in *APL* systems, since entering the name of a program in the active workspace causes it to run; it is simply a matter of a valid *APL* statement being entered by the user.

Any *APL* statement that will execute in the active workspace can be a statement in an *APL* program. Thus it is normal to test algorithms one statement at a time in immediate execution mode before storing them as lines of a program. Immediate execution of statements is a benefit to be expected of an interpretive language processor. It is such an important benefit that in some non-*APL* systems there are separate interpretive language processors solely for testing and debugging (i.e., in addition to the compiler that generates the production version of the tested code). The existence of separate interpreters and compilers for other programming languages raises the question: "How efficient is the *APL* interpreter?" Rather efficient, as will be seen below.

Programs exist to process data, and while some programs get by with small amounts of data, an important measure of a computer system is how much data it can process at one time. In general, the more data that can be referred to at one time by a program, the simpler the program will be. This results from less need for control structures in the program to iterate a solution through repetitions of the fundamental algorithms acting on segments of the data. All data used by *APL* statements is dynamically managed in the active workspace so that the space used by the data can be reused as soon as the data is no longer needed. In a conventionally compiled program, a data array is declared to occupy a certain amount of space. It occupies this space for the entire program execution—even if the array is needed only by a few lines of code constituting one step in the algorithm. Some programmers will actually reuse such an array one or more times elsewhere in their program to save execution space—which does not make the program easier to document and maintain! In *APL*, local variables are automatically erased upon return from a subroutine, and there is an executable erase that can be used (but is rarely needed) right in the subroutine or main program.

The *dynamic storage allocation* in *APL* systems allows an array, or variable, to become larger or smaller at any time. The array is always exactly the size needed by the data being processed. This exact-size quality eliminates the need for accessory variables in programs that keep a count of the number of rows or columns in a table (a considerable coding simplification). It also means that as one array gets smaller, space is immediately available to be used by another array that may be getting larger. Since the language processor does not need to know the size and shape of arrays beforehand, the *APL* programmer is relieved of having to use declaration statements to specify data type or data size and shape. Arrays are allowed to change size, shape, and data type any time a statement reassigns the array variable.

It may be claimed that some documentation is lost by not requiring variable declarations in the program code. However, the rank and type of an array is often quite obvious from its context in an *APL* statement. If it is not, and the programmer believes the code should note these specifications, he is encouraged to add a comment explaining the variable's attributes. Such a comment is likely to be more helpful to the reader than a program statement—like the DIMENSION statement in FORTRAN—that only tells how big the data can become.

### The Symbol Table: Signpost to All Identifiers

All *APL* programs, whether main programs or subroutines, are called *functions*. The names of functions and variables are called *identifiers*. All identifiers are cataloged with descriptive and location information in the *symbol table*. The language processor keeps the symbol table completely up to date as each statement executes, because some statements will create new variables and functions as well as change the size of existing variables. The

programmer does not explicitly manipulate the symbol table, although most
*APL* statements implicitly reference and modify the symbol table entries.
Actually, most *APL* programmers know little or nothing of the existence of the
symbol table, and the explanation in this paper is only for those systems-
oriented people who are interested in how the language processor works.

Perhaps the most obvious use of the symbol table is in workspace storage
management. The location of all items in the workspace is maintained in the
symbol table along with information about each item's status. For example,
when returning from a subroutine, all the local variables of the subroutine are
flagged "to be removed". The actual removal and reorganization of the space
waits until an *APL* statement needs to create an array requiring more space
than is available in a contiguous block. At that time, items in the workspace
that are still in use are moved next to each other and items flagged for removal
are discarded. This process is known as "garbage collection". Garbage collection is timed asynchronously. It occurs not when garbage is created, but when
the space occupied by the garbage is needed for an array or function.

Other uses of the symbol table support various *APL* language features and
language processor efficiencies. For example, the fact that the symbol table is
maintained in real time during execution provides late binding of identifiers.
Thus, in this program statement:

```
'25A1, 12CF10.2, CF13.2' □FMT (NAMES;NUMS)
```

the identifier *NUMS* could be either a variable or a function. During debugging,
*NUMS* might be a workspace variable to test the program until completion of
the application module that will manage the application data. When that
module is completed, a function *NUMS* could be defined in the workspace,
perhaps like this one:

```
     ∇ NUMBERS ← NUMS
[1]    NUMBERS←□FREAD DEPTFILE,CURRENTΔDEPARTMENT
     ∇
```

The format statement above continues to operate without modification,
because the language processor does not make a syntactic distinction between
a variable and a function that has no argument and that returns an array
result. At the moment of execution, it is clear from the context in the
workspace what *NUMS* is, because there is always only one current (visible)
definition of any identifier. Late binding of identifiers and interpretive
execution allow the application implementer to test changes in his application
design or coding with a minimum of typing and waiting at the keyboard.

More than one item in a workspace can be named with a particular
identifier, but only the most recently created item will be referred to by an
*APL* statement. A given identifier could be a global function or variable and it
could be local to one or more functions currently executing. Only if an
identifier is declared as *local* in a function header statement can there be more
than one item with the same name in a workspace. (There is a declaration
statement in *APL* after all—only one—and it is the function header statement
that declares the function's syntax and its optional local variables.) When a
function is called, the local identifiers in the function header statement are
marked in the symbol table so that when a value or function is first defined in
the function for the local identifier, it does not disturb the previous definition
of the identifier, but rather creates a new item referred to by the identifier. An
*APL* statement always references the most recent item created for any
identifier. If there is no local definition in the currently executing function, the
reference is to the most recently defined variable or function with this

identifier. "Most recently defined" implies a scan backward through the chain of function calls to see which, if any, calling function localized (and defined) this identifier. If no calling function localized the identifier, the global definition is used.

Thus *APL* uses "umbrella localization". That is, an identifier defined as local in a function protects the previously defined items with this identifier, but is available to be read or modified in any functions called by this function—unless one of the called functions localizes this same identifier. When execution "returns" from this function, all the local identifiers are flagged to be erased in the symbol table, and the most recent previous definition of the identifier is again revealed for reference by *APL* statements.

When formal parameters are passed to functions (subroutines), the *APL* language uses "call by value". That is, no action in the subroutine can modify the array specified as the argument to the calling function, because the arguments of the function are considered local variables inside the function. For example, if

```
[9]     I←1
[10]    XG←COMP2 I
[11]    ISQ←I*2
```

calls this function:

```
     ∇ RESULT←COMP2 NUM
[1]    RESULT←NUM
[2]    NUM←NUM+1
[3]    RESULT←RESULT,NUM×2
     ∇
```

the calculation on line [11] will use a value of 1 for *I*. Of course, line [2] does change the local variable *NUM*, which uses as its starting value the same data as was in *I* when the function was called.

This call by value is considered a very important protection for functions that call each other. However, when the arguments to functions are large arrays requiring thousands of bytes of storage, the CPU time required to set up the local variable arguments—and the very important space taken up by them—can be costly, because often a function will look at but not modify its arguments. If the arguments are not modified, the duplicate copy of the array is unnecessary. However, the symbol table is used to circumvent the inefficiencies of this form of duplication. Without disturbing the *APL* language definition of protecting the arguments to functions, the language processor uses the symbol table information to establish synonyms for arrays. If one array is assigned to another name, as in

```
    X2←X1
```

the entries for both *X*1 and *X*2 in the symbol table will point to the same data stored in the workspace. Thus, *X*1 and *X*2 are two different names for the same data, or synonyms. This will continue to be the case until either *X*1 or *X*2 is assigned a new array—even one that differs only minutely from the other—at which time the reassigned identifier will point to its new version of the data. Use of such synonyms reduces CPU time spent on data replication; it also saves space in the workspace and postpones the need to "collect garbage".

When a function is called, its argument local variables are not given duplicate copies of the data arrays supplied to the function; rather, the argument local variables are treated as synonyms to the data array arguments until the argument local variables are modified by an assignment. The synonym feature—sometimes called data chaining—was not part of early *APL* implementations. Without it, when coding in a cramped workspace, it was necessary to use a less readable style of function coding in which arguments were not explicitly named in the header. Instead, data to be used by the function was made available through global variables.

The synonym feature provided by having the symbol table maintained in real time gives the protection of call by value with the space and CPU time savings of call by name (when these savings are possible).

Because of the protection of arguments supplied to a function as it is called and the protection of local variables used to control an algorithm, functions can be used recursively with no effort on the programmer's part other than to localize variables to control the flow of processing. Since it is good practice in any case to localize all variables not needed outside the function, *APL* functions are naturally recursive without any extra effort or caution.

Another way in which the symbol table allows increased efficiency is that the language processor passes a pointer to data for the result of a calculation when the calculation happens not to modify the data given to it. Take, for example, the following statement:

$XCOMP \leftarrow B/XTABLE \times 10$

If $B$ happens to contain a scalar (single element) 1, or even if it contains all 1's and no 0's (as it well might, in some cases), the compression function ($/$) does not create a new data array. That is because with a left argument such as these, compression does not change the data. The symbol table already points to the temporary array result of $XTABLE \times 10$, so the identifier $XCOMP$ is made to point to this same array, which is then no longer considered temporary because there is an identifier referring to it.

### *APL* Interpreter Efficiency: A Contradiction in Terms?

Is it a contradiction to use "efficient" and "interpreter" to describe the same language processor? It need not be. *APL* language processors started out with some powerful strengths and development has continued on them for over ten years. New ones are still being developed. This paper has already looked at several ways in which efficiency of execution has been designed into the language processor.

What further efficiencies should be considered? Efficiency may be considered in terms of the availability and use of particular resources such as CPU time, main memory space, disk memory space, high-speed swapping device space, terminal ports or telecommunications ports, terminals, development programmer time, application user time, and so on. Installations will have varying assortments of resources in short supply, which therefore must be used "efficiently".

Many systems managers are conditioned to think of efficiency first in terms of CPU time used, since this was uniformly expensive when computers first came into use. In recent years, CPU speeds have increased; thus the bottleneck in a system today might more likely be the number of disk accesses per second, or the number of page faults per second. On some systems the high-speed or low-speed input/output capacity may be used up before CPU usage approaches saturation.

As a general technique, interpretation is not always a poor choice. For example, it takes a lot of hardware circuitry to implement every 370 instruction in a CPU. For smaller models of the 370—up to the 370/148—the hardware logic gates do not implement a 370 at all. Rather, they implement a simpler machine capable of emulating (interpreting) a 370. The emulation code is stored in fast, read-only memory control store. The CPU determines which 370 instruction is to be performed. Then, using a (rather complicated) subroutine of fundamental machine instructions (microcode) from the control store, the CPU emulates the 370 instruction. Considering their performance-per-cost, 370/148s and 4331s have their rightful place in the hardware lineup.

Another example of hardware interpretation that is dear to the pocket-books of its lucky users is the *APL* assist microcode option available on 370/148s and 370/138s. This feature speeds up execution of the *VS APL* language processor by implementing, in extended control store, additional CPU "instructions" much more powerful than 370 instructions and specially designed to replace sections of Assembler code in the *VS APL* language processor. The hardware does not implement these instructions with additional logic circuitry; again, they are subroutines of microcode instructions. This is interpreting at the hardware level, and it causes a 370/148 to considerably outperform a 370/158 when executing *APL* programs.

During program debugging and testing stages, the CPU time saved by not having to compile the language source code is very considerable. For jobs that do not run many times in production mode, the CPU savings alone completely cost justify *APL*.

Perhaps the discussion so far sounds like an apology for a slow language processor that uses a lot of CPU time. The fact is that one can easily find benchmark programs to show that FORTRAN, for example, is faster than *APL*. But it is just as easy to come up with benchmark programs showing that *APL* executes faster than the best code from optimizing compilers. This standoff quickly resolves to the wise saying: "Use only benchmarks that are representative of one's actual workload." Sometimes that is hard to do, since one's actual workload may not yet be coded in *APL*. So the systems manager continues to be wary of claims about interpretive language processors, even after hearing that great effort has been spent to make them use less CPU time.

It is worth looking more carefully at considerations of speed. Usability of the language by humans should be taken into account, because this is a very important speed factor too: "How much people time is needed to design, implement, document, and maintain applications in one language versus another?"

An interpretive language processor is a collection of carefully coded algorithms whose processing efficiency is as high as possible, given the resources used to develop algorithms. Existing *APL* language processors on IBM computers execute subroutines coded entirely in Assembler language for greatest speed. The language supported by the interpreter invokes a sequence of these algorithms. To achieve "processing efficiency", the ratio of time spent executing the carefully coded algorithms to time spent deciding which algorithms to execute should be high. *APL* programs are stored in the workspace in partially translated code strings in which all identifiers (function and variable names) have been resolved into pointers to symbol table entries. Relatively few *APL* symbols and pointers in a code string need be parsed to invoke powerful execution routines. In the following example, only 25 code string elements contain the statement:

```
T1←NAMES[(NAMES[;ιρNV]∧.=NV)/ι1↑ρNAMES;]
P1← P2   [(   P2 [;ιρP3]∧.=P3)/ι1↑ρ   P2 ;]      (shows pointers)
   AB  C  DE     F GHIJ KLMNO PQRSTUV   W XY      (25 elements)
   21  2  11     2 1111 21111 2111111   2 11      (31 bytes)
    1     2         3 45    6     7 89            (9 functions)
```

Only 31 bytes of code need be parsed to invoke the 9 execution subroutines to evaluate the statement. (Byte count and function count rules are for the XM6-based $APL \star PLUS$ System; other systems may vary slightly.) What does this statement accomplish?

> "Store in table $T1$ the complete names from table $NAMES$, which are selected because their leading characters are identical to the caracters in $NV$."

The flexibility in this program statement is noteworthy. The table $NAMES$ can have 0, 1, 2, 3, or 10,000 rows (or names). The lookup candidate in $NV$ can be expressed with minimum truncation. That is, if "JONES, ROB" uniquely distinguishes an entry, the entire entry "JONES, ROBERT JAMES, JR." need not be entered in $NV$. Conversely, if $NV$ contained only "JO", $T1$ will contain all names beginning with "JO", whether there are 0, 1, 2, 3, or thousands of them. No rank, type, or size declarations have been made for the variables $T1$, $NAMES$, or $NV$, because none are needed. This same statement will work whether $NAMES$ is 1, 2, 3, 20, or hundreds of columns wide.

Efficiency in $APL$ is a consequence of the use of powerful primitive functions: larger blocks of processing are meaningfully conveyed with briefer code statements. This produces two important efficiencies. First, the interpreter spends less time parsing statements than in a language with less powerful functions, and relatively more time doing "useful work"—that is, working directly upon data. Second, and perhaps more importantly, the programmer spends less time writing and maintaining the shorter code statements!

Processing efficiency in $APL$ execution routines gets a lot of development attention. Often there are alternative execution subroutines for a particular $APL$ primitive function. The subroutine actually executed will be chosen based on the amount of data to be processed, whether the data is integer or floating point, and so on. In the previous example, the table lookup (the $\wedge$ . = matrix inner product) uses an algorithm especially optimized for character data. Also in that figure, $/ \iota$ is recognized as a special composite function and executed by a single subroutine, although the $APL$ language defines compression $(/)$ completely independently of the index generator $(\iota)$.

The use of alternative execution subroutines to achieve processing speed for the simple arithmetic primitive functions (such as $+, -, \times, \div, \lceil, \lfloor$, and $\star$) goes as far as generating object code tailored to the exact data given with each function call. This object code is discarded after its one use. Generation and execution of object code for such simple arithmetic is much faster than a generalized subroutine execution, except when very little data is given with the function. Where five or fewer data elements are given, the "old-fashioned", but in this case faster, general subroutine is used.

The $APL$ language abounds with powerful primitive functions. The following simple statement:

```
CUMSUMS←+\TABLE
```

produces cumulative sums for each row of $TABLE$ and stores them in $CUMSUMS$, a table with the same number of rows and columns as $TABLE$. As always, storage allocation for the tables—and special cases for empty, or very large, tables—is not the concern of the programmer.

$APL$ interpreters are highly engineered for processing speed. Their ability to surpass the speed of optimized FORTRAN (or other compiled languages) in many instances is based on the fact that a small selection of powerful $APL$

primitives does a job that may require many pages of FORTRAN. The FORTRAN object code produced from these pages of source code has to compete with carefully tuned, hand-coded *APL* execution routines called with a modest overhead of parsing concise statements.

While presently available interpretive language processors are fast enough to be very useful, competition between software suppliers continues to improve the speed of execution. Indeed, *APL* language processors are beginning to appear that generate and save object code for every statement so that subsequent executions are faster than interpretive execution. As these language processors become available for the CPU of the manager's choice, the issue of processing speed will disappear. The use of *APL* will then become even more desirable, given all its other advantages.

### Manipulating *APL* Programs: Poof, It's a Program

"Quick, call me a taxi!" "All right, already, you're a taxi."

As this old joke suggests, magical transformations unlock many possibilities for the application implementer. Perhaps the most useful program transformation is a general change of state from executable program (compiled if need be, linked, and loaded in the execution area) to data that a companion program can modify, and back again to executable program. This allows an executing program with self-knowledge to modify its subroutines. Such modifications can be as simple as storage management to free up execution space occupied by infrequently used (large) programs, or as complicated as creating programs to perform contingent, case-dependent code selection and optimization for efficient execution.

A less complicated but frequent use of program-to-data and back-to-program transformations is in *APL* programs that are themselves program development aids and that modify a program while it is in the data state. The program development aids in *APL* systems will continue to grow in versatility without the need for intervention of a systems programmer.

In addition to conveniently formatted program listings with various cross-reference tables (comparable to the listings available to an Assembler programmer—except that they are much shorter!), *APL* application implementers use program development aids of the type exemplified in the Appendix at the end of this paper. These programming aids recognize the syntactic rules of *APL* and can make useful organizational and syntactic changes to a program as well as perform traditional editing chores. There is, of course, a system-provided function editor quite suitable for simple entry and modification of programs.

The *APL* language processor uses a stack to store the control information for the execution in process. An execution may halt with a processing error during debugging. Another execution can be started, and when it is finished, the original execution can be restarted. This allows the use of programs to help analyze and correct problems that occur during debugging. If a program will not halt where it needs to be analyzed, program stops can be set to force a halt. Program traces can be set to cause the language processor to display intermediate results and the flow of processing as each selected statement executes.

Certain data conditions and external events can cause errors that normally halt execution. However, the *APL* application implementer has language and system features permitting him to maintain processing control when an error occurs, treat the error condition if he knows what measures to take, and keep on processing. This "exception handling" allows simplification of the control structures of some sequences of program code, since the program does not have to test for obscure cases of bad data. Exception handling allows the application designer to further protect the end user from the unexpected events that can occur during processing, including those events caused by the user not following directions!

### The File System: Unlimited Storage

The active workspace can be, and often is, permanently saved. While workspaces can contain data, workspaces are saved primarily to save the programs in them. The need for data organization and storage goes beyond having variables in a workspace. In 1971 STSC released its *APL∗PLUS* File Subsystem, which has become the one to which other *APL* file systems are compared. The STSC file system is well documented elsewhere, but a brief summary is in order here.

The items stored in a file are entire arrays from a workspace. Every attribute of the array—its rank, shape, type, and all its data—is stored in the file as a single entity, called a component. An array stored in a workspace is stored as a variable with an alphanumeric identifier. The variable name that might be assigned to an array when it is stored in a workspace is not part of the file component. It is identified in the file by its position number in the sequence of components. This is appropriate, because it is often useful to process many components identically with an algorithm that repeats once for each component. This is done by reading the components into the active workspace one at a time and storing them in the same variable on each iteration of the algorithm.

Components of a file can be randomly read or replaced by specifying the component number. A component can be replaced with a completely different array component—different in rank, shape, type, and size. Multiple files can be tied, or "open" at one time. If correctly planned, multiple users can update the same file concurrently. The system provides access tools to control the sequence of updates and prevent one user from modifying the file until another user completes his update.

Files are completely private when created, but after creation, the file owner can allow carefully controlled (with passnumber protection), fine-grained access to users of his choice. For example, the file owner can allow one user to read the file with one password; allow other users to append to the file (but not read it) with another password; and allow certain maintenance users to read, append, *and* erase the file.

Considerable development effort has gone into designing a file system that cooperates with the multiuser scheduler for maximum system throughput. One technique is to coordinate the swapping of users with the expected completion of file operations. Multiple file operations proceed concurrently.

The file system interface presented to the *APL* programmer is compatible with overall *APL* language design considerations. The file operations are invoked with system functions that behave like *APL* language primitives in syntax and error messages. All file operations can be done under program control.

### A Summary Statement: *APL* Is Cost Effective

In the early days of *APL*, it acquired a reputation for being "for mathematicians and scientists only". This was partly due to the extended character set and partly to some system support limitations of early implementations (e.g., lack of a file system, lack of an output formatter, and small active workspace size).

*APL* service companies such as STSC have welcomed use by mathematicians and scientists, but over the years business users have come to account for more and more of the usage (currently 80 to 90 percent for STSC). The very users who should care the most about cost comparisons are the ones who use *APL* the most. Probably it is because of *APL*'s effectiveness!

## Appendix—*APL* Program Development Aids

This appendix lists some of the program development aids frequently used by users of STSC's *APL\*PLUS* Service. All of these programming aids are *APL* programs that use the program-to-data transformation ($\square VR$) and the data-to-program transformation ($\square DEF$). The programming aids work on the data that represents the *APL* program under consideration.

Workspace 11 *TOOLS* contains several functions that search and/or manipulate other functions. Following are brief descriptions for each of the functions in workspace 11 *TOOLS*.

- The function *BRKOUT* modifies a given function to break out embedded assignments into individual statements. For example,

  ```
  H←ρ□FREAD(R←1↑F),C←F[1+O←ι1]
  ```

  would become

  ```
  O←ι1 ◊ C←F[1+O] ◊ R←1↑F ◊ H←ρ□FREAD R,C
  ```

- The function *FNIDS* searches a given function for identifiers in certain categories (locals, labels, direct assignments, indexed assignments, or □ names). Combinations of identifiers may also be specified (e.g., intersection, union, and complement).

- The function *LOCALIZE* localizes specified functions in a given function.

- The function *ORDLOC* reorders the local identifiers in the header of a given function.

- The function *RELABEL* modifies a given function to use the set of labels *L*1, *L*2, and so on. This function also converts occurrences of *THISL* and *NEXTL* to their corresponding labels. (Also see <u>*RELABEL*</u>.)

- The function *SNUFF* removes comment text from a given function.

- The function *UNPAREN* removes superfluous parentheses from a given function.

- The function *XREF* displays a cross-reference of a given function.

- The function <u>*RELABEL*</u> modifies a given function to use the set of labels <u>*A*</u>, <u>*B*</u>, and so on. This function also converts occurrences of *THISL* and *NEXTL* to their corresponding labels. (Also see *RELABEL*.)

Workspace 11 *FNED* contains the function *FNED*, which edits functions quickly and conveniently, including those whose lines are longer than workspace or terminal widths. *FNED* uses conventions that provide:

- ordinary string searching or syntactic element searching
- single or multiple replacements
- large deletions, moves, copies, and insertions.

Workspace 11 *FNR* contains the functions *FNREPL* and *BY*, which can be copied into the active workspace. These functions are used to modify programs by replacing one character string with another. Their syntax is

'*function list*' *FNREPL* '*old*' *BY* '*new*'

where both '*old*' and '*new*' are character vectors; '*old*' must not be empty, but '*new*' may be empty; '*function list*' can be a character array of any rank (nominally a vector), with the individual function names separated by spaces (nominally), new-line characters, structural significance (rows of a matrix), or any combination of the three.

*FNREPL* searches all unlocked functions in '*function list*' for the syntactic elements represented in '*old*'. For each function in which *FNREPL* detects '*old*', an indication of how many occurrences is given and '*old*' is replaced by '*new*' in that function.

Workspace 11 *WSS* contains the functions *WSFIND* and *WSSHOW*, which (when copied into the active workspace) are used to find or show all occurrences of a character string. Their syntax is

*WSFIND* '*characterstring*'
*WSSHOW* '*characterstring*'

Only unlocked functions are searched. *WSFIND* prints the function names, followed by the line and print position in the line. If the character string appears more than once in the line, an indication is given. *WSSHOW* prints the function name and the number of occurrences of the character string in the function; it then prints the text of each line in which the character string occurs.

Workspace 11 *WSSEARCH* contains the functions *SEFIND* and *SESHOW*, which (when copied into the active workspace) find or show all consecutive occurrences of the syntactic elements represented in the right argument in all unlocked functions in the workspace. Their syntax is

*SEFIND* '*characterstring*'
*SESHOW* '*characterstring*'

For example, the expression

*SEFIND* '*BCD 234*'

would find '*BCD 234+5*' or '*A+BCD 234*', but would ignore '*BCD 2345*' and '*ABCD 234*'. *SEFIND* prints the function names, followed by the line and print position in the line. If the character string appears more than once in the line, an indication is given. *SESHOW* prints the function name and the number of occurrences of the character string in the function, and then prints the text of each line in which the character string occurs.

*Murray Spencer joined STSC in 1970 as branch manager of the company's Washington, D.C., office. He subsequently held the positions of branch manager in San Francisco, APL applications analyst, and manager of product planning and support. Spencer is currently manager of small computer products for STSC.*

*Prior to joining STSC, Spencer was a systems programmer for Bell Telephone Laboratories and an EDP product planner for RCA Information Systems. He has a B.S. in applied mathematics from Clemson University.*

Fred B. Lear and John W. Myrna

# Evaluating Telecommunications Networks

With the availability of packet carriers and specialized common carriers, you, the communications manager, have viable alternatives to meeting your network needs inhouse. "Should you use a packet or specialized carrier rather than doing it yourself? How do you evaluate your options? What, in fact, are your options?"

Over the years, STSC has asked these questions. After considerable technical and financial study, we concluded that the most effective approach for us was to use a mix of packet carrier services with a central inhouse network. We would like to share our analysis, experience, and conclusions with you. Though the conclusions you reach may be different from ours, our analysis and experience should prove useful.

### Some Background on STSC

To set the stage we'd like to outline STSC's experience in the communications area. This will help you understand the problem we were addressing when looking at the options.

STSC was founded in 1969 to provide an interactive computer time sharing service based on the *APL* programming language. We decided on a national marketing strategy, which was uncommon at that time. This required a national network from the start. We originally used a simple Time Division Multiplexer network, but we quickly outgrew it. As we increased the trunk speeds to 4800 BPS and expanded our services to cover smaller cities, we became painfully aware of the limitations of the telephone company's network and the quality of available modems and multiplexers.

We eagerly evaluated each new communications offering, hoping that it would hold the solution to our problem. Alas, none solved all of our problems completely, so we were forced to combine offerings that would collectively meet our needs.

Through the years, STSC's communications service has evolved to meet the needs of its customers. The table below shows the growth in this area from 1972 through 1979.

| 1972 | Used Western Union Data Communications Service. |
| 1973 | Reviewed and rejected inhouse minicomputer networking. |
| 1974 | Began using specialized common carriers--MCI and DATRAN. |

|      | Interfaced to the TYMNET network. |
|------|-----------------------------------|
| 1975 | Began using DDS. |
|      | Became the first user of the minicomputer-based SMART/MUX. |
|      | Became the first customer of TELENET. |
| 1976 | Converted to Infotron multiplexers (240, 180). |
| 1977 | Added Infotron smart multiplexers (780). |
| 1978 | Installed Comten 3670 front ends, with RPQ code for demuxing (A.M.X.). |
| 1979 | Upgraded to Comten 3690 front-end processors. |

To this day, we are still searching for the system or technology that will solve the bulk of our problems with one bold stroke.

In 1977, we had reached a pivotal point in our network planning and felt that there were three approaches available to us:

- Develop and extend our inhouse network using intelligent multiplexers.
- Leave the network business entirely and use only a packet carrier.
- Use some combination of the two approaches.

We determined which approach to take based on the answers we found to the following questions:

- What were our objectives?
- What were our options?
- How should we evaluate the options?

Of course, these three questions apply to just about every decision made in business.

### STSC's Objectives

Our primary communications objective was to provide an acceptable, cost-effective means of connecting user terminals to our host computers. The importance of understanding the company's objective cannot be overemphasized. To determine the best way to meet our objective, we considered the following questions:

- What type of terminals must we support?

    low-speed asynchronous?

    high-speed bisynchronous?

    polled bisynchronous?

- Where is access required?

    in major cities?

    in small, out-of-the-way plant locations?

    internationally?

- What service level is acceptable?

    are users generally insensitive to errors?

    are users very sensitive to errors?

    are users very sensitive to system availability?

- What is the volume and distribution of usage?

  a few hours per month from many locations?

  hundreds of hours per month from a few locations?

- What are the characteristics of usage?

  short holding times with dial access?

  hardwired terminals logged on all day?

- What is an acceptable cost?

  less than long distance?

  less than using a local minicomputer?

## STSC's Options

As mentioned before, our three options were to build and operate an inhouse network, use a commercial Value-Added Network (VAN) such as the packet carriers TELENET and TYMNET, or use some combination of the two.

## STSC's Evaluation Process

How did we evaluate the options? We used five basic criteria:

- cost of service
- quality of service
- scope of service
- service sparkle (image)
- the ever popular "other".

What follows is a discussion of the five criteria and issues STSC considered in 1977. Even today, STSC continually reevaluates its communications needs in terms of these considerations.

1.  Cost of Service

The cost of providing service is based on the location of users, the usage profile, and the volume of usage. One way to characterize the *location* of users is high density, low density, and off-net. A high-density location for a packet carrier is usually a major city such as New York. Because of the large number of users sharing common facilities, the cost per user of providing service is less than it is in a low-density location. The packet carriers, therefore, can charge less because of economies of scale. In addition, they may choose to charge less for competitive reasons.

In most systems there are users in locations not serviced by the network. In our case, these are typically small branch offices of client corporations whose major usage is on the network. The relatively low-volume usage from these locations makes some variation of long distance—such as WATS—an acceptable, though relatively expensive, method of support. We were amazed to find that this small percentage of our usage represented 29 percent of our costs.

The *usage profile* has a dramatic effect on the cost of using a packet carrier. The number of characters transmitted per hour and the number of characters per transaction has a noticeable effect on the final bill, since the carrier's charge is based on those factors.

The *volume of usage* affects cost in three ways. First, the cost of the computer's telecommunications front end must be amortized over the total traffic. As the front end typically has a large, fixed element of cost, the greater the number of usage hours, the lower the cost per hour. Second, packet carriers require a connection to the network--another fixed monthly expense to be amortized. And third, with sufficient volume from a given location the packet carrier may give a price cut and inhouse equipment may be better utilized.

What is a typical breakdown of network costs? The figures in Table 1 are derived from an analysis of providing 20,000 hours of service per month in 90 cities in the United States and Canada. For the analysis, the network was assumed to be 100 percent inhouse or 100 percent packet carrier. For the assumed volume and distribution of usage, a 100 percent packet carrier approach was projected to cost 20 percent less than the equivalent inhouse network. Although the percentages will differ for a different combination of cities and volume, it is still instructive to review costs in this way.

| Table 1 — A Cost Comparison | | |
|---|---|---|
| | Inhouse | Packet Carrier |
| Staff | 14% | 6% |
| Front-end Processor | 8% | 12% |
| Off-Net Access | 29% | 3% |
| Network | | |
| Long Lines and Modems | 20% | |
| Multiplexers | 10% | |
| Local Lines and Data Sets | 9% | |
| Site Rental | 4% | |
| High-Density | | 34% |
| Low-Density | | 42% |
| Van Connection | | 3% |
| Other | 6% | |
| | 100% | 100% |

Looking at Table 1, you will note how large the staff expense is for the inhouse network (14 percent of total expenses). These expenses are much lower for packet carriers, because the carrier provides his own staff and, since the carriers are available in so many cities, there are fewer users off-net.

Economies of scale will decrease costs. As total volume increases in a part of the network, the use of long lines, local lines, datasets, and modems increases. As usage increases, the average cost per usage hour will decrease.

Another cost consideration is that the packet carrier's domestic charges are not dependent on distance. The packet carrier will charge the same amount for one hour of usage in the city where the computer is located as it charges for one hour of usage in a city on the other side of the country. Since long-line rates are distance sensitive, the cost of providing service via an inhouse network increases with increased distance from the host. Thus, a packet carrier may provide the lowest cost for a national network, while an inhouse system may be better for a regional network.

There are additional costs for installation, maintenance, training, software, and equipment. In a dynamic network like STSC's, where we are constantly adding or deleting parts, installation charges can actually exceed the regular monthly charges. In this case, there is an advantage in using a packet carrier.

One additional concern is how to prepare for growth in usage volume. Packet carriers charge for usage as it occurs, so if you must double your usage in a city, you simply do so. With an inhouse network, however, there are new local lines and datasets to be ordered and installed, equipment to be upgraded, and so on.

2. Quality of Service

STSC examines three measures of quality of service: reliability, availability, and response time. *Reliability* is defined as the probability that a user will complete his work without being disconnected by the network. We consider values greater than 97 percent to be acceptable. *Availability* is defined as the probability that a user will be able to connect to the host during scheduled hours. We consider an availability greater than 98 percent to be acceptable. *Response time* is defined as the time the network adds to the user's interaction. We consider values less than one second to be acceptable.

Packet carriers have characteristics that should provide high availability and reliability. They use minicomputers to detect and correct line errors, redundant equipment to minimize outages, and a large number of local-dial lines in each location. Where an inhouse network might be able to provide 90 percent availability, a packet carrier (because of the larger number of lines in each rotor group) could provide 99 percent availability.

However, the response time on a packet carrier tends to be longer than on an inhouse network. This is generally due to the fact that the packet carrier routes users through more intermediate nodes. Another potential problem is that a company's need for increased capacity in a given city may not concur with the packet carrier's schedule for an upgrade, resulting in longer lead times to respond to growth needs. Similarly, mean time to fix problems can become extended, primarily due to the coordination effort necessary between the numerous parties involved.

3. Scope of Service

In comparing VANs such as TELENET and TYMNET, it is important to determine how many of the cities serviced by you are directly served by the VAN. You should also verify that the terminals and features used in your network are supported; for example, in 1977 we desired support for the IBM 3767 and for transmissions of up to 120 characters per second (CPS).

4. Service Sparkle

Our decisions also consider a number of items that may be best described as vendor "sparkle". If poorly handled, these details can be a major irritant to users. For example: "What is the sign-on ritual? How many steps are involved to sign on? How solid is the automatic baud rate detection? If a user makes an error when connecting to the network does he have to hang up and dial again? Does the network support multiple hosts? Does the packet carrier cater to specific needs?" (In our case, one special requirement is the support of *APL* terminals.)

5. Other Considerations

We include a number of other considerations in our decisions. The terms of the contract and its conditions are important as is the availability of technical assistance and the guaranties available on service and price. In addition, there are several broader considerations, such as:

- What are future product directions?
- What economies of scale apply? Today a packet carrier may be ideal, but in a couple of years the same may not be true.
- Reducing the size of inhouse staff may be irreversible.
- Does it make sense to have a networking capability as part of corporate vertical integration?
- Who has control over cost, quality, and innovation?
- Does using a packet carrier affect corporate image?

- Will building and supporting an inhouse network detract from other opportunities, or drain management resources?
- Does using a packet carrier increase vulnerability?
- How flexible will future services be?

## STSC's Decision

After much consideration of the technical and financial aspects of communications, STSC decided to use an inhouse network, supplemented by a VAN. Eighty percent of the network load is handled inhouse; the other 20 percent is handled by packet carriers.

You might well ask: "What has happened since this decision was made?" For one thing, the primary packet carrier we chose was slower in meeting our needs than we had anticipated. Consequently, we were unable to move the substantial share of usage to the carrier as planned.

On the other hand, the rapid expansion of the packet carriers (particularly internationally) has been an asset to us, allowing us to substantially reduce our off-net expenses. We also have relied on the packet carriers to provide special services to our customers, such as 33.33 CPS access for IBM 3767 terminals and 120 CPS dial access. Both of these services would have been expensive to add to our network. In addition, TYMNET has served as a backup to our own network. We have relied on the packet carriers to smooth sudden, but temporary, increases in usage. This has saved us the high installation costs of rapidly expanding our own network.

## Conclusion

STSC has reaffirmed the value of the packet carriers. They are an integral part of our network. However, with our scale of usage it appears that it will always make sense for us to use a substantial inhouse network.

One last point is that, as a communications manager, you should determine whether you actually have a need for a network. If you have only one application that requires an extensive network, or your network requirements are low, you should consider running the application on a time sharing service.

As has been said before, but is so true, there are no simple solutions—only intelligent choices.

*Fred Lear joined STSC in 1979 as manager of communications. He is in charge of STSC's international telecommunications network, which provides access to the APL\*PLUS Service in over 200 cities throughout the world. Prior to joining STSC, he spent eight and one-half years with Boeing Computer Services, where his positions included operations manager (Philadelphia), Washington area communications manager, and supervisor of hardware configurations.*

*Lear attended the Institute of Computer Management for one year and also holds certificates from several IBM and COMTEN training programs.*

*John Myrna joined STSC in 1971 as manager of operations; in this position he organized STSC's Computing Center and nationwide communications network.*

*He was subsequently promoted to manager of communications in 1973, director of development and design in 1975, director of development in 1977, and to his current position as vice president of development in 1979.*

*Myrna directs STSC's Operations Group and is a member of its Executive Committee and Technical Management Committee. He is responsible for the production and delivery of computing and telecommunications services and for the development of new applications, products, system features, and technologies.*

*Myrna holds a B.S.E.E. degree from the New Jersey Institute of Technology and an M.S.E.E. degree from Montana State University.*

Michael E. Handelman

# Managing an *APL* Installation

In operating and managing an *APL* installation, many complex problems arise. We at STSC, Inc., have addressed these problems and, in this paper, I will present our solutions to you. For purposes of discussion, I have divided the process of developing and operating an *APL* service into four distinct areas: software requirements, hardware requirements, commercial considerations, and staffing requirements.

## Software Requirements

Running an *APL* service is similar to operating any other form of computer service; the major difference is the software. Software requirements, which affect all other areas of the operation, are the operating system, the supporting software, and upgrades and other changes.

1. Operating System

An exhaustive analysis was performed by STSC to determine which *APL*-supporting operating system, of all those currently on the market, best fit our particular requirements. IBM's OS/MVT and VM systems proved superior in our ratings. Although VM consumes more resources than other systems investigated, it is an extremely powerful system, and is both reliable and truly dedicated to teleprocessing. OS/MVT, although a batch-oriented system, has been modified by STSC to be a highly reliable and stable operating system. STSC currently operates both OS/MVT-based and VM-based services.

2. Supporting Software

The reliability of any operating system depends on the supporting software. It is necessary for supporting software to be as "bug-free" as possible to ensure satisfactory support of both systems development and pure applications. A stable operating system and an excellent record of vendor support are critical components of bug-free supporting software. STSC has developed a System Support Team (SST) to diagnose problems and determine their origins, whether caused by hardware, the operating system, or STSC. Our team is staffed with dedicated system programmers who recognize the need to keep their knowledge and abilities current with fluid technology and stringent company standards. The benefit is minimal down time and a diminished need to rely on other sources—including the vendor—for problem solution.

3. Upgrades

Upgrades and other *APL* system changes must successfully complete three preparatory stages before being installed on STSC's production system.

The first stage involves the identification of a problem and formulation of a solution or upgrade by our design team. In stage two, our development team installs the potential upgrade on a system identical to our production system. Once the potential upgrade is proven reliable, its modules (code) are passed to SST personnel who perform a technical walk through (TWT) in stage three. When the code has been debugged, stage three results in an upgrade that has survived rigorous testing procedures and standards. An upgrade, having met the challenges of the three-stage preparatory system, is finally incorporated into our production system. It is important to note that the ability to back out of any modification at any stage of the process is designed to be as simple as possible.

## Hardware Requirements

Continuing advances in technology, coupled with outstanding price and performance improvements, have caused the hardware area of data processing to change at an astonishing rate. For example, the capabilities of STSC's Amdahl 470V/6 Central Processing Unit (CPU) are astounding when compared with units available just fifteen years ago. Technological advances such as IBM's new 64-bit chip show that for hardware the future is just beginning.

For advocates of *APL*—who are sharing in the resultant interactive language boom—the industry is showing new life and growth. At STSC, we have emphasized the importance of keeping abreast of changes and trends in the industry. Attendance at seminars, the reading of trade journals, and active interface with vendors are encouraged as valuable learning tools. Awareness of hardware requirements for the CPU and peripherals also requires investigation, planning, implementation, and monitoring.

1.  Central Processing Unit

In a teleprocessing environment, the CPU—the core of any system's performance—must be constantly monitored to determine if it is overused. When overused, specific bottlenecks must be identified. At STSC we use a hardware monitor designed by TESTDATA and software modified by STSC to provide these results. This enables us to determine the type of upgrade necessary (e.g., more swapping devices rather than more memory or another disk controller to decrease channel busy status occurrences). All this permits the fine tuning of the system to attain optimal use.

2.  Peripherals

When discussing hardware requirements we must also mention peripherals. For an *APL* installation, the major form of storage is online storage. This includes swapping devices and file storage units, but excludes communications controllers that are regarded as a separate system in today's world. Tape drives, printers, and card readers are also made available, of course, but their importance is low in a telecommunications system.

Swapping devices—high-speed, fixed-head disks with low storage capability—are used to establish storage areas proportionate to the workspace size. (Workspace size is the actual size of real memory assigned to each user when logged on to *APL*.) Although virtual systems allow for swapping to relatively low-speed storage devices, it is a process that slows down the response time to the end user. Therefore, as the number of users or workspace size increases, high-speed swapping devices become a necessity in keeping pace with user needs. It is the duty of the paging or swapping manager to monitor the performance of the swapping function. Knowing the optimal number of users and the size of real memory on the system, the swapping manager can determine when low-speed swapping is occurring, and when additional high-speed swapping devices would benefit system response time.

File storage of user data, normally kept on an online storage device, must be flexible. Although user data may be stored on tape, cards, or other types of machine-readable media, these methods are entirely unacceptable for normal, interactive use in this era of instant computing. Recognizing the current three- to six-month lead time involved in the acquisition of new hardware disk modules, we must maintain a constant awareness of user storage needs. Only by carefully plotting historical and current usage can proper storage planning be accomplished.

When planning the back-up considerations of file storage, archival and emergency needs must be examined. STSC currently performs nightly incremental back-ups that copy files to a tape, and include any file updates performed that day. A full dump, a tedious process that places all disk files on tape, is run once a week—usually on Friday night. The tape created by the dump is scanned to check for any tape errors or other improper processing. All of the file disk packs are then taken offline and a new set put online. Next, a full restore is run to copy all information from the tapes that were used for the full backup to the new set of disk packs. The results of these procedures are two sets of tapes (one of which is stored offsite in a fireproof vault) and two sets of disk packs.

These backup and restore procedures illustrate the great care that is taken to preserve the integrity of user data. This is all performed as standard procedure for users of our *APL\*PLUS* Service.

## Commercial Considerations

Commercial considerations are all nontangible items required to support the user community. They include the billing method, scheduling, hardware reliability, and system security.

1. Billing Method

When viewing commercial considerations, it is important to understand the billing method. In addition to charges for online and offline storage, communications needs, and any special services provided, actual CPU and related costs must be calculated. These are presented through Computer Resource Unit (CRU) charges. The CRU is a unit of measure, developed on a base central processor, which is portable to other CPUs by adapting the measure to allow for quantitative differences in machine capabilities. The CRU not only measures the time involved in executing a program, but also recognizes all potential resource usage, thereby simplifying billing through reduction to a simple rate.

2. Scheduling

Scheduling of computer resources—the ability to assign load according to a set of priorities—is another important factor. The most important consideration is the scheduling of external or billable users versus internal or nonbillable users. For example, to make the system load sensitive, user sign-on identifications can be biased so that external users are assigned a high-priority level and internal users a low-priority level.

During light to moderate usage periods, users are unaffected by the priority scheduling. However, during heavy usage, resource availability is weighted in favor of external users. Simply, as resource requests are made they enter a queue and are identified by a timestamp and a user priority level. Adding the priority level to the timestamp determines the access priority. Since the queuing system adheres to first-in-first-out (FIFO) guidelines, an external user who submits a request less than the predetermined number of timestamps after an external user will have first access to available resources.

A hypothetical example of biasing user identifications, using a .0 priority level for external users and a .3 priority level for internal users, is presented in Table 1. STSC uses a similar type of load-sensitive system to maintain excellent response time for our customers.

| Table 1 — Biasing User IDs: An Example | | | | | | |
|---|---|---|---|---|---|---|
| Order of Requests | 1 (ext.) | 2 (int.) | 3 (ext.) | 4 (ext.) | 5 (int.) | 6 (int.) | 7 (ext.) |
| Timestamp | 1.1 | 1.3 | 1.4 | 1.5 | 1.7 | 1.9 | 2.1 |
| Priority Level | +.0 | +.3 | +.0 | +.0 | +.3 | +.3 | +.0 |
| Biased Timestamp | 1.1 | 1.6 | 1.4 | 1.5 | 2.0 | 2.2 | 2.1 |
| Biased Order of Access | 1 | 4 | 2 | 3 | 5 | 7 | 6 |

## 3.　Hardware Reliability

In conjunction with providing rapid response time, systems must be available and reliable. One method of assuring both availability and reliability is to maintain redundant hardware. Since economics do not allow 100 percent redundancy, an effective manager must determine the optimum percentage of redundancy. Each system must be rated on importance to the normally operating system and the impact of any resulting operational degradation due to loss of the component.

An example of the process is typified in rating a disk controller versus a single disk unit. Loss of a controller could cause the loss of a whole string of disks—up to 32 drives. When compared to the loss of a single unit, a back-up controller is justified. Further, the primary and back-up controllers could split the 32-unit disk string, each controlling 16 drives. Not only would this afford optimal performance through two-channel switching, but each controller would back up the other allowing improved response time and a back-up disk controller in case of failure of one of the units.

## 4.　System Security

System security is another important consideration in running an *APL* service. In defining and implementing security measures, both physical security and software security must be considered.

The physical security of computer installations is a growing concern, and the marketplace is responding with a variety of security systems. A brief list of considerations regarding the physical security of an installation, and some possible remedies are given below.

- *Machine room access.* Limited access to computer facilities can be attained through the installation of a card key or electronic lock system. These systems can allow entry to a secure waiting area where a guard or receptionist screens individuals before admittance to more highly classified areas. Alarms should, of course, be placed on all doors to and from the facility.

- *Fire protection.* The best method currently available is a Halon fire protection system in conjunction with a cross-zoned detection smoke-protector system. When two detectors in separate cross-zones are activated, an alarm sounds, access doors are automatically closed, and the time-delayed Halon system is enabled. If determined to be a false alarm, the time delay provides for manually aborting release of the Halon. Detectors for this system should be inside the ceiling and below all raised flooring for maximum effectiveness.

- *Water detection.* Although professed to be waterproof, underfloor cables can present a hazard if subjected to water leakage. Water detectors are inexpensive compared to the cost of potential water damage.

- *Sealed room.* The machine room should be sealed against the entry of outside water leakage and dust. The facility designer must anticipate water leakage from floors above the machine room and should plan for the installation of a drainage system under the raised flooring.

With a significant rise in the incidence of computer crime, physical security alone does not offer sufficient protection of resources. Software security is rapidly becoming a prime concern. The most visible software security measure in an *APL* installation is the sign-on password; users must understand the significance of password protection. Each user should be as possessive of his password as he is of his toothbrush or any other highly personal property. Further protections have been added to the *APL∗PLUS* System, as described below:

- Both workspaces and files can be locked with a password.

- Files cannot be addressed by anyone other than the owner, unless the owner overrides the default by specifically giving access to other users.

- By applying privileged levels, the owner of a file can give others permission to read, add, modify, copy, or delete file information (or any combination of these).

- A daily report of possible system security violations is produced. As an added feature of the *APL∗PLUS* System, STSC can set a limit on the maximum number of such incidents allowed during a single user's session. If this limit is exceeded, a "burglar" alarm is triggered to notify the *APL∗PLUS* System Operator of a possible violation, and pertinent information is displayed.

Physical and software security are critical components of an effective security system, but properly executed manual procedures are equally as important. These manual security procedures provide an effective buffer for the automated physical and software security measures. Operator logs, for example, provide a narrative of daily occurrences at the installation and have proved to be valuable security tools.

### Staffing Requirements

Staffing requirements can be divided into three areas: Operations, Communications, and Systems. Figure 1 depicts the organization chart for an *APL* installation, and the sections that follow describe each area in more detail.

1. Operations

Operations at STSC is comprised of all personnel who run the machine room. This excludes Communications staff, but includes the receptionists, clerks, and computer operators who handle day-to-day operations. In an *APL* installation, the operator not only handles normal duties such as mounting tapes, running consoles, operating high-speed printers, and maintaining trouble logs, but also acts as a system user. The operator must both run *APL* user programs and interface with the users, incorporating a knowledge of overall operations with more detailed knowledge of specific operations. Training in the specific aspects gives the operator confidence in his abilities and gives the user confidence in the overall operation.

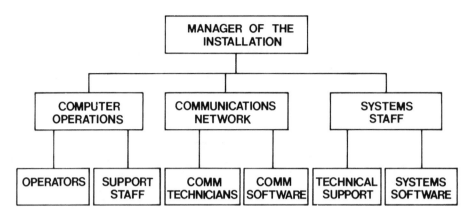

**Figure 1—Organization Chart for Operations**

Candidates for the position of *APL* operator are carefully evaluated, based on willingness and desire to learn. Although past experience and knowledge of operations, hardware, and operating systems is important, being open to new learning experiences is the quality that will allow growth in the position. At STSC, we view computer operators as entry or junior-level personnel who, with dedication and training, can find rewarding careers in the data processing field.

2. Communications

Communications requirements, which should include all real-time communications support, differ among installations. In a small installation, the Operations and Communications functions can be easily combined. In a larger installation, however, the two should be separate and distinct functions. Responsibilities of Communications personnel should encompass installations, upgrades, network maintenance, and terminal hardware support. Communications personnel should also support communications software which includes development, maintenance, and the interface with both Operations and vendors.

3. Systems

Systems staff at STSC comprises a Technical Support Team (TS) and a Systems Support Team (SST).

TS staff are systems experts who deal with users at all levels. TS is responsible for maintaining system centralization, carrying out special projects and programs, providing customer interface that cannot be handled by Operations, and furnishing all non-*APL* support. TS also provides training and designs tools for all users.

SST staff must possess a high level of technical ability to be fully responsive to the wide range of problems that are encountered. Additionally, the main departmental function—system upgrades—must be allocated according to individual capabilities. Specific areas of an upgrade include thorough testing and debugging, a technical walk through, complete documentation, a weekly upgrade cycle, and fast back-out and recovery procedures. Further,

SST staff provide training and develop tools for the other departments in the Computing Center.

## Conclusion

The most important consideration in managing an *APL* installation is service to the user. Quality service can only be provided if the installation is reliable and the organization is qualified. Thus, there must be adequate coverage of the Operations, Communications, and Systems areas of the organization. Additionally, security measures must be constantly monitored to ensure the privacy of users' files and programs. To foresee and prepare for future needs, a planning analyst should—under the auspices of the manager—direct full-time effort to capacity planning and software monitoring.

The single most important, yet most overlooked, influence on service is the people. A manager must maintain a responsive team of qualified professionals backed with a strong training program, especially for entry-level staff. The effective installation manager recognizes the direct correlation between the quality of support staff and the quality of service provided by the installation.

*Michael Handelman joined STSC in 1979 as manager of operations for the STSC Computing Center. Prior to that he had several years' experience at the George Washington University Computer Center, where from 1976 until 1979 he was the supervisor of computer operations.*

*Handelman holds B.B.A. and M.B.A. degrees from George Washington University.*

**Janet H. Faltz**

# An Overview of Reporting
# And Formatting in *APL*

Report formatting is the process by which raw data is transformed into a pleasing and readable format. Ideally, the data is presented so that its full import is obvious to the reader and key information can be extracted easily from the report. This may involve manipulating the data in some way, such as performing calculations on it or changing the order in which it is presented, or it may require adorning the data with explanatory material that will assist the reader in understanding its content.

Computers *should* be ideal tools for aiding in the process of reporting. Data—the reason for the existence of a report in the first place—can be manipulated by computers in large quantities, at amazingly fast speeds, and with virtually no probability of error. However, the embellishment of the data is often a nontrivial task.

In the *APL* environment, character data is presented exactly as it is defined, allowing for the effects of terminal printing width. Numeric data is displayed according to a set of fairly complex conventions that may differ from one *APL* implementation to another, and may be subject to change. Even this is an improvement upon other computer language environments, where the process of removing data from the heart of the machine and displaying it elsewhere can be painful. The skillful *APL* programmer can manipulate *APL* data-display conventions to his advantage, but the less sophisticated user must either have *APL* formatting tools available or be content with system conventions.

*APL* formatting tools should assist the user in many ways. For example, they should provide the ability to:

- Mix text with numeric data, such as in report titles, row names, column headings, and footnotes.
- Display numeric data in a format different from its internal representation; for example, round decimal data and display it as integer data.
- Display decorative text such as currency markers, percent signs, and commas.
- Handle several data arrays concurrently.
- Control the precision of numeric display.
- Support patterned data formats.

The format primitive (⍕), sometimes called "thorn", is familiar to many users of *APL* implementations. When used monadically, format produces a character array whose visual appearance is identical to the original data. Thus, for character data, monadic format produces no changes; for numeric data, it is subject to system conventions.

```
      A←3 5ρ'BLUE RED   GREEN'  ◊  A
BLUE
RED
GREEN


      ▼A
BLUE
RED
GREEN

      ι10
1 2 3 4 5 6 7 8 9 10
      ρι10
10

      ▼ι10
1 2 3 4 5 6 7 8 9 10
      ρ▼ι10
20
```

When used dyadically, format also produces character output, but allows control over the precision and spacing applied to the data. Pairs of control numbers are the left arguments to dyadic format, where each pair applies to one scalar, one element of a vector, or one column of a matrix right argument. These control numbers specify the width of the resultant formatted field and the data type and precision of the presentation.

```
      TABLE
1.05            4.55         2.8          3.5
1.4             0.35         4.2          4.2
5.6             2.45         3.15         5.25

      4 0 ▼ TABLE                 Integer format.

   1    5    3    4
   1    0    4    4
   6    2    3    5

      4 1 6 2 6 3 8 4 ▼ TABLE      Fixed-point format.

1.0  4.55 2.800  3.5000
1.4   .35 4.200  4.2000
5.6  2.45 3.150  5.2500

      3 ▼ TABLE                    Default width.

1.050 4.550 2.800 3.500
1.400  .350 4.200 4.200
5.600 2.450 3.150 5.250
```

By producing character output, the format primitive provides the first step in report generation. Only one array may be passed to format at a time. Furthermore, if decorative text or titles are desired, they must be forcibly inserted into the character data result.

```
      SALES
1401     300.2    416.3    299.5    317      245.5    247.5
1765     247.5    299.6    300.2    416.3    299.5    317
1900     416.5    444      506.6    509      511.1    499.6
2316     267.5    397.5    305.4    399.6    399.6    417.5

      4 0 8 2 8 2 8 2 8 2 8 2 8 2 ▼ SALES
1401 300.20 416.30 299.50 317.00 245.50 247.50
1765 247.50 299.60 300.20 416.30 299.50 317.00
1900 416.50 444.00 506.60 509.00 511.10 499.60
2316 267.40 397.50 305.40 399.60 399.60 417.50
```

```
        ρ 4 0 8 2 8 2 8 2 8 2 8 2 8 2 ▼ SALES
4  52

        FINAL←(52↑'                    SIX MONTHS SALES DATA'),[.5]' '
        FINAL←FINAL,[1] 52↑' REP    JAN      FEB      MAR      APR      MAY        JUN'
        FINAL←FINAL,[1] 4 0 8 2 8 2 8 2 8 2 8 2 8 2▼SALES
        ⎕TCNL ◇ FINAL

             SIX  MONTHS  SALES  DATA

        REP    JAN      FEB      MAR      APR      MAY      JUN
        1401   300.20   416.30   299.50   317.00   245.50   247.50
        1765   247.50   299.60   300.20   416.30   299.50   317.00
        1900   416.50   444.00   506.60   509.00   511.10   499.60
        2316   267.50   397.50   305.40   399.60   399.60   417.50
```

On other *APL* systems, formatting capabilities such as alpha (α) go a few steps further than the format primitive by supporting patterned data display and some decorative text.

On STSC's *APL*PLUS* System, the function ⎕*FMT* provides all the facilities listed above as desired features of a formatting tool. ⎕*FMT* allows concurrent formatting of many arrays; allows character arrays to be formatted at the same time as numeric arrays; provides patterned data display; allows automatic handling of report titles, column headings, and row names; supports decorative text; and supports absolute and relative tabulation. ⎕*FMT* is a dyadic system function whose representation is

$$result ← \text{'formatstring'} \quad ⎕FMT \quad (data1; data2; . . .; datan)$$

where '*formatstring*' contains the instructions that control the display of the data arrays and determine where special features will be invoked in the display. Each part of the format string (excluding tabs and blank spaces) applies to one scalar right argument, one element of a vector argument, or one column of a matrix argument specified in the data list. For example,

```
        COLORS← 3 5ρ'RED  GREENBLUE '
        COLORS
RED
GREEN
BLUE


        QUANT←5

        NUMBERS←3 2ρ 1.25 6.3 1.4 7.45 0.65 3.95
        NUMBERS
    1.25          6.3
    1.4           7.45
    0.65          3.95

        OUTPUT←'5A1,X4,I1,X2,F3.1,X2,F4.2' ⎕FMT (COLORS;QUANT;NUMBERS)
        OUTPUT
RED       5  1.3  6.30
GREEN        1.4  7.45
BLUE         0.6  3.95

        ρOUTPUT
3  21
```

A complete description of ⎕*FMT* is beyond the scope of this paper. The reader is referred to the publication entitled *Formatting in the APL*PLUS System* (STSC, 1977) for more information. Several examples showing key features of ⎕*FMT* follow.

Pattern Editing:

```
      PHONES← 3 1ρ3016578220 9194932478 9144286910
      PHONES
3016578220
9194932478
9144286910

      'G⊂(999) 999-9999⊃' ⎕FMT PHONES
(301) 657-8220
(919) 493-2478
(914) 428-6910
```

Parentheses around Negative Numbers:

```
      MAT
¯54.48      47.67      74.91     ¯68.1      ¯44.265
 10.215     54.48      34.05     ¯57.885     71.505
 61.29      23.835     ¯6.81      57.885    ¯27.24
 51.075     61.29      78.315     30.645     20.43

      'M<(>N<)>Q< >F9.3' ⎕FMT MAT

(54.480)    47.670     74.910    (68.100)   (44.265)
 10.215     54.480     34.050    (57.885)    71.505
 61.290     23.835     (6.810)    57.885    (27.240)
 51.075     61.290     78.315     30.645     20.430
```

Floating Dollar Signs:

```
      'M<($>N<)>P<$> Q< >F9.2,X2' ⎕FMT MAT

($54.48)    $47.67    $174.91    ($68.10)   ($44.26)
 $10.22     $54.48     $34.05    ($57.88)    $71.51
 $61.29     $23.84     ($6.81)    $57.89    ($27.24)
 $51.08     $61.29     $78.32     $3.65      $20.43
```

Check Protection:

```
      MONEY
100.45 1.53 17.99 4055.75

      'R⊂*⊃CLP⊂$⊃F10.2' ⎕FMT MONEY
$100.45***
$1.53*****
$17.99****
$4,055.75*
```

Accounting Notation:

```
      'M< >N< CR>Q< DR>F10.2,X2' ⎕FMT MAT

54.48 CR    47.67 DR   174.91 DR   68.10 CR    44.26 CR
10.22 DR    54.48 DR    34.05 DR   57.88 CR    71.51 DR
61.29 DR    23.84 DR     6.81 CR   57.89 DR    27.24 CR
51.08 DR    61.29 DR    78.32 DR    3.65 DR    20.43 DR
```

Workspace 1 *FORMAT* on STSC's *APL\*PLUS* System contains functions that allow you to place titles and row and column names on a report. In the following example, we will format with ease the report obtained from a previous example using the functions *CENTER* and *COLNAMES* from workspace 1 *FORMAT*.

```
      SALES
1401    300.2    416.3    299.5    317     245.5    247.5
1765    247.5    299.6    300.2    416.3   299.5    317
1900    416.5    444      506.6    509     511.1    499.6
2316    267.5    397.5    305.4    399.6   399.6    417.5
```

```
     ∇ R←FORM DATA;FS
[1]    FS←'I4,6(X2,F6.2)'
[2]    R←FS CENTER 'SIX MONTHS SALES DATA' ◇ R←R,[1] ' '
[3]    R←R,[1] FS COLNAMES '∘REP∘JAN∘FEB∘MAR∘APR∘MAY∘JUN'
[4]    R←R,[1] FS □FMT DATA
     ∇
```

□TCNL ◇ FORM SALES

SIX MONTHS SALES DATA

| REP | JAN | FEB | MAR | APR | MAY | JUN |
|-----|-----|-----|-----|-----|-----|-----|
| 1401 | 300.20 | 416.30 | 299.50 | 317.00 | 245.50 | 247.50 |
| 1765 | 247.50 | 299.60 | 300.20 | 416.30 | 299.50 | 317.00 |
| 1900 | 416.50 | 444.00 | 506.60 | 509.00 | 511.10 | 499.60 |
| 2316 | 267.50 | 397.50 | 305.40 | 399.60 | 399.60 | 417.50 |

The system function $□FMT$ is an extremely powerful formatting tool for *APL* technicians. Its use requires familiarity with *APL* data arrays, *APL* syntax, and $□FMT$ commands and capabilities.

There is also a great need for formatting tools for non-programmers. These tools should allow the businessman to focus on the key elements of the desired report: the data and the verbal information. The businessman should not have to be concerned with the technical aspects of the supporting system. Two such facilities provided by STSC—QUICKPLAN™, The Quick Planning and Reporting System, and the *EMMA* Report Generator—are discussed in papers that appear elsewhere in this book: "QUICKPLAN: A Reporting Tool for the Non-Programmer" and "The *EMMA* Report Generator".

*Janet Faltz started with STSC in 1974 as a marketing representative and is currently branch manager of STSC's Southeast Branch located in Chapel Hill, North Carolina. Before joining STSC she worked as an applications programmer and publications editor at the University of North Carolina Computation Center and as a management information systems analyst for Continental Can Company.*

*Faltz has a B.A. in mathematics from Douglass College and an M.A. in educational technology from Columbia University.*

**David L. Hopkins**

# QUICKPLAN: A Reporting Tool for the Non-Programmer

Reporting. What is it? Who does it? Most importantly, how does QUICKPLAN™, STSC's Quick Planning and Reporting System, meet the requirements of a reporting system? These are the questions I propose to answer.

Reporting is the process of organizing and presenting data or information in a useful form, with one or more purposes in mind. Reporting is done by virtually everyone, from elementary school students reporting "current events" to large corporations reporting to their shareholders. Reports are as varied as their creators and users, and can contain any combination of text, pictures, graphs, plots, and tables of numbers.

In business and government, a simple report can be generated by an analyst working with pen and paper and, perhaps, a calculator. The report so generated will probably be typed to appear more uniform and legible. Or, the analyst will take a set of specifications for a report, with a request for computer resources, to his company's data processing center.

Both of these procedures, however, have obvious drawbacks. The typist may make mistakes, and the process of correcting them is often time consuming and annoying. Requesting reports from the data processing center may be time consuming as well, as there will typically be many other demands placed on the center. Furthermore, adjustments or changes to the report specifications are more difficult to accomplish. In both cases, turnaround time may not be as quick as the report user would like.

What the businessman needs is often more than either of the above methods can provide. He needs the ability to produce reports using data that may be entered specifically for a particular report, or that may be retrieved from an existing data file. In either case, substantial data calculations or manipulations may be required to complete a report.

In other words, the businessman needs access to all sorts of data, and he needs to be able to work with that data. He wants the capability to present the data in many different, and sometimes unexpected, formats. And, most importantly, he wants the resulting reports available in a timely manner. A system that meets these requirements is more than a reporting mechanism—it is a tool with which the businessman increases his productivity and the accuracy of his decisions.

If this is all within reach by using high-speed computers (and it is), then why doesn't everyone with access to a computer perform his own report generation? The answer to this question is not the lack of native intelligence on the part of the average user; the answer is, however, related to intelligence. That intelligence is the method of accomplishing the task.

In a batch computer environment, the user may find it necessary to learn such programming languages as COBOL, FORTRAN, or PL/1. In addition, he has to contend with the detailed mechanics of how information is entered into the computer (on punched cards, for example). He is also subject to the turnaround time. Even in a time sharing environment, languages such as *APL* prove to be too complex for the businessman to use directly. Too often, a businessman finds it necessary to take the additional time necessary to learn and use commands and symbols that bear little relation to the finished report.

Let's look at a typical, though simplified, business report (see Figure 1). Though reports have widely varying formats, this report has a common format. It presents numeric data in rows across the page and columns down the page. The rows and columns have labels, and the report has titles at the top and comments at the bottom.

| CAPITAL COMPARISON FOR MIDWEST BANKS | | | |
|---|---|---|---|
| BANK | CAPITAL TO ASSETS | CAPITAL ($ MILLION) | DEBT TO CAPITAL % |
| BIG BANK | 4.4 | 501.0 | 25.0 |
| FRED'S BANK * | 4.6 | 1,903.0 | 22.4 |
| BANCO DEL ORO BANK | 5.1 | 40.0 | 15.0 |
| WHY BANK * | 5.2 | 54.0 | 24.2 |
| FAST BANK | 5.3 | 217.0 | 25.4 |

*AS OF MARCH 31, 1979.

**Figure 1—A Typical Report**

Ideally, the user who wishes to create a report like that shown in Figure 1 should be concerned only with describing the key components and specifying the order in which those components should appear. This ideal situation is rarely the case, though, as most businessmen do not have the proper tools. QUICKPLAN was developed to provide the tools. Its English style commands, simplifying assumptions, and full database interaction make it a natural tool for reporting.

To see firsthand how QUICKPLAN meets the requirements of a useful reporting tool, we will use the system to create the report shown in Figure 1. After signing on to STSC's *APL∗PLUS* System, we access the QUICKPLAN System and the tools it provides:

```
)LOAD 333 QUICKPLAN
SAVED  . . .
```

Next, we create a filing area called *QUICK* for the Report Generating System (RGS) and its data and programs.

```
GPCREATE
G/P SYSTEM NAME?  QUICK
 9999999 QUICK CREATED.
```

Now we're ready to create the RGS, which we'll call *BANK*. The RGS is used to store information for report titles, headings, line names, line numbers, and data.

```
        BUILDRGS
RGS NAME:   BANK
HOW MANY COLUMNS?
□:
        3
BANK CREATED.
```

With these steps completed, we are ready to enter the specific information for our report. It is important to note that the above steps are necessary only when setting up a report for the first time. Many reports can be generated using the same "file" (*QUICK*) and the same RGS (*BANK*).

Next, let's enter the character information for our report (titles, column headings, and line names). For each item, we must specify a number (used for later reference), the justification (left, right, or centered), and, of course, a name. Line names also offer two additional options for the data that will appear in each line—formats and scale factors—but we will not use these options.

```
        ENTERTITLES         First we enter the titles.

RGS NAME:   BANK
DEFAULT: LJUST, CENTER, RJUST   C
SEQUENTIAL?   NO
ENTER TITLE NUMBER
□:
        12
12:  |CAPITAL COMPARISON FOR MIDWEST BANKS
ENTER TITLE NUMBER
□:
        END
MORE?   NO
TITLE NAMES STORED.
```

```
        ENTERHEADINGS       Next we enter the headings.

RGS NAME:   BANK
ITEMS TO BE ENTERED: NAME, FORMAT, SCALE:   NAME
DEFAULT - LJUST, CENTER, RJUST:   R
USE ⊂, ∩, OR ⊃ TO OVERRIDE DEFAULT. USE ← FOR NEW LINE
SEQUENTIAL?   NO
ENTER HEADING NUMBER
□:
        0
0 NAME:   |⊂BANK←  ̄ ̄ ̄ ̄
ENTER HEADING NUMBER
□:
        1
1 NAME:   |CAPITAL TO ASSETS← ̄ ̄ ̄ ̄ ̄ ̄ ̄ ̄ ̄ ̄ ̄ ̄ ̄ ̄ ̄ ̄ ̄
ENTER HEADING NUMBER
□:
        2
2 NAME:   |CAPITAL←($MILLION)←  ̄ ̄ ̄ ̄ ̄ ̄ ̄ ̄
ENTER HEADING NUMBER
□:
        3
3 NAME:   |DEBT TO CAPITAL←        ∘/∘ ←  ̄ ̄ ̄ ̄ ̄ ̄ ̄ ̄ ̄ ̄ ̄ ̄ ̄ ̄ ̄
ENTER HEADING NUMBER
□:
        END
MORE?   NO
HEADINGS STORED
```

```
        ENTERLINES          And, finally, we enter the line names.

RGS NAME:   BANK
ITEMS TO BE ENTERED:  NAME, FORMAT, SCALE:   NAME
SEQUENTIAL?   NO
ENTER LINE NUMBER
□:
        10
10 NAME:   |BIG BANK
```

```
ENTER LINE NUMBER
□:
       12
12 NAME:  |FRED'S BANK*
ENTER LINE NUMBER
□:
       20
20 NAME:  |BANCO DEL ORO BANK
ENTER LINE NUMBER
□:
       24
24 NAME:  |WHY BANK*
ENTER LINE NUMBER
□:
       31
31 NAME:  |FAST BANK
ENTER LINE NUMBER
□:
       END
MORE?  NO
LINE NAMES STORED.
```

Now we can try a "first cut" at our report. All we need to do is enter a simple program that specifies the order in which the components should be printed:

```
    ∇REPORT
[1]  FIELDS 26 18 18 18    ⍝FIELD WIDTH FOR PRINTING COLUMNS
[2]  TITLES 12 0 0         ⍝PRINT TITLES 12 0 0 (0 PRODUCES A BLANK LINE)
[3]  HEADINGS 0 1 2 3      ⍝OVER THE COLUMNS, PRINT HEADINGS 0 1 2 3
[4]  LINES 0 THRU 99       ⍝PRINT VALID LINES IN THE RANGE 0 TO 99
[5]  ∇
```

We run our report program at this point to check the format of the report (the resulting "report" is shown in Figure 2):

```
    REPORT


                  CAPITAL COMPARISON FOR MIDWEST BANKS


                                                CAPITAL      DEBT TO CAPITAL
    BANK                 CAPITAL TO ASSETS      ($MILLION)         °/°
    ____                 _____      _____    _____

    BIG BANK                     0                  0               0
    FRED'S BANK*                 0                  0               0
    BANCO DEL ORO BANK           0                  0               0
    WHY BANK*                    0                  0               0
    FAST BANK                    0                  0               0
```

**Figure 2—Checking the Report Format**

If the report format is correct, we can begin to enter the data. A simple data input program like the one given below shows us what data must be entered.

```
    ∇INPUT
[1]  GETSYSPGM 'PENTERDATA'
[2]  1 2 3 PENTERDATA 0 THRU 99
[3]  ⍝ ENTER DATA IN COLS. 1 2 3 FOR LINES 0 THRU 99
[4]  ∇
```

We run the input program and enter the appropriate data:

```
    INPUT
10: BIG BANK  = 0 0 0
□:
     4.4 501 25
```

```
12: FRED'S BANK*  = 0  0  0
□:
      4.6 1903 22.4
20: BANCO DEL ORO BANK  = 0  0  0
□:
      5.1 401 15
24: WHY BANK*  = 0  0  0
□:
      5.2 540 24.2
31: FAST BANK  = 0  0  0
□:
      5.3 217 25.4
```

We modify our report program slightly to add cosmetic additions such as spacing and comments.

```
      ∇REPORT1
[1]   'ALIGN PAPER'◇PAUSE  ⍝ STOP TO LET USER ALIGN PAPER
[2]   FIELDS 26 18 18 18
[3]   FORMAT '1'  ⍝ SHOW ONE DECIMAL PLACE
[4]   TITLES 12 0 0
[5]   HEADINGS 0 1 2 3
[6]   LINES S,(0 THRU 99),S,S  ⍝ 'S' GIVES BLANK LINE
[7]   COMMENT'*  AS OF MARCH 31, 1979.'
[8]   ∇
```

Finally, we run the modified report program, and we have a finished report as shown in Figure 3.

REPORT1

```
                  CAPITAL COMPARISON FOR MIDWEST BANKS


                                          CAPITAL     DEBT TO CAPITAL
                                          ($MILLION)      °/°
      BANK               CAPITAL TO ASSETS --------  ----------------
      ----               -----------------


      BIG BANK                  4.4           501.0         25.0
      FRED'S BANK*              4.6         1,903.0         22.4
      BANCO DEL ORO BANK        5.1           401.0         15.0
      WHY BANK*                 5.2           540.0         24.2
      FAST BANK                 5.3           217.0         25.4



      *  AS OF MARCH 31, 1979.
```

**Figure 3—The Finished QUICKPLAN Report**

QUICKPLAN can do much more than produce reports, since it contains its own database manager called the GET/PUT facility. Data is stored with *PUT* commands and retrieved with *GET* commands. The user need not be concerned with the structure of files; he addresses all data items by names that he has chosen. GET/PUT databases can be shared, and many people can simultaneously put data into a database or retrieve data from it.

To expand our example, let's assume that one QUICKPLAN GET/PUT database contains data about banks. It might contain all the operating data on every bank in the United States, or in a specific state. Once this database exists, the user can select data that meets any given criteria. In our example the report was for midwest banks, but we could as easily have selected data for another region or for banks with greater than a specified capital level. If data were stored in the database by year, we would have yet another dimension in our database. The user could then produce reports for specified time periods.

Having selected any subset of the stored data, the user can perform calculations and produce reports, or put the calculated data back in the database for later access. The possibilities for manipulating and reporting data become endless. Better yet, these possibilities are all within the reach of QUICKPLAN and its database system.

## Conclusion

Stepping back from the mechanics of QUICKPLAN, let's repeat the necessary elements of a complete reporting system. We can then decide whether QUICKPLAN meets these requirements.

- The reporting system must be clear, concise, and unambiguous.

- It must contain all the necessary commands, including the selection criteria, to facilitate interaction between the user and the databases in which relevant data is stored.

- The user should not be asked to deal directly with the underlying programming language (in our case, $APL$). That is, all error messages and data manipulations should be handled by the user-oriented language of the reporting system.

- The system should be column or line oriented, or both, and should provide headings for columns and lines.

- Numbers should be presented, by default, with standard business notation (using dollar signs, commas, parentheses, and decimal points).

- The system should prevent the user from doing harm to a database.

- The system should allow the user (and the database manager) to change anything he has done—easily and quickly.

- Finally, the reporting system should be compatible with other systems written in the same language so that the systems can be easily linked.

When these requirements are met, the reporting system will best meet the needs of the businessman. It will also be a useful tool for programmers.

QUICKPLAN does, in fact, meet these requirements. Furthermore, one can easily learn to use QUICKPLAN. In one day, the average person can master QUICKPLAN's reporting capabilities. Little additional time is required to learn the database management capabilities.

Let's return to the original questions. It is fairly obvious what reporting is. With QUICKPLAN, the answer to "Who does it?" is "Anyone with a need for reports, a few minutes, and access to a terminal". Does that sound too simple? If so, that's because QUICKPLAN makes business reporting so simple that most users can master the system in a day.

*Dave Hopkins earned his B.S. in computing and information science at Trinity University in Texas, where he worked part-time for two years at the university's computing center. After receiving his M.B.A. from Southern Methodist University, Hopkins joined STSC in 1978 as an applications consultant.*

*Hopkins has developed many customized QUICKPLAN reporting systems for STSC customers, particularly for major oil and energy producing companies located in Houston.*

Robert R. DeCloss

# The *EMMA* Report Generator

In physics we learn that an "erg" is a unit of energy or work. The ERG System (*EMMA*™ Report Generator System) allows a user to define and obtain numerous reports easily and quickly, making his work more productive, and saving him the time and effort spent otherwise collecting that data.

ERG is a system designed for non-programmers who, with a surprisingly small "vocabulary", can generate virtually unlimited reports in formats they specify. For that reason, ERG is particularly useful to management. Management's reporting requirements vary almost daily. Since ERG requires no programming, an executive can define reports and have them in minutes.

The ERG System operates from an *EMMA* file. *EMMA* (Extended Management Macros in *APL*) is a proprietary collection of programs developed by STSC to manipulate, select, replace, and compare data. In contrast to *EMMA*, ERG has only a few user programs, which I will explain a bit later. First, I would like to share some of the history of ERG's development.

ERG was the result of a great design process; we spent *hours* considering alternatives and options. Here is how it all began:

One of our clients needed many different kinds of reports for its management. They had been using PERT*PLUS, STSC's Interactive Project Management System, but they had come to realize that the system was solving only parts of their problem at an expensive price. One Friday afternoon, they gave us a list of the capabilities they wanted. For example, they wanted to be able to print different columns and have data paged for easy separation and distribution to different departments. They also wanted the ability to total columns of data based on a major category and to subtotal based on a subcategory.

From this "wish list" we had a better idea of what the client's needs were. When we went to see the client on Monday, we proved that we had not only satisfied their needs, but had also added the capability for the user to format his own reports.

After the client registered mild shock at the speed with which we had solved their problem, we asked if our design was acceptable. It was; we were off and running; and ERG was born!

I suppose I could be accused of heresy, but I believe a majority of products and packages are developed in this way—at least a majority of useful products. *APL* is the only language I'm aware of that will let you accomplish what I've just described. With *APL* you can have results within a couple of hours of receiving ideas from a client. The client reviews the initial design, and usually thinks of additional requirements. After input and suggestions from both sides, you go back and add some "features" (a technical term for "bells and whistles"). Soon you've met the client's requirements, and probably given him much more!

The best way to substantiate my claims of the value and simplicity of ERG is to describe its characteristics.

The current version of ERG (others are under development) works from a single *EMMA* file. It can be installed quite easily by anyone who understands the basic concepts and nomenclature of the system.

That brings me to an extremely valuable overall design consideration in any product or package I develop: ease of use. This may be an overused phrase, but I *do* go to great lengths to avoid computer jargon and to implement ideas that fit the customer's business, *not* the computer business. But, I digress.

To return to ERG, five of the main user programs are

- *REPORT*—A conversational program that asks what fields to print, how to sort the data, what fields to total, where to put page breaks, and what field to break on within a page.

- *SUMMARY*—A program similar to *REPORT*. The only difference is that the data is summarized and no detail information is printed. Break totals and page totals are printed on the report.

- *PRINT*—A program that prints a previously created report. The report specified can be printed at a terminal or can be submitted for printing on a remote, high-speed printer.

- *DIRECTORY*—A program that displays all report files currently existing.

- *ERASE*—A program that erases a report file.

To store the report information, the user fills out a worksheet and enters the information into the system. Editing features allow the user to set or change formats or column headings very easily. Once satisfied with the headings, formats, tables, and names, the user saves the information. A variety of reports are now ready for production, waiting only for a request from the user.

In generating reports, a user must become familiar with the following eight concepts.

- print fields
- sort fields
- page break field
- page total fields
- break field
- break total fields
- selection criteria
- report name.

Most of these concepts are relatively straightforward and become second nature quickly.

The *print fields* specify the columns of data the user wishes to display in the report. The *sort fields* indicate how the printed fields should be sorted, in major to minor order. The sort fields *do not* have to be included in the print fields.

The *page break field* is used to force a new page every time the specified column of data, after being sorted, changes. The *page total fields* allow the user to specify which columns of data are to be totaled before each page break. (If no page breaks are specified, the user is prompted for grand total fields rather than page total fields.)

The *break field* allows a subtotal within a page break field. Thus, a user can get branch totals within each cost center or subtask totals within each task. The *break total fields* allow a user to select which columns of printed fields are to be subtotaled. Page total fields can be different from break total fields.

Now, for the only slightly complex part of the whole system—selection criteria. The *selection criteria* specify what data is to be printed, using abbreviations of English words such as: *FROM, BETW, EQ, GT* (greater than), *AND,* and *OR.*

Parentheses can be used to alter a definition or form complex statements. For example:

*SELECTION CRITERIA:*   **(SAL BETW 1000 2000) AND EARN GT 100000**

For experienced *APL* programmers, the same selection criteria can be specified using raw *APL*:

*SELECTION CRITERIA:*   **(SAL>1000)∧(SAL<2000)∧EARN>100000**

Let's consider an example. Suppose we want to generate a report that prints the cost center, branch number, employee number and name, employee salary, and revenue generated by each employee. We want to sort it by cost center and by branch within cost center, and we want only cost centers less than 400. We are only interested in the top producers, so we want only those who have generated year-to-date revenues in excess of $130,000.

Here is all we do:

```
      )LOAD 9999999 ERGDEMO
SAVED  . . .
      REPORT
PRINT FIELDS:  HELP
VALID FIELD NAMES AND NUMBERS ARE LISTED BELOW:
(NOTE: WHEN USING NAMES YOU MUST USE A COMMA AS A SEPARATOR).
CC=1  , BR=2  , EMP=3 , NAME=4 , SAL=5  , DATE=6, EARN=7 , STATE=8

PRINT FIELDS:  CC,BR,EMP,NAME,SAL,EARN
SORT FIELDS:  CC,BR
PAGE BREAK FIELD:  SKIP
GRAND TOTAL FIELDS:  SAL,EARN
BREAK FIELD:  CC
BREAK TOTAL FIELDS:  SAL, EARN
SELECTION CRITERIA:  (CC LT 400) AND (SAL FROM 1000 3000) AND EARN GT 130000
REPORT NAME:  MYREPORT
REPORT TITLE:  TOP PERFORMERS FISCAL YEAR 1980
FIRST SUBTITLE:  (SPACE,RETURN)
DONE
```

After entering the report specifications in this manner, you can run the program *PRINT* and produce the report, as shown in Figure 1. Using slightly different report specifications, and other ERG options not demonstrated here, you can produce many variations of this basic report.

I can't stress enough how easy it is to use ERG. The user does not have to learn a programming language, nor does he have to figure out what a work file is or even how to create one. All the user has to know is what data should appear on the report, and in what order. This gives each user more time to review reports containing exactly the information he wants to see—no more and no less. Each report is customized so that the user sees only the columns and headings pertinent to him. Managers don't get detailed reports crowded with data that doesn't interest them, or worse, annoys them.

```
OFFICE PRODUCTS SERVICE COMPANY
TOP PERFORMERS FISCAL YEAR 1980

PAGE 1; 2/19/80

      COST   BRANCH  EMPLOYEE   EMPLOYEE               EMPLOYEE   DOLLARS
    CENTER   NUMBER    NUMBER       NAME                 SALARY    EARNED
    ------   ------  --------   --------               --------   -------
       311        1      1137   FLANIGAN, JOAN            2,900   136,500
       311        3      1069   RYAN, KAREN E.            1,600   133,500
       311        3      1087   ESKINAZI, KEVIN          1,600   147,500
                                                       --------  --------
                                                          6,100   417,500

       332        4      1107   GURGOLD, JOHN            2,800   144,000
                                                       --------  --------
                                                          2,800   144,000

       341        1      1115   DAAR, ARLENE             2,700   138,500
       341        1      1007   CARTER, CLIF             1,000   137,500
       341        1      1122   CHANDLER, JAK            2,700   138,000
       341        1      1108   WEAVER, JEFF S.          2,500   143,500
       341        3      1028   KARPF, ELEANOR T.        1,300   133,000
       341        3      1098   KRANISH, RON S.          1,200   132,000
                                                       --------  --------
                                                         11,400   822,500
                                                       ======== =========
                                                         20,300 1,384,000
```

## Figure 1—A Sample ERG Report

The combination of ERG and *APL* provides managers with a powerful tool for producing reports that meet their requirements, even if those requirements change daily. Furthermore, valuable information is provided on time and at a very reasonable price. What better way to work? That is the key to ERG—making work better and easier.

*Bob DeCloss joined STSC in 1973 as a programmer. He took a leave of absence in 1975 to become treasurer of the Irwin Trading Company and Irwin Management Company, but later in 1975 rejoined STSC in the APL Development Department. Since 1978 he has been the branch manager of STSC's Denver office.*

*DeCloss co-authored with Roy A. Sykes, Jr., a paper for the APL75 Conference in Pisa, Italy, titled "EMMA : Extended Management Macros in APL" (APL75 Conference Proceedings, ACM, 1975). In 1977 he wrote the EMMA Reference Manual (STSC, 1978). He has designed and implemented several systems dealing with report generation, database management, and construction accounting.*

*DeCloss has an M.A. in mathematics from Claremont Graduate School.*

Richard W. Butterworth

# When *APL* Is Inappropriate

The use of *APL*, or any high-level programming language, can be inappropriate for a given application, particularly when the use of a different language offers a lower *overall* cost to achieve the objectives of the user and the application. From this somewhat over-simplified beginning, we will discuss several issues that help determine when *APL* (or any high-level language) is appropriate. These issues frequently become the deciding factors in choosing a programming language.

Of course, there are few, if any, hard and fast rules in a field whose technology is changing so rapidly. The following discussion and examples will provide some principles that can be examined when resolving the issue of whether *APL* is appropriate.

## Program Readability

The primary issue in language choice is *program readability*. For purposes of this discussion, program readability refers to the inherent difficulty and associated costs of reading a program, determining precisely what the programmer intended the program to do, and executing the program. This issue includes not only "people" readability (a person learning the input, process, and output characteristics), but also "machine" readability (the initial interpretation of the program into machine-executable code and subsequent executions of the program). As might be expected, high-level languages favor people readability, while low-level languages favor machine readability.

The issue of readability fits naturally into the concept of a program's total life-cycle cost. A program's life-cycle cost can be viewed as the sum of its people readability costs and its machine readability costs. The former might be measured in manhours, and the latter in machine cycles. These two costs are determined by the amount of "reading" the program is subject to over it's life and the associated costs. Hence, a program that is read primarily by machines, such as a system utility, will have life-cycle costs dominated by machine readability costs. Conversely, a program read primarily by people, such as a program for quantitative support of management decisions, will have life-cycle costs dominated by the people readability costs. Proper language selection, then, entails knowing the program's intended use and environment and selecting the language that minimizes the composite costs.

Foretelling total people readability costs is a subjective process. People readability costs, for example, include not only the original programmer's time, but also the time of subsequent persons (programmers and users) who need to understand the program from a conceptual, technical, or operational viewpoint. These costs are usually underestimated.

People readability costs also contribute heavily to a program's development cycle time, since during the development phase a program is read almost exclusively by people. In a linguistic sense, as with high-level spoken languages, a high-level programming language greatly assists the communication of ideas among designers and programmers, thereby reducing the time it takes to understand the problem. This asset, and the ease of translating the algorithmic concepts into executable programming statements, shortens development time significantly. This suggests that some programs requiring short development cycles may be infeasible unless undertaken in a high-level language.

Machine readability costs are equally difficult to estimate. The primary factors are the cost of machine resources and the execution cost of the program. Though CPU power is becoming increasingly cheap, additional machine cycles cannot always be purchased. For example, many products today contain dedicated microcomputers or minicomputers; the application environment is precisely defined and the CPU power restricted. Another example sometimes occurs with the Federal Government, which occasionally chooses low-level languages for their ability to conserve CPU resources made scarce not by financial or architectural restrictions, but rather by an extremely slow procurement process. Thus, machine readability, like people readability, may be constrained by a variety of cost parameters. These parameters, which include opportunity costs as well as actual costs incurred, usually have highly subjective attributes.

## Readability and the Performance Issue

The life-cycle costs of computer applications are then a combination of the reading costs incurred by people and machines. To minimize expected total cost, a compromise is usually sought between costs of software development and maintenance, and costs of hardware capacity and sophistication. *APL*, with its natural ability to manipulate data arrays and its user-oriented implementations, offers distinct benefits in reducing software development costs. Predictably, *APL* is most effective in applications such as modeling systems and decision support systems, where software development costs are highest. In these systems, primary design criteria are ease of use, ease of program adaptability, a short development cycle, and frequently, a customized approach.

Today, however, a majority of computer applications are characterized by repetitive processes. Programs that are changed infrequently and that do not require interactive processing are less able to take advantage of *APL*'s assets. Moreover, on most implementations, the interactive interpreter makes it difficult to move these processes out of the very busy (and, consequently, the most expensive) prime operating time.

The current trend toward distributed processing provides another example where programs are duplicated to run at many locations or on many machines at the same location. This reduces software cost per unit hardware cost, and creates leverage for low-level languages. Take, for example, the system supporting a large retailer's point-of-sale terminals. Hardware costs are amplified many times by the number of terminals involved, but software, once written, is likely to remain very stable. It is clear from this discussion that the language issue cannot be decided outside the application's context.

In current machine architecture, which requires that a programmer's code be reduced to common machine code before execution, the performance requirements of a program can become a major issue in language selection. Some programs are read primarily by machines; programmers read the code only for development and maintenance and the end users do not read it at all. In these cases, machine performance is a main concern, and a low-level language is clearly preferred. Examples of this are utilities such as file sorts, random number generators, and internal checks and balances.

A different example involves a scientific simulation project. The operation and maintenance of emergency diesel generators at nuclear power plants were simulated to study the effect of the maintenance and test plan on the generators' reliability and availability. Though extensive documentation of the program was not required, people readability was an issue, since the model being simulated was not completely specified and was likely to undergo change.

These factors would appear to indicate that *APL* would be a good programming language for the project. However, performance became the deciding issue, as the precision of the results depended heavily on multiple replications over long horizons. A few short programs had to be executed hundreds of thousands of times to evaluate each scenario. Consequently, the associated machine costs became a limiting factor to the system's use. FORTRAN was finally chosen as the programming language for the project; the random number generator was provided by the host compiler, probably in Assembler language. The complexity of the model precluded any low-level language approach, due to the people readability issue.

A secondary issue in the simulation project was machine portability (i.e., the ability to move and maintain an application on two or more computer systems). The portability requirement, while essentially a machine readability issue, is usually resolved by using a high-level language. In this case, *APL* was not available on the alternate system, but FORTRAN was. The FORTRAN simulation program, when moved to the alternate installation, ran and duplicated earlier results with a change to only one line of source code.

Another type of problem not generally handled in *APL* is the linear programming (LP) problem. Linear programs are comprised of "matrix generators" that develop application data in a canonical LP format. The LP problem, an optimization of a linear function of independent variables subject to linear constraints, is then solved using the simplex algorithm, or some variation of the simplex technique. Finally, the solution is translated back into the terms of the problem and output reports are produced.

Although LP problems are characterized by matrix data structures, only relatively small problems (those having 50 or fewer equations) seem suited to an *APL* approach due to the nonlinear increase in iterative computations. Even when an LP problem is small, other factors must also be present to suggest an *APL* solution (e.g., a fluid problem definition requiring constant revision).

## Readability and the Intelligence Issue

As the prerequisite intelligence of a program increases, so does the need for increased people readability. (The word "intelligence" in this paper refers to a program's ability to handle complex sets of logical rules and to deal gracefully with unanticipated input.) Complex ideas are difficult to communicate with the limited "vocabulary" of low-level languages and are nearly impossible to grasp by reading a program written in a low-level language. Just as high program intelligence generally supports the use of a high-level language, low program intelligence generally favors use of a low-level language (i.e., the non-*APL* solution).

An example of a low-intelligence task that can become expensive when undertaken in *APL* is large-volume record processing to update and maintain a database. Large personnel systems, for example, usually maintain a record on each individual, perhaps in a sequential dataset consisting of many tapes. The database must be updated weekly, or even daily, and update reports must be produced. The procedures for performing such updates are relatively simple; consequently, the matrix manipulation capabilities of *APL* would be largely under utilized. The machine expense associated with constant interpretation of the code to simply process the next record creates a situation in which the system's overall cost is dominated by the machine readability of the program.

It is worth noting, however, that non-*APL* programs can build *APL* databases that can subsequently serve many information needs. These databases generally condense entity data into frequency of occurrence data that summarizes the activity. Such databases can become excellent sources of top-down management information, supporting the increasingly popular decision support systems (DSS).

In our experience, two personnel systems have been implemented in this manner. One tracks 30,000 persons and the other tracks over 500,000 individuals. In both systems, *APL* was judged inappropriate for the database development because of the large number of record manipulations required. However, management models that used the data *were* developed in *APL* specifically to obtain ease of model development and flexibility. This illustrates that large systems can easily contain applications appropriate for both non-*APL* and *APL* programs.

In fact, it is typical in large application systems for *APL* to be appropriate for some programming tasks, but not for others. One such case is a flight-routing system called OPARS (Optimum Path Air-Routing System). OPARS provides flight plans on a production basis for a subset of the Navy's flight community. Flight plans are requested a few hours before flight time by naval weather personnel or flight personnel, but seldom by computer personnel. To request a flight plan, the user responds to a few questions in an interactive terminal session. The result of the session is a request file, which is forwarded to a batch input queue. The flight plan is printed at the user's terminal five to ten minutes later, and can be revised if necessary before takeoff.

The flight plan consists of an optimum routing from point of departure to point of arrival. The criterion for optimality is minimum fuel consumption, which may be subject to user constraints such as mandatory fly-overs or fly-arounds, or use or nonuse of FAA jet routes. Wind and temperature forecasts from real-time databases are used to develop a dynamic network to which a shortest path branch-and-bound algorithm is applied. The final result is a formatted flight plan showing the suggested routing, expected fuel consumption, forecasted winds enroute, and a checkpoint schedule.

Because of the machine performance issue, *APL* was inappropriate for the production version of this shortest path network optimization program. The nature of the network algorithm, which sequentially examines arcs for potential inclusion in the shortest path, precluded the use of "matrix-type" calculations, and suggested a "looping" design instead. However, *APL* was used during the design effort to test the network and algorithm design concepts by developing a prototype program for the optimization. The *APL* program contributed to a proof of concept, but was relatively inefficient for repetitive execution of the algorithm in a large-scale production environment.

*APL* was also found to be inappropriate for implementing the main flight-routing program, which begins with the request input file and terminates with a formatted flight plan file. In spite of the complexity of the program, the performance issue was overriding. The number of flight plans to be prepared daily could not be forecasted; however, as system activity increased, the number was expected to grow from between 10 and 20 plans to between 100 and 500 plans. Given the turnaround requirement of 10 minutes, the application required a language that kept machine performance high and machine readability costs low. The languages selected were FORTRAN (for the flight routing) and Assembler (for the input/output operations).

The interactive request generator, though developed in FORTRAN because of institutional constraints, was a suitable candidate for *APL* implementation. This interface had to be interactive and "user friendly", had to handle sparse amounts of data, and had to have a fair amount of intelligence to determine whether requests were well formed and complete. Requirements for this program were expected to change as system capabilities were added or temporarily suspended—another factor favoring the use of *APL*.

## Conclusion

The readability theme of this presentation focuses on the reading and interpretation costs of programs. Readability costs are accumulated by machines, in machine cycles, and by people, in manhours. The key to resolving the language issue is to look at the relative costs of having the program read by people and by machines. If the life-cycle program costs will be dominated by machine costs, *APL* may not be the best language choice, in spite of its more productive use of people's time.

Language choices are still likely to be somewhat subjective, however, as factors affecting hardware costs and personnel costs continually change. Examples of factors directly influencing the choice of *APL* are the decreasing costs of hardware, the continual improvements to the *APL* interpreter, and the possibilities of bringing native hardware operations structurally closer to *APL* primitive operations. In the foreseeable future, however, many situations will arise where compelling cases can be made for low-level language approaches. The best solutions, *APL* or not, will capitalize on the assets of both high- and low-level languages, in composite solutions.

Some points discussed in the examples are summarized as follows:

- General support utilities, such as file sorts, are good candidates for non-*APL* implementation.

- Simple tasks that require little intelligence and emphasize high-volume processing (e.g., sequential record updates) are generally not recommended for *APL* implementation.

- Real-time performance requirements of complex tasks may not permit a responsive solution with *APL*. These applications tend to become "expensive" to implement because of a somewhat constrained language choice.

- Portability, which usually favors the high-level language approach, can work against *APL* until such time as *APL* is implemented on a wider range of machines.

- Hybrid solutions offer numerous benefits. While *APL* has many attractive features, there are valid and compelling reasons to select other languages for certain system segments to complement the segments written in *APL*.

*Richard Butterworth, technical director of the Advanced Analytical Applications Division of SEI, is experienced in operations research, with specific interests and applications including military manpower analysis, energy systems reliability, statistical time-series forecasting, and interactive decision support systems. At SEI he led the development of DELIS, the Navy's Executive Level Information System, and OPARS, a global Navy flight-routing system.*

*Prior to joining SEI, Butterworth was associate professor of operations research at the Naval Postgraduate School, where he developed a new course in interactive computing. He holds a Ph.D. in operations research from the University of California at Berkeley.*

**Thomas A. Gull**

# Managing Outside Computer Services:
# An Organizational Relationship

## The Basic Relationship

If you are a time sharing coordinator or an important user of an outside computer service, your organization holds you responsible for meeting certain objectives. These objectives may be quite specific, or they may be very general. In either case, you are responsible for using resources to meet those objectives, and your management will examine the difference between the costs of resources used and the value derived from those resources.

The resources allocated to you may include budgeted funds, personnel, supplies, and time. Availability of these resources may give you the option of buying various services from another organization. When you use an outside computer service, you are going to build a business relationship between two organizations, and that relationship must be carefully managed.

In real life, of course, the "relationship" between two organizations really can be thought of as some function of all the personal relationships between members of the organizations. These personal relationships, however, work well when there is general agreement on why the people interact on a continuing basis. This agreement occurs when goals have been set by the leaders of each organization, the goals are supported by members of both organizations, and everyone can see that the personal interactions help meet those goals. In effect, this is a "business relationship" regardless of the goal of either organization.

Simply stated, your organization is going to get services and pay for them in some way. You, personally, are not receiving or paying for services; by the same logic, no one person in the vendor organization is serving you and being paid for it. Your understanding of the distinctions between organizational relationships and personal relationships has a huge effect on the quality of the service you will receive.

## Identifying the Common Ground

Whether a vendor is a profit or non-profit organization, goals will have been defined for the entire organization. When you first choose an outside computer service, spend some time ferreting out those corporate goals. For a vendor shooting for monetary profit, the goals may be well publicized and easy to understand. A non-profit vendor may survive with vague goals, though some research or service groups have very clear objectives. You do not know if you can get service from a vendor until you know what they want in trade for that service. As harsh as it may sound, your goodwill by itself may not keep you on as a client of a service having difficulty meeting its goals. In other words, getting services free sets up an unbalanced relationship in which you will have little or no influence when circumstances change. You will get what you pay for.

When you know what motivates the vendor to give you service, you can examine your available resources to see if you can afford the service you need. Most vendors will prefer to deal with organizations that can contribute to meeting goals at some significant level. For example, getting service from a giant firm can be a problem if you would be its smallest client. You should be realistic about what you expect to spend on computer services, since this will give your vendor an honest picture of what resources to set aside for your use. Your estimates of what you will need will be used by the vendor to manage the allocation of his resources; bad estimates may contribute heavily to bad management in either organization, perhaps increasing your costs or even preventing you from meeting your objectives.

Common ground for any business relationship has four main components:

1.   What services does your organization need?

2.   What can you pay for those services?

3.   Can the vendor provide those services?

4.   Are you giving the vendor enough incentive to provide those services?

This approach implies that you will receive the most useful service when you and the vendor can both (1) meet your respective goals, and (2) avoid using resources unnecessarily. If you have identified the common ground correctly, you should be able to predict what level of service you will receive from any vendor.

## Communications with the Vendor

Your vendor will assign one or more persons to work with you and your organization. Your basic communications with the vendor organization will go through this assigned person, so you must be able to deal effectively with this representative of the vendor. You will receive the best service when both of you take the time to identify the "common ground", and this process requires honesty and skill. If you have trouble dealing with the assigned person, ask for another representative.

As you work with your representative, be aware of what organizational goals he has been given. In a company like STSC, for example, the marketing representative has been hired to increase revenue at a reasonable expense. That is the focus around which decisions will be made. However, the manner in which goals are met will vary widely from vendor to vendor. For example, one vendor may sell only machine time and provide no other services. Another vendor may provide machine time, consulting, educational programs, and so forth.

The overall quality of a computer service is actually more dependent on the manner in which the service is delivered than on the hard economics of the vendor's goals. To have a complete picture of what service a vendor will deliver to you, you should consider not only the vendor's goals, but also his business philosophy and his level of involvement with the customer.

Some vendors concentrate on high business volume mixed with low personal service. Their favored customers will probably not interact much with the marketing representatives. Other vendors may concentrate on medium level volume coupled with high personal service. In the former case, vendors will not have many highly trained support personnel available, since personalized service is discouraged. In the latter case, there will be support personnel spread throughout the organization.

The presence or absence of support personnel and a listing of the resources available to a marketing representative, and, therefore, to a customer, can outline a company's basic business philosophy very clearly; these factors are a direct communication to you describing how a vendor intends to meet his goals. If his intentions don't match your needs, look for another vendor.

When you work with a marketing representative for an *APL*-based service company, there is a subtle trap both you and the marketing representative can fall into. In some cases, particularly when using *APL*, your representative may have enough technical skill to solve many of your problems directly. This may give you the impression that the representative can, and should, personally solve all your technical problems. In practice, it is better to hold the representative responsible for obtaining the resources you need, without necessarily being the resource himself. This distinction in attitude helps to ensure that the business relationship between your two organizations is not overdependent on the skill and goodwill of one or two individuals.

Overdependence on one person seems to be fairly common in the *APL* environment. The productivity of each *APL* analyst is very high compared to, say, a FORTRAN or COBOL analyst, and many projects are completed from start to finish by only one person. If you, as the user, deal only with that person, you are encouraging bad habits in your vendor that may ultimately hurt both organizations.

For example, if you have a vendor build a general ledger system in *APL*, it may take only one person to do the job. During development of the system, communications about concerns will go to that person. When the system is completed, a crucial moment occurs. If you continue to call the developer when something needs changing or fixing, none of the other vendor personnel will gain experience with the project. The net effect is that you will get quick service only as long as the developer remains available; should he move on, your vendor may lose the ability to serve you easily on that project.

The average analyst using *APL* works so quickly that customers are usually convinced that the analyst assigned to their project is uniquely competent, and so the customer prefers to be served by that analyst. Since many customers may feel this way, the cumulative effect upon the analyst can be devastating. Actually, a professional analyst works in such a way that another analyst could easily deal with many of the questions asked about a project. It is part of the analyst's job to complete projects with advice from other analysts, with the expectation that others will modify or support the project in the future. If there is such interaction, the vendor organization is able to give you good service even if a particular analyst is on vacation or has switched jobs.

For example, the Washington, D.C., marketing branch of STSC handles customer needs by assigning a different person each day to screen incoming phone calls. Problems taking up to roughly 20 minutes to solve are handled directly by the "hotline" person. More complex problems are referred to the appropriate marketing representative or to the manager of the branch technical resources. These complex problems can then be worked into a flexible schedule involving the entire branch. If one analyst is on vacation, a customer will be readily and effectively served by another STSC analyst, and problems of overdependence on one person disappear.

## Conclusion

You can get the computer services you need from an outside vendor, but you will need to analyze such a relationship carefully. The crucial distinction suggested in this paper involves the difference between organizational and personal relationships. If your job involves meeting organizational objectives, then your relationship with an outside vendor should focus at that level. Some ways of working person-to-person seem effective but actually will not help you accomplish your job. Your vendor should be aware of this fact, and the organizational structure of the vendor ought to reflect an ongoing concern with what makes good business sense. If you lay the ground rules for a business relationship, personal relationships between members of the two organizations are likely to be effective and comfortable.

Dealing with an outside computer service effectively involves using an organizational approach and having the willingness to communicate honestly with your vendor's representatives. Ideally, those representatives should approach you in the same manner.

*Tom Gull joined STSC in 1974 and has held positions as an applications consultant, marketing representative, and account manager. In his current position as an applications consultant manager he is responsible for managing the technical resources of the Washington, D.C., branch office, including the scheduling and planning of technical consulting activities. Gull has also helped develop and implement new business methods and applications and acts as a liaison between marketing and the Design and Development Department.*

*Gull graduated from Cornell University in 1974 with a B.A. in sociology.*

Frank Vogt

# Selecting and Managing Outside Computer Services

Selecting and managing outside computer resources effectively is important to business and government users of computer applications. It is an interesting and complex task that requires juggling a diverse assortment of components including hardware, software, maintenance, technical support, communications, training, and documentation.

Proper management must cover the entire cycle of outside services; that is, the *selection, utilization,* and *termination* processes. *Selection* is the process of evaluating, comparing, and contracting with the vendors to service one's applications. *Utilization* is the day-to-day procurement of the services selected. *Termination* is the end of such utilization—normally due to the end of an application (in its present form), a transition to an inhouse system, or a transition to another outside vendor.

Note the phrase "day-to-day procurement of services". It is important to bear in mind that such services are generally ordered "by the drink" and that the source of supply can vary throughout the life of an application—that is, one can always "go to another bar".

This paper will highlight some critical aspects of choosing and managing outside computer services. The points presented are intended to stimulate and help organize the thinking of the person undertaking this task. The presentation will be grounded largely in government terminology and philosophy; this is due to my background as a government teleprocessing user and my current involvement in implementing existing government procedures for competitive acquisition of such resources.

Government awareness and policy have evolved considerably in this area during the past few years. Much has been learned, often at painful expense. It is hoped that this paper will help readers, from both the public and the private sector, to avoid going through the same trials.

We will address the following topics:

- connect/communications
- storage
- processing
- software
- performance
- account administration role.

The management of *connect/communications* is critical to many applications. The marketplace offers a variety of coverage, pricing plans, and types of service.

The selection of baud rates to be used is a basic decision; charges by suppliers will vary by baud rate, by the volume of data transmitted, or both. Terminal availability will be a strong factor in this decision.

One approach to data transmission is to employ intelligent terminals in an application. Using intelligent terminals means that data can be entered locally at leisure, corrected later, and finally transmitted to the remote service in a very efficient fashion.

Some applications may justify a distributive network or more sophisticated equipment to collect and perform a portion of the data manipulation locally. Some may justify a user-implemented network to supplement or optimize the use of a supplier's network.

A decision must be made concerning bulk terminals; cost tradeoffs must be considered when determining whether to lease or share lines and whether to rent or purchase equipment.

Approximately 20 to 25 percent of teleprocessing charges fall in the area of connect/communications.

*Storage* has been judged by many to be the most misused and abused aspect of remote computing services. It is available in many different forms. Immediate Access Storage (IAS) can be purchased by the character—either at one pricing plan or by the track, sector, or pack at rates that differ considerably.

Offline storage may be the better choice for part of an application; the data can be kept on magnetic tapes or on the client's own mountable disk pack. In either case, large savings will be realized. It is crucial for the client to determine how long he can wait to access his various files and what guarantees the vendor will make regarding mount and read time.

Old versions of programs on data files should be policed regularly; meticulous archiving practices can enormously benefit budget and operations. "Junk files" should be moved to a very low cost medium for later cleanup.

Often the operating system or database management system will allocate and control storage. This can result in some surprisingly large storage charges and thus should be monitored carefully.

Storage charges constitute 20 to 30 percent of charges to the average user.

*Processing* costs typically are responsible for about half of the dollars spent by users of outside computing services. Understanding prime and nonprime pricing structures can lead to a noticeable decrease in costs as well as an increase in throughput. For example, west coast users might get better performance at reduced costs from an east coast mainframe by running large jobs at the end of the work day.

Proper use of batch processing and established priorities is essential. Discipline is also essential to this aspect of an application.

The benchmark programs employed in the process of selecting outside services should be carefully chosen to test the capability, timing, and pricing of the system appropriate to the client's needs. Without a benchmark, processing costs will be essentially unknown.

Choice of *software* is of major importance. The remote service vendor is usually the best source of software support pertinent to his system; the user should make his needs clear to the vendor. Client needs and vendor support must be blended carefully.

A recent General Accounting Office estimate quoted $8.00 per line for software development in languages such as FORTRAN and COBOL. With a language as powerful as *APL*, the number of program lines required is greatly reduced, but the per line costs may be higher. At these rates, it is crucial to use skilled personnel to get the most from your software development expenditures.

After programs are in place, it is important to create a system for the modifications that will be required as needs change. Assistance from remote service vendors varies in price, availability, and quality. This service, and the availability of vendor-written software, are deciding factors in selecting or using a remote service. Prewritten application packages can result in dramatic savings. But much of the prewritten software will entail an extra charge forcing a rent, create, or buy decision.

The *performance* of a remote system should be looked at very carefully, both when it is selected and throughout its usage. The hardware and operations will be managed by the vendor—not the client's own staff. Run times should be measured and monitored, as should job costs. A variance resulting in budget or mission problems must be dealt with. It is often a good idea to get post-selection benchmark runs to police performance and justify possible billing adjustments.

Any remote service usage, regardless of size, requires *account administration*. This duty could be full time or simply a portion of a particular user's responsibilities.

The account administrator should control user identifications to permit proper access; work with management to estimate and justify expenditures; verify billings by benchmark runs as well as by actual usage; monitor storage and access patterns to optimize the use of available pricing plans; monitor priority usage and assign priorities based on management goals; track and project usage for budgeting purposes; and work with the remote service vendor.

A "single-point interface" with the vendor need not be a rule, but it will enhance the relationship with the vendor, reduce redundant queries, and enable trends to be recognized and remedied.

Proper management of outside computer resources is not a trivial task. Basic common sense will rule, but familiarity with the services provided and a comprehensive approach are required.

*Frank Vogt is currently an independent telecommunications consultant and a general partner in TSP Training Associates. He previously worked as a technical advisor for the General Services Administration (GSA). In this capacity, he acted as a negotiator on many contracts for GSA's teleprocessing services program. He assisted in developing a structure for evaluating time sharing service vendors for the government's procurement services.*

*Vogt has a B.A. in mathematics from the College of Steubenville and has done graduate work in mathematics at Denver University. He served as an officer in the Air Force and previously worked as a mathematician with the Navy, as an operations research analyst for the Army, and as a data system manager for the state of Ohio.*

Clif Kranish

# Converting External Datasets
# Into *APL* Files

*APL* files on STSC's *APL\*PLUS* Time Sharing System are structured to
work efficiently with the powerful primitive functions of the *APL* language.
Consequently, it is often useful to convert data files produced on other
computer systems or by programs written in other languages into *APL* files so
that the data can be accessed and manipulated by *APL* programs. This paper
describes methods used at STSC to perform these conversions.

### What Is an *APL* File System?

On early *APL* systems, such as *APL\360*, the only way to store data was
as a variable in the *APL* workspace. While this was satisfactory at first, it was
soon found to be too restrictive, since all data for an application had to fit into a
single workspace. In fact, the most common criticism of the *APL* language was
that "*APL* couldn't handle large amounts of data". It didn't seem to matter
how much the workspace size was increased; as long as there was an upper
limit, *APL* programmers quickly reached it.

Another problem with early *APL* systems was that there was no way for
*APL* to get at data produced by programs in other languages, even if these
programs were running on the same computer as the *APL* system. The often
heard complaint was that "*APL* couldn't talk to the rest of the world". The
only way to make this data accessible to *APL* programs was to type it in at a
terminal.

Other shortcomings of early *APL* systems were their inability to store and
retrieve data under program control and their cumbersome procedures for
sharing databases among several users.

To address these problems, most commercial vendors of *APL* developed
file subsystems to go along with their *APL* systems. These file subsystems
allowed data to be stored outside the workspace and made managing large
amounts of data much easier. Although each single data object was still
limited by the size of a workspace, there was no real limit on the total amount
of data that could be stored.

In 1970, STSC offered one of the first *APL* file subsystems, called the
*APL\*PLUS* File Subsystem. Soon after, other vendors such as Burroughs and
Digital Equipment Corporation (DEC), offered files with their *APL* systems.
Although the storage and access methods are different, all of these systems
store data outside the workspace.

One important advantage of storing data outside the *APL* workspace is
that programs written in other languages can access the data. In effect, the

*APL* file systems opened a "window" to the rest of the world. Data could be interchanged between *APL* programs and other languages.

## What Is an *APL* File?

An *APL* file is made up of components containing *APL* data that can be stored as variables in a workspace. Thus an *APL* file can contain components of different rank, shape, or data type. Data is stored outside the *APL* workspace, and the amount of data is not subject to workspace size constraints. System functions are used to transfer data between files and workspaces.

Most *APL* users aren't concerned with the internal representation of data or the use of different data types (except for the distinction between character and numeric data). Conversion from one numeric data type to another is done automatically.

However, the internal representation of data *does* affect the amount of storage required for an *APL* data item. It often affects the amount of computer resources required to perform some arithmetic operations on the data. The data representation is also important when considering a conversion from some external medium to an *APL* file.

All data stored on a computer is represented internally as a sequence of binary (0 or 1) values or *bits*. The meaning of each bit sequence depends on the type of data it represents. Most systems based on *APL\360*, including the *APL*PLUS* System, support four different data types. The four *APL* data types and the number of bits required for a single value are

- Boolean—1 bit
- Character—8 bits
- Integer—32 bits
- Real—64 bits.

## Why Is Conversion Necessary?

External files, called *datasets*, are structured differently from *APL* files. These datasets are described in terms of logical *records*. For example, for a dataset on 80-column punched cards, each card is a logical record. For a dataset on magnetic tape the records may be grouped into *blocks* for efficient storage and processing.

To use *APL* programs to process data on external datasets, the datasets must first be converted into *APL* files. For external datasets consisting entirely of data in one of the four *APL* data types, conversion can be accomplished without interpretation using a simple batch program. The program reads the data on the cards or tape and appends the data to an *APL* file.

Sometimes, however, it is necessary to convert external datasets that contain more than one *APL* data type, or that contain data types that don't exist in *APL* (e.g., packed decimal). To convert these datasets, more sophisticated techniques are required. STSC offers one such technique, known as the File Conversion Generator (FCGEN).

## How the File Conversion Generator Works

Data in an external dataset is described in terms of *fields* and *records*. Each field generally contains one type of information. These fields often have different data representations depending on the type of data that is stored. For example, one field in a personnel file may contain social security numbers, another field may contain names.

A record contains the information for a single entity in the file. For example, one record in a personnel file may contain the social security number, name, and other information for one individual. A programmer using COBOL or other high-level languages includes, as part of the program that processes the data, a description of each field in the input record.

To convert an external dataset into an *APL* file, the user must specify how the various fields and records are to be handled. This could be done using a program written in a language other than *APL*, but not without great difficulty. The special nature of *APL★PLUS* System files makes it difficult to deal with *APL* data representations in languages other than *APL*.

In addition, the *APL★PLUS* System provides special security checks not available with the OS/MVT operating system under which it runs. Consequently, it is advantageous to write the initial conversion program in *APL*.

But what about the COBOL programmer who is unfamiliar with *APL*? It seems unfair to ask him to learn *APL* so that he can write a conversion program.

This is where FCGEN proves most useful. FCGEN is a package of *APL* subroutines that are used to write an *APL* conversion program. The unique characteristic of FCGEN is that its subroutines accept data descriptions in notation closely resembling that commonly used in COBOL for describing record formats. Other *APL* programs check the *APL* conversion program for syntax and consistent specifications and generate a COBOL program, which actually performs the file conversion.

Advantages to this approach are twofold:

- The notation used in the *APL* program is familiar to both COBOL and *APL* programmers.

- Indirect generation of the COBOL conversion program allows the user to take advantage of the security checks provided on the *APL★PLUS* System.

In writing the *APL* conversion program, the user must specify the following information.

- *The fields in the input record to be converted.* Each field in the input record is listed. If the field is to be converted, the *FIELD* statement is used. For fields that are to be skipped, the *FILLER* statement is used.

- *The records to be converted.* Normally each record from the input dataset is read and converted. To select only certain records, an *OSFILE* statement is used. Records can be selected by specifying the first or last record to be read or by specifying that every *n*th record is to be read.

- *The records to select, by field values.* It is often useful to select only certain records by the values of certain fields. For example, if the value of an "amount" field is zero, that record could be ignored by using a *DISCARD* statement.

- *The data type and length of each field.* Each field of the input record can contain character data or numeric data in decimal or other representations. Each field description must include the data type and length in standard COBOL notation.

- *The translation of character data.* Character data on external media is generally not in the *APL* character representation, but in EBCDIC or ASCII. A standard translate table has been defined for characters with a direct correspondence. For example, the digits 0 to 9 and the uppercase letters A to Z are translated to their *APL* equivalents. For special graphics, "reasonable" translations are defined. Extensions or changes to the default translate table can be made using the *TRANSLATE* statement.

- *The distribution of data in a file.* When converted to an *APL* file, data is stored in file components as numeric or character matrices with values from successive records occupying successive rows of a matrix. Character and numeric values must, of course, occupy separate components. However, it may be useful to store a field in a component of its own if it is to be accessed frequently, or it may be useful to store related fields in the same component. The distribution of fields into *APL* file components is specified by using *TARGET* statements.

- *The file structure.* The data can be directed to several different files or to consecutive components of a single file.

- *The blocking factor.* The maximum number of input records to be stored in a single component is specified with the *BLOCKING* option. A large blocking factor will be more efficient in that it will require fewer file accesses, but the resulting components will require more workspace area when manipulating the data. If the file is ordered by a certain field, it may be useful to start a new component when the value of that field changes. This is done with the *NEWBLOCK* option.

- *The name of the summary file.* As part of the conversion process some error checking is performed. Defects such as incorrect characters, translation errors, nonnumeric values in numeric fields, numeric overflow, and magnetic tape errors are reported in a summary file.

## Sample Conversion Program

The following sample input file contains six records. Arrows indicate the field breaks.

```
ALBANI        5000ODENSE        1859
CARLSBERG     2900HELLERUP      1847
CERES         8000AARHUS        1856
FAXE          4640FAKSE         1901
THOR          8000AARHUS        1910
TUBORG        2900HELLERUP      1847
↑             ↑    ↑            ↑
```

The records of the sample input file are processed with the following FCGEN program.

```
      ∇ DKBREW
[1]    APLFILES BLOCKING 5
[2]    '12345 SUMMARY' GETS SUMMARY
[3]    '12345 DATA' GETS CHARDATA
[4]    '12345 DATA' GETS NUMDATA
[5]    F1:FIELD 'X(10)' ⍝ BYTES 1-10 NAME
[6]    F2:FIELD 'S9(4)' ⍝ BYTES 11-14 CODE
[7]    F3:FIELD 'X(10)' ⍝ BYTES 15-24 LOCATION
[8]    F4:FIELD 'S9999' ⍝ BYTES 25-28 EST
[9]    FILLER 'XX' ⍝ LOGICAL RECORD LENGTH IS 30
      ∇
```

The program creates three files: a summary file to report the outcome of the conversion and errors, if any; a file to collect character data; and a file to collect numeric data. All four fields of all six records are converted.

## Conclusion

FCGEN allows programmers to control the way in which external datasets are converted into *APL* files. Many different data representations can be converted into *APL* data using FCGEN. In addition, both *APL* and COBOL programmers can easily write the conversion programs using simple FCGEN notation.

*Notes*

1.  C. Kranish, STSC Working Memorandum No. 127, *FCGEN—File Conversion Generator,* (STSC, 1978).

2.  L. Gilman and A. J. Rose, *APL: An Interactive Approach,* (Wiley, 1976).

*Clif Kranish joined STSC as an operator/programmer and is currently a senior programmer in the company's Technical Support Group. He participated in the design and development of STSC's Source Level Transfer System, which provides a means for transferring a workspace from one APL system to another. He also participated in the implementation of STSC's File Conversion Generator (FCGEN) and authored Working Memorandum No. 127, FCGEN—File Conversion Generator (STSC, 1978).*

*Kranish currently provides support for programs written in PL/1, COBOL, and 370 Assembler, as well as APL. He has taught introductory APL courses for STSC personnel and customers and currently teaches introductory programming at George Washington University.*

*Kranish has a B.S. in systems and information science from Syracuse University and is currently pursuing a master's degree in computer science at George Washington University.*

John A. Estep, Richard C. Geden,
Jack S. Reynolds, and Howard M. Sternlieb

# A Fully Automated Interface between Systems In Boston and Bethesda

This paper describes the evolution and implementation of a fully auto-mated interface that transfers data from the Gillette Safety Razor Division in Boston, Massachusetts, to STSC in Bethesda, Maryland. The interface runs weekly and requires no involvement from a user at a time sharing terminal.

The Safety Razor Division (SRD) at Gillette has implemented a manufac-turing resource planning system that runs on STSC's *APL*PLUS* Time Sharing Service and that is based on STSC's Comprehensive Manufacturing Control System, CMCS™ (see notes 1 and 2). Before this implementation, some of the inventory balance information required by CMCS was already being maintained by a Purchasing and Material Reporting System running on Gillette's inhouse IBM System/370, Model 158 computer. Gillette and STSC personnel developed—in stages—an interface that now automatically trans-fers status of open purchase orders and raw material inventory from Gillette's system to STSC's system.

## Interface Specifications

When the interface specifications were developed two years ago, the CMCS installation was in its early stages. Contributing to the specifications were STSC representatives, SRD's Manufacturing Systems and Production and Material Control Departments, and Gillette's Management Information Systems (MIS) Department. An interface of this kind had not been previously attempted at Gillette, and its development had to be coordinated with the CMCS installation. Consequently, it was important to involve both users and systems personnel.

The group defined the following steps (similar in concept to manufactur-ing process routings) through which each purchasing transaction was to progress:

1. Issue purchase requisition.
2. Issue purchase order.
3. Receive material.
4. Inspect material.
5. Dispose of rejected material and post accepted material to stock.

The users selected a pilot group of parts, monitoring their progress step by step using the CMCS worksheet facility and manually posting information from the inhouse system to CMCS. This simulation identified conceptually the tasks that the interface would be required to perform. It also helped the users develop their own procedures, giving them confidence in their ability to use the system to accomplish their tasks. The group determined that the information should be passed weekly from Gillette's system to CMCS.

Gillette's MIS and Manufacturing Systems Departments then developed two programs—one for each end—incorporating the lessons learned from the simulation. On Gillette's end, the program created two files containing purchase order progress and material status transactions. On STSC's end, the program validated the transactions and used them to update the CMCS database. Activity transactions (rather than a snapshot of status) were used in the initial implementation because the information could be captured easily and required only minor changes to Gillette's existing systems. This approach did require, however, some duplication of the Purchasing and Material Reporting System's logic at STSC's end. With *APL*, this task was accomplished with little difficulty.

### Transmission

With the programs in place, the only task remaining was to actually move the data. At first the data was written to tape and physically carried to STSC. However, the resulting two-day turnaround did not meet Gillette's timing requirements. To save time, Howard Sternlieb of SRD's Manufacturing Systems Department introduced a Hewlett Packard 7260 table-top card reader. The information was punched on cards, read into the card reader (which was connected to an ordinary time sharing terminal), and transmitted to STSC over the telephone lines at 300 baud and later at 1200 baud. This cut down the cycle time considerably—from two days to as little as two hours. Unfortunately, the card system was susceptible to line noise and card jamming, so it was necessary for someone to "babysit" the terminal. Sometimes the job took as long as half a day.

The next improvement came with the elimination of the card reader and the direct transfer of data from a disk file on Gillette's system to a disk file at STSC. This was accomplished using two facilities:

- STSC's High-Speed Data Terminal Service (HSDTS), which moves data at high speed (2400 or 4800 baud) in either direction between STSC and a HASP terminal (see note 3).

- The HASP Remote Workstation (HRWS) program. (HRWS, which was originally the IBM program HASP.RMI360, was extensively modified by the University of Iowa and has been further modified by STSC).

HRWS is run as an ordinary batch job on Gillette's system, but it copies the two files from disk to the computer's communications interface, which the operator has connected (by dialing) to STSC. HRWS makes Gillette's computer appear to be a HASP terminal to STSC's system. HRWS and HSDTS reduced turnaround time for the transmission to approximately 12 minutes.

### Complete Automation

Once the transmission time was reduced to an acceptable level, we turned our attention to STSC's interface program, which verifies the data received and updates the CMCS database. The program was interactive, requiring a user to sign on, run it, and answer a lengthy series of questions. This process was inconvenient, since it meant that the one person responsible had to sign on every Monday by 7:30 AM (the file transmission took place on Saturday) to complete the database update before other users arrived. Since the data was coming from a file—not from the operator—the answers to the questions were invariably the same every week. This was a good opportunity for automation using STSC's Deferred Execution System, a facility which allows the automatic scheduling of production jobs (see notes 4 and 5).

The goal for this part of the interface was to have the update performed automatically each week. The job had to be completed by 7:30 AM every Monday, and it had to be performed without user intervention. By running the job as a "deferred task", we could not only free the user from the drudgery of entering repetitive data, but we could also take advantage of the substantial discount available to deferred jobs with batch priority.

Before automation of the CMCS update, the following procedure was performed on a weekly basis:

1. Gillette's computer operations staff initiates HRWS, which transmits the data.

2. HASP updates the *APL* files.

3. A Gillette user runs the interface program, which updates the database and prints the reports.

4. The Gillete user "cleans up" and prepares for the next transmission.

To complete file updates and generate reports by 7:30 AM on Monday, we were having the data transmitted (step 1) sometime over the weekend. This still left steps 3 and 4 in the above procedure as obvious candidates for automation.

To automate these steps it was necessary to examine the procedure more carefully and make some changes. First, it was necessary to insert a new step between steps 2 and 3. This new step was to verify the completion of the transmission and the creation of the *APL* files (i.e., to verify the successful completion of steps 1 and 2). In fact, this verification was already being performed. It was, however, a simple check at the beginning of the interface (step 3). By automating the data transmission, we had introduced some uncertainty into the procedure; that is, we could not know exactly when, over the weekend, the transmission would be performed. Consequently, the verification step became a more important part of the procedure.

The second change in the procedure was to separate (in step 3) the generation of the reports from the printing of the reports. We decided not to automate the final printing of the reports; instead this task was left for the end user to complete on Monday morning.

With these changes implemented, the procedure looked as follows:

1. Gillette's computer operations staff initiates HRWS, which transmits the data.

2. HASP updates the *APL* files.

3. A deferred task verifies the successful completion of steps 1 and 2.

4. The deferred task runs the interface program, which updates the database and generates the reports.

5. The deferred task "cleans up" and prepares for the next transmission.

6. A Gillette user prints the reports.

Now, with the additional automation of steps 3 through 5, all file updates and report generations are performed before Monday morning. The only exception to this is on rare occasions when the data transmission fails over the weekend, or when there is some system problem that prevents steps 3 through 5 from being run as scheduled.

The automation of steps 3 through 5 in this procedure was accomplished using STSC's Deferred Execution System. This system allows users to request that *APL* programs be run at some future time. A key feature of the system is that submission and monitoring of the deferred jobs is accomplished with *APL* programs. This makes it possible for one deferred job to submit additional deferred execution requests. In this way, a job that is to run on a regular basis (weekly, in the case of our interface) can perpetuate itself indefinitely into the future without any involvement from the end user.

A secondary goal of the automation was to take advantage of the lower CRU (Computer Resource Unit) rates offered for deferred overnight processing. This presented a problem because the lower rates apply only if the job is run with a batch priority class. This means that the actual scheduling of the job is left up to the Deferred Execution System. Uncertainty regarding when the deferred task would run, together with uncertainty regarding when the data would be transmitted, presented the only complication in automating the interface.

We resolved our problem by scheduling two overnight jobs each weekend. One job runs on Saturday night and performs the interface if, in fact, the data was transmitted on Saturday. The other job runs on Sunday night and does nothing if the interface was successfully completed on Saturday. If, however, the data was not transmitted until Sunday, the Sunday night job performs the interface.

At first glance, it might seem easier to have just one job on Sunday perform the interface. With this approach, you would not have to worry about when the data was actually transmitted. Indeed, this approach was considered and rejected because of the possibility of a system problem occurring on Sunday that would prohibit the interface from successfully running. The "two-job" approach was selected because it gives the system two nights to complete the interface, and therefore increases the probability of its being successfully completed by Monday morning.

Once the two-job approach was selected, the only task that remained was establishing conventions for each job so that it could communicate its progress to other jobs and to the end user on Monday morning. With these conventions established, the weekly procedure was quickly and easily automated.

### The Future

The last step in the automation of Gillette's interface is to convert from processing purchase transactions to transferring a snapshot of the entire file. The transaction approach currently being used has two principal disadvantages: (1) the logic is complex and expensive to maintain, and (2) recovery from failures is hampered by the lack of a clean restart point. Snapshot logic is simple and recovery from failures is accomplished by merely rerunning the job.

The transaction approach can be more suitable than the snapshot approach when the volume of data involved is significantly less using the transaction approach. For Gillette, the amount of data is the same using either approach. The switch to the snapshot approach did, however, require writing a new interface program at each end, but the logic has proved so simple that the task was accomplished in less than three days. At this writing, final testing is in progress.

### Conclusion

Interface development is a combined systems and user effort. Specifications must be clear and represent a consensus; results must be closely monitored.

During each stage of development at Gillette, the interface continued to provide vital inventory status information to CMCS so that planning could proceed. Gillette's interface has evolved in the direction of maximizing the use of computer system capabilities and reducing clerical involvement. At the same time, each improvement in the interface has reduced both the time to transfer the information and the cost of operating the interface.

An important side benefit of the interface effort at Gillette is the relationships established between Gillette's users and systems personnel and STSC's representatives. These relationships not only aided the interface effort, but have also proved invaluable in other work undertaken by these groups.

*Notes*

1. R. G. Brown, *Materials Management Systems: A Modular Library*, (Wiley, 1977).

2. *Comprehensive Manufacturing Control System User's Guide*, (STSC, 1978).

3. J. J. Prats, Working Memorandum No. 104, *High-Speed Data Terminal User's Guide*, (STSC, 1978).

4. J. G. Wheeler, *Deferred Execution Reference Manual*, (STSC, 1979).

5. J. G. Wheeler, *Deferred Execution User's Guide*, (STSC, 1979).

*John Estep joined STSC in 1977 and is currently a materials management consultant, responsible for the sale, customization, installation, and support of systems for finished goods management, production and capacity planning, and production control. Prior to coming to STSC, he worked in operations research and systems design for the Talon Division of Textron and for the Connecticut General and Massachusetts Mutual life insurance companies.*

*Estep holds a B.S. in mathematics from Allegheny College and an M.S. in electrical and computer engineering from the University of Massachusetts, where he is currently a candidate for a Ph.D.*

*Dick Geden has worked with the Gillette Company for over 11 years. He previously managed the Blade Dispenser Loading Department and Machine Shop Planning Department, and was the project manager for MRP (Material Requirements Planning) development. Currently he is manager of manufacturing systems.*

*Geden holds a B.S.B.A. degree from Boston College and an M.B.A. from Babson College. He is a certified practitioner of APICS, the American Production and Inventory Control Society.*

*Jack Reynolds is currently an applications consultant manager in STSC's Boston office. Before joining STSC, he was with IBM where he learned APL and developed expertise in a variety of database design and data storage and retrieval techniques. Recently he completed installation of a portfolio management package for an insurance company, and he is currently directing development of an inventory cost accounting system for a national manufacturing firm.*

*Reynolds holds a B.A. in mathematics from Dartmouth College.*

*Howard Sternlieb is currently a technical coordinator in the manufacturing systems department of Gillette Company's Safety Razor Division. He has responsibility for all technical aspects of computing, including programming, hardware selection, user support, and inhouse education. Sternlieb joined Gillette in 1974. He previously worked as manager of sales support with Wang Laboratories, and as a senior materials analyst at Honeywell.*

*Sternlieb earned his B.S.B.A. from Northeastern University and his M.B.A. in computer science from Boston College. He is on the staff of the Computer Information Systems Department at Bentley College.*

Robert E. Cook

# Making the Inhouse Decision:
# Some Considerations

As the popularity of *APL* grows, more *APL* users are looking beyond the traditional *APL* time sharing vendors for alternative ways of getting the computer power they need. Because of the dramatic decline in the per function cost of computer hardware over the past ten years, large users question the variable costs of commercial time sharing. They search for ways to lower and bound costs for *APL* and other time sharing usage.

To objectively evaluate the alternatives to commercial *APL* time sharing, more than hardware costs must be examined. A full understanding of the time sharing vendor's environment must be reached, as well as a reasonable understanding of the hardware and system software environments. Making a decision to move a series of *APL* systems from commercial time sharing to an inhouse processing environment, without detailed investigation of these various environments, is a disservice not only to the *APL* user, but also to the general management of the user's enterprise.

The scope of this discussion does not permit a detailed investigation of the relative merits and drawbacks of commercial *APL* time sharing versus an inhouse processing environment. Rather, a "road map" to and "background briefing" for this kind of investigation will be provided from the perspective of the *APL* time sharing vendor. A brief discussion of the vendor environment, the hardware environment, and the software environment will be provided, together with observations concerning the trends in technology and pricing that should be considered when evaluating the long-term implications of alternative means of delivering *APL* computer power.

When an analyst evaluates the environment of an *APL* time sharing vendor, he usually assumes that the vendor is fully aware of technological trends and will act in his own best interests to ensure the continued viability of his particular approach to business. The continued trend toward reduced hardware cost per computing function, when viewed on a relative CPU cycle-cost basis, makes the inhouse time sharing environment quite attractive. However, the time sharing vendor provides much more than a CPU service; in fact, CPU power is a relatively minor portion (less than 10 percent for STSC) of the cost. Although most commercial *APL* vendors find it convenient to charge customers in terms of CPU (or "CRU") usage, services such as "free" customer training and "free" telephone customer assistance are bundled into the seemingly simple charges. The analyst must consider the impact of removing these "free" services from the user environment.

When pricing an inhouse *APL* service, the analyst must also consider the disruption caused by removal of ancillary software services; ancillary software is seldom provided in a readily installed form by the hardware vendor. Prime examples of this are the administrative or "housekeeping" software that provide services such as file backups, accounting and billing, sorting and merging, and high-volume printing. These functions are of critical importance to only a small subset of the total user population and, therefore, might be easily overlooked in an evaluation.

Additionally, *APL* language enhancements and proprietary application software—the most important assets of an *APL* time sharing vendor—are often woven into many of the user's own application programs. This transparent, proprietary software is usually designed to enhance the already high productivity of *APL* programmers and, for that reason, is of great value to users. The cost of losing this proprietary software must also be factored into the ultimate investment decision.

The hardware environment, of the costs to be discussed, is probably the least complex. Hardware prices will continue to plunge. Not only will prices for CPU power drop, but relative prices for all kinds of storage will also drop. Again, one must assume that the hardware vendors will act in their own best interests and protect the viability of their enterprises.

If hardware prices are to continue their downward trend, and if the costs of hardware manufacturers are to remain relatively constant, where will the manufacturers get their profit margin? At least some of the margin will come from economies of scale based on increased sales volume. Before long, however, competition for market share will drive high-volume hardware prices down, again squeezing the profit margins of the hardware vendor.

One method available to assist the hardware vendor in addressing this quandary is a substantial increase in the use of microcode or firmware to implement application and system software. The use of proprietary microcode both improves system performance and allows the hardware vendor to establish a proprietary edge that permits reestablishment of high-margin pricing.

A careful investigation of the true long-term costs of an inhouse hardware/software alternative to commercial *APL* time sharing must include a recognition of the trends established by the hardware vendors toward "unbundled", or individual, pricing of all proprietary system and application software. This unbundling implies a dramatic increase in the price of software vended by the manufacturer. A *Computerworld* article (Lundell, "Software for IBM 4300 May Cost More than Hardware", *Computerworld*, 30 April 1979) documented that software charges from IBM could exceed hardware charges for an IBM 4300-series computer over the life of the system. This trend, and the costs associated with it, must be recognized by the time sharing user community in investment analyses.

The single most important consideration in evaluating alternative means of delivering *APL* computing power is software—both system software and *APL*-related software. Proprietary application software may also have relevance to this decision.

With regard to software, response time is a major consideration. It is impossible, or at least unrealistic, to plan on maintaining a "happy" *APL* user community with terminal response time of more than two seconds for a trivial terminal command. This is an extremely important consideration, since users will reject an otherwise robust and well-rounded *APL* system if the terminal response time is unacceptably high.

The competition of an inhouse *APL* system is usually the commercial time sharing system that preceded it; users measure the new system accordingly. At STSC, for example, a 0.5-second response time is the standard at which the acceptability of terminal response is measured. A two-second response time—a

400 percent degradation from STSC's standard—appears to be a reasonable measure of the tolerance of the *APL* user community in an inhouse *APL* environment.

A primary question, then, must be "What operating system or system control program (SCP) is best suited for delivering acceptable response time in an interactive terminal environment?" After a full calendar year of testing, STSC concluded that IBM's VM/370 SCP is the best available choice. VM/370 (or its unbundled successor) is a superior interactive time sharing system with terminal response time in the two-second range. Moreover, it is adequate for an ancillary, low-volume batch workload. IBM OS/VS2 (MVS) was also carefully evaluated and then rejected as an *APL* processor. In the opinion of STSC, MVS is a superior system for batch processing and an adequate system for an ancillary, low-volume interactive time sharing workload (if five-second terminal response time is acceptable to the user community).

It is important that a fully supported SCP be used rather than a heavily modified, unsupported operating system such as DOS. The trends toward firmware and microcode options mentioned earlier necessitate a system approach that will allow the user to take advantage of at least some of the relative economies offered by the hardware vendors' microcode, without impacting the system's ability to process the *APL* workload.

In summary, weighing the relative benefits of an inhouse decision requires thorough investigation, especially of the less obvious aspects of providing *APL* processing facilities. Too often, decisions are based on insufficient data and fail to recognize the true costs associated with them. Complete, indepth analysis, careful planning, and superior plan execution are critical to the successful conversion of the user community to the alternative system.

*Bob Cook joined STSC in 1977 as director of corporate planning and has been vice president of market development since April 1978. His current responsibilities include project management for STSC's inhouse APL systems marketed for use on IBM-compatible hardware. Cook previously held management positions with Basic Four Corporation, Boeing Computer Services, and U.S. Time Sharing, Inc.*

*Cook earned a B.S. in mathematics from Indiana University of Pennsylvania and an M.S. in business administration from George Washington University.*

Michael F. C. Crick

# Variations in $A^{\text{pl}}$ Flat Major

This paper is a personal survey of the interesting features found in *APL* systems produced by IBM and other mainframe manufacturers such as Control Data Corporation (CDC) and Burroughs. It is intended to give the audience a general view of what is going on outside the cozy environment of STSC's *APL*PLUS* System.

## Overview

Most users work with one or perhaps two different *APL* implementations and, thus, rarely have the opportunity to see a large variety of *APL* systems. As an independent consultant, I am in the position of working with one version of *APL* one week and a different version the next. I would like to share with you some of my personal observations.

In the short space allotted it is clearly not practical to provide a detailed comparison of all available versions of *APL*—nor would such a comparison be very interesting. What I have attempted to do here is discuss a selected set of *APL* systems and to present only those details that to me seemed interesting and memorable. I shall thus discuss in turn *APLSV*, *VS APL*, *APLUM* (CDC), *APL/700* (Burroughs), *APLSF* (DEC), and Harris *APL* all in relation to STSC's *APL*PLUS* System (see note 1).

## Is IBM Drowning in Its Own Alphabet Soup?

IBM has two major *APL* systems at this time: *APLSV* (*APL* Shared Variables) and *VS APL* (Virtual Systems *APL*). *APLSV* is a descendant of the famous XM-6 version from which the STSC implementations of the *APL*PLUS* System are derived. *VS APL* is IBM's official Program Product. It is much cleaner internally since it was written from scratch, whereas *APLSV* evolved from a series of earlier implementations. *VS APL* relies on its host system to provide many services such as swapping and terminal support, whereas *APLSV* provides its own. The new version of the *APL*PLUS* System running under VM is an extension of *VS APL*. The *APL* on the 5110 and 5120 is a direct crib of *APLSV*.

Current IBM implementations are mainly notable for what they do not have. There is no support for the diamond statement separator ($\Diamond$), for error trapping, or for anything corresponding to Automatic Control of Execution (ACE), a proprietary product of STSC that provides the system facilities necessary to run production programs automatically without a user signed on at a terminal. Additionally, the file systems offered by IBM are very hard to use and have significantly fewer capabilities than those offered by STSC.

At present, IBM is suffering a severe case of schizophrenia about *APL*. The idea evolved early in the development of *APL* that it was a "scientific language"—a fact reflected in STSC's original name, "Scientific Time Sharing Corporation". Since *APL* was designed as an extension of mathematics, that assumption was not unreasonable. Yet, everyone who has contact with the real commercial world knows that *APL* has in practice triumphed as a commercial language. IBM's persistence of the vision of *APL* as a scientific or engineering language only shows how far IBM is out of touch with reality.

The illusion of schizophrenia is further fostered by the fact that IBM has, at this writing, both two *APLs and* two groups working on *APL*—the research group at Watson Research Center in Yorktown Heights, New York, and the development group in San Jose, California.

IBM is developing an interesting research version of *APL* at Yorktown Heights that supports operators, non-simple and homogenous arrays, and many other major new features (see note 2). What the development group is doing is not known. Whether IBM can get its act together and produce a single new *APL* that reflects the reality of user requirements remains to be seen.

## Contrast at Control Data

The first versions of *APL* distributed by CDC were total disasters. An unofficial version written by Jim Burrill and Clark Weidmann at the University of Massachusetts (*APLUM*) moved in to fill the void. CDC now recognizes *APLUM* as the official CDC *APL* and has sole rights to distribute the product. The University of Massachusetts has complete control of development.

CDC *APL* operates under a handicap—Control Data machines are scientific machines and not commercial machines. CDC machines are poor at manipulating bit and character data, and their operating system is not designed for major file-sharing applications.

We all know the sort of person who is "handicapped" by being very short (or very tall), or by being from a foreign country. A person with such a handicap usually responds by trying harder and being more adaptable. That is how I would characterize *APLUM*. The implementers, as outsiders, were always insecure. They *had* to do a better job despite the limitations of the hardware and software they had.

The result is an *APL* that is everywhere characterized by what I think of as "good" design. Their innovations are always extremely clean and logical, and they have managed to avoid perpetuating many of the strange features of *APL* that have been supported over the years almost as acts of faith.

For example, why are certain *APL* operations such as )*COPY* only permitted as manual operations? In the days of Automatic Control of Execution, this makes no sense. Some vendors have bypassed this limitation by allowing the execute primitive (⍎) to operate on system commands or by sharing a variable with the input stack. *APLUM* has done it right. It uses □*LOAD,* □*COPY* and the whole implementation is "clean". Other *APLs* should copy this approach.

Why does every major *APL* lack a decent context editor? Context editors are usually to be found as functions or perhaps as part of the host system. *APLUM* has integrated the context editor into the standard *APL* editor. Again the implementation is simple and clean. Another feature other *APLs* should copy.

Why do most *APLs* force you to preallocate space for symbols and the stack, not to mention the shared variable processor or the user workspace?

*APLUM* has one pool that is allocated automatically as needs dictate. If the pool runs out, the system asks the host for a bigger swap area in which to run itself—all performed automatically with no user intervention. This is a design standard that other *APL*s should emulate where possible.

*APLUM* has an extremely simple form of error trapping and its batch support is reasonably good. Its main defects are the curious and idiosyncratic file system and the lack of support for the diamond statement separator. It is very fast for floating-point operations, but can take forever to perform such character operations as catenating two character arrays.

Overall, the group at the University of Massachusetts has done a superb job. Despite the unsuitability of the host machine and the operating system, and despite their lack of clout as a group external to CDC, they have produced an excellent *APL*. Their current direction is toward developing an *APL* compiler to let *APL* compete with FORTRAN and perhaps ultimately be accepted by engineers.

## Burroughs and *APL/700*

Burroughs *APL* is another non-IBM *APL* that is worth considering in some detail. It is a "liberal", user-friendly *APL* that owes much of its character to Jim Ryan. It has numerous minor but useful extensions—many of which deserve to become a permanent part of the language.

For example, *APL/700* supports set operations. These are perhaps more useful than one might suspect. The most common use is to eliminate duplicates from a set of numbers thus:

```
(ι0) ∪ ARRAY
```

It would seem logical to define a monadic form of union (unique?) to eliminate the need for the ι0 on the left.

*APL/700* has introduced the use of assignment as an operator, taking any scalar dyadic function as its left argument. For example:

```
I+←1                    (Meaning I←I+1.)
```

This feature comes into its own when the variable being incremented has a large and complex subscript. Curiously, catenate is not allowed with this construction—one might have thought that would be the most useful case.

*APL/700* has extended transpose (to turn vectors into column matrices) and reshape (to operate on empty vectors). The axis operator has also been extended to operate on scalar dyadic functions thus:

```
      (2 3ρι12)+[1] 10 20 30
11 22 33
14 25 36
```

This eliminates the need for a lot of wasteful reshaping and should be used more widely.

*APL/700* offers reasonable support for ASCII terminals using a visually pleasing character substitution approach. On an ASCII terminal one can enter:

```
X <IS> 3 4 <RHO> <IOTA>12
```

There are also a number of useful extensions to tracing and editing that are not described easily, but are very useful. The file system uses special symbols such as ⊞ and ⊟. There are some new goodies like "pop", "map", and compress. The file system is generally like that of STSC's *APL\*PLUS* System, differing only in detail. For example, files are accessed by name rather than by tie number, and security is handled by the host rather than by access matrices. *APL/700* does not support the diamond statement separator and generally shows up poorly when benchmarked. This is partly compensated for by the fact that Burroughs machines can support a large number of central processors on one system.

In 1977 Jim Ryan went to work at Data Resources, Inc., but he is now back at Burroughs working on SYBIL—a new language derived from *APL* which uses words instead of special characters. The new language will have an extended notion of workspaces known as namespaces. Meanwhile, *APL/700* is fully supported by a separate group at Burroughs.

### Diversity at DEC

If *APL/700* bears the stamp of Jim Ryan, DEC's *APLSF* bears the stamp of Alan Perlis. As developed by the group at Carnegie-Mellon University in the early seventies, DEC *APL* was ahead of its time. Now that the rest of the world has caught up, DEC *APL* has been forced to do a certain amount of back-tracking to become consistent with everyone else. There are, for example, three format functions in the language—the official IBM "thumbtack" (⊤), a version of □*FMT* (using the symbol $), and the pioneering monadic encode (⊤) that will now probably be phased out.

For the same reasons, execute may be performed by $\epsilon$, $\perp$, or ♠. Not only may one execute system functions, but one may also execute a character matrix. This brings *APL* closer to LISP, where data and functions are all the same thing.

My favorite extension is the omega function, which performs a "where" operation as shown below:

$$\omega B \ \leftrightarrow \ B/\iota\rho B$$

$$\omega \ 1 \ 0 \ 1 \ 1 \ 0 \ 1$$
$$1 \ 3 \ 4 \ 6$$

This is particularly useful when *B* is a complex expression. I gather that this primitive is being phased out to allow for future inclusion of alpha and omega as defined by Kenneth Iverson.

*APLSF* has an elaborate file system that uses special symbols, system functions, and system variables—powerful but messy. There is no support for the diamond statement separator. As a whole, DEC *APL* illuminates the pitfalls one faces for being *too* liberal. It must have been infuriating as well as gratifying to those at Carnegie-Mellon to see IBM use many of their ideas in slightly modified form.

Another DEC innovation is to provide two levels of *APL* at different prices. The inexpensive beginners version lacks certain enhancements, notably the file system. A major disadvantage of *APL* compared with other major languages is that it comes in only one size. Nobody selling shoes or houses of only one size would stay in business, but in the case of *APL* the general policy has always been all or nothing. The market for a small, carefully chosen subset of *APL* has not been properly served.

We must commend DEC for its pioneering efforts to expand the language. Just as the first platoon out of the trenches suffers the heaviest casualties, DEC has had to pay the penalty for being first.

### Doing It Straight at Harris

If *APLSF* is liberal, the new Harris *APL* is conservative. One is reminded of the eager new member of the club whose dress is always a little too correct and who can be relied upon never to raise an eyebrow. Such an attitude probably befits a newcomer—only the old guard can break new ground and get away with it.

The new Harris *APL* is quite impressive. Its file system is very close to that of STSC's *APL\*PLUS* System, as is its support for error trapping. It supports batch processing, and shared variable support is imminent.

The only real differences are the use of $\Box ST$ and $\Box TR$ for stop and trace, and a variant definition for the diamond symbol. On Harris *APL*, if three statements are placed on a line, the next line gets the line number plus three rather than the next sequential number, as on the *APL\*PLUS* System. Thus, diamond can be considered as an instruction to the function display module rather than as a piece of punctuation. One cannot write:

$$\rightarrow NEXTL \; IF \; B > 5 \quad \Diamond \quad 'B \; IS \; TOO \; SMALL' \quad \Diamond \quad \rightarrow E5$$

This, and the fact that Harris *APL* does not support $\Box FMT$, would appear to make conversion from STSC's *APL\*PLUS* System to Harris *APL* infeasible for major applications, despite the correspondence of most other features. Conversion from Harris *APL* to STSC's system, on the other hand, is likely to be particularly easy.

Harris *APL* is fast—impressively so according to their benchmarks. One should be aware that this speed is achieved in part by doing all numeric operations in floating point, with 39 bits (11 decimal places) of precision. This makes Harris *APL* unsuitable for financial applications requiring precision to the penny for large dollar amounts.

### ...And What About the *APL\*PLUS* System?

Since this presentation was prepared at the request of STSC, I have assumed, possibly incorrectly, that all readers are familiar with the *APL\*PLUS* System. The discussion has been largely in terms of how other *APL* systems compare to the *APL\*PLUS* System. This is because the *APL\*PLUS* System is a recognized leader in the *APL* community; what STSC does, others copy.

There are many new developments in *APL*, and STSC is a major force in initiating them. Since I write this paper without being privy to what STSC is going to unveil at its April 1980 conference, to talk at length about the unique features of the *APL\*PLUS* System would be to talk about those features that others have not yet copied. Much work is going on in areas like relations, support for systems on different hardware, systems software, and generalized arrays. Other presentations in this book (e.g., "Nested Arrays: The Tool for the Future") address these subjects in detail.

*Notes*

1.   The latest manuals for the *APL* systems discussed are properly obtained by contacting the local sales office of the company involved.

2.   J. A. Brown, "Evaluating Extensions to *APL*", *APL79 Conference Proceedings* and *APL Quote Quad*, Vol. 9, No. 4, June 1979.

*Michael Crick is an independent software consultant and financial advisor in Seattle, Washington. His involvement with APL began while he was employed by IBM, where he received an outstanding contribution award for his efforts in the development of APL (CMS). Crick was also instrumental in the development of MAINSTREAM−APL at Boeing Computer Services and was branch manager of the Seattle office of I. P. Sharp Associates.*

*Crick holds both a B.Sc. and M.Sc. from the University of London.*

**Robert L. McGhee and James G. Wheeler**

# Travels in VM Land:
# A Virtual *APL* Primer

> **Virtual** *adj.* Existing or resulting in essence or effect
> though not in actual fact, form, or name.
>
> —*American Heritage Dictionary.*

Many of our readers will already know that VM stands for "Virtual
Machine", but far fewer will have a clear grasp of just what the term means to
them as *APL* users. Simply introducing the idea of a machine may worry some
*APL* users. STSC's *APL∗PLUS* System running under OS/MVT has traditionally isolated the user from the details of *real* machines, for *APL* naturally
tends to make the computer on which it is executing invisible to the user. A
programmer can work successfully on the *APL∗PLUS* System without thinking about computers at all; instead, he can imagine that he has a magic
terminal that executes *APL*, and he can let things go at that.

There are many positive things to say about this isolation, in particular
the way it lets the programmer keep his thoughts on the conceptual, problem-
solving plateau instead of worrying about physical hardware or the internals
of software. But this isolation also tends to limit the types of solutions that the
programmer can choose. Three of the biggest limitations are these:

1.  *APL* programs cannot access data that is used by programs
    written in other programming languages. Traditional *APL* pro-
    vides no means for an *APL* program to use the same data as a
    program written, say, in FORTRAN.

2.  This isolation from other languages also prevents *APL* users from
    enjoying the use of software packages that are not written in *APL*
    (and, all chauvinism aside, some of the best software around is
    written in other languages).

3.  A less awesome limitation, but still an irksome one, is that *APL*
    traditionally has a fixed workspace size. This severely limits the
    size of the data objects that can be used by an *APL* program and
    often requires that applications be divided into multiple work-
    spaces.

Using STSC's *APL∗PLUS* VM System, an *APL* programmer can conquer
all of these limitations and still enjoy the full problem-solving power of *APL*.
VM is, however, unfamiliar territory to most *APL* users and the bookcase full
of manuals on the subject may discourage the uninitiated, no matter how
much they may want to exploit the new capabilities VM offers.

The purpose of this paper is to present the basic concepts involved in using VM. Because of the size of the subject, we will not try to present even the minimum knowledge needed to be a successful VM user. Instead, we will try to convey the basic ideas needed for a user to feel at home learning about VM and understanding it intuitively. We will present three different views of VM:

1. *The virtual machine perspective.* This is the "hardware" point of view. Since VM simulates a private computing center for each user, this perspective is essential to understanding the capabilities of the virtual machine.

2. *The software perspective.* Working in VM means moving into and out of the *APL* environment. This perspective is important in understanding the relationships among the various software environments of the VM system.

3. *The APL user's perspective.* Our interest in VM is due primarily to the way it complements and extends the power of *APL*. We will use a case study of transferring an *APL* workspace to VM to show just how valuable these new capabilities can be.

## The Virtual Machine Perspective

The central idea behind VM, indeed the one that gives it its name, is the *virtual machine.* VM/370 simulates a complete, private computing center for *each* time sharing user. Simply by signing on to VM (a process known as "logging on"), you can in effect obtain the exclusive use of hundreds of thousands of dollars worth of computer equipment. Of course, it's almost all virtual hardware, which means that it will not perform as briskly in real time as actual equipment. But since *APL* users are quite accustomed to doing without real-time capability, no significant sacrifice is involved. In fact, considering that one real computer is giving each of its many users the illusion of having a personal computer, the performance is really quite good.

Each user's virtual machine is configured at log-on to a predetermined initial configuration. A typical VM user at STSC might be given the following virtual hardware at log-on:

- An IBM 370-series mainframe (CPU) with 512 kilobytes of main storage.

- An "operator's console", which is simply the terminal that the user is using.

- A virtual line printer (known to most *APL* users as a "high-speed printer").

- A virtual card reader (*APL*ers who gasp at this idea should catch their breaths before reading the next item).

- A virtual card punch (how else would we produce virtual card decks for the virtual card reader?)

- Three virtual disk drives, otherwise known as Direct-Access Storage Devices, or DASDs.

This virtual hardware can be put to a number of good uses, giving the user the following capabilities and more:

- Printing files by *spooling* them to the virtual line printer, in a manner similar to that provided by the Fileprint Facility on STSC's OS/MVT system. The files are printed on real paper by a real high-speed printer shortly after the spooling operation is "closed".

- Transmitting files to other virtual machines (i.e., other VM users) by punching virtual card decks for them. In reality, the "cards" are records in system spool files that magically appear in the "input hopper" of the other user's virtual card reader.

- Reading virtual card decks from the virtual card reader, completing the transfer of files between virtual machines. Virtual card decks are not the only means by which data can be transferred from one virtual machine to another, but they are useful for sending a file to another user when that user is not signed on.

- Reading from and writing to files residing on virtual disk drives. These disks may belong to the user's virtual machine or may be shared by other users.

- Disconnecting the console (i.e., the terminal), leaving the virtual machine running; this provides a facility comparable to the Detached Execution Facility available on STSC's OS/MVT system.

In VM jargon, a virtual disk drive is referred to as a *minidisk*. This term reinforces the concept that minidisks are in fact portions of real disks dedicated to specific users. The term "virtual disk" is discouraged because, unlike virtual main storage, the amount of permanent storage available on minidisks cannot be altered by the user.

The three disks typically available to the user at log-on are

- The user's private minidisk, called the A disk.

- A system minidisk, called the S disk, containing system software.

- Another system minidisk, called the Y disk, containing system and application software.

The A disk contains the user's private files and the user is permitted to both read from and write to this disk. The A disk is analogous to an *APL* user's private library. In fact, the user's private saved workspaces are presently stored on this disk.

The S disk and Y disk are analogous to public libraries in an *APL* system. Both are read-only disks in that the user can read files from the disk but not modify the files. All virtual machines have access to these disks. The S and Y disks contain such things as the *APL* interpreter, the FORTRAN compiler, and applications like SCRIPT (a text formatter developed by the Department of Computer Services at the University of Waterloo), BMDP (Biomedical Computer Programs, P-Series), and SPSS™ (Statistical Package for the Social Sciences).

Each minidisk contains a number of *files*. Unlike *APL*, where files store only *APL* data values, these files are of many different types and are used for widely varying purposes. Some files contain data, and a wide variety of different data formats are possible. Other files contain compiled programs that can be invoked by using the file name as a command. Still other files, called EXECs, are programs made up of sequences of VM system commands.

The user's virtual hardware configuration can be selectively modified as needs for resources change. For example, the typical virtual machine that we have discussed is illustrated in Figure 1. The size of the user's *APL* workspace is directly related to the amount of main storage in his virtual machine. If this user finds he does not have a big enough workspace, he can increase the amount of main storage to, say, two megabytes. If he needs a large amount of temporary file space, he can create a new virtual disk drive (this file space is lost at sign-off). If he needs a tape drive to read from or write to a tape, he can have a *real* tape drive attached to his virtual machine. After performing these actions, the same virtual machine would have the configuration shown in Figure 2.

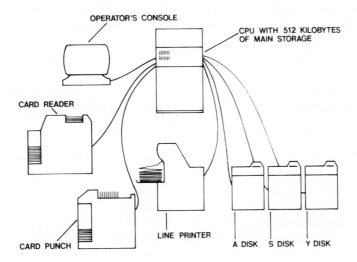

**Figure 1—Typical Default Virtual Machine**

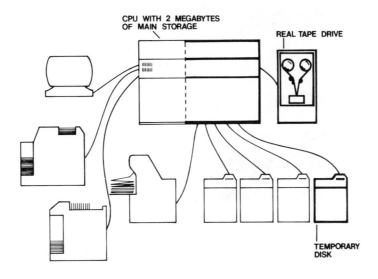

**Figure 2—Reconfigured Virtual Machine**

## Software Perspective

The VM/370 operating system is divided into two main components—the Control Program (CP) and the Conversational Monitor System (CMS). CP's role is management of the real hardware; system resources are distributed among users so that each has the illusion of controlling a full-scale, private computer. CMS is an operating system designed to give the time sharing user a friendly and yet versatile way of working in the virtual machine created by CP. While it is possible to run different operating systems under CP (including STSC's

OS/MVT system), CMS has been built specifically to run efficiently in a
virtual machine and to serve a single user at a single terminal.

CMS runs under the control of CP, providing interactive use of various
applications and language processors, notably the *APL∗PLUS* System interpreter. CMS processes commands entered from the terminal, including CMS
and CP commands. By using the proper tools, it is also possible to execute some
CP and CMS commands from within the *APL* environment.

This hierarchy of environments and the various routes between them can
be very confusing to the new VM user, particularly one who has previously
been accustomed to using *APL* on a system that provides only *APL* computing.
To help the reader develop an intuitive sense of the hierarchy and relationships between the multiple environments, we'll use a spatial and architectural
model.

In this model, we'll imagine that a virtual machine is equivalent to a
house. The real computer can be considered a small community of many users,
each living in a private house (see Figure 3). The control program CP can then
be thought of as the main street in this community. Each user enters his
private house from the street and departs it by the same route.

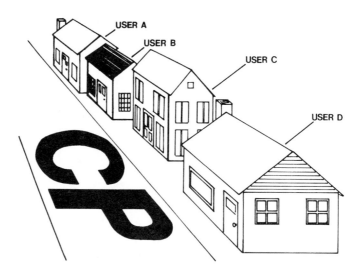

**Figure 3—Main Street in VM Land**

Logging on to the VM system is accomplished by communicating with CP.
The CP command LOGON is roughly equivalent to a request to "build me a
house". Each user has a set of master blueprints stored in a CP directory, and
CP constructs the user's default house according to these blueprints. As can be
seen from Figure 3, different users can have houses of different sizes and types.
If a user wants to change the size of his house, he must "move out" temporarily
while the old house is torn down and CP builds a new one.

The walls of the houses provide ample isolation and privacy for each user,
and each user's computing is done entirely within the boundaries of his own
house. Facilities exist for appropriate interaction between houses (virtual
machines); these will be described a little later. Communication and transfer of
data between houses requires mutual cooperation, however. One user cannot
invade someone else's house or impinge on his privacy without invitation.

Each user's private minidisk is something like a storage shed in the back yard (see Figure 4). The user can put things in the shed and retrieve them at will, and what he stores in the shed is his own business. Extending this analogy, the system (S and Y) disks are more like department stores down the street. The user can get merchandise (data from files) *from* the department store, but most users never supply anything *to* the department store.

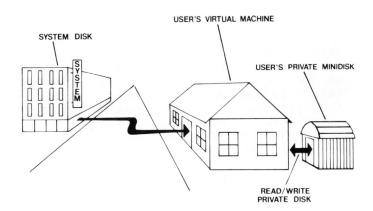

**Figure 4—Relationships of Private and System Disks**

It is possible for one user to give another user a key to his storage shed by setting a password on his private disk and supplying the other user with that password. A read-only password gives other users the ability to retrieve things from your private disk, which is something like allowing your neighbors to borrow your lawnmower from your storage shed while insisting that they not stash any of their own garden supplies there. A read/write password gives neighbors permission to both store in and retrieve from your storage shed. The storage-shed analog also holds in that one user can use another user's storage shed, even when that user is not currently "at home" (signed on). Note that once you've given someone a key, you cannot prevent him from giving the key to others. You can, however, keep everyone out of your storage shed by changing the padlock (password).

Giving out keys to storage sheds is only one of the ways that data can be shared between houses. If you want to give a copy of a file to another user without giving him a key to your storage shed, you can use the technique of *spool punching*. This is like using a parcel service to send a package to someone else's house. Using the CP command DISK DUMP, you give the "CP Delivery Service" a "package" containing a copy of your file on virtual punched cards (which are punched on your virtual card punch). As is customary with any good parcel service, the CP Delivery Service does not deliver any packages without the recipient's permission and only when the recipient is "at home". Thus, spooling is a good way to transfer data to virtual machines that are not currently signed on. When the recipient logs on, he is notified by CP that a package is waiting. By executing the CP command DISK LOAD, the recipient accepts delivery of the package and stores its contents in his own storage shed. (From the hardware perspective, the user loads punched cards into a file using his virtual card reader).

The other way of communicating between virtual machines is the Virtual Machine Communication Facility (VMCF), which is more like a telephone service. With VMCF, two virtual machines can have a conversation, sharing data immediately. The advantage of VMCF is that the data is transferred at once instead of waiting to be delivered. The disadvantage, as with the telephone, is that the other user has to be at home to answer the phone. VMCF cannot be used directly by CMS commands, but it can be built into application packages. In fact, a facility exists whereby *APL* users can transfer data via VMCF.

The boundary between the inside and the outside of the house neatly defines the respective roles of CP and CMS. All of the transfer between houses is handled by CP. The role of CMS is to manage the activity *inside* the house. Figure 5 shows a view of the interior environment of a virtual machine. Within the house, CMS is the main hallway. Leading off from the hall are separate rooms, each of which is a distinct computing environment. The *APL* room is the one that concerns us most, but there are also many other rooms, including the BASIC room, the COBOL, FORTRAN, and PL/1 compiler rooms, the SPSS room, the BMDP room, and many others. In most cases, one enters one of these rooms from CMS and can move to another room only by leaving the room and walking down the hall to the other door.

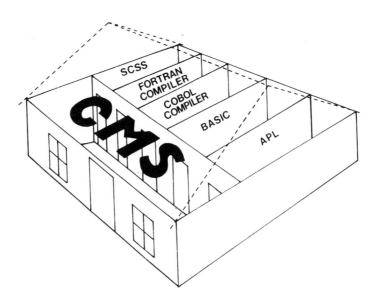

**Figure 5—Inside the User's Computing Environment**

Notice that the *APL* room in Figure 5 has no windows, only the door into the CMS hallway. This implies that when one is within the *APL* environment, one is isolated from CMS and the outside world of CP and the other virtual machines. *APL* users do not always have to be isolated, however. At the time that the user enters *APL* from CMS, he can specify the creation of a workroom of a certain size within the *APL* environment. This workroom houses *auxiliary processors*, which are programs that can interface *APL* to the outside world.

There is a window between the auxiliary processor and the rest of the *APL* environment. Data and commands can be passed through this window to the auxiliary processor. The auxiliary processor can then relay the data or commands to the outside world through other windows. The window through which *APL* communicates with the auxiliary processor is formally called a *shared-variable interface.*

Several different auxiliary processors are available and each has different capabilities. Some perform special-purpose computation on the data passed from the *APL* environment and pass the results back through the window to *APL*. Other auxiliary processors, such as the one shown in Figure 6, have other windows into the CMS hallway or even into the outside world. Using these auxiliary processors, an *APL* user can execute many useful CMS and CP commands, read from and write to files in the "storage shed", and so on. One cannot, however, enter the FORTRAN compiler through an auxiliary processor, because using the compiler requires leaving the *APL* environment. (It *is* possible to automate the movement from *APL* to FORTRAN and back again using an auxiliary processor.) One auxiliary processor even uses the VMCF to permit conversation with another user in the *APL* room of another house.

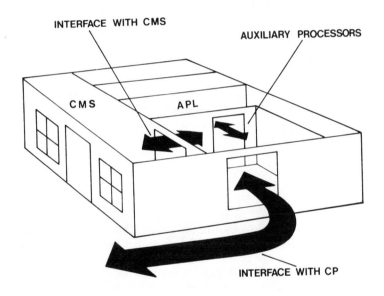

**Figure 6—Auxiliary Processors Interface *APL* to Outside World**

### The *APL* User's Perspective

We will show the *APL* user's perspective on VM by demonstrating a process that many users who begin working under VM will wish to perform— transferring a workspace from another *APL* system onto STSC's *APL★PLUS* VM System. The process of producing a copy of a workspace from another *APL* system and transferring it to tape will not be described here; see Working Memorandum No. 125, *Source Level Transfer Using the Workspace Interchange Standard* (STSC, 1978) for details. We will assume that the tape has been produced, delivered to the STSC Computing Center, and catalogued into its tape library.

The demonstration begins at the point where we log on to VM to install the transfer workspace. The first step is to dial the STSC network number and enter the terminal speed-setting character; the system then responds:

```
TYPE SYSID
VM)
VM CONNECTED

VM/370 ONLINE

CP
```

At this point, we are in the CP environment, but we do not yet have a virtual machine defined. By logging on, we ask CP to construct our virtual machine:

```
LOGON USER
ENTER PASSWORD:
XXXXXXXX
LOGON AT 12:24:23 EST TUESDAY 02/12/80 05201
CMS VER 5.07.008 -- 11MAR79
R; T=0.01/0.01 12:24:26
```

Now, we have entered the front door of our house and are in the CMS "hallway". Our terminal is now controlling our default virtual machine.

To enter the *APL* environment from CMS, we use the CMS command APL. We also specify an optional argument to the APL command that asks for a large shared storage space to be used by an auxiliary processor in the transfer process.

```
APL 150K
APL015I INSUFFICIENT STORAGE FOR MINIMUM-SIZED WORKSPACE.
R; . . .
```

This is an error message meaning, in effect, that the size of the *APL* room containing the auxiliary processor workroom exceeds the size of our house. The amount of main storage in our default virtual machine is not enough. The CP command QUERY STORAGE can be used to find out the current size of the virtual machine. Although we are now in the CMS hallway, CMS recognizes the CP command and passes it outside to CP.

```
CP QUERY STORAGE

STORAGE = 00512K
R; . . .
```

The report indicates that we currently have 512 kilobytes of main storage in our virtual CPU. Here's a fine chance to exploit our ability to increase the size of our virtual machine. In a matter of moments, we can double the amount of main storage:

```
DEFINE STORAGE 1024K
STORAGE = 01024K
AUTOIPL CMS
CMS VER 5.07.008 -- 11MAR79
R; . . .
```

Now, with this larger machine, we can try again to enter the *APL* environment with a large shared storage space:

*APL 150K*

> *APL*PLUS SERVICE*

*CLEAR WS*

Now, we can further change our virtual machine configuration by adding a tape drive, which we will need to read the transfer workspace from tape. The *APL*PLUS* VM System Operator can attach the tape drive to our virtual machine after mounting the transfer tape for us.

> *)OPR PLEASE MOUNT TAPE VOL 123ABC, BIN NO. 1234 AS 181. THANKS.*
*SENT*

Now, we wait for the operator to fetch the tape from the tape library, mount it on a tape drive, and attach it to our virtual machine at virtual address hex '181'. The process usually takes a few minutes, and a message is displayed when the tape drive is ready.

*TAPE 181 ATTACHED*
*MESSAGE FROM OPERATOR:  TAPE MOUNTED AND READY. /OPR*

The tape drive is now ready to use and, since we're monopolizing a real tape drive, we should finish the job promptly. The first step in installing the transfer workspace is making sure the present workspace is clear.

> *)CLEAR*
*CLEAR WS*

To get ready to read the data from the tape, we'll use Auxiliary Processor 100, the CMS/CP Command Processor. It provides us with a means of executing CMS and CP commands from within the *APL* environment. On STSC's VM Service, this auxiliary processor is set up for us each time we enter the *APL* environment. We communicate with the auxiliary processor by a technique known as *shared variables*, an explanation of which is beyond the scope of this paper. (For a tutorial on shared variables, see the paper entitled "Using Shared Variables and Auxiliary Processors in *VS APL*", which appears elsewhere in this book.)

> *X←'CMS' ◊ 100 □SVO 'X'*
2

The preceding statements *shared* the variable *X* with the auxiliary processor. *X* will now serve as a means of communicating with CMS through the auxiliary processor. We will use the CMS command FILEDEF to define the tape (TAP1) as a CMS file named SLT:

> *X←'FILEDEF SLT TAP1 SL1 VOLID 123ABC (RECFM U BLOCK 32760)'*
> *X*
0

The value of *X* has changed to 0, indicating that the FILEDEF command has been executed successfully. Now that we can treat the tape drive as if it were a regular CMS file, we can use the source level transfer functions in workspace 99 *SLT* to install the workspace:

```
      ⎕ERASE 'X'
      )COPY 99 SLT SLTIN
SAVED  . . .
      'TRANSWS' WSIN 'SLT'
```

The left argument to *WSIN* is the name of the workspace as it is recorded on the tape. The right argument is the CMS file name identifying the tape. *WSIN* uses Auxiliary Processor 110, the CMS Disk Input/Output Processor, which lets an *APL* program read from and write to a CMS file (in our case, the tape drive).

*WSIN* produces a lot of output, not shown here, as it installs each transferred function and variable in the active workspace. The following message is displayed when the installation is complete.

```
')ERASE SLTIN' AND SAVE THIS WS WITH PROPER NAME

      )ERASE SLTIN
      )WSID TRANSWS
WAS CLEAR WS
      )SAVE
. . . TRANSWS
```

Now, we will use the CMS/CP command processor to detach the tape drive. The operator is responsible for attaching the tape drive, but we can detach it ourselves.

```
      X←'CMS' ◊ 100 ⎕SVO 'S'
2
      X←'CP DETACH 181' ◊ X
TAPE 181 DETACHED
0
      )OPR PLEASE DISMOUNT TAPE AND SCRATCH IT.  THANKS
SENT
```

## Conclusion

We hope these perspectives have whetted the reader's appetite for the new tools and techniques available to the *APL* programmer working in the VM environment. Many programmers have bemoaned the traditional isolation of *APL* from the rest of the computing world. Perhaps VM, with the aid of auxiliary processors, will help bridge that barrier.

There are, of course, those *APL* enthusiasts who believe that the isolation of *APL* from other programming environments is beneficial and who would rather not bother with other programming languages. For them, techniques exist to make the VM operating system as invisible as is on STSC's other system, while still giving them the benefits of large workspaces. VM's benefits thus extend to proponents of either philosophy.

*Bob McGhee joined STSC in 1973 as a marketing representative and is currently a systems programmer in the company's System Product Department. In this position, he packages, installs, and supports STSC's system software products.*

*McGhee received his B.S. degree in electrical engineering from Virginia Polytechnical Institute. Before coming to STSC, he developed electronic instrumentation at DuPont, commercializing an ultrasonic imager and solving production problems in a spectrophometer using APL simulation. He is currently interested in applications of APL operators in electrical engineering.*

*As a design specialist for STSC, James Wheeler is responsible for the design and specification of user-visible features of the APL\*PLUS System. Before joining STSC in 1977 as a technical writer, Wheeler taught scientific writing at the State University of New York at Buffalo, where he also worked on computer techniques for literary analysis. As a technical writer, Wheeler wrote the Automatic Control of Execution (ACE) series of manuals and prepared the manuals for the VM/370 version of the APL\*PLUS System. An avid APL programmer, Wheeler developed the text-editing system used by STSC to produce its photocomposed manuals.*

*Wheeler's background includes current graduate studies in computer science at the University of Maryland, an M.A. in English from the State University of New York at Buffalo, and a B.A. in art from the University of Maryland.*

**Mark L. Osborne**

# Using Shared Variables and Auxiliary Processors in *VS APL*

The use of shared variables and auxiliary processors in *VS APL* permits the integration of programs written in *APL* with programs written in other languages running in the CP/CMS environment. Processors are available to execute CMS and CP commands; stack CMS input; access CMS, QSAM, and VSAM files; communicate between virtual machines; and control input/output lines. Other processors can be built to interface with any operation in the CP environment.

Particularly useful is access to the file systems that run in the CMS environment, giving *APL* a way to share large volumes of data with programs written in FORTRAN, PL/1, COBOL, and other languages. These include a large number of commercially available application packages such as SCSS™ (SPSS™ Conversational Statistical System) and MPSX/370 (Mathematical Programming System Extended).

The CP/CMS Stack Input Processor provides a means for passing control in and out of the *APL* environment. Using this processor, an *APL* function can stack *APL* and CMS commands that checkpoint the *APL* environment, cause exit from the *APL* environment, and then invoke CMS commands, EXEC files, or executable program modules. Typically, a CMS EXEC is used that invokes a program. When the program completes, the EXEC stacks a series of commands to resume in the *APL* environment.

Any named variable can be used as an interface between the *APL* environment and an auxiliary processor. A variable is established as a "shared" interface through use of the system function $\Box SVO$. Once this is done, communicating with the auxiliary processor is simply a matter of referencing the variable or assigning values to it. The values have different effects, depending on the auxiliary processor being used. Another system function, $\Box SVC$, can be used to impose control on the sequence of accesses of the variable. Finally, the system function $\Box SVQ$ is provided to query the status of shares.

A brief description of these functions is in order. They are more completely documented in the manual *APL Language* (IBM, 1978).

$r \leftarrow p \ \Box SVO \ n$

An offer to share the variable named in *n* is extended to the auxiliary processor identified by the numeric value in *p*. The explicit result is known as the *degree of coupling*. A result of 2 indicates that the offer is matched by an offer from *p*. A result of 1 indicates that the offer is currently unmatched. If the share is successfully matched, communication has been established between the *APL* environment and the auxiliary processor. Multiple shares can be established with one use of $\Box SVO$ when $p$ is a vector of auxiliary processor numbers and $n$ is a matrix of variable names.

$r \leftarrow \Box SVO\ n$

The degree of coupling is returned for each variable named in $n$. Note that a result of 0 is valid if no offer has been made by or to the active user for a variable named in $n$.

$r \leftarrow c\ \Box SVC\ n$

An access control setting is established for the shared variable named in $n$. This setting is the logical-or of the four-element Boolean vector $c$ and the last access setting specified by the share partner. The explicit result is a Boolean vector representing the new access setting. The access setting controls how the shared variable is used by inhibiting multiple uses by one share partner without specific intervening action by the other share partner (a share partner may be either a user or an auxiliary processor). When an element of the access setting is 1, it inhibits use in the following way:

- The first element of the access setting inhibits two successive assignments by partner A without intervening access (assignment or reference) by partner B.
- The second element inhibits two successive assignments by partner B without intervening access by partner A.
- The third element inhibits two successive references by partner A without an intervening assignment by partner B.
- The fourth element inhibits two successive references by partner B without an intervening assignment by partner A.

The arguments can be extended to matrices, in which case each row of $c$ must contain an access setting for the variable whose name is in the corresponding row of $n$.

$r \leftarrow \Box SVC\ n$

The current access settings for the variables named in $n$ are returned as an explicit result.

$r \leftarrow \Box SVR\ n$

The existing share offers for variables named in $n$ are retracted. The explicit result is a vector containing the degree of coupling of each variable before the retraction.

$r \leftarrow \Box SVQ\ p$

If $p$ is an empty vector, the explicit result is a vector of processor numbers of auxiliary processors extending share offers to the user. If $p$ is a vector of processors, the result is a matrix of names of the variables offered by those processors, but not yet matched by the user.

Most uses of auxiliary processors in *VS APL* include the following sequence of steps:

- Initialize the shared variable. The initial value communicates information to the auxiliary processor, such as the name of a file and various processor options.

- Extend the share offer to the processor. The resultant degree of coupling is usually two, since most (but not all) auxiliary processors extend a return share automatically. An application program should check this returned value to be sure the offer was reciprocated.

- Access the shared variable to check the return code from the auxiliary processor. This will verify that the processor options specified were valid. The form and values returned here are dependent on the processor being used.

- Proceed to access and or reference the shared variable according to the conventions of the auxiliary processor. Note that use of most processors does not require setting of the access vector, since the auxiliary processor generally sets the necessary access.

- Retract the share when the interaction with the processor is finished.

Now for some examples of shared variable and auxiliary processor use:

*APL*

> *APL*PLUS SERVICE*

*CLEAR WS*

First, we initialize the variable *DMK* with a value that indicates that we want to pass commands to CP. $\square SVO$ is used to share the variable with Auxiliary Processor 100; the result of 2 is the degree of coupling and indicates that AP100 matched our offer. *DMK* has a *return code* as its value when next referenced, and the value of 0 indicates that all is well.

```
      DMK←'CP' ◇ 100 □SVO 'DMK'
2
      DMK
0
```

```
      DMK←'Q SET'          What are our virtual machine options?
MSG ON , WNG ON , EMSG TEXT, ACNT ON , RUN OFF
LINEDIT OFF, TIMER OFF , ISAM OFF, ECMODE ON
ASSIST ON SVC NOTMR, PAGEX OFF, AUTOPOLL OFF
IMSG ON , AFFINITY NONE , NOTRAN OFF
VMSAVE OFF, AUTOBEGN OFF, AUTOIPL ON
```

```
      DMK←'SET EMSG ON'      We want to see complete error
                            messages from CP and CMS.
```

```
      DMK←'Q SET'          Did SET EMSG work?
MSG ON , WNG ON , EMSG ON , ACNT ON , RUN OFF
LINEDIT OFF, TIMER OFF , ISAM OFF, ECMODE ON
ASSIST ON SVC NOTMR, PAGEX OFF, AUTOPOLL OFF
IMSG ON , AFFINITY NONE , NOTRAN OFF
VMSAVE OFF, AUTOBEGN OFF, AUTOIPL ON
```

CMS commands can also be executed by AP100. This time we'll initialize another variable to indicate CMS and offer the share.

```
      DMS←'CMS' ◇ 100 □SVO 'DMS'
2
      DMS
0
```

```
      DMS←'LIST (DATE'              Tell us what files we have.
FILENAME FILETYPE  FM  FORMAT    RECS BLOCKS   DATE    TIME
EDITAPL  EXEC      A1  V    14      6    1   2/12/80  16:18
EDIT2    VSAPLWS   A1  F   800     15   15   2/12/80  16:05
LEFTWS   VSAPLWS   A1  F   800     11   11   2/12/80  17:22
MAILING  ADDRESS   A1  F    80      6    1   2/12/80  15:08
SVDEMO   SCRIPT    A1  F    80    125   13   2/12/80  15:08
```

```
      DMS←'TYPE MAILING ADDRESS'         Display a file.
```

```
MARK OSBORNE (MLO)
STSC, INC.
7316 WISCONSIN AVE.
BETHESDA MARYLAND 20014

PLACE IN VMDEV MAIL SLOT
```

*MAILING ADDRESS* is a must for anyone who wants his computer printouts mailed to him. It is simply a file with the filename *MAILING* and the filetype *ADDRESS*. It must have no more than eight lines, and no line can be more than 30 characters long. It is automatically tagged on all printouts generated by your virtual machine. *MAILING ADDRESS* can be created with the CMS editor.

```
      DMK←'Q UR'       Ask CP about the status of our unit record devices.
RDR  00C ALL    NOCONT NOHOLD    EOF        READY
PUN  00D STD    NOCONT NOHOLD COPY 01       READY
     00D FOR SVDEMO1  DIST SVDEMO1
PRT  00E A001   NOCONT NOHOLD COPY 01       READY
     00E FOR SVDEMO1  DIST SVDEMO1
```

Let's put any printer output we generate "on hold". We can then query the printer (at virtual address hex `'00E'`) to be sure the hold worked.

```
      DMK←'SPOOL PRT HOLD'

      DMK←'Q 00E'
PRT  00E A001   NOCONT   HOLD COPY 01      READY
     00E FOR SVDEMO1 DIST SVDEMO1
```

Next, let's define a print file the way AP111 (QSAM I/O) likes 'em.

```
      DMS←'FILEDEF PRINT PRINTER(RECFM V BLKSIZE 132'
```

```
      DMS←'Q FILEDEF'    We get that right?
PRINT     PRT            Guess so.
```

```
      PRINTV←'PRINT (APL'      Initialize a variable for AP111.
```

*PRINT* corresponds to the name specified in the *FILEDEF* command; *APL* is a translate option.

```
      111 □SVO 'PRINTV'      Share it.
2
```

```
      PRINTV      Check the return code.
0
```

Good. Now we'll write something directly to the print queue:

```
      PRINTV←'THIS LINE GOES DIRECTLY TO MY PRINT QUEUE.'
      PRINTV←'WHEN WE RETRACT THE SHARE, THE PRINT FILE IS CLOSED.'
      PRINTV←'IF WE RELEASE THE HOLD WE SET ON THE PRINTER,'
      PRINTV←'THIS FILE WILL PRINT ON THE LINE PRINTER AT THE'
      PRINTV←'STSC COMPUTER CENTER.'
      PRINTV←'SINCE WE WON''T GET TO SEE THAT, WE''LL CHECK OUR PRINT'
      PRINTV←'QUEUE AND TRANSFER THE PRINT TO OUR VIRTUAL CARD READER.'
      PRINTV←'FROM THERE, WE CAN READ THE TEXT INTO A CMS FILE AND'
      PRINTV←'TYPE IT AT THE TERMINAL.'
```

     □*SVR 'PRINTV'*     *Retract the share.*
PRT FILE 3163  FOR SVDEMO1  COPY 01    HOLD
2                       *Looks promising.*

     *DMK*←*'Q PRT ALL'*     *Ask CP if there's a spool file for us.*
FILE FORM RECDS COPY HOLD DATE  TIME  DIST     NAME      TYPE     ROUTE
3163 A001 000009 01  USER 02/12 21:14 SVDEMO1    *Nine lines. Looks right.*

     *DMK*←*'TRANS PRT RDR 3163'*     *Transfer it to our reader.*
PRT FILE 3163 TRANSFERRED FROM SVDEMO1
0001 FILE  TRANSFERRED

     *DMK*←*'Q RDR ALL'*     *Is it there?*
FILE FORM RECDS  ORIGIN   HOLD DATE  TIME  DIST     NAME TYPE
3163 A001 000009 SVDEMO1  USER 02/12 21:14 SVDEMO1

     *DMK*←*'CHANGE RDR 3163 NOHOLD'*     *Better take it off hold to read.*
0001 FILE  CHANGED


Now, we'll read this spool file from the virtual card reader to a CMS file named *FOO FILE A* (the good stuff is always named *FOO*).

     *DMS*←*'READ FOO FILE A'*
DMSRDC738I RECORD LENGTH IS '132' BYTES.    *Just as we suspected!*

     *DMS*←*'LIST (DATE'*     *The file FOO should now show up here.*
FILENAME FILETYPE  FM  FORMAT   RECS BLOCKS   DATE     TIME
EDITAPL  EXEC      A1  V    14     6      1  2/12/80 16:18
EDIT2    VSAPLWS   A1  F   800    15     15  2/12/80 16:05
LEFTWS   VSAPLWS   A1  F   800    11     11  2/12/80 17:22
MAILING  ADDRESS   A1  F    80     6      1  2/12/80 15:08
SVDEMO   SCRIPT    A1  F    80   125     13  2/12/80 15:08
FOO      FILE      A1  F   132     9      2  2/12/80 21:23

     *DMS*←*'TYPE FOO FILE'*     *Let's see what's in it.*
THIS LINE GOES DIRECTLY TO MY PRINT QUEUE.
WHEN WE RETRACT THE SHARE, THE PRINT FILE IS CLOSED.
IF WE RELEASE THE HOLD WE SET ON THE PRINTER,
THIS FILE WILL PRINT ON THE LINE PRINTER AT THE
STSC COMPUTER CENTER.
SINCE WE WON'T GET TO SEE THAT, WE'LL CHECK OUR PRINT
QUEUE AND TRANSFER THE PRINT TO OUR VIRTUAL CARD READER.
FROM THERE, WE CAN READ THE TEXT INTO A CMS FILE AND
TYPE IT AT THE TERMINAL.


And my fingers never left my hands! And now, for a finale, the disappearing file trick:

     *DMS*←*'ERASE FOO FILE'*

     *DMS*←*'LIST'*     *Let's use the short form.*
EDITAPL  EXEC      A1
EDIT2    VSAPLWS   A1
LEFTWS   VSAPLWS   A1
MAILING  ADDRESS   A1
SVDEMO   SCRIPT    A1


Sure enough, the file *FOO* is gone. Now, we need only retract both outstanding shares and we're done.

     □*SVR 2 3*ρ*'DMKDMS'*
 2  2

     )*OFF HOLD*
R; *T*=1.22/4.35 21:30:36

### *EDIT2* Workspace

The *EDIT2* workspace contains a set of functions to be used in conjunction with the CMS EXEC, *EDITAPL*, to edit *APL* functions or character matrices with the CMS Editor. (The functions in the *EDIT2* workspace are listed in the Appendix at the end of this paper.) To use this facility, simply type:

        *EDIT 'fnname'*

The argument *fnname* is the name of the function or variable you wish to edit. You will then be placed in the CMS editor. When you enter the editor command *FILE*, your function will be moved back into the original workspace and you will resume in the *APL* environment.

The facilities used to achieve this are the CMS File Auxiliary Processor (AP110), the CMS Stack Input Processor (AP101), and the CP/CMS Command Processor (AP100).

A running example of the use of the functions in this workspace follows. We will edit the function *APPEND* by converting the representation of the function to a CMS file. Then we leave *APL*, move into the CMS environment, invoke the CMS editor, change the function-representation file, reenter *APL*, read the edited file, and define the function in the workspace. All of the file manipulations and movement between environments is done automatically. The user enters only the commands for the CMS editor.

```
APL
        APL*PLUS SERVICE
CLEAR WS
        )LOAD EDIT2
SAVED   16.13.12 02/13/80
        EDIT 'APPEND'
R; T=0.45/1.27 17:05:58
EDIT APPEND VRAPLFN A
EDIT:
T *                     Type entire file.

TOF:
R←MAT APPEND VEC;COLS
A CATENATES A VECTOR VEC AS A NEW ROW OF MATRIX MAT.
COLS←(ρVEC)⌈1↓ρMAT

MAT←((1↑ρMAT),COLS)↑MAT

R←MAT,[⎕IO] COLS↑VEC


EOF:
TOP                     Move back to top of file.
TOF:
N                       Move to next line.

R←MAT APPEND VEC;COLS

R R←M CATENATE V;COLS           Replace with this line.

N
A CATENATES A VECTOR VEC AS A NEW ROW OF MATRIX MAT.
CH/ VEC / V /           Change VEC to V.

A CATENATES A VECTOR V AS A NEW ROW OF MATRIX MAT.
CH/ MAT./ M./          Change MAT. to M.

A CATENATES A VECTOR V AS A NEW ROW OF MATRIX M.
N                       Next line.

COLS←(ρVEC)⌈1↓ρMAT
CH/MAT/M/* *            Change all occurrences of MAT to M.

COLS←(ρVEC)⌈1↓ρM
M←((1↑ρM),COLS)↑M
R←M,[⎕IO] COLS↑VEC
EOF:
```

```
LU/1↓                    Search from bottom to top; locate next occurrence of 1↓.
COLS←(ρVEC)⌈1↓ρM
CH/VEC/V/                 Change VEC to V.

COLS←(ρV)⌈1↓ρM
CH/VEC/V/* *                        Do it for all occurrences (from current line on).
R←M,[⎕IO] COLS↑V
EOF:
LU/1↓                    Locate 1↓ again.

COLS←(ρV)⌈1↓ρM
CH/1↓/¯1↑/                Change.

COLS←(ρV)⌈¯1↓ρM
EDIT:
FILE                     Rewrite the file; exit from the editor.
R; T=0.17/0.62 17:10:52
        APL*PLUS SERVICE
CLEAR WS
SAVED  . . .
CATENATE DEFINED


        ⎕VR'CATENATE'
    ∇ R←M CATENATE V;COLS
[1]  ⍝ CATENATES A VECTOR V AS A NEW ROW OF MATRIX M.
[2]  COLS←(ρV)⌈¯1↓ρM
[3]  M←((1↑ρM),COLS)↑M
[4]  R←M,[⎕IO]COLS↑V
    ∇


     )WSID
IS EDIT2
     )OFF HOLD
R; T=0.48/1.28 17:11:31
```

## Appendix—The *EDIT*2 Workspace

The functions used in demonstrating how the CMS Editor can be used to edit an *APL* function are listed in this appendix.

```
∇ EDIT NAME;WSID;SINK;VAR
[1]  ⍝  ALLOWS EDITING OF AN APL FUNCTION OR CHAR MATRIX VIA THE CMS EDITOR.
[2]  ⍝  NAME CONTAINS THE FUNCTION OR VARIABLE NAME OR THE NAME OF
[3]  ⍝  AN UNDEFINED OBJECT.
[4]  WSID←⎕WSID ⍝  SAVE THE WS ID.
[5]  ⍝  GET VARIABLE REPRESENTATION OF OBJECT NAMED IN NAME.
[6]  VR←GETVR NAME
[7]  ⍝  WRITE VR TO CMS FILE NAME,' VRAPLFN A'
[8]  VR WRITE NAME
[9]  ⍝  STACK COMMANDS TO SAVE WS, EXIT APL, AND INVOKE EDAPLFN EXEC.
[10] REEDIT:STACKEDIT
[11] ⍝  READ FILE NAME,' VRAPLFN A'
[12] VR←READ NAME
[13] ⍝  RE-ESTABLISH FUNCTION OR VARIABLE IN ORIGINAL FORM.
[14] ⍝  BRANCH TO REEDIT IF USER WANTS TO RE-EDIT INVALID FN.
[15] →REEDIT IF VR FIX NAME
[16] ⍝  ERASE NAME,' VRAPLFN A'
[17] ERASE NAME
    ∇


    ∇ VR←GETVR NAME
[1]  ⍝  PLACE ENTITY NAMED IN NAME INTO VARIABLE VR.
[2]  ⍝  IF IT IS A FUNCTION, THE CANONICAL REPRESENTATION IS PLACED IN VR.
[3]  ⍝  IF IT IS A CHARACTER MATRIX, THE VALUE IS ASSIGNED TO VR.
[4]  ⍝  IF IT IS AN UNDEFINED NAME, VR IS CREATED AS A 1 BY 130
[5]  ⍝  ARRAY CONTAINING THE NAME.
[6]  ⍝  IF IT IS ANYTHING ELSE, AN ERROR MESSAGE IS PRINTED AND
[7]  ⍝  AN EXIT IS TAKEN.
[8]  ⍝  THE ORIGINAL NAME CLASS IS SAVED IN VAR FOR USE WHEN THE
[9]  ⍝  OBJECT IS RE-ESTABLISHED FROM THE EDITED FILE.
```

```
[10]    →(0 2 3 =VAR←⎕NC NAME)/NONENT,VARIABLE,FUNCTION ◇ →BADNAME
[11]  NONENT:VR← 1 130 ρ130↑NAME ◇ →0
[12]  VARIABLE:VR←⍕NAME ◇ →BADNAME IF(' '≠1↑0ρVR)∨2≠ρρVR ◇ →0
[13]  FUNCTION:VR←⎕CR NAME ◇ →0
[14]  BADNAME:'ARGUMENT MUST BE NAME OF FN, CHARACTER MATRIX, OR UNDEFINED' ◇ →
      ∇


      ∇ VR WRITE NAME;OUT
[1]   ⍝  VIA AP110 (CMS FILE PROCESSOR), WRITE VR TO FILE NAME, 'VRAPLFN A'
[2]   ⍝  INITIAL VALUE OF SHARED VARIABLE IS FILENAME AND OPTIONS OF
[3]   ⍝  U (UNFORMATTED), AND APL (TRANSLATION FOR FULL CMS APL CHARACTER SET).
[4]    OUT←(8↑NAME),' VRAPLFN A(U APL'
[5]   ⍝  EXTEND SHARE AND CHECK DEGREE OF COUPLING AND RETURN CODE.
[6]    →ERROR IF 2≠110 ⎕SVO 'OUT'
[7]    →ERROR IF 0≠1↑OUT
[8]   ⍝  WRITE VR ONE LINE AT A TIME.
[9]   TOP:→END IF 0=1↑ρVR ◇ OUT←VR[⎕IO;] ◇ VR← 1 0 ↓VR ◇ →TOP
[10]  ⍝  RETRACT SHARE AND EXIT.
[11]  END:SINK←⎕SVR 'OUT' ◇ →0
[12]  ERROR:'ERROR WRITING TO ',(8↑NAME),' VRAPLFN A' ◇ →
      ∇


      ∇ STACKEDIT;STACK
[1]   ⍝  STACK THE NECESSARY COMMANDS IN THE CMS STACK TO SAVE THE WS,
[2]   ⍝  EXIT FROM APL, AND INVOKE THE CMS EDITOR.
[3]   ⍝
[4]   ⍝  INITIALIZE VARIABLE AND SHARE IT.
[5]   ⍝  LIFO (LAST IN FIRST OUT) WILL CAUSE COMMANDS TO BE EXECUTED
[6]   ⍝  IN REVERSE ORDER.  APL SPECIFIES THE CMS CHARACTER SET TRANSLATION.
[7]    STACK←'CMS(LIFO APL' ◇ SINK←101 ⎕SVO 'STACK'
[8]   ⍝  NOTE:  THE FOLLOWING COMMAND IS NOT STACKED BUT TAKES EFFECT WHILE
[9]   ⍝  THE STACK IS BEING READ.
[10]   STACK←'HT' ⍝  HALT TYPING WHILE READING FROM STACK.
[11]  ⍝  STACK INVOCATION OF OUR EDIT EXEC.
[12]   STACK←'EDITAPL ',(8↑NAME),' VRAPLFN A'
[13]   STACK←')OFF HOLD' ⍝  TO EXIT FROM THE APL ENVIRONMENT.
[14]   STACK←')SAVE' ⍝  SAVE THE WS.
[15]   STACK←')WSID EDTEMP' ⍝ GIVE WS A FIXED NAME SO EDIT EXEC CAN )LOAD IT.
[16]  S∆STACKEDIT←RESUME1 ⍝ STOP AT THIS LINE. NEXT READ WILL BE FROM STACK.
[17]  ⍝  WHEN THE EDITOR IS EXITED, EDITAPL EXEC WILL STACK AN
[18]  ⍝  APL COMMAND AND A →RESUME1.
[19]  ⍝  WE RE-ESTABLISH THE SHARE WITH AP101 SINCE IT WAS LOST WHEN WE
[20]  ⍝  LEFT APL.
[21]  RESUME1:STACK←'CMS(LIFO APL' ◇ SINK←101 ⎕SVO 'STACK'
[22]   STACK←'HT' ⍝  HALT TYPING AGAIN.
[23]   STACK←'→RESUME2' ⍝  AFTER EXECUTING )WSID, RESUME EXECUTION HERE.
[24]   STACK←')WSID ',WSID ⍝  WE'LL WANT TO RE-ESTABLISH WS NAME.
[25]  S∆STACKEDIT←RESUME2 ⍝  STOP HERE SO WE READ )WSID FROM STACK.
[26]  RESUME2:STACK←'RT' ⍝  RESUME TYPING.
[27]   SINK←⎕SVR 'STACK' ⍝  RETRACT SHARE.
      ∇


      ∇ VR←READ NAME;IN;TEMP
[1]   ⍝  VIA AP110 (CMS FILE PROCESSOR), READ FILE NAME,' VRAPLFN A'
[2]   ⍝  INITIAL VALUE OF SHARED VARIABLE IS FILENAME AND OPTIONS OF
[3]   ⍝  U (UNFORMATTED) AND APL (TRANSLATION FOR FULL CMS APL CHARACTER SET).
[4]    IN←(8↑NAME),' VRAPLFN A(U APL'
[5]   ⍝  EXTEND SHARE AND CHECK DEGREE OF COUPLING AND RETURN CODE.
[6]    →ERROR IF 2≠110 ⎕SVO 'IN'
[7]    →ERROR IF 0≠1↑IN
[8]   ⍝  INITIALIZE VR, THEN READ SUCCESSIVE RECORDS TILL WE GET AN EMPTY ONE.
[9]    VR← 0 0 ρ' '
[10]  TOP:→END IF 0=ρTEMP←IN ◇ VR←VR APPEND TEMP ◇ →TOP
[11]  ⍝  RETRACT SHARE AND EXIT.
[12]  END:SINK←⎕SVR 'IN' ◇ →0
[13]  ERROR:'ERROR READING FROM ',(8↑NAME),' VRAPLFN A' ◇ →
      ∇
```

```
      ∇ REED←VR FIX NAME;TEMP
[1]   ⍝  RE-ESTABLISH THE ENTITY VR WITH THE NAME CONTAINED IN VARIABLE NAME.
[2]   ⍝  IF IT WAS A VARIABLE USE AN EXECUTED ASSIGNMENT.
[3]   ⍝  IF IT WAS A FUNCTION OR UNDEFINED, USE ⎕FX.
[4]   ⍝  IF THE FUNCTION CANNOT BE RE-ESTABLISHED, ASK USER IF THEY
[5]   ⍝  WANT TO RE-EDIT THE FUNCTION.  SET REED TO 1 IF SO.
[6]    REED←0
[7]    →FN IF 2≠VAR ◊ ⍕NAME,'←VR' ◊ →0
[8]   FN:TEMP←⎕FX VR ◊ →FXERR IF ' '≠1↑0↑TEMP ◊ TEMP,' DEFINED' ◊ →0
[9]   FXERR:'⎕FX ERROR: ',⍕TEMP ◊ →0 IF REED←'Y'=1↑AKI 'REENTER EDIT ? '
[10]   'FUNCTION TEXT IS IN VARIABLE <VR>'
      ∇


      ∇ ERASE NAME;DMS
[1]   ⍝   VIA CMS COMMAND PROCESSOR, ERASE THE FILE NAME,' VRAPLFN A'
[2]    DMS←'CMS' ◊ SINK←100 ⎕SVO 'DMS'
[3]    DMS←'ERASE ',(8↑NAME),' VRAPLFN A'
[4]    SINK←⎕SVR 'DMS'
      ∇


      ∇ R←MAT APPEND VEC;COLS
[1]   ⍝  CATENATES A VECTOR VEC AS A NEW ROW OF MATRIX MAT.
[2]    COLS←(ρVEC)⌈1↓ρMAT
[3]    MAT←((1↑ρMAT),COLS)↑MAT
[4]    R←MAT,[⎕IO] COLS↑VEC
      ∇


      ∇ R←AKI TXT
[1]   ⍝ A SIMPLE MINDED PROMPTING FN.
[2]   ⍝ DISPLAYS TXT AND RETURNS USERS INPUT.
[3]    ⍞←TXT ◊ R←DROPLB ⍞
      ∇


      ∇ R←DROPLB X
[1]   ⍝ DROP LEADING BLANKS FROM X.
[2]    R←(∨\X≠' ')/X
      ∇


      ∇ R←A IF B
[1]    R←B/A
      ∇
```

The CMS EXEC *EDITAPL* is used in conjunction with the *APL* functions above:

```
EDIT ∊1 ∊2 ∊3
∊BEGSTACK LIFO
→RESUME
)LOAD EDTEMP
APL
END
```

*Mark Osborne joined STSC in 1974 as a systems programmer and is currently manager of the company's VM Development Group. At STSC he implemented chained variables and managed the System Support Team for one year. More recently, he implemented an interpreter interface for the VS APL demonstration project file system.*

*Osborne learned APL while working at GTE Laboratories, where he built a digital logic simulator for a large-scale integration project and was responsible for installing, maintaining, and modifying GTE's APL/360 and APLSV systems.*

**Stuart A. Bell**

# Practical *VS APL*—FORTRAN Interfacing

This paper describes a practical means for interfacing a FORTRAN program with a *VS APL* workspace or series of workspaces. The interface described is conceptually easy to understand, not difficult to implement, and provides complete control of the FORTRAN and *VS APL* environment. Data is shared between the two environments and sufficient control information is available to let the application user control the phasing of the application.

The paper contains examples of code that is easy to follow but lacks elegance. In each *VS APL* workspace, one function is illustrated independently of the others and separated by sufficient comments to permit clear understanding of the desired concepts.

## Background

Historically, the *APL* family of dialects existed in a world by itself. Unique data structures, unusual input and output conventions, and isolated data-management techniques resulted in the generation of "closed" applications. These applications became large and sophisticated in many cases, but generally all the data had to be available at the beginning of the application and the results had to be managed totally by *APL* throughout the life of the application. Attempts to mate the excellent features of *APL*'s data handling with the more traditional packages such as large linear programming systems were often contrived and difficult to use.

The introduction of shared variables and Time Shared Input/Output (TSIO) files into the *APL* environment created opportunities for importing and exporting much larger amounts of data. Soon after the introduction of shared variables, several installations began permitting *APL* applications to submit batch jobs in a stream. The ability to submit batch jobs in this way allowed an *APL* application to control the more traditional batch-type jobs. Hybrid applications began to evolve. This step forward permitted interface between *APL* applications and preexisting non-*APL* applications.

However, shared variable TSIO applications required a batch/*APL* interface and presented a foreign environment to the end user accustomed to the near immediate response of a well-tuned *APL* system. Batch scheduling delays of several hours were often experienced between the time the *APL* segment completed and the time the batch segment was scheduled and ran to completion. Additionally, the two different environments required vastly different systems skills, since the mastery of Job Control Language can be a full time project for specialists in that area.

The introduction of *VS APL* into the conversational time sharing environment simplified the interface problem between *APL* and non-*APL* segments of an application. It became quite practical to consider *APL* segments of an application as closed routines to be used where the unique advantages of *APL* can be employed. It also became practical to integrate *APL* and non-*APL* applications. The majority of development code can be done in *APL* and the older code can be retained as long as its value exceeds the rewrite costs.

The feature of *VS APL* that makes such applications practical is its single-service nature. Each user of *VS APL* is served by a single copy (conceptually) of the *APL* environment, and the user retains complete control of the entrance into and exit from that environment. For example, a *VS APL* terminal user can create a file using the Shared Storage Manager (slightly different from the Shared Variable Manager) and exit from *VS APL* to the native TSO or CMS environment. The file can then be edited by the system editor or serve as input to another application program (the FORTRAN Compiler, for example). All this can take place with a unified command set covered by the system's macro processor: CLIST in the TSO environment, or EXEC in the VM/CMS environment.

It is important to understand that when using *APL*, the Shared Storage Manager, *VS APL*, and the entire application package library run conversationally under control of the terminal session. It is this control that makes the examples that follow possible. *VS APL* can stand aside and permit programs written in other languages to execute for the duration of an application process.

## Examples

The clearest method of illustrating the unique feature of *VS APL* is by way of a contrived example. In this example, a sample terminal session is shown along with supporting functions and a user-written command file (EXEC) that are transparent to the terminal user.

In the sample terminal session, a user of IBM's Conversational Monitoring System, VM/CMS, logs onto the system and enters the application process via a pseudo-command QLOAD. This command invokes a user-written EXEC file. The QLOAD EXEC executes as follows:

```
&STACK HT
&STACK FIFO )LOAD SAB.LOADWS
EXEC APL
```

The QLOAD EXEC procedure quietly enters the *VS APL* environment, suppresses the welcoming banner from *VS APL*, and loads the initial workspace *LOADWS*. In the EXEC statements, the & character signifies that the next command is an EXEC directive. The HT command signifies "halt typing", and its effect is to turn off terminal output. The second &STACK directive places the material following it into a console stack in First-In-First-Out order. The lines stacked in the console stack eliminate the need for the user to enter these commands from the terminal keyboard. While the stack in not empty, the system will read lines of stacked input and treat them as if they had been keyed from the terminal. The remainder of the text, )LOAD SAB.LOADWS, is read by *VS APL*. It is a normal *APL* load command that causes the workspace to be loaded without the user's participation. Since terminal output is disabled, the user need not be aware that he has moved into *APL* or that the workspace has been loaded.

The workspace's latent expression executes *STARTUP*, whose first action is to counter the "halt typing" request issued in the QLOAD EXEC. This is done by invoking the stack auxiliary processor, AP101, and specifying the RT (resume typing) command. This auxiliary processor makes it possible to load the console stack from within the *APL* environment, producing an effect equivalent to the &STACK command in the QLOAD EXEC.

```
      ∇ STARTUP;STACK
[1]     STACK←'CMS (APL BEG'
[2]     0 0 ρ101 □SVO 'STACK'
[3]   ⍝ SHARE <STACK> WITH AUXILIARY PROCESSOR 101, AND
[4]   ⍝ DISCARD THE RESULT OF □SVO.
[5]     STACK←'RT' ⍝ RESUME TYPING
[6]     0 0 ρ□SVR 'STACK' ⍝ CLEAN UP AFTER MYSELF
[7]     'THIS IS A SAMPLE FUNCTION'
[8]     'ENTER CHANGEWS TO ENTER ANOTHER WORKSPACE'
      ∇
```

*STARTUP* also displays instructions to the terminal user:

```
THIS IS A SAMPLE FUNCTION
ENTER CHANGEWS TO ENTER ANOTHER WORKSPACE
```

```
      )WSID
IS SAB.LOADWS
```

At this point, entering *CHANGEWS* causes another workspace to be loaded. The *CHANGEWS* function performs the actual workspace transfer by stacking an HT and a )*LOAD* command in a manner similar to the QLOAD EXEC.

```
      ∇ CHANGEWS;STACK
[1]   ⍝ THIS FUNCTION QUIETLY LOADS ANOTHER WORKSPACE.
[2]     STACK←'CMS (APL BEG'
[3]     0 0 ρ101 □SVO 'STACK'
[4]     'YOU WILL NOW ENTER THE WRITEAPL WS'
[5]     STACK←'HT' ⍝ SUSPEND TERMINAL OUTPUT FOR AWHILE.
[6]     STACK←')LOAD SAB.WRITEAPL'
      ∇
```

The stack input processor can also be used to pass application values between workspaces by stacking the values prior to transfer and reading them into the second workspace or alternate language application. In our sample terminal session, however, no parameters are passed since each workspace is essentially independent.

By executing *CHANGEWS*, the terminal session user enters the workspace named *WRITEAPL*. The latent expression executes *STARTWS*, and a message is displayed as shown:

```
      CHANGEWS
```

```
ENTER 'WRITE' TO START A PROGRAM THAT WRITES A FILE FOR
READING FROM FORTRAN.  ENTER 'FORTRAN' TO ENTER THE FORTRAN
ENVIRONMENT.  READ THE FILE USING THE PROGRAM <APLREAD>.
MORE INSTRUCTIONS FOLLOW (FROM FORTRAN):
```

Again, *STARTWS* must execute the RT (resume typing) command before the user's next terminal input. This function could be performed by a general utility but is included here for clarity.

```
      ∇ STARTUP;STACK
[1]   ⍝ THIS FUNCTION STACKS AN RT 'RESUME TYPING' AND PRINTS INSTRUCTIONS.
[2]     STACK←'CMS (APL BEG'
[3]     0 0 ρ101 □SVO 'STACK'
[4]     STACK←'RT'
[5]     0 0 ρ□SVR 'STACK'
[6]     'ENTER ''WRITE'' TO START A PROGRAM THAT WRITES A FILE FOR'
[7]     'READING FROM FORTRAN.  ENTER ''FORTRAN'' TO ENTER THE FORTRAN'
[8]     'ENVIRONMENT.  READ THE FILE USING THE PROGRAM <APLREAD>.'
[9]     'MORE INSTRUCTIONS FOLLOW (FROM FORTRAN):'
      ∇
```

The *WRITE* function, listed below, is the most complex of the functions in the illustration. It creates a file in external format for later reading by another language processor (in this case, FORTRAN).

```
     ∇ WRITE;OUTPUT;CMS;TEMP
[1]    0 0 ρ100 □SVO CMS←'CMS' ⍝ SHARE A VARIABLE WITH THE CMS COMMAND
[2]  ⍝ PROCESSOR AND THROW AWAY THE SHARE RESULTS
[3]    CMS←'ERASE SAMPLE APLFILE' ⍝ ERASE THE OLD COPY OF THE SAMPLE FILE
[4]    0 0 ρ□SVR 'CMS' ⍝ RETRACT THE SHARE
[5]    OUTPUT←'SAMPLE APLFILE (192 FIX' ⍝ USE FULL APL-EBCDIC TRANSLATION
[6]  ⍝ THE DEFAULT FILETYPE IS VARIABLE - WE WANT FIXED FILES.
[7]    0 0 ρ110 □SVO 'OUTPUT' ⍝ THROW AWAY SHARE RESULTS
[8]    0 0 ρOUTPUT ⍝ AND INITIAL REFERENCE OF FILE
[9]    OUTPUT←80↑'THIS IS A SAMPLE FILE' ⍝ THE FIRST SPEC DETERMINES THE BLKSIZE
[10]   'ENTER DATA UNTIL TIRED AND END WITH A <CR>'
[11]   →NEXTL IF 0=ρTEMP←⍞ ◇ OUTPUT←80↑TEMP ◇ →THISL
[12]  ⍝ RETRACT THE SHARE - READ AND ECHO THE DATA
[13]   0 0 ρ□SVR 'OUTPUT'
[14]   OUTPUT←'SAMPLE APLFILE (192' ⍝ RE-SPECIFY FOR RESHARE
[15]   0 0 ρ110 □SVO 'OUTPUT' ⍝ AND RE-OFFER FOR INPUT
[16]   0 0 ρOUTPUT ⍝ THROW AWAY INITIAL VALUE SHOWING SPECIFICATIONS OF FILE
[17]   →NEXTL IF 0=ρTEMP←OUTPUT ◇ □←60↑TEMP ◇ →THISL ⍝ TRIM TO FIT ON 3270
[18]  ⍝ END OF FILE IS INDICATED BY A SHAPE OF 0.
[19]   0 0 ρ□SVR 'OUTPUT' ⍝ AND CLEAN UP AGAIN
     ∇
```

Lines [1] through [4] erase any file of the same name *'SAMPLE APLFILE'*, if any exist. If this is not done, the material being entered will be written to the end of the existing file. The same format specifications must be used when appending data to an existing file or the material may be unreadable. Also, any shared variables associated with the file must be retracted prior to erasing it. In the CMS environment, severe damage may be done to the file tables and Shared Storage Manager if a file is renamed or erased when it is also shared.

Line [5] establishes the file name, format, and conversion options, mapping each element of □*AV* into a unique external character. In most cases, the external characters are the obvious ones, namely A-Z and 0-9. Other conversion options and several functions are available to translate from one of these character sets into another. The *FIX* parameter indicates that the file is to contain fixed-length records and that each record is to be padded to the length of the first record.

Line [7] establishes the actual share. At this point, an empty file exists containing fixed-length records of a yet unspecified size and having the name *'SAMPLE APLFILE'*. Any set of eight or fewer characters can be used for either part of the name.

Line [8] is not really necessary for files that are to be read. If the result were printed, it would be a four-element vector containing the condition code of the share, a pointer to the first record to be read, a pointer to the first record to be written, and the blocking factor of the file (0 1 1 1, in our case).

Line [9] establishes the file as a fixed-length file with 80 characters per record.

Line [11] reads in the actual data and assigns it to a temporary variable. When only a RETURN is entered, the shape of the input vector is zero, indicating the end of terminal input in this application.

After completing the input, line [13] retracts the share and closes the file. Lines [14] through [19] read the file back, trimming the displayed data to 60 characters to fit conveniently on the screen of a video-display terminal.

The function *FORTRAN* listed below causes the application to exit from the *VS APL* environment, run a previously compiled FORTRAN program (named *APLREAD*), and reenter *VS APL*. Line [4] of the function instructs the stack processor to place the material on a push down stack in such a manner that the last command entered is the first executed. The commands HT and HX are exceptions to the stacking rule—they are executed immediately.

```
    ∇ FORTRAN;STACK
[1]   ⍝ THIS FUNCTION LINKS AND ACCESSES <SAB>'S 'A' DISK, INVOKES THE
[2]   ⍝ FORTRAN PROGRAM <APLREAD> FROM <SAB>'S DISK AND FINALLY REENTERS
[3]   ⍝ APL.  ALL QUIETLY (HOPEFULLY).
[4]     STACK←'CMS (LIFO APL'
[5]     0 0 ρ101 ⎕SVO 'STACK'
[6]     STACK←'HT' ⍝ SHUT OFF PRINTING OF THE FOLLOWING MATERIAL
[7]     STACK←'EXEC QLOAD'
[8]     STACK←'APLREAD'
[9]     STACK←')OFF HOLD' ⍝ THIS EXITS FROM APL INTO CMS ENVIRONMENT
[10]    0 0 ρ⎕SVR 'STACK' ⍝ RETRACT SHARE AND UNSTACK THE STACK
    ∇
```

The FORTRAN program *APLREAD* is listed below. It has already been compiled and set up so that it will begin running when its name is used as a command in the CMS environment. No external job control language or command language is used. The calls to OPSYS provide the necessary pointers to the disk file and the terminal.

```
C
C       THIS PROGRAM USES THE COMPANION WORKSPACE WRITEAPL TO CREATE A FILE
C
        INTEGER RECNO,MSG(20)
C
C       SET UP THE NECESSARY DEFAULT FILEDEFS:
C       FT05F001 - READ (5,XXX) - TERMINAL INPUT
C       FT08F001 - WRITE (8,XXX) - TERMINAL OUTPUT
C       FT10F001 - READ (10,XXX) - DISK INPUT - FROM VS APL
C
C
C       OPSYS IS AVAILABLE IN OBJECT FORM ON DON'S 'S' DISK
C
        CALL OPSYS('$'.'FILEDEF FT08F001 TERM$',IRET)
        CALL OPSYS('$','FILEDEF FT05F001 TERM$',IRET)
        CALL OPSYS('$','FILEDEF FT10F001 DISK SAMPLE APLFILE$',IRET)
   10   READ (10,100,END=20) MSG
  100   FORMAT (20A4)
        IF (MSG(1).EQ.FLAG) GO TO 20
        WRITE (8,200) MSG
  200   FORMAT (20A4)
        GO TO 10
   20   STOP
        END
```

After reading in the file, this routine exits back to CMS and executes the QLOAD EXEC that was stacked by line [7] of the function *FORTRAN*.

## Conclusion

The examples in this presentation are obviously contrived and have no practical value as written. In an actual application, the *VS APL* workspaces could prepare input for a package such as a statistical reduction program or a linear programming model.

Canned packages that have evolved over many years are often very efficient internally but cumbersome to use. *APL* permits ease of use through human-engineered interface, but sometimes lacks the sophisticated support routines present in a full-service data processing environment.

*VS APL* permits the programmer to take advantage of the "best of both worlds"—human engineering through *APL* and applications processing through preexisting batch packages—in a smooth and efficient operating environment.

*Stuart Bell, head of systems and operations with Sigma Data Services, Inc., is currently managing a data processing installation at the Goddard Modeling and Simulation Facility in Greenbelt, Maryland. Bell has been working for over ten years in systems programming and real-time systems design. He was previously employed by Computer Science Corporation and STSC, Inc.*

*Bell holds a B.S. in physics from Drexel University in Philadelphia and has done graduate work in computer science at the University of Florida, University of Maryland, and Johns Hopkins University.*

Mary Lou Fox

# Optimization Modeling Systems:
# An *APL*/MPSX Interface

Virtual Machine Facility/370 (VM/370) is a very versatile operating system from the perspective of the optimization modeling system designer. In the VM environment, it is possible to interface the interactive and computational power of *APL* with the advanced, high-performance software component MPSX/370 to create user-oriented modeling systems for solving complex optimization problems. This paper will illustrate such a system, albeit a trivial one.

### Optimization Problems

Optimization problems are those that seek to find a best solution among many feasible solutions to a set of constraints that are often numerous, complex, and conflicting. Some objective is sought, such as maximizing profits, minimizing costs, or minimizing fuel consumption. Typical optimization problems include:

- Investment problems such as finding the best investment strategy given many possible opportunities.

- Transportation problems such as finding the best route and schedule for trucks going between several warehouses.

- Production problems such as determining the best mix of products to produce, given constraints such as raw material costs and factory limitations.

Mathematical programming is a proven technique for solving optimization problems. A model of the problem is built that involves an objective function and a number of constraints; that is, a number of equations and inequalities. The solution to the problem is the *best* of the many feasible solutions, the one that maximizes (or minimizes) the objective function and satisfies all constraints. Usually the sheer number of constraints makes solving an optimization problem impossible without a computer.

### MPSX/370

IBM's MPSX/370 (Mathematical Programming System Extended) is a proven, state-of-the-art software system for solving optimization problems. MPSX/370 consists of a series of Assembler macros and procedures that are efficient, powerful, and reliable.

MPSX/370 requires as input a card deck containing the row, column, and right-hand side values of the model matrix. MPSX/370 is executed by calling a control program that consists of macro and procedure calls to MPSX to solve the problem. During the optimization process, a solution file is created, recording the optimal seeking process and the final solution. Additional features of MPSX/370 include a report generator and restart procedures. Solving a model using MPSX/370 requires computer sophistication—it is not for the casual user.

## Optimization Modeling Systems

An interactive user-oriented modeling system for optimization problems using MPSX usually contains the following:

- An interactive program that accepts data in a straightforward format that is comfortable for the user.

- A database of information that can be updated and stored over a period of time.

- A matrix generator program that creates the correct mathematical model for the problem, and translates this into the card deck for MPSX/370.

- An MPSX Control Language Program that contains the macro and procedure calls to find the optimal solution.

- A report writer program to interpret the solution file and print the solution in a report format easily understood by the user.

VM/370 is an excellent operating system for optimization modeling because it permits communication between programs written in *APL*, FORTRAN, PL/1, and Assembler. Thus a typical modeling system might have an interactive data input program written in *APL*; a database consisting of CMS files; a matrix generator written in *APL*, PL/1, or FORTRAN; a CMS EXEC procedure that calls the MPSX/370 control program; and an *APL* program to print reports. What is remarkable from the perspective of the typical *APL* user is that all of the above programs can be executed automatically from a single *APL* program.

On the VM system, *APL* can communicate outside its environment with the virtual processor. The vehicle for this is the set of auxiliary processors available in *VS APL* that makes it possible to do the following from within the *APL* environment:

- Create CMS files that can be read by FORTRAN, PL/1, or Assembler programs.

- Read CMS files that have been created by a program written in one of these languages.

- Set up a sequence of commands to exit from the *APL* environment, run a CMS EXEC procedure, and return to *APL* in a way that is automatic and transparent to the user.

Table 1 illustrates the data used in a simple model on the VM system. This example, a linear model of oil refinery operations, is quite simple and really does not require MPSX/370 to solve. Yet it illustrates the facets of a modeling system for the purposes of this discussion.

The problem is this: At regular intervals, a refinery wants to know how much of each type of raw gasoline it should blend to make each of its products—regular and premium gasoline—to maximize its profit. Costs and selling prices fluctuate greatly, so that the blend that is most profitable in one time period may not be the most profitable blend in the next.

The modeling system discussed here is designed to allow the refinery to enter costs and other relevant data. The system uses a linear model of the refinery's operations and solves it using mathematical programming techniques.

### Table 1 — Oil Refinery Operations

| Gasoline | Octane Rating | Refinery Capacity (in barrels) | Vapor Pressure |
|----------|---------------|-------------------------------|----------------|
| Type 1   | 108           | 30,000                        | 4              |
| Type 2   | 90            | 20,000                        | 10             |
| Type 3   | 73            | 40,000                        | 5              |
| Premium  | 95            |                               | 6              |
| Regular  | 85            |                               | 9              |

### The Model

The solution to the problem is that combination of values of each variable below that produces the maximum profit:

$R1$      number of barrels of raw gasoline of type 1 to be used in the regular gasoline blend.

$R2$      number of barrels of raw gasoline of type 2 to be used in the regular gasoline blend.

$R3$      number of barrels of raw gasoline of type 3 to be used in the regular gasoline blend.

$P1$      number of barrels of raw gasoline of type 1 to be used in the premium gasoline blend.

$P2$      number of barrels of raw gasoline of type 2 to be used in the premium gasoline blend.

$P3$      number of barrels of raw gasoline of type 3 to be used in the premium gasoline blend.

The profit to be gained from the production of the gasoline blends is the difference between the selling price of the particular blend and the cost of the raw gasoline for each variable above (see Table 2).

### Table 2 — Gasoline Cost and Selling Price

| Gasoline | Cost | Selling Price |
|----------|------|---------------|
| Type 1   | $35  |               |
| Type 2   | $25  |               |
| Type 3   | $20  |               |
| Premium  |      | $30           |
| Regular  |      | $27           |

Using the costs in Table 2, the profit equation becomes

```
PROFIT = ¯8R1 + 2R2 + 7R3 - 5P1 + 5P2 + 10P3
```

The model also includes *constraints* that restrict the values of the variables. In this problem, there are three basic constraints: octane ratings, refinery capacity, and vapor pressures.

Octane constraints require that the octane rating of a blend be at least 95 for premium and 85 for regular. The inequalities that reflect this are for regular gas:

```
108R1 + 90R2 + 73R3 ≥ 85(R1 + R2 + R3)
```

or:

    23R1 + 5R2 - 12R3 ≥ 0

and for premium gas:

    108P1 + 90P2 + 73P3 ≥ 95(P1 + P2 + P3)

or:

    13P1 - 5P2 - 22P3 ≥ 0

Capacity constraints restrict the amount of each type of raw gasoline that can be produced at the refinery.

Gas Type 1:

    R1 + P1 ≤ 30000

Gas Type 2:

    R2 + P2 ≤ 20000

Gas Type 3:

    R3 + P3 ≤ 40000

Vapor pressure constraints require that the gasoline blends have sufficiently low vapor pressure. The inequality for regular gas is

    4R1 + 10R2 + 5R3 ≤ 9(R1 + R2 + R3)

or:

    ⁻5R1 + R2 - 4R3 ≤ 0

and for premium gas:

    4P1 + 10P2 + 5P3 ≤ 6(P1 + P2 + P3)

or:

    ⁻2P1 + 4P2 - P3 ≤ 0

Additional constraints could be introduced, such as a minimum production schedule to meet existing contracts:

| Gasoline | Contractual Obligations (Minimum Production) |
|---|---|
| Premium | 8000 |
| Regular | 3200 |

The corresponding constraints would be for regular gas:

    R1 + R2 + R3 ≥ 3200

and for premium gas:

    P1 + P2 + P3 ≥ 8000

A last set of constraints requires the nonnegativity of barrels produced:

    R1 ≥ 0, R2 ≥ 0, R3 ≥ 0, P1 ≥ 0, P2 ≥ 0, P3 ≥ 0

Thus the final model expressed as a programming problem would be given as follows:

Maximize:

    PROFIT = -8R1 + 2R2 + 7R3 - 5P1 + 5P2 + 10P3

subject to:

$$
\begin{array}{rcl}
23R1 + 5R2 - 12R3 & & \geq 0 \\
13P1 - 5P2 - 22P3 & \geq & 0 \\
R1 \qquad\qquad + \quad P1 & & \leq 30000 \\
R2 \qquad\qquad + \quad P2 & & \leq 20000 \\
R3 \qquad\qquad + P3 & \leq & 40000 \\
-5R1 + R2 - 4R3 & & \leq 0 \\
- 2P1 + 4P2 - P3 & \leq & 0 \\
R1 + R2 + R3 & & \geq 3200 \\
P1 + P2 + P3 & \geq & 8000
\end{array}
$$

and:

$$R1, \ R2, \ R3, \ P1, \ P2, \ P3 \ \geq \ 0$$

## Modeling System

A modeling system for this refinery would allow the user to easily enter the costs, selling prices, and contractual obligations of the gasolines. In addition, the system would return the result in report format. Such a system is illustrated below with the sample inputs from the above discussion. Figure 1 shows the report containing the results.

```
        REFINERY
ENTER  COSTS OF GAS TYPES: 1, 2, 3
☐:
        35 25 20
ENTER  SELLING PRICE OF PREMIUM AND REGULAR GAS
☐:
        30 27
ENTER  MINIMUM PRODUCTION (CONTRACTS) FOR PREMIUM AND REGULAR GAS
☐:
        8000 3200
ENTER  OCTANE RATINGS FOR GAS TYPES 1, 2 AND 3, PREMIUM AND REGULAR GAS
☐:
        108 90 73 95 85
ENTER  VAPOR PRESSURE FOR GAS TYPES 1, 2 AND 3, PREMIUM AND REGULAR GAS
☐:
        4 10 5 6 9
ENTER  REFINERY CAPACITY FOR GAS TYPES 1, 2 AND 3
☐:
        30000 20000 40000
```

```
                    PRODUCTION SCHEDULE - GASOLINE BLENDS


                            PREMIUM                    REGULAR
                     BARRELS PRODUCED    COST    BARRELS PRODUCED    COST
        GAS TYPE (COST)

            1    ($35)    5028.6      175,861       14,971.4    $523,999

            2    ($25)       0.0            0       20,000.0    $500,000

            3    ($20)    2971.4      $59,428       37,028.6    $740,572


    TOTAL PRODUCTION:     8000.0     $235,289       72,000.0  $1,764,571


                              PROFIT


    GAS BLEND    BARRELS PRODUCED     COST        SALES        PROFIT

    PREMIUM           8000         $235,289    $240,000        $4711

    REGULAR         72,000       $1,764,571  $1,944,000     $179,429

    TOTAL:          80,000       $1,999,860  $2,184,000     $184,140
```

**Figure 1—Optimization Results**

What is interesting from the perspective of this paper is that what is happening during the execution of the *REFINERY* program is totally transparent to the user. As far as the user is aware, he signs on to *VS APL* and runs a program *REFINERY*, which produces a report. In fact, the following chain of events have occurred:

1. The user enters the *APL* environment, loads a workspace, and executes an *APL* program *REFINERY*.

2. The user enters run-dependent data.

3. An *APL* matrix generator subprogram is executed, creating the model matrix.

4. A CMS file is created using Auxiliary Processor 110. This file contains the card image of the model matrix required as input to MPSX. Figure 2 illustrates this file.

5. A "stack" of commands is created to exit from *APL*, run a CMS EXEC, and return to *APL*.

6. The CMS EXEC calls the MPSX macros. Figure 3 illustrates a portion of the solution file created by the MPSX macros.

7. Execution returns to *APL* and begins the report program. The solution data for the report is read from the CMS solution file using Auxiliary Processor 110.

```
1MPSX/370 V1M4 PTF7    MPSCL EXECUTION
0SECTION 2 - COLUMNS
- NUMBER  .COLUMNS  AT    ...ACTIVITY...  ..INPUT COST..  ..LOWER LIMIT.  ..UPPER LIMIT.  .REDUCED COST.
0    10   R1      BS    14971.42857     8.00000-        .               NONE           .
     11   R2      BS    20000.00000     2.00000         .               NONE           .
     12   R3      BS    37028.57143     7.00000         .               NONE           .
     13   P1      BS     5028.57143     5.00000-        .               NONE           .
A    14   P2      LL         .          5.00000         .               NONE           .
     15   P3      BS     2971.42857    10.00000         .               NONE           .
1MPSX/370 V1M4 PTF7    MPSCL EXECUTION
0EXIT - TIME =    0.05
```

**Figure 3—MPSX Solution File**

## Conclusion

This paper illustrates the construction of an optimization modeling system that combines the powerful, interactive potential of *APL* with the rich variety of the VM/370 environment. Much more complex modeling systems have been developed using these techniques. A quite sophisticated system can be written in VM/370 whereby the only user-required command is the log-on command. All the subsequent commands to enter the *APL* environment, load a workspace, run an *APL* program, exit from *APL*, run a CMS program, return to *APL*, load a workspace, run a program, and log-off can be handled *automatically*. VM/370 is a truly remarkable operating system!

```
NAME GAS FREE
ROWS
 N  PROFIT
 L  GAS1
 L  GAS2
 L  GAS3
 G  POCTANE
 G  ROCTANE
 L  RVAPOR
 L  PVAPOR
 G  CONTRACT
COLUMNS
 R1  PROFIT  -8
 R1  GAS1  1
 R1  ROCTANE  23
 R1  RVAPOR  -5
 R2  PROFIT  2
 R2  GAS2  1
 R2  ROCTANE  5
 R2  RVAPOR  1
 R3  PROFIT  7
 R3  GAS3  1
 R3  ROCTANE  -12
 R3  RVAPOR  -4
 P1  PROFIT  -5
 P1  GAS1  1
 P1  POCTANE  13
 P1  PVAPOR  -2
 P1  CONTRACT  1
 P2  PROFIT  5
 P2  GAS2  1
 P2  POCTANE  -5
 P2  PVAPOR  4
 P2  CONTRACT  1
 P3  PROFIT  10
 P3  GAS3  1
 P3  POCTANE  -22
 P3  PVAPOR  -1
 P3  CONTRACT  1
RHS
 MIX  GAS1  30000
 MIX  GAS2  20000
 MIX  GAS3  40000
 MIX  POCTANE  0
 MIX  ROCTANE  0
 MIX  RVAPOR  0
 MIX  PVAPOR  0
 MIX  CONTRACT  8000
ENDATA
```

**Figure 2—CMS Card Image File**

*Mary Lou Fox, currently an applications analyst in STSC's Management Technology Division, has been an active user of APL since 1968. At STSC she is responsible for the design, development, and implementation of user-oriented modeling systems and software tools. Before joining STSC she was a research associate at Fairfield University, responsible for the design and development of*

*APL applications, including the university's APL libraries, CAI (Computer-Assisted Instruction) courses, instructional applications, and simulations.*

*Fox has a B.S. in mathematics from Boston College, a master's in math education from Fairfield University, and a master's in computer science from Polytechnic Institute of New York.*

Christian Hocquet and Gerard Lacourly

# Real-Life Applications of VM/370

Société de Traitements et de Services Conversationnels, the French distributor for *APL*PLUS* Service, has for the past 18 months been promoting and supporting VM/370 products and services. VM provides a much wider range of facilities than those available on OS-based *APL* systems, and some of these facilities will be illustrated via the four different applications discussed in this paper.

*EOLE* is a programming package designed and developed for opinion research via surveys, with applications in the behavorial sciences. The major features and capabilities of the package are described below:

- *EOLE* can process large arrays resulting from questionnaires (up to 30,000 respondents with up to 50 questions each).

- Analytical features range from simple cross-tabulations to advanced statistical analyses—segmentation, typology, and factor analysis.

- The input data is bulk processed to convert it to a more convenient internal format, and subsequent studies are performed on the converted data.

- The main file need not be kept online. Instead, facilities are provided so that the user can manage the archived data directly.

The system was implemented using *VS APL* on a VM system for several reasons. The user (who is a behavioral scientist, not a computer scientist) had a distinct preference for using *APL*, and the ability of *VS APL* to process very large arrays (as contrasted with the ones available in *APL* implementations with fixed workspace sizes) made it easy to manage the data in a natural fashion. And, because VM is an interactive system rather than a batch system, the user maintains full control, in real time, of his data.

A major application in energy flow control employs linear programming to optimize the production of hydroelectric plants. The application has three major steps: collecting, controlling, and processing the input data; linear programming analysis; and the post-processing of results to prepare management and engineering reports. Originally, the entire application was prototyped in *VS APL* (including the linear programming model). However, because of the vast amount of data involved, we decided to use MPSX 1370 (IBM's Mathematical Programming System Extended) for the linear programming step. This produced a system with the best mix of features: it kept the flexibility and ease of change for the input and output processing, and employed auxiliary processors (APs) to communicate with MPSX. MPSX itself is a highly developed linear programming system; its use greatly improved processing speed.

A major French manufacturing company had independently developed a personnel management system several years ago on an OS-based *APL* system that featured files resembling those of the *APL\*PLUS* System. After much operating experience, they decided to adapt the application to *VS APL* on the *APL\*PLUS* VM System. The main reasons for the change were (1) data could be moved more easily from non-*APL* storage to the file system of the *APL\*PLUS* VM System than to OS-based *APL* files, and (2) the file-sharing capabilities of the *APL\*PLUS* VM System were more flexible.

A consulting firm specializing in economic and statistical analyses sought a computer service both for processing their clients' applications and for creating and offering new software packages. After evaluating several computer service suppliers, they chose *APL\*PLUS* VM Service for the following reasons:

- It provides access to several programming languages (FORTRAN, COBOL, and PL/1 were the most important).

- It offers several well-known statistical packages such as the Biomedical Computer Programs, P-Series (BMDP); the Statistical Analysis System (SAS); and the SPSS™ Conversational Statistical System (SCSS™).

- It provides advanced tools for conversational programming of new applications.

- It gives the user full control of the machine environment when he needs it.

The four applications described above give many of the reasons why our clients like *VS APL* and VM. From our vantage point, as suppliers of the service, we see the following benefits:

- VM is a real-time system with a wide range of capabilities.

- Most commercially available VM/370 systems, such as the *APL\*PLUS* VM System, feature numerous application libraries and well-developed tools for rapid application programming in a variety of programming languages.

- While VM systems are fundamentally interactive, it is easy to change the interfacing mechanism so that applications can be run either in the traditional interactive mode, or (using predefined calling sequences) in a mode resembling batch or remote batch processing.

In the early days of VM/370 usage, it was often disparagingly said that one had to be a computer scientist to be able to use VM. This is no longer the case, for there are many cataloged procedures that can be invoked to tailor the system (as the user sees it) to match his own skills. Thus, the computer novice, who is interested only in applying predeveloped programs to his data, uses the system at one level, while the professional data processing person has access to the full scope of the system—a system that gives more facility and flexibility than the naked machine itself.

Perhaps the most significant benefit of VM is the ease with which one can develop the various phases of an application in whatever language is most appropriate. The user can be confident that transferring data, or sharing files among phases of processing, is convenient, not prone to error, and well-disciplined.

*From 1975 to 1978 Christian Hocquet was an applications consultant at CISI (Compagnie Internationale de Services en Informatique), where he developed database applications in personnel database management and medical laboratories data management using an IMS DB/DC System. At CISI he also managed the programming methodology and technical support groups and a development group using IMS. In 1978 Hocquet joined the Société de Traitements et de Services Conversationnels, an independent distributor of APL\*PLUS Service in France. Hocquet is currently an applications consultant manager at the Société.*

*Hocquet has a master's degree in computer science and a doctorate in management science.*


*Gerard Lacourly has been managing director of the Société de Traitements et de Services Conversationnels since 1978. In this capacity, he manages all activities of the company, an independent distributor of APL\*PLUS Service in France. Before joining the Société, Lacourly was head of the APL Department at SLIGOS and held several management positions with CISI (Compagnie Internationale de Services en Informatique).*

*Lacourly has a graduate degree in electrical and mechanical engineering from the Ecole Nationale Superieur d'Electricite et de Mecanique, a doctoral degree in mathematical statistics from the Institut Superieur de la statistique at Paris University, and an M.A. in applied mathematics from Harvard University.*

Brian C. Hagenbuch

# *APL* and the Relational Model of Data

When *APL* first appeared, many people thought of it as a "toy" language. While it was well suited to scientific applications involving complex calculations on relatively small amounts of data, it was completely unsuitable for business applications involving relatively simple calculations on large amounts of data. Time has shown this *opinion* to be false. Today the primary use of *APL* is in the very realm where it was once thought to be unsuitable—business data processing.

Some reasons for the success of *APL* in the business environment follow:

- The extraordinary expressive power of the language is as well suited to straightforward calculations as it is to more arcane sorts of computing.

- Most *APL* time sharing systems now include facilities to aid the programmer of business applications: file processors for storing large amounts of data outside the *APL* workspace, formatting utilities to reduce the cost of enhancing output, and other miscellaneous system enhancements such as shared variables.

- As the *APL* programming community gained experience with business applications, software libraries evolved to simplify the task for future system developers. Many *APL* time sharing systems now include routines (and even general-purpose application packages) to deal with file management, financial analysis and planning, inventory control and material requirements planning, and so on.

While for many the initial attraction to *APL* was its expressive power, the evolution of system facilities and *APL* software is what made the migration of *APL* into the realm of business data processing possible. Today we are on the verge of the next stage of evolution of *APL* time sharing—the marriage of *APL* with database management.

The 1970s have been aptly called the decade of the database. The use of computers in business has led to an increased awareness of the potential value of information. To realize this potential value a new kind of software emerged—the database management system (DBMS). The goals of a DBMS are to allow diverse applications to access a common collection of data and to allow these applications to be developed more easily, more inexpensively, and more flexibly than would be possible otherwise. DBMSs attempt to achieve these goals in several ways.

One of the most important ways is through *data independence*. Data independence refers to the insulation of application programs from the details of how their data are stored. *APL* programmers enjoy quite a bit of data independence in that they need not be concerned with such matters as how a matrix of numbers is actually represented within the *APL* system. Users of DBMSs can be similarly unconcerned with how their databases (usually much more complex than matrices) are represented internally.

Consider the advantage of being able to refer to "the salaries of the employees in department 50", rather than "the values in components 31 through 40 that correspond to occurrences of 50 in components 61 through 70". The notion of data independence goes further than this, however. In addition to freeing application programs from the details of the *physical* representation of the database, many DBMSs supply forms of *logical* data independence, thus allowing different applications to view the same data with entirely different logical organizations. (One man's field is another man's record.)

Another important advantage of a DBMS follows from the notion of logical data independence; to wit, the ability to avoid duplication of data. Without benefit of a DBMS, it is common to find two or more applications working with separate copies of the same data. Whether this is due to conflicting access requirements (the need for different logical views of the data) or just the lack of communication between application designers, the result is the same. In addition to the obvious increase in storage costs, the risk that these separate copies will not stay the same is introduced. As the copies drift apart, the applications will inevitably produce inconsistent results. Avoiding this risk is one of the main attractions of DBMSs.

A sophisticated DBMS will also provide capabilities such as:

- Programming language interfaces that allow access to the DBMS from familiar environments and that make possible the development of complex procedures using the data.

- Maintenance and utility programs that free the application programmer from the need to develop special solutions to routine problems.

- Data reorganization facilities that improve storage and performance characteristics.

- Data security and integrity controls that help ensure that data is maintained in a correct and consistent fashion.

- Sharing capabilities that allow applications to support multiple users without concern for interlocks and other such items.

- Access controls that protect the privacy of sensitive information.

- Restart capabilities that eliminate the need to adopt obscure recovery tactics within individual applications.

- Tuning capabilities that allow the performance of the DBMS to be balanced dynamically as new applications are incorporated and old ones retired.

Although *APL* applications that incorporate many of these capabilities are occasionally written, they always address fairly specific problems. Thus, while new applications often benefit from techniques used in old ones, the new ones must usually be designed and written from scratch. The situation is one in which the substantial part of the effort of developing an application is aimed at maintaining the data for the application, rather than at solving the real-world problem. The need for a database management capability for *APL* applications is clear.

But what should an *APL* database management capability look like? The discussion above concentrated on the common characteristics of DBMSs.

Obviously, not all DBMSs are alike. In addition to superficial differences in the features they provide, DBMSs differ dramatically in the way they represent data to users; that is, in their choice of a *data model*. It is here that we will concentrate our discussion.

All DBMSs represent data as simple collections of related items. Such collections are usually called records and might, for example, contain the number, name, salary, and date of hire of an employee. The term *data model*, however, refers not to records, but to the way collections of records are organized. There are three data models used in current systems. While some systems claim to support more than one model, most can be neatly classified as either *hierarchical, network,* or *relational.*

In the *hierarchical model,* records are organized according to a simple *tree structure.* A typical record is seen as subordinate to one record and as superior to a collection of records. For example, consider an enterprise that is organized into departments, each of which is solely responsible for several projects. These projects are, in turn, individually staffed. In a hierarchical database for this enterprise, a project record could be subordinate to a record associated with the department charged with the project, and superior to a group of records, each of which is associated with an employee who works on the project. This organization seems quite natural in many contexts, and it conveniently supports a wide range of applications.

The *network model* may be viewed as a generalization of the hierarchical model. It organizes records according to what is called a *plex structure.* A plex structure is one in which a typical record may have several superior as well as several subordinate records. If the example above were changed slightly so that several departments could share the responsibility for a single project (and a single employee could work on several projects), the network model would seem a more natural choice for handling the data.

In both the hierarchical and network models, a database is represented in terms of two distinct kinds of conceptual objects: *records* and *links* between records. The *relational model* differs from both the hierarchical and network models in that it omits the concept of a link between records. Rather, records are organized into tables. Each table is a collection of unique records of the same type; that is, all the records in a table have the same field descriptions. Within the relational model the effect of links between records is achieved by reference to the values stored in the records.

An example may help make this distinction clearer. In the hierarchical structure described above, there are five "objects" to consider:

1. Department records containing department number (*DNO*), department name (*DNAME*), and budget (*BUDGET*).

2. Links relating each department to a set of project records.

3. Project records containing project number (*PNO*), project name (*PNAME*), and budget (*BUDGET*).

4. Links relating each project record to a set of employee records.

5. Employee records containing employee number (*ENO*), employee name (*ENAME*), salary (*SAL*), and date of hire (*DOH*).

We can represent this hierarchical scheme as follows:

*DEPARTMENT(DNO,DNAME,BUDGET)*

One *DEPARTMENT* links to many *PROJECT*s

> *PROJECT(PNO,PNAME,BUDGET)*

One *PROJECT* links to many *EMPLOYEE*s

> *EMPLOYEE(ENO,ENAME,SAL,DOH)*

In the relational model, the "one-to-many" links of the hierarchical model can be expressed as data items in the subordinate records. Thus, a relational version of the hierarchical scheme might look like:

> *DEPARTMENT(DNO,DNAME,BUDGET)*

> *PROJECT(DNO,PNO,PNAME,BUDGET)*

> *EMPLOYEE(PNO,ENO,ENAME,SAL,DOH)*

(Underlined data items are keys; that is, they have unique values within the table in which they appear.) Thus, by reference to the *PNO* value of an employee record, we may uniquely identify the project records to which it is linked, and similarly the department to which a project is linked.

The example of a network structure may also be recast in the relational model. Recall that in the network example the "one-to-many" links of the hierarchy are replaced by "many-to-many" links. We might represent a network scheme as:

> *DEPARTMENT(DNO,DNAME,BUDGET)*

Many *DEPARTMENT*s link to many *PROJECT*s

> *PROJECT(PNO,PNAME,BUDGET)*

Many *PROJECT*s link to many *EMPLOYEE*s

> *EMPLOYEE(ENO,ENAME,SAL,DOH)*

In the relational model, this more complicated structure can be represented as follows:

> *DEPARTMENT(DNO,DNAME,BUDGET)*

> *DEPTVSPROJ(DNO,PNO)*

> *PROJECT(PNO,PNAME,BUDGET)*

> *PROJVSEMP(PNO,ENO)*

> *EMPLOYEE(ENO,ENAME,SAL,DOH)*

The important observation here is that, in the relational model, some of the structural characteristics of the other models (links) are recast simply as contents of the basic structure common to all the models (the record). This simplification is apparent in data manipulation languages designed to work with the relational model, and is one of the main benefits of the relational approach.

While all three data models are capable of expressing the same range of interrelationships between records (procedures exist to recast one model in terms of another), the relational model has clear advantages for *APL*. The "tables" of the relational model are quite similar to the arrays handled by *APL*. Further, the lack of nonrectangular link structures makes the relational model seem "more natural" to *APL* programmers.

To my knowledge, there are no current implementations in which *APL* is effectively interfaced with a relational DBMS (although the time is ripe). Nevertheless, the results of the work that led to the relational model can be of immediate benefit to the designer of database applications in *APL*. Foremost among those results is the concept of *normalization*. Normalization is a database design technique with the goal of simple, consistent representation of the relationships inherent in the data for an application. Although normalization techniques are applicable to all the data models discussed, they are most easily understood and applied in the context of the relational model.

Most discussions of the relational model deal implicitly with tables in what is called "first normal form" (1NF). 1NF simply means that the value of a particular field in a particular record is *atomic*; that is, cannot be decomposed into a simpler form. (A non-atomic value would, itself, be a table.) 1NF, therefore, deals with the structure of tables. Higher normal forms are more interesting in that they deal with the meaning of tables. It is impossible to look at a table and tell whether, for example, it is in third normal form, unless you have some additional information about the real-world situation represented by the table. Take, for example, the following table:

| DEPARTMENT | COURSE | STUDENT |
|------------|--------|---------|
| ENGLISH | LIT210 | JONES |
| ENGLISH | LIT210 | BLAKE |
| PHYSICS | OPTICS402 | JONES |

The table is meant to represent a real situation in which students are enrolled in courses offered by the departments in a university. What is not apparent from the table alone is the fact that a particular course is always offered by one and only one department. In light of this fact, some system designers (even those not familiar with normalization techniques) may feel uncomfortable with our table. Some problems they might uncover include:

- The association between a department and a course that it offers cannot be represented in the table unless at least one student is enrolled in the course. There is nowhere in the table to record the fact that the *MATH* Department offers *ALGEBRA*102 until some student enrolls in the course.

- Correspondingly, when the last student enrolled in a course drops it and the pertinent record is deleted, additional information is lost. If Jones decides to drop *OPTICS*402, we'll also lose track of the fact that *OPTICS*402 is offered by the *PHYSICS* Department.

- In the course of updating values in the table, it is possible to violate the correspondence of departments to courses. Suppose *BLAKE* decides to move from *LIT*210 to *OPTICS*402. Unless the associated change to *DEPT* is made at the same time, we may find that *OPTICS*402 is offered by both the *PHYSICS* and *ENGLISH* departments, in violation of our knowledge of the real state of affairs.

In the terminology of normalization theory, our table suffers from three kinds of anomalies: insertion anomalies, deletion anomalies, and update anomalies. These problems can be solved by recasting the table as two separate tables:

| DEPARTMENT | COURSE |
|------------|--------|
| ENGLISH | LIT210 |
| PHYSICS | OPTICS402 |

| COURSE | STUDENT |
|--------|---------|
| LIT210 | JONES |
| LIT210 | BLAKE |
| OPTICS402 | JONES |

Each of the new tables is in what is termed fourth normal form. The original table was not. (It was, however, in third normal form.) As a result of the further normalization of our table, it is now free from the anomalies described above.

Normalization theory is too complex a topic to treat here in detail. It is, nevertheless, worth the attention of anyone who designs databases. What it amounts to is a formalization of "common sense design". It is especially appropriate in the *APL* environment, where the native data structure is the rectangular array.

For excellent discussions of normalization theory (and the whole area of database management), the reader is directed to the two books listed in the notes at the end of this paper.

## Conclusion

The continuing success of *APL* in business data processing is due not only to the power of the language itself, but also to the ever increasing range of system facilities designed to aid the application programmer, and to the expertise of the *APL* programming community. Computerized information systems have led the business community to appreciate the immense value of accessible, well-organized information. To keep pace, *APL* time sharing systems must eventually be extended to include the capabilities of a DBMS. In the meantime, it would behoove the designer of database applications in *APL* to look into the general area of database management. Of particular interest is the relational model of data and its associated discipline of normalization.

*Notes*

1.  James Martin, *Computer Database Organization*, Second Edition, (Prentice-Hall, 1977).

2.  C. J. Date, *An Introduction to Database Systems*, Second Edition, (Addison-Wesley, 1977).

*Brian Hagenbuch studied physics at Pennsylvania State University for one year before transferring to St. John's College in Annapolis, where he earned his B.A. in liberal arts. He then spent a year with Leasco Response, Inc., a time sharing vendor, working on an interactive file management system. In 1974 Hagenbuch joined STSC as an applications consultant, and in 1978 he joined STSC's Applications Development Department, where he is currently an APL applications analyst.*

*At STSC, Hagenbuch has taught APL courses for STSC personnel and customers and worked on several application development projects. He recently completed a study on database management in APL.*

# Part 2

# The General Management Viewpoint

John E. Suwara

# *APL* Tutorial
# For General Management

With labor costs to business—especially for white-collar and managerial workers—rising steadily, it becomes more and more important to make people productive in all areas. What *APL* does, and does well, is to make people more productive in implementing computer solutions. It is not uncommon for people working with *APL* to improve their speed in implementing applications by a factor ranging from 5 to 15. This is particularly true for "quick and dirty" applications where an immediate answer is needed on a one-time basis.

This paper is derived from seminar material presented in a single day to nontechnical managerial personnel. Its purpose is to provide the reader with a sense of what it is *APL* does to speed the work of its users, with particular reference to some of *APL*'s uses in a business context.

## Why *APL*?

*APL* came into being in the late 1950s because of a Harvard University mathematician's search for a more effective way to express certain algorithms. In working with conventional mathematical notations, Kenneth Iverson had found them to be inconsistent; he also found he had to step out of mathematics and use English to represent phenomena such as sorting. He looked into the computer languages that were then available and also found them to be inconsistent.

Being resourceful, Iverson invented his own notation—a notation that also serves as a very elegant computer programming language. His invention is sometimes called Iverson's Notation, but is more commonly known as *APL* (a programming language). Iverson's starting point for *APL* was conventional mathematics. From it, he developed a notation that is mathematical in nature but has a richness and consistency that allow it to be applied to a wide variety of commercial and scientific applications. This notation, by the way, allows sorting to be represented.

In 1962 Iverson set forth his notation in a book called *A Programming Language* (Wiley, 1962). At about the same time Iverson joined IBM, where he worked on applying *APL* to the expression and solution of problems in a variety of disciplines. In 1965 IBM implemented Iverson's *APL* notation on a computer for the first time. This initial implementation—using an IBM System/360 computer and *APL* as an interactive programming language— was so good that it was until just recently IBM's mainline *APL* product.

Moreover, it is the "granddaddy" for the *APL* currently offered by most time sharing companies that use IBM-type equipment, including STSC.

*APL* at IBM was originally an underground phenomenon. However, in the early 1970s it achieved such widespread use that it gained formal product support at IBM. Today *APL* is the most widely used interactive system at IBM.

The reason *APL* has achieved wide acceptance at IBM and other large companies is that it is an exceptionally powerful computing language. It derives its power first of all from the fact that it is *interactive*. *APL* users are online, working directly and immediately with the computer. This means that *APL* can be readily used by people in their daily work; they can "get on" the system and get results fast. An interactive capability immediately improves productivity. Furthermore, users do not have to be expert programmers, nor do they have to be familiar with a lot of data processing jargon to use *APL*.

*APL* is powerful because it is *concise*. A one-line statement in *APL* is the equivalent of many lines of code in other programming languages. *APL* is powerful because it is a *rich* language. Built into it are more than 40 "primitive" operations that can be run by simply typing the appropriate symbol on the *APL* keyboard. These primitives go far beyond the standard addition and subtraction to functions that allow sorting by various criteria, identification of maximums and minimums, logarithms, and so on. And *APL* is powerful in its *consistency*. *APL* primitive functions can be consistently applied both to varying quantities of data and to varying configurations of data.

*APL* may also legitimately be termed a *universal* programming language. A first look at *APL* can easily give the impression that it is great for scientific applications, but not very useful for business applications. In fact, STSC's original name was *Scientific* Time Sharing Corporation because the founders had that impression. In actuality, *APL* is extremely well suited to handling business applications. This is because a surprisingly large number of business applications involve tables and *APL* is strongly table oriented. For example, most budgeting applications are table oriented; I've personally written approximately fifteen budgeting applications in my eleven years of selling and writing *APL* systems. In fact, the principal example we will work through will be a budgeting application.

Last, and perhaps most importantly, *APL* is a language that allows its users to deal with data *dynamically*. The same program that can be used to handle three numbers can also be used to handle a hundred or even several thousand numbers. During a given run, the user can change matrix sizes. Rows and columns can be added; they can also dynamically be deleted. *APL* has a whole set of primitives for dynamic data management.

Now let's take a look at *APL* in action. We go to the terminal and sign on to STSC's *APL*PLUS* System. We type

```
    3 + 4
```

press the RETURN key, and immediately get back:

```
7
```

*APL* is in "desk-calculator" or immediate execution mode, and we can perform operations such as:

```
    7 - 2
5
    3 ÷ 4
.75
    6 × 2
12
```

Note that the computer's responses are printed at the left margin of the paper. When it is our turn to enter a statement, the terminal automatically creates a six-space indent and "waits" for our input.

The foregoing are scalar to scalar operations—that is, operations on individual numbers. Addition, subtraction, division, and multiplication are available directly on the keyboard and are "scalar dyadic primitive functions".

Such a demonstration shows the highly interactive nature of *APL*. Each time we type a statement and press the RETURN key, the information is transmitted from the terminal over a telephone line to the computer. The computer then processes the statement and returns the answer. All of this takes place in less than a second. This type of responsiveness is typical of *APL* interactions and is part of what makes them so powerful.

*APL* can be extended in a consistent fashion to work with groups of numbers. Suppose a company has three products and last year's sales for these products are 8, 13, and 16. We want to know what happens if current sales increase 10 percent over last year's. We enter:

```
1.1 × 8 13 16
```

and get back:

```
8.8 14.3 17.6
```

The computer has multiplied 1.1 × 8, 1.1 × 13, 1.1 × 16. This is a scalar to vector (chain of numbers) operation.

If the sales expenses associated with each product are 5, 6, and 8, then the gross sales margin would be

```
8 13 16 − 5 6 8
3 7 8
```

In this case, the group of numbers on each side of the subtraction function are subtracted element by element: the 5 from the 8, the 6 from the 13, and the 8 from the 16. This is a vector to vector operation.

What is reflected in these operations is the consistency of *APL* and the way in which its primitive functions can be consistently applied to varying quantities of data. The examples happen to involve vectors of three numbers. They could just as well have contained three hundred or three thousand numbers—such is the capacity of *APL*.

## Variables and Assignment

There are two main features of a digital computer that make it such a powerful tool. One is that it can store very large amounts of data; the other is that it allows the user to run defined procedures against that data. The term commonly applied to these defined procedures is "computer program".

In *APL*, the basic way data is defined and stored is through the use of *variables*. To assign one or more values to a variable such as *SALES*, we use the *assignment* function, an arrow (←), as follows:

```
SALES←4 5 6 4
```

From now on, every time we type *SALES*, the computer will return the values we entered:

```
SALES
4 5 6 4
```

We can perform scalar to vector operations on the variable *SALES*. Suppose sales go up by 10 percent and we want to know what the resulting sales figures are

```
1.1 × SALES
4.4 5.5 6.6 4.4
```

The computer has multiplied each element of *SALES* by 1.1.

We can also assign the result of a mathematical expression to a variable. For example:

```
GRTH←1.1 × SALES
```

In this case, the computer does not respond to what we enter. However, it does store the information in the variable *GRTH*, and if we now type in *GRTH* we will get back 1.1 × *SALES*:

```
GRTH
4.4 5.5 6.6 4.4
```

The answer is not lost somewhere in the innards of the computer. The ease of getting output from *APL* will be particularly appreciated by users familiar with other programming languages.

*APL* is "human engineered"; throughout its structure and operations, the *APL* language reflects a concern for *people* and how they can use computers more effectively. As much as possible it is designed to free its users from thinking about the computer and let them focus on implementing their applications.

To continue, we can define a variable called *EXP* for sales expenses:

```
EXP←2 3 2 1
```

To obtain gross margins, we enter:

```
GM←SALES − EXP
GM
2 2 4 3
```

A variable name, incidentally, can contain up to 77 alphabetic or numeric characters; however, it must always start with an alphabetic character.

## Dynamic Nature of *APL*

Thus far we have seen *APL* operating with variables of stable size. *APL* also makes it extremely easy to change the size of a variable. For example, suppose we want to add sales figures for three more products to our variable *SALES*. Sales are 10, 9, and 8 for the three new products. We add these figures as follows:

```
SALES←SALES,10 9 8
```

Now, if we look at *SALES* we see that the additional figures are included:

```
SALES
4 5 6 4 10 9 8
```

The comma specifies this enlarging operation (,10 9 8)—known as catenation. By means of catenation, the variable *SALES* has changed its size—or, in *APL* terminology, its "shape"—from four elements to seven. We have simply added three elements to the end of the vector *SALES* and stored the expanded vector back in *SALES*. We can do the same thing for *EXP*:

```
EXP←EXP,6 4 7
EXP
2 3 2 1 6 4 7
```

Suppose we need to know the number of elements in a variable. Do we have to print them out and count them? Not at all. *APL* offers a primitive function on the keyboard that allows us to determine the number of elements. This is the *shape* function (ρ). Thus:

```
ρSALES
7
     ρ3 4 6 7
4
```

## Indexing

We have seen how *APL* allows operations to be performed on entire vectors; it also makes it possible to select and work with one or more elements within a given vector. This is done by means of the *indexing* (also known as subscripting) function, represented on the *APL* keyboard as brackets [ ]. Let's look at *SALES*:

```
     SALES
4 5 6 4 10 9 8
```

We can address any number in *SALES* by specifying the location that number occupies within the vector (first from left, second from left, etc.). For example, if we want to look at the sales figures for the second product in *SALES*, we enter:

```
     SALES [2]
5
```

Or, if we want to look at the sales figures for the third and fifth products, we enter:

```
     SALES [3 5]
6 10
```

This ability to address specific locations can be used to *change* information as well as to display it. For example, to change the sales figures in the fourth, fifth, and seventh locations of *SALES*, we enter:

```
     SALES [4 5 7]←6 8 9
```

This assigns new values to the locations specified so that looking once again at *SALES* we see it now contains the new values:

```
     SALES
4 5 6 6 8 9 9
```

## Extension of *APL* to Matrices

A two-dimensional matrix is nothing more than a table. To define a matrix in *APL*, we simply specify to the system the number of rows and columns we want the matrix to have. To do this, we turn again to the *APL* primitive function ρ, as follows:

```
     MAT←3 2 ρ 1 2 3 4 5 6
     MAT
1 2
3 4
5 6
```

This is the dyadic or *reshape* function of ρ. It takes the elements on its right (1 2 3 4 5 6) and rearranges them according to the specifications on its left (3 2)—that is, in 3 rows and 2 columns.

Just as it does with vectors, *APL* allows us to readily perform standard arithmetic operations on entire matrices. Thus, if we want to increase the values in *MAT* by 10 percent, we enter:

```
     1.1 × MAT
1.1 2.2
3.3 4.4
5.5 6.6
```

We can address any specific location in *MAT* by entering, for example:

```
     MAT [2;1]
3
```

This gives us the value for the data located in the second row, first column.

We can change values in *MAT*:

```
     MAT [2;1]←9
     MAT
1 2
9 4
5 6
```

We can create a second matrix called *MEXP*:

```
     MEXP←3 2 ρ 1 1 2 1 1 1
     MEXP
1 1
2 1
1 1
```

and subtract its contents from those of the first matrix:

```
     MAT - MEXP
0 1
7 3
4 5
```

We can store the result in the variable *OUT* by entering:

```
     OUT←MAT - MEXP
     OUT
0 1
7 3
4 5
```

## Reduction and Scan

One of *APL*'s most useful functions—used extensively in business applications—is *reduction* (/). What reduction does is reduce an array of data to a single element. Returning to our variable *SALES*, suppose we are interested in knowing the total sales for all products. In *APL* we simply enter:

```
     +/SALES
47
```

This returns the sum of all the numbers in *SALES*. This is known as *plus reduction*. In combination with the shape function (ρ), plus reduction can be used to determine value averages by means of an extremely concise expression:

```
     (+/SALES) ÷ ρSALES
6.7142857
```

Here we take the sum of the values in *SALES* and divide it by the number of elements in *SALES*. This is the classic illustration of *APL*'s power. The equivalent FORTRAN or BASIC program usually contains 10 or more statements.

Reduction is not confined to plus reduction. It can be used with any valid *APL* primitive dyadic function. A practical example would be to define a variable called *INT* that contains annual interest rates for four years:

```
     INT←.1   .12   .14   .15
```

To obtain the compound interest rate for the four-year period, we use *times reduction*:

```
     ×/1+INT
1.615152
```

In the same family of functions as reduction is *scan* (\). Scan performs a series of partial reductions. *Plus scan* calculates a series of partial sums.

Suppose we define a series of monthly sales for six months:

```
     MSALES←3 2 8 4 9 3
```

To obtain the cumulative sales for each month, we use plus scan:

```
    +\MSALES
3 5 13 17 26 29
```

Returning to the compound interest example, we can apply *times scan* to get the cumulative compound interest at the end of each year:

```
    ×\1+INT
1.1  1.232  1.40448  1.615152
```

## Writing a Program Using *APL*

It was stated earlier that digital computers derive a great deal of power from their ability to run defined programs against large amounts of stored data. How are such programs defined in *APL*? In *APL*, another name for a program is *function*. Programs are called defined functions. Defining a function extends the capability of the computer. Let's assume that we want to concentrate on calculating averages. We can define a function to do this for us, as shown below:

```
     ∇Z←AVG X
[1]  Z←(+/X)÷ρX
[2]  ∇
```

By typing in the *del* (∇), we inform the *APL* system that we are leaving immediate execution mode and entering a mode that allows us to define our own programs (called function definition mode). After entering the function, we type another ∇ to switch us back to immediate execution mode. In between the two ∇s we have defined a function named *AVG* that will accept data through *X* and display the result through *Z*. Now when we enter:

```
    AVG SALES
6.7142857
```

we call on a predefined function called *AVG* to manipulate the *SALES* data.

The next step is to take what we have learned about defining and storing data and about defining functions and apply it to an actual *APL* application: building a small budgeting system.

## System Definition

The first requirement is to define the system. With a real-world application, we would consult with the application's user to work out this definition. The key at this stage is to determine what kind of output is desired and in what format it is to be reported. From that information we can work backwards and decide where the data is to come from and what processing is necessary to get it in the desired format. Figure 1 shows the kind of report our budgeting application will be designed to produce.

An important part of determining the report format is to define the relationships between the rows and the columns in the report. We must specify which data is to be entered and which is to be calculated. From this information we can now design the system and write the programs.

## Writing the Programs

We will write three programs: one to enter the data, a second to perform the specified calculations, and a third to print the report.

First, we will write the data storage program. We define a program that will create a two-dimensional matrix or table to store numbers (statement [1]) and that will then enter the appropriate numbers (statements [2] through [10]).

```
                           STSC SAMPLE BUDGET
                           FISCAL YEAR 1980


                      QTR    QTR    QTR    QTR
                       1      2      3      4        TOTAL

   APL REVENUES        input . . . . . . . . .
   CONSULTING          input . . . . . . . . .
   SOFTWARE            input . . . . . . . . .

   TOTAL REVENUES      calculated totals . . . . . . . .


   SALARIES            input . . . . . . . . .
   TRAVEL              input . . . . . . . . .
   TELEPHONE           input . . . . . . . . .
   OFFICE SPACE        input . . . . . . . . .
   OTHER EXPENSES      input . . . . . . . . .

   TOTAL EXPENSES      calculated totals . . . . . . . .


   PROFITABILITY       calculated (rev - exp)  . . . . .
   YTD PRF             calculated (ytd of prf) . . . . .
   o/o EXP/REV         calculated (exp ÷ rev)  . . . . .
   o/o SAL/REV         calculated (sal ÷ rev)  . . . . .
```

**Figure 1—Sample Budget Information**

```
      ∇ENTER
[1]    D←14 5ρ0
[2]    'ENTER APL REVENUES' ◊ D[1;]←5↑☐
[3]    'ENTER CONSULTING REVENUES' ◊ D[2;]←5↑☐
[4]    'ENTER SOFTWARE REVENUES' ◊ D[3;]5↑☐
[5]    ⍝ ENTERING EXPENSES
[6]    'ENTER SALARIES' ◊ D[5;]←5↑☐
[7]    'ENTER TRAVEL' ◊ D[6;]←5↑☐
[8]    'ENTER TELEPHONE' ◊ D[7;]←5↑☐
[9]    'ENTER OFFICE SPACE' ◊ D[8;]←5↑☐
[10]   'ENTER OTHER EXPENSES' ◊ D[9;]←5↑☐
[11]   '' ◊ 'END OF INPUT'
[12]  ∇
```

Second, we define the program that performs the calculations:

```
      ∇CALCULATE
[1]    D[4;]←+/D[1 2 3;]        ⍝ TOTAL REVENUES
[2]    D[10;]←+/D[5 6 7 8 9;]   ⍝ TOTAL EXPENSES
[3]    D[11;]←D[4;] - D[10;]    ⍝ PROFITABILITY
[4]    D[;5]←+/D[;1 2 3 4]      ⍝ TOTAL COLUMN
[5]    D[12;]←+\D[11;]          ⍝ YTD PROFITABILITY
[6]    D[12;5]←D[11;5]          ⍝ FIXUP YTD TOTAL COLUMN
[7]    D[13;]←100×D[10;]÷D[4;]  ⍝ o/o EXP/REV
[8]    D[14;]←100×D[5;]÷D[4;]   ⍝ o/o SAL/REV
[9]    'END OF CALCULATIONS'
[10]  ∇
```

Last comes the program to print the report. To write this program we will use STSC's enhanced utility programs for report formatting to format titles, column headings, and row names.

The first thing we will do is copy these formatting utilities from the public library in which they are stored. This is done by entering:

```
     )COPY 1 FORMAT
SAVED  . . .
```

Now we write the *REPORT* program:

```
      ∇REPORT
[1]   'ALIGN PAPER - PRESS RETURN' ◊ T←▯
[2]   FS←'20A1, 5CBF10.2'
[3]   FS CENTER 'STSC SAMPLE BUDGET'
[4]   FS CENTER 'FISCAL YEAR 1980'
[5]   ''
[6]   FS COLNAMES '//QTR/QTR/QTR/QTR'
[7]   FS COLNAMES '// 1/ 2/ 3/ 4/TOTAL'
[8]   RN←20 ROWNAMES '-APL REVENUES-CONSULTING-SOFTWARE'
[9]   RN←RN,[1] 20 ROWNAMES '-TOTAL REVENUES-SALARIES-TRAVEL'
[10]  RN←RN,[1] 20 ROWNAMES '-TELEPHONE-OFFICE SPACE'
[11]  RN←RN,[1] 20 ROWNAMES '-OTHER EXPENSES-PROFITABILITY'
[12]  RN←RN,[1] 20 ROWNAMES '-YTD PRF-○/○ EXP/REV-○/○ SAL/REV'
[13]  FS ⎕FMT (RN;D)
[14]  ∇
```

We can put these three programs together in a little system called *MAIN* by entering:

```
      ∇MAIN
[1]   ENTER
[2]   CALCULATE
[3]   REPORT
[4]   ∇
```

That's all it takes. Our budget application is now complete. Applying this simple package of three programs to the appropriate financial data will quickly produce the report shown in Figure 1.

## Conclusion

This paper has offered a brief overview of *APL* syntax and style with a view to illustrating the programming language's singular economy and power. With *APL*, users can implement applications many times faster than is possible with other high-level programming languages. We have seen some of the quick, practical applications possible with *APL*; there are many, many more that make people more productive in implementing computer solutions. And nothing is more crucial in today's competitive business environment than increasing "people productivity".

*John Suwara joined STSC in 1975 and was a branch manager and regional manager before he assumed his current position as vice president of western U.S. marketing. Suwara previously worked as a systems engineer and marketing representative for IBM. He is a co-founder of TSR, where he worked from 1969 to 1974.*

*Suwara holds a bachelor's degree in electrical engineering from City College of New York and a master's degree in electrical engineering from New York University. He also completed courses at St. John's University toward an M.B.A.*

Linda Alvord

# *APL* in the
# High School Curriculum

Since 1967, we at Scotch Plains-Fanwood High School in New Jersey have been actively developing a new approach to teaching mathematics. We have incorporated *APL*, with its traditional symbolic notation, into the teaching of mathematics at the secondary level. Based on our experiences, I would like to share with you a few of my reasons for believing that *APL* expands, as well as expresses, the concepts normally developed in a high school mathematics program, and consequently offers students exposure to numerous career options.

The study of *APL* has immediate value to students because it makes mathematics more real to them. With the addition of *APL*, mathematics may be perceived as more comprehensive, but it also becomes more applicable, exciting, and relevant. Students and teachers benefit in two ways. First, teaching and learning secondary school math becomes a more exciting, and therefore a somewhat easier, process. Second, the important concepts learned in math courses are more apt to be extended—by the students themselves—to the world around them.

One significant goal of teaching mathematics is to encourage students to develop and use a written symbolic language to communicate abstract ideas. *APL* not only provides an excellent mathematical language to cover all high school math concepts, but it also provides an excellent means for demonstrating the use of a computer programming language.

In a recent lesson on probability and statistics, we considered a moderately complex problem: finding all possible sums that could be obtained if three dice—one tetrahedron (4 faces), one icosahedron (20 faces), and one dodecahedron (12 faces)—were tossed. The sample contains 384 possible outcomes. To count the number of times any specific sum could occur is quite tedious. With *APL*, we used arrays of data and produced the expected values. By creating a frequency table, we actually experienced the sampling process. Using *APL* notation alone, without executing expressions at a terminal, the students were able to understand the relevant aspects of the problem. Increased understanding is a major benefit of using *APL* in the learning process.

As a student's knowledge of a language increases, visual images will often appear in his "mind's eye" as expressions are read and understood. The clarity of each *APL* expression, combined with the visualization of results at a terminal, can have dramatic effects on the thinking and learning process. Just as there seems to be some magical moment when one begins to think in terms of a new (spoken) language, there is a parallel jump in using *APL* to process numeric data and learn mathematics. Difficult concepts are more easily understood as they are worked through using *APL*, because the student can "see" each step of a problem sequentially.

Diagrams or pictures are often very helpful when learning mathematical concepts. Again, *APL* lends itself nicely. Using outer product ($\circ . \times$), for example, we can illustrate the "how" and "why" of complex multiplications.

The use of *APL* in our mathematics curriculum has provided more significant motivation for our students to explore mathematics and related fields. Moreover, they do so in creative ways not typically inspired by conventional teaching techniques. They find that their experiences relate to science, psychology, sports, theoretical mathematics, and other fields. The inspired investigation of these diverse areas leads to career opportunities often not formerly considered by students.

A student with a fundamental knowledge of *APL* can easily begin a computer-oriented career. At least two recent graduates have been employed by the computer science department of Bell Telephone Laboratories immediately after graduation. Consider that this occurred without their having college degrees or specialized training. Another student had a sufficient start in his education to complete both his graduate and undergraduate work in only four years.

Although many students leave high school long before their careers are shaped, their introduction to *APL* and computers at the high school level provides them with a more substantial mathematical background and a foundation for understanding computer systems. And perhaps more important in the long run, the exposure to *APL* presents them with diverse career opportunities for the future.

*Linda Alvord has been chairperson of the Mathematics Department at Scotch Plains High School, New Jersey, for the past 18 years and has taught mathematics for 21 years. In 1968, assisted by fellow teachers, Alvord developed an APL teaching program that has been running successfully ever since.*

*Alvord has a B.A. from Montclair State College, an M.A. from Columbia Teachers College, and is currently enrolled in a doctoral program at Rutgers University for creative arts in education.*

Andrew D. Luzi

# A Business School's Approach
# To Better Business with *APL*

It is no secret that government and business are becoming increasingly more dependent on computers in all management functions. Business schools—to "stay in business" as well as to provide a relevant education to their students—are increasingly realizing the value of offering practical coursework in computers to students studying all areas of business.

Once a school has made such a commitment, two general objectives are likely to emerge:

1. Students should be knowledgeable in, and comfortable with, the use of a business-oriented computing language.

2. The use of that language should be incorporated into coursework across disciplines to strengthen students' skills with the language and to enhance the content of the individual courses and the entire business program.

My experience in teaching and using *APL* in a business school shows me that *APL* is an ideal language for meeting these objectives. Benefits are obtained not only by students, but also by professors, future employers, and the business school itself.

Students benefit in ways I will make clearer later. Basically, they gain a general knowledge of computers and specific knowledge of a programming language. Through the use of computers, they also gain deeper insights in related subject matter, such as accounting, marketing, and operations research.

Professors benefit because their jobs are made more interesting, though not necessarily easier. It is easier, however, to point out the value of particular course material if you can make it *both* interesting and relevant. There are obviously numerous ways professors can use computers for their own personal research and class management.

Potential employers save time and money when they are able to hire a person already knowledgeable in the use and value of computers.

The business school that offers practical coursework in computers is aware of the benefits that accrue when it notes the number of applications per opening for each entering class and the average profile of the applicants. Students carefully evaluate business schools. One of their criteria for selection is how well business schools can sell their "product"—the students—to employers. An increasingly large factor in that transaction is how well equipped students are to enter the business world and contribute. Relevant experience is highly desirable, and knowledge of computers is still one of the best attributes a graduating student can have. Schools that offer the best, and most relevant, business experience will attract potential employers and, consequently, the best students.

At Pennsylvania State University we have introduced the use of computers in several courses. We have found that a one-semester course in computing and introductory *APL* provides the necessary background on which to build practical coursework in various disciplines.

For example, one accounting course requires a major project using *APL* for personal computing, terminal remote batch processing, text editing, and *APL* programming. Students work alone and in groups to complete projects, which may take as long as three or four weeks. The modular aspect of *APL* function syntax allows a group to partition the project so that everyone obtains programming experience. Having the students program in parallel paths forces a thorough understanding of project design before the project begins.

Perhaps a more interesting, but equally successful, use of *APL* at Pennsylvania State University is student participation in projects outside specific coursework. A student, or group of students, acts as a consultant to a company or government agency. Because these projects are undertaken in real-world settings, they can result in part-time employment. The high probability of having their own ideas actually implemented serves as an excellent motivation for students. In most cases, the potential outside users attend the final student demonstration of the project.

Examples of past projects include setting up:

- A radioactive material inventory.
- A history of human exposure to radioactive material.
- Payroll deduction tables for use by a manual payroll system.
- Inventory systems for a small car dealership.
- A patient history and hearing-aid selection system (to be presented at the Pennsylvania Speech and Hearing Association).
- A program to predict student enrollment (through analysis of a questionnaire filled out by all accounting majors).
- Computer-aided instruction programs to teach students advanced *APL* concepts.

The students and the school benefit when the objectives mentioned earlier are met through coursework and extracurricular work such as that described. Students gain a deeper knowledge of programming and the subject material, because writing programs and designing systems requires a solid understanding of concepts and relationships, not simply facts or formulas.

An example of this is the student who, while programming an accounting package for a small car dealership, exclaimed: "I don't know enough accounting!" The programming project forced him to recognize his lack of knowledge, to ask for help, and to complete a self-study of advanced accounting before continuing to program. Students are motivated to do this extra work because they know the value of hands-on experience and feel a sense of accomplishment when a project is done well.

In conclusion, classroom projects and assignments using computers introduce students to interactive computing, allow for development of interpersonal communicative skills, reinforce real-world and classroom concepts in an applied environment, and provide the student with experience that can be used beneficially in future employment.

*Andrew Luzi is an assistant professor in the Department of Accounting and Management Information Systems at Pennsylvania State University. He holds an M.S. and a Ph.D. in accounting, both earned at the University of Kansas. Luzi is currently involved in research on developing audit systems for the Pennsylvania Department of the Aging. Research interests include a process concept of control and controls, quantity accounting: an interactive model, systems training in the public sector, and the relationship between performance information systems and group problem solving processes.*

*Luzi is a member of the American Accounting Association, the National Association of Accountants, and ACM.*

Mary Lou Fox

# Computer-Assisted Instruction
# At the Undergraduate Level

During the past two decades the instructional use of computers at universities and colleges has mushroomed. Professors and researchers have long recognized the benefits of using computers in their own professional endeavors. Now there is increasing recognition that the use of computers by students during their undergraduate years also has great value.

Part of the value lies in removing the mystique about computers and in increasing students' awareness of the potential benefits and problems associated with the ubiquitous use of computers in a technologically advanced society. But, more importantly, using computers in instruction fundamentally alters approaches to learning in many subject areas and has broad implications for the future careers of students who learn in this fashion.

In my experience as an instructor of computer programming and applications at Fairfield University, I have found there are significant benefits associated with students' exposure to, and use of, the *APL* language and programming concepts. The concise expressions and algorithmic nature of *APL* allow fundamental concepts of computing to be learned without the obfuscation of programming details. The fundamentals of *APL* are easily and quickly learned, thus allowing students to tackle worthwhile problems within a reasonable period of time.

At Fairfield University, all students with a business major and most students with a mathematics, science, or social science major study *APL* in a one-credit course in their freshman year. This early exposure to computing serves two important purposes. One is to introduce students to computing so that they will have a basic knowledge of a computer's capabilities and so they can use that knowledge during their undergraduate career. The second purpose is to help students discover that computing is an exciting and worthwhile career. Making this discovery during the freshman year permits students to orient their studies and career goals in this direction. Not all students want to be programmers, but many may want to include computing as an integral part of their future. This desire comes from a growing recognition of the usefulness of the computer as a tool in learning and problem solving.

Fairfield University's approach to learning is reinforced with the widespread use of computers in the instructional process in many subject areas. Some examples illustrate this point:

- Freshmen studying chemistry are tested on prerequisite skills in mathematics and chemistry during orientation. Students requiring remedial help are told to sign on to the Computer-Assisted

Instruction (CAI) programs, which are written in $APL$ and which attempt to remove the deficiencies in the student's background.

- Students studying chemistry or mathematics frequently attend laboratory sessions in the terminal room. During these sessions $APL$ is used to illustrate basic concepts such as limits or derivatives, to grind out terms of series to demonstrate convergence or divergence, or to develop algorithms to solve problems such as plotting a great circle course for a ship. Emphasis is on problem solving and clear, concise algorithms.

- Sophomore sociology majors find that one of the three weekly classes in the required statistics course is held in the terminal room. The usual approach to statistics involves a great deal of calculation with too little understanding of what is being computed! In this new approach, students quickly learn to use $APL$ to calculate statistics. This introductory course focuses on a database of sociological research data, and on the correct use and interpretation of statistical tests to report on this database. Feedback from students has indicated that interest in this traditionally dull subject is quite high. Students enjoy analyzing real data and making judgments based on statistical tests. They become quite involved in the quantitative aspects of sociology.

- A biology professor conducts a course on ecology and the environment. He complements the lectures with field trips and computer laboratory sessions. The topic of water pollution is viewed from the perspective of field trips to a pond and a river, and students use a computer model to simulate effects of pollution in bodies of water. The computer model, written in $APL$, permits students to thoroughly explore many problems that can only be alluded to in a lecture. Students enjoy experimenting with this and other models as they attempt to solve realistic problems that generally could not be solved without such models.

- Some students find that their interests lie in the area of computer applications or computer science. The initial exposure to $APL$ gives the students experience in manipulating data arrays and provides a firm foundation in clear, concise algorithmic expression. This is a great aid in further study of other programming languages, data structures, and applications.

The examples above illustrate how students can become deeply involved in subject matter when an interactive $APL$ computing system is used in the learning process. The key benefits of instructional computing are summarized below.

1. Instructional computing emphasizes problem solving using realistic problems not generally within the grasp of undergraduates.

2. Instructional computing focuses on clear and concise algorithmic expression.

3. Instructional computing motivates students to learn more about a subject and to become more deeply involved in the learning process.

Students who have been actively involved with computing during their undergraduate years frequently seek career opportunities in this field. Some areas where they have sought opportunities include:

- Graduate work in computer science or diverse quantitative areas such as operations research, management science, statistics, biostatistics, econometrics, and financial analysis.

- Teaching computer programming and applications.

- Employment in computer programming, systems analysis, the broad range of application areas, systems programming, or computer systems design.

- Medical research on the myriad possibilities for using computers in medicine, such as monitoring patients and implanting microcomputers.

- Research and data analysis.

- Scientific computing and numeric analysis.

- Developing modeling systems to solve problems in areas as diverse as economics, the environment, medicine, business, criminal justice, and traffic safety.

- Developing financial planning systems, forecasting systems, and financial analyses.

- Development of instructional computing applications that include drills and practice sessions, tutorials, computer-assisted testing, simulations, and games.

As our society becomes increasingly dependent on computers, students who can work with computers, develop and use algorithms effectively, and deal with quantitative analyses will increase their career opportunities dramatically.

*Mary Lou Fox, currently an applications analyst in STSC's Management Technology Division, has been an active user of APL since 1968. At STSC she is responsible for the design, development, and implementation of user-oriented modeling systems and software tools. Before joining STSC she was a research associate at Fairfield University, responsible for the design and development of APL applications, including the university's APL libraries, CAI (Computer-Assisted Instruction) courses, instructional applications, and simulations.*

*Fox has a B.S. in mathematics from Boston College, a master's in math education from Fairfield University, and a master's in computer science from Polytechnic Institute of New York.*

Gayle E. Abbott

# Career Growth
# In an *APL* Environment

*APL* is a powerful and efficient tool that can be used in a multitude of environments to accomplish a wide range of tasks. Originally the language was primarily thought to be useful for scientific or mathematical applications. In the past ten years, however, STSC and other *APL* service companies have enhanced the language to increase the efficiency of automated applications in a business environment. Typical examples include financial planning systems and manufacturing and material requirements planning systems. The advent of features such as Automatic Control of Execution (ACE) has dramatically expanded the ability of *APL* applications to take on "batch-like" characteristics, when appropriate.

In looking at careers, the addition of *APL* programming skills to one's background can open the door to a wider range of opportunities than would otherwise be available. While the knowledge of other programming languages can also lead to career growth, *APL* has distinct advantages. The ease with which one can learn the language allows one to seek interesting and rewarding jobs a very short time after the initial introduction to the language. Other key advantages include the relative "newness" of *APL*, the rapidly growing popularity and use of the language, and the diversity of the applications written in *APL*.

These are some of the reasons why *APL* is emphasized at STSC. It has been found, however, that skill in *APL* alone is not sufficient for career growth. In some cases, individuals are brought into STSC without any specific knowledge of *APL*, but with a desire and aptitude to learn the language.

*APL* is a tool that, when combined with other skills and characteristics, can provide a wide range of career opportunities. Most companies have a greater demand for qualified personnel than the marketplace can supply. This phenomenon—which is expected to continue well into the 1980s—provides many opportunities for the individual with initiative. While emphasis is placed on recruiting individuals with bachelor's or master's degrees, pertinent work experience, or both, opportunities also exist for those with technical training or a high school diploma. A key factor is evidence of initiative—indicated perhaps by the pursuit of additional education on one's own or involvement in special projects. The emphasis on college degrees has arisen from the need for flexibility and a broad understanding of the business environment.

The other skills and personal characteristics that have been found to complement technical skills are communications skills (both written and oral); specialized knowledge in a field such as finance, insurance, or manufacturing;

pride in personal accomplishments; a positive attitude; the ability to work independently with minimal supervision, yet function as part of a team; the ability to accept responsibility; and the ability to think analytically.

Once we find individuals with these qualifications, what can we do to retain them? It is important for corporations to recognize individual career objectives and to make the best use of them in meeting corporate objectives. A key point is flexibility—companies need to be flexible in defining jobs and career opportunities. Definition of career progression opportunities is a common request made by data processing personnel today. Limited definition of career paths, combined with unlimited opportunities, provides an environment where an individual need only change companies to satisfy career and personal needs. It is a challenge to the industry to provide a means for educating data processing personnel in career planning and for assisting them in defining and achieving their goals.

Responsibility for career development rests at three levels—on the Personnel Department, on the employee, and on the employee's manager. It should be noted that top management is responsible for providing a climate that encourages and is open to career development.

The role of the Personnel Department (or its equivalent) is to provide the resources. It can provide assistance on planning a career and can counsel employees by answering questions or by asking questions designed to "guide" the employee. Personnel is a resource only. It cannot set the path an employee is to follow; it can only present the options.

Each employee has the primary responsibility for his own career development. He must determine where he has been and where he wants to go, evaluate his needs, communicate his career intentions to the organization, and negotiate his career.

The employee's manager must learn to move from the role of "boss" to that of career counselor. The manager must be open to discussing an employee's needs and desires, strengths and weaknesses, career opportunities, and the skills that need to be acquired or enhanced to meet the employee's career objectives.

Career paths in the data processing industry need not be clearly defined. To do so would take away flexibility. Creativity and initiative—factors that are highly valued in many jobs and that STSC feels have been a crucial ingredient in the success of the company—would be reduced. While some positions require guidelines and structure, many are flexible, giving the individual the freedom for initiative and creativity. It is found throughout the structure, however, that it is important to unleash motivation by ensuring that work has a purpose, that it allows the full use of abilities and education (note the term "abilities", rather than "experience"), and that it allows some measure of autonomy and decision making. In addition to being challenging, positions should involve full project responsibility wherever possible.

Career development or progression does not refer just to movement from one position to another, but to the molding and shaping of positions, when appropriate, to provide for individual needs and to use the individual's abilities. It is important for jobs to be designed so that each person is challenged and needs to stretch a little to succeed. Job expansion and lateral as well as upward movement should be recognized and encouraged. The variety of duties and responsibilities in a general job classification (e.g., programmer) must be recognized, as well as movements between different departments in the company (e.g., from a technical to a sales department).

Frequently it is seen how individual career growth parallels the career growth of the organization. As an organization grows, so do its needs and the variety of opportunities—it only takes personal initiative for an individual to seize these opportunities and grow himself. As mentioned earlier, it is the individual who works to broaden his knowledge and skills who will grow in his career and who will find the greatest number of options for growth available to him.

A broad range of jobs are available in the data processing industry. Any of these might be highly suitable for the individual with skills in *APL*. Positions start at the clerical or technician level (that point where most people with only a high school diploma or limited technical training might begin) and run to professional and managerial positions that emphasize any combination of higher education and experience. Opportunities exist in applications and systems programming, product and system development, communications, consulting, sales, management, or any combination of these.

Thus far we've covered the career benefits of *APL*, the opportunities available in the marketplace, and the need for career development. One might well ask: "How are opportunities communicated, and how are individual abilities recognized at a corporate level?" At STSC, we have (or are in the process of developing) the following systems to aid our internal communications and career development program:

- All job openings are currently announced via an online system (which was, of course, written in *APL*). Descriptions of most jobs and the required qualifications are entered into the system as soon as the jobs become available. Any employee can access current job openings by simply loading a workspace. Openings are posted for a minimum of one week or until the job is filled. In addition to informing internals of opportunities available to them, it provides a means whereby employees can refer qualified friends. This system has worked extremely well, resulting in a significant amount of lateral and upward movement.

- Communication between managers and employees is encouraged and emphasized. In addition to ongoing interaction, a performance evaluation system exists to encourage interaction and stress individual development. Performance reviews are scheduled every six months and are usually separated from salary reviews by at least three months. The latter guideline is set so that preoccupation with salary is avoided and development is emphasized. In addition to reviewing performance against individual standards set at the preceding review, these sessions allow discussion of skills the employee needs to acquire, methods for acquiring them, and the employee's own feelings regarding his career. It is necessary to devote adequate time to performance evaluations, since they are a key to career growth and planning.

- A recent development, not yet finalized, is a personnel database or skills inventory file. The system contains biographical summaries of all employees. If a job arises that requires a certain key skill, the database can be accessed to see which employees have the required background. For instance, if you wanted to see which employees have an engineering background, you would load the workspace and request "engineering". The database can also be accessed by type of degree, college attended, name, previous employers, skill, or title—to name just a few.

- Lastly, a career development folder is in preparation. This pamphlet, which will be available to all employees, will provide assistance in evaluating and defining career experiences and goals. It will also provide a broad definition of opportunities available within the company, and it will describe the related, required, or desirable qualifications. In summary, the folder will be a resource manual, assisting employees in the responsibilities they have for planning their careers.

Training must be mentioned, if only briefly, as an important segment of the career management process. Training programs can strengthen existing skills; develop new skills; or orient individuals to a concept, job, or organization. Internal training and company support of continuing education (as expressed by tuition aid, seminar attendance, and a liberal leave of absence policy) are important.

## Conclusion

We have discussed the characteristics important to career development, the definition and responsibilities of the career planning process, and the components of a working career management system. Career planning is important in the data processing industry, and it can work effectively. The key factors are flexibility, initiative, and creativity. *APL* is a useful tool both in the formal career planning system and as a skill that an individual can use in any number of environments, for any number of purposes. *APL* is another highly marketable skill that can and does increase the opportunity for exciting, challenging, and varied careers.

*Gayle Abbott has been director of personnel at STSC since August 1978. Prior to joining STSC, she was personnel manager for the Computer Network Corporation and a personnel specialist for the Food and Drug Administration.*

*Abbott has a B.A. in political science from American University and has completed coursework toward an M.B.A., also at American University. She is active in numerous professional associations and recently authored an article, "Headhunting", which appeared in the Roundtable Discussion Section of the October 1979 issue of* Insiders' Letter, *published by International Computer Programs, Inc.*

**Ollie Chambers**

# The Upjohn Company
# Customized Financial Planning Model

The modern business era is one of international conglomerates (with their common multicurrency, multibusiness lines) and worldwide inflation. These factors make automated financial planning systems a must for financial planners. These systems must invariably be somewhat sophisticated, very flexible, and accessible from many different geographic locations.

Few companies have the inhouse expertise and staff to provide the kind of intermittent low-cost support required by most financial planners. Because of this, many companies like Upjohn have turned to time sharing vendors such as STSC, Inc. In this paper I will give you a brief overview of my unit's involvement with STSC and our expectations for the future.

Before I get too involved with our financial planning system, let me give you a brief overview of the Upjohn Company.

In 1979 Upjohn had annual sales of about $1.5 billion and net earnings of $149 million. As shown below, we have seven major divisions with, for financial planning purposes, a total of 17 separate businesses.

1. Domestic Pharmaceutical Business Group
   - U.S. Prescription Medicine Business
   - U.S. Consumer Products Business
2. U.S. Pharmaceutical Chemical Business
3. International Business Group
   - Pharmaceuticals Business
   - Animal and Plant Health Business
   - Pharmaceutical Chemical Business
4. Agricultural Business Group
   - U.S. Animal Health Business
   - Vegetable Seed Business
   - Agronomic Seed Business
   - Florida Farm Supply Business
   - U.S. Plant Health Business
   - Poultry Breeding Business
5. Chemical Business Group
   - Polymer Chemicals Business

- Urethane Systems Business
- Fine Chemicals Business
6. Upjohn Healthcare Services
7. Clinical Laboratory Business

The Upjohn planning process (see Figure 1) starts with strategic planning where the divisions decide what they want to do. Next comes resource planning to determine the capital requirements and to develop a financing plan that determines where we will obtain the necessary capital. Before approval is granted, financial plans are presented to our senior management for comparison with corporate financial objectives.

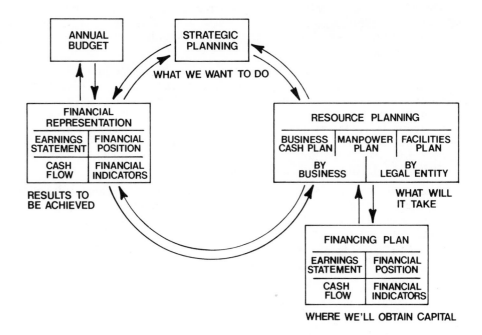

**Figure 1—The Upjohn Company Long Range Planning Process**

We rely heavily on a customized financial planning model that was developed with STSC using their *APL\*PLUS* Service and the modeling language available in their Financial Planning System (FPS). The Upjohn model has the following characteristics:

- It is a time sharing application accessed in several geographic locations (e.g., Michigan, Connecticut, Texas, and California) via remote terminals.

- It is operated by professionals and accounting technicians.

- It is cost effective—a forecast costs about $40 and a merge costs about $35.

- It is highly user oriented and heavily prompted.

- It is coordinated by a one-man corporate staff located in Kalamazoo, Michigan.

- It is adaptable to changes in accounting principles or management preferences.

- It includes three years of historical data and five years of forecast data.

- Its output includes a complete set of financial statements—income statement, balance sheet, cash flow, and ratios.

Like most Fortune 500 companies, the Upjohn Company has had some form of financial planning for several years. In 1968 our efforts were mostly manual and limited to a five-year projection of earnings. We produced only income statements for our seven divisions. By 1970 we were using a "canned" package offered by Citibank to prepare balance sheets and cash flow statements to accompany the income statements for the seven divisions and Agronomic Seed Growers. In addition, we were able to perform consolidations and to conduct limited sensitivity analyses.

By 1973 we were getting pretty serious about financial planning. We expanded our planning to cover our business worldwide for a ten-year period. Our senior management began to play formalized objective-setting and feedback-generating roles.

It was at this point that we ran into problems; it became evident that a customized model was an absolute necessity. Citibank could not accommodate our operating management's desire for tiered financial statements and historical data, and a task force was organized to select a company that could best meet our needs. After several weeks of hard work, six finalists were chosen. They were International Timesharing Systems (ITC), National CSS, Comshare, Cyphernetics (now ADP), First National Citibank/General Electric, and Scientific Time Sharing Corporation (now STSC, Inc.).

Although we had a lengthy list of detailed musts and wants, we had but two groups of basic requirements. First, we needed the ability to generate tiered financial statements. These statements would provide four levels of earnings: earnings by business responsibility, earnings by division responsibility, net earnings before corporate allocations, and net earnings.

The second group of requirements dealt with flexibility. They are described below.

- *Flexibility in detail.* We required 20 revenue categories, 150 operating expense categories, and 25 inventory categories.

- *Flexibility in forecasting.* We needed the ability to express forecasts in dollar amounts, growth rates, percent of sales, percent of cost of goods, and percent of any related variable. We also needed numerous special forecasting codes.

- *Flexibility in output.* We needed the ability to produce income statements, balance sheets, cash flow statements, and financial ratios. We also needed the ability to select information by line or by statement, to produce tiered statements by responsibility, and to footnote statements as appropriate.

There were several things we liked about STSC. Their development costs were by far the lowest, and they could meet our tight development schedule. Their *APL$\star$PLUS* Service was by far the most powerful, and the Management Technology Division could provide support for their proprietary language enhancements. Further, their FPS modeling language used English-language commands rather than symbols, and they offered onsite support.

There were, however, some factors involved with choosing STSC that we didn't like. At that time, STSC was a young company; it had only been in business since 1969 and had been profitable for only two years. Consequently, the organization was thin; they lacked Citibank's experience and financial expertise, and they had not yet demonstrated the ability to provide a strong consolidation capability. In addition, several terminals would have to be replaced to accommodate the *APL* programming language. As you can see from this paper, we chose STSC to develop our system.

In 1975 our customized model was developed. It included full allocation of expenses and assets, identification of earnings and cash flow by responsibility, inclusion of historical data, and graphics.

Since 1975 we have focused on the content of our planning and development efforts. We have also developed several other customized financial planning models: the Eighteen-Month Quarterly Cash Flow Forecasting Model and the Post-Planning Review Model.

We began our transition from form to content in 1976 with emphasis on a capitalization/earnings ratio, improved communications and internal consistency, and a six-step senior management review process.

Our focus on content expanded in 1978-1979, emphasizing reduced planning costs and condensed presentations, return on net assets, post-planning review data, industry data, and operating management follow-up.

Because we did not want our divisional staffs to have to become familiar with too many programming languages, we have subsequently used STSC for much of our capital evaluation work including an economic evaluation model, a lease versus buy model, a post-evaluation model, and a capital aggregation model.

We are very pleased with the service we have received from STSC, and look forward to continuing to work with them in the future. In fact, we are currently waiting for them to perfect a graphics package that will allow us to achieve the quality of terminal graphics required to support our post-planning review efforts.

In closing, let me summarize the major reasons I support working with a time sharing company like STSC for financial planning:

- Development costs are relatively low and projects are completed on time.

- Operating costs are truly flexible, since projects can be discontinued when and if unfavorable cost/benefit ratios appear.

- The flexibility of *APL* and of the FPS modeling language makes it easy for us to use these languages in meeting special project requirements.

- Their system can be accessed throughout the United States and in many locations throughout the world, thus facilitating communication with staff in remote locations.

- They provide capable onsite support to take care of unforeseen problems and new requirements.

*Ollie Chambers, currently manager of corporate long-range planning at The Upjohn Company, has been in the finance and accounting areas of the company since he joined the financial management program in 1972. Drawing on his experience with internal auditing, information systems, product profitability analysis, capital expenditure requests, budget preparation, property accounting, accounts payable, and cash flow management, Chambers was instrumental in guiding STSC's implementation of Upjohn's long-range financial planning system. He currently uses that system to analyze and present the consolidated long-range plan to senior management each year.*

*Before joining Upjohn, Chambers worked as an economist in the U.S. Office of Management and Budget and with Southern Pacific Railroad. He earned his M.B.A. from Indiana University after graduating from the University of Oregon's School of Economics.*

Randall S. Robinson

# Financial Planning Applications
# Of *APL* in J. Ray McDermott

In the McDermott company, Operations Research (OR) is a chargeback department that does analytical studies and advanced computer system development for corporate, group, and division managers. Recently our OR business has been booming. One important reason for the boom, I think, is that we apply and aggressively promote *APL*.

This paper briefly discusses two key inhouse financial systems that we have implemented employing *APL*: the FINANCIAL INFORMATION NETWORK, which encompasses three different multiuser reporting systems; and the SHORT-TERM INVESTMENT PORTFOLIO SYSTEM, which is a single-user system composed of four related programs emphasizing analysis.

I'll begin my discussion with a few comments about our general approach to *APL*-based financial system development. Then, for each of the two selected financial systems, I'll discuss system features, experience in development and implementation, and current status.

## Background Information about McDermott

J. Ray McDermott is an energy services company. Our operations are organized into two multinational units—McDermott and Babcock & Wilcox (B&W).

The McDermott operating unit serves the oil and gas industry, primarily in marine projects. Major activities include the construction of offshore platforms and the laying of undersea pipelines.

B&W builds steam-generating systems for electric utilities. In addition, B&W manufactures related products such as industrial boilers and specialty steel tubing.

During fiscal year 1979 (ended 31 March 1979), the company realized $3.14 billion in revenue and employed approximately 61,000 people.

## Why and How We Use *APL*

The main reason we in OR like *APL* is that we believe it provides a lot more bang for the buck. That is, when preparing a time sharing/interactive computer program—the type of program which usually seems best in applications pursued by OR—we feel *APL* enables us to do the job much faster and with much less expense charged back to the user than other computer languages.

Underlying the basic advantages of speed and lower cost are considerations probably well known to *APL* enthusiasts. Since *APL* is naturally interactive, it hastens all coding, including the coding of input and output routines for users. Furthermore, *APL* frees the system designer from the need to design in bits-and-bytes detail; it permits him to design, instead, in terms of spreadsheets, tables, and similar application-oriented concepts.

When compared with other programming languages, *APL* is often said to speed up design and coding by a factor of five to ten. We have estimated a gain in our own productivity of about that order of magnitude. We attribute the gain in speed to inherent capabilities of raw *APL*, to adopting good practices, such as organizing code into modules and having simple conventions for variable names, and to drawing upon a library of general functions—particularly groups of functions constituting general higher-level languages (for financial planning, database management, plotting, statistical modeling, and so on).

Our own approach to system development using *APL* is, I suspect, about the same as that taken by the majority of *APL*ers. I mention highlights here to indicate our endorsement of this approach.

In conventional, pre-*APL* system development the following procedure might be followed: plan every detail before you start coding; have the user certify that the plan contains exactly what he wants; proceed with coding; and require that the user go through a formal request process if he wishes to make a change after coding has begun. The language very likely is COBOL.

Because *APL* facilitates rapid coding, its use has allowed us to adopt a different approach: begin coding early; and move ahead in steps, with code running at each step, and with each step more advanced than the one before. A key difference is that we actually encourage the user to propose improvements, or perhaps just change his mind, at any and all stages of development. We think making operational code available to try out and think about—in a series of steps—matches the typical user's preference for working with tangible, realistic examples and improving them in successive evaluations.

The bottom line of our *APL*-oriented approach is that it produces, we believe, really superior results while taking less time and costing less.

**Financial Applications**

Before describing the selected financial systems, I'd like to note two general points about our financial applications.

First, at McDermott we see many promising financial applications of *APL*. And, although the best probably is yet to come, our company already has experienced the favorable impact of *APL* programming in a variety of areas. In addition to the financial network and investment portfolio projects, there have been *APL* projects related to such important company functions as divisional financial planning, divisional cash-flow forecasting, and corporate screening of proposed capital expenditures.

The second point has to do with what often is called "decision support". For years, managers and specialists have discussed their belief that really big payoffs will come from computer applications which support management decisions—especially large dollar-value decisions.

The basic purpose of computerization in a decision-support application is, you might say, to improve the depth and overall quality of the analysis management looks at when considering decision alternatives. Through its ability to handle data retrieval and "number crunching", the computer can conveniently do certain types of useful analysis that wouldn't be attempted manually. Some examples are forecasting by complex methods, developing "what if" projections, finding the best plan among a large number of possible plans, and including risk or uncertainty in the analysis.

Members of our OR Department certainly subscribe to the proposition that decision-support applications promise large payoffs; after all, decision support is our specialty. *APL* makes the development of decision-support systems much more practical because of the factors enumerated before—faster development and program modification, plus lower total cost.

I think the ideal arrangement is one in which the bread-and-butter aspects of an application (e.g., accounting, consolidation, and reporting) are combined with the decision-support aspects in a single, coordinated system. We have been striving for this in our financial network and investment portfolio systems.

### Acknowledgment

The systems to be described were made possible by the combined efforts of many different individuals in user departments and the OR Department. So I am writing on behalf of a large group of contributors, sponsors, and supporters in McDermott.

### The Financial Information Network

#### 1. System Description

The Financial Information Network consists of three similar, computer-based systems (programs and procedures) covering three similar, but nevertheless different, applications.

The *Business Planning Model-2 System (BPM-2)* generates financial reports for the annual business plan, covering financial histories, forecasts, and analyses. BPM-2 is used primarily by the Corporate Controller, Corporate Planning, and all B&W divisions and groups. The *Quarterly Forecast and Analysis System,* utilized by the Corporate Controller and all B&W divisions and groups, prepares quarterly financial reports, again including histories, forecasts, and analyses. The *Capital Planning and Analysis System* produces quarterly capital investment reports (with histories, forecasts, and analyses). Users of this system are the Corporate Controller plus all B&W divisions and groups. Top management reviews selected reports from all three systems.

All programs in the Financial Information Network are available online and used interactively. The term "network" refers to the fact that each system ties divisions, groups, and the corporate office together via telephone communication with a central computer. The transmittal of information from one unit to another in this network can be accomplished in minutes or even seconds.

#### 2. Features

The basic idea of the Information Network is summarized as follows. First, every user—whether in the corporate office, a group, a division, or a subsidiary—communicates with the same central computer. Strict privacy is provided to each user, however. Each user has his own files and workspaces in which he can prepare, check, and revise his reports. Results are released to a higher level only when the user authorizes it. Second, every user gains entry to the system through a terminal. The computer responds immediately most of the time, day or night. Reports can be produced on a terminal or on a high-speed printer.

The Network's technical features are quite interesting, I believe. But the most important point about capabilities is that the Network accomplishes certain things management wants accomplished. Here, then, is a brief list of pertinent management requirements together with a summary of how the Network satisfies those requirements:

- *Reduce manual workload, especially at the corporate level.* Computerization eliminates many time-consuming manual activities. Time saved is greatest in connection with consolidations, analyses entailing extensive calculations, and report revisions following changes in input data.

- *Speed up transmission of information.* Network replaces the previous procedure of mailing reports, which involved days of delay, with transmission by phone, which takes only minutes.

- *Obtain more and better analyses.* Previously, it was felt that participants spent so much time preparing reports they had little time to think about them. Also, there was corporate reluctance to add new analysis-and-reporting requirements for fear of increasing already heavy workloads. After Network implementation, time was freed to reflect upon contents, and it became easier to add requirements without overwhelming users.

- *Have rapid turnaround when data is changed.* Formerly, it was slow going, and sometimes not feasible before a deadline, to revise all affected calculations and reports when input data was changed. The Network facilitates making such revisions very quickly.

- *Improve accuracy and consistency of reports.* In manual, pre-Network systems, undetected errors arose occasionally during the conversion of input data into reports. Furthermore, people at divisional, group, and corporate levels occasionally disagreed about the latest values for a given information item. Now, in the Network, data-to-report errors are essentially eliminated. Also, all people authorized to see a given item look at the same value.

- *Implement new reporting requirements quickly and uniformly.* When new reporting requirements are established, the Network speeds up implementation and ensures uniform compliance. This is true because the user needs only to learn new inputs (if any); the Network handles all revised calculations and report formats.

- *Achieve smooth operation in the Network, even though personnel working hands-on at terminals may begin without experience and may have a high turnover rate.* Among numerous Network aspects intended to simplify life for terminal operators are (1) general procedures in the three systems are similar—if an individual knows one system, he can readily learn the other two; (2) complete written instructions are available; (3) the OR Department periodically conducts training sessions at user locations; (4) OR encourages every user to telephone for help immediately when any problem arises; (5) system programs extensively check user inputs and respond with informative messages if mistakes are found; (6) special edit routines help operators to easily revise online data; and (7) for less experienced users there are full prompts to guide data entry, while for more experienced users there are fast entry procedures.

- *Allow Network systems to be easily modified and reasonably efficient.* Changes in line items, report formats, and other application details are being introduced at a rapid pace, which calls for speed in making system enhancements. Such speed is achieved because of the power of *APL*, the adoption of good coding practices, and the use of a library of coding aids. Operating efficiency—another important goal—is pursued through design and coding choices and regular cost monitoring.

- *Protect confidentiality of sensitive information.* Access to data in the Network is strictly controlled according to established ground rules.

## 3. Development and Implementation

Development of BPM-2, the first Network system, started in March 1977, sponsored jointly by Corporate Planning and the Corporate Controller at Babcock & Wilcox. After a crash effort on the part of two OR staff members responsible for design and coding, actual use of BPM-2 began at divisions in early June and continued thereafter; debugging was essentially completed in July.

Even though development was rapid, the initial version of BPM-2 incorporated many advanced features, including: privacy for each user; operational on both *APL* and non-*APL* terminals; procedures involving action by a terminal operator (e.g., entering data, writing reports, creating and erasing files) were designed to keep the novice operator out of serious trouble; instructions for any selected operator action could be displayed at the terminal; provided flexibility to users in grouping and regrouping information; provided for consolidation; and enabled users to pass information along, thereby connecting divisional, group, and corporate levels.

Since BPM-2 represented a radical departure from past reporting practices, its "installation in the field" deserved special attention. Each user was visited by an OR staff member who gave an onsite demonstration and later kept in close touch as the user's actual BPM-2 work progressed. Users phoned OR immediately to report problems, and solutions were found quickly in most cases. Onsite demonstrations and telephone problem solving proved extremely productive, so they were continued as the Network expanded to include other systems.

BPM-2 operated well in 1977 and, while undergoing occasional modification, has operated well ever since. The good results from BPM-2, plus other factors, led B&W's Corporate Controller to authorize the development of the quarterly and capital systems in September 1978.

BPM-2 initially contained reports that were very similar to those of its predecessor manual system. The quarterly and capital programs, on the other hand, started with a wholesale revision of reports, including the addition of schedules that were thought to be too much work for a manual system. Development of the two new systems slowed drastically for several months during a period beginning in late September, when B&W corporate functions were being moved from New York to McDermott headquarters in New Orleans. Things eventually settled down so that by March 1979, three OR staff members, working part time on this particular project, had the programs operational.

Since March 1979, the quarterly and capital systems have been in regular use for quarterly reporting throughout B&W. Some modifications were made after March, and then, between December 1979 and January 1980, all programs including BPM-2 were revised to implement basic reporting changes desired by management.

### 4.  Status

The BPM-2, quarterly, and capital systems that make up the Financial Information Network are now well-established production programs in the B&W side of J. Ray McDermott.

Various additions and extensions to the system are under consideration. For example, since the programs reside on the same computer, in the same *APL* language, it is realistic to plan capabilities which coordinate several applications. If a monthly reporting system were added, for instance, monthly actuals reported in that system could be fed by computer into the quarterly actuals needed in the quarterly system. Or, if a general inquiry feature were added, the user could retrieve and work with data of his choice (where authorized) from any or all systems. Other examples of possible enhancements are pen-plotter graphics, aids for corporate "what if" projections to assess business strategies, cash-flow forecasting routines, and extension of the Network to cover the rest of the company.

### Short-Term Investment Portfolio System

### 1.  System Description

The Short-Term Investment Portfolio System, like the Financial Information Network, is a group of related online  interactive computer programs covering similar but different applications. It is not called a network because normally there is just one user location—the Corporate Treasurer's Department. Of course, users can access the programs from different geographic locations should they wish to do so.

All elements of the system help with administration of McDermott's Short-Term Investment Portfolio, managed by the Corporate Treasurer's Department. The *Database Program for Operating and Accounting Reports* draws from online records of individual investment transactions plus additional data to provide standard daily and monthly reports, and customized unscheduled reports, on investment operations and accounting. The *Database Program for Performance Analysis* uses the same database to provide standard monthly and unscheduled reports that give an in-depth analysis of investment performance. The *Investment Alternative Evaluator* (or Swap Program) produces unscheduled analytical reports pertaining to daily investment decisions. These reports show detailed analyses of anticipated investment performance, based on user assumptions about future interest rates, cash flows, and buy, hold, or sell actions. The program allows a user to evaluate single investments or groups of investments. The *Strategy Program* generates unscheduled analytical reports pertaining to monthly portfolio strategy. This program finds a superior monthly strategy and reports on its anticipated performance, based on user assumptions regarding future interest rates, cash flows, and policy restrictions. It also compares strategies derived by the program with other strategies proposed by the user.

### 2.  Features

The basic purpose of the Portfolio System is to help sustain and improve investment performance. Management felt—and we in OR agreed—that a really good system should pay for itself many times over, because McDermott's short-term portfolio is comparatively large. A small percentage change in performance has a big dollar impact.

Some of the managerial needs listed for the Financial Network applied here too. In this case, the main requirements were to: handle more work, both routine and advanced, without overwhelming personnel; improve control by supplying more complete and timely status information; and improve and document investment decisions by performing more extensive analysis.

The following are highlights of specific features in the four programs implemented thus far.

- *Database Program for Operating and Accounting Reports.* The terminal operator procedures built into the Database Program are designed, as in the Financial Network, to be simple and trouble free, while allowing a lot of flexibility. Using these input/output procedures, Treasury personnel enter data and run reports daily, when convenient.

  Reports can be obtained in two ways. One is through the program's special Generalized Inquiry System (GIS) capability, which enables the user to select exactly what he wants from the data stored in the computer, and then develop customized reports on that selected information. The other way is to call for a prespecified report (e.g., a maturity schedule). There is flexibility even with a prespecified report because the user can select any desired data on which to run the report (e.g., select active time deposits in just the largest of the various short-term portfolios; run a maturity schedule). Numerous prespecified reports cover the gamut of investment activities, and more reports can be added if the need arises.

- *Database Program for Performance Analysis.* This portion of the Database Program is a group of prespecified reports, together with additional required input data, that permit doing a comprehensive analysis of investment performance, similar to the indepth analysis now commonplace for pension funds. The reports describe performance in McDermott's various portfolios and then compare that performance with benchmarks, based on other actual portfolios and on indexes. Aspects covered include the usual three dimensions: rate of return, safety, and liquidity.

- *Investment Alternative Evaluator (Swap Program).* This program, currently not linked to the database, helps make projections of anticipated investment performance. Its purpose is to give fast, on-the-spot assistance to a manager who is analyzing different investment choices under active consideration. A single possible choice, or possible course of action, is called an "investment alternative" in the program. The swap—selling a current holding and reinvesting in a replacement—is just one of many types of alternatives that can be analyzed.

  The program handles various types of holdings (e.g., time deposits and bonds), alone or in combination. It permits the user to look at any number of different investment alternatives, each of which may involve one holding, a sequence of successive holdings, or any group of holdings. It converts interest-rate forecasts into forecasts of market prices. Alternatives can be stored. The user has substantial control over input and output; for instance, he can readily edit data previously entered, select full or fast prompts, and adjust the specific kinds of information included in reports to match his immediate interests.

- *Strategy Program.* In this application, the term "strategy" refers to a plan showing how much will be invested, held, and sold (where policy permits trading) in each broad category of investment, month by month over some period of time. An investment category is a combination of type (e.g., time deposits) and maturity (e.g., six months to maturity).

Analysis begins with one or more forecasts—supplied by the user, not by the program—of future interest rates and cash flows. The user also stipulates details of various policy restrictions on investment action, such as a restriction to maintain desired liquidity. The program then makes three basic analyses available. First, it employs the computational method of linear programming (LP) to find the strategy that maximizes anticipated rate of return. This is done for every forecast, and entails a separate analysis for each combination of policy restrictions the user wishes to consider. Second, when the user has a particular strategy in mind, he can evaluate it in the "simulation" portion of the program, which shows the performance of a proposed strategy given any selected forecast. The third basic option is a more complex LP analysis in which the user recognizes uncertainty and risk by assigning probabilities to alternative forecasts.

## 3. Development and Implementation

After preliminary investigation, including visits outside McDermott to see what others were doing, development of the four programs began in April 1979. The level of effort varied from month to month. On average, the full time equivalent of about 1.5 OR staff members worked on the project during the last 12 months.

Several milestones along the way were: Swap Program (version 1) completed in June 1979; Treasury personnel began entering real data into the database in October 1979; Strategy Program (version 1) completed in December 1979; Database Program for Operating and Accounting Reports (version 1) completed in February 1980; and Database Program for Performance Analysis (version 1) completed in March 1980.

During development, Treasury staff members collaborated closely with OR staff, usually through daily discussions. The result was programs which, while high powered, are very practical.

## 4. Status

Since the four implemented programs are still new, as can be seen from the milestone dates above, we do have a backlog of desired refinements and enhancements. In addition, project plans call for considering the possibility of adding separate programs to help with tasks such as storing and analyzing investment research data, forecasting interest rates (or at least obtaining a better understanding of them), and providing more advanced analysis in support of daily investment decisions and strategy formulation. Consideration may also be given to building separate programs focused on cash-management topics beyond investment—debt, cash forecasting, customer financing, and foreign-exchange exposure, for example.

## Conclusion

The Financial Information Network and the Short-Term Investment Portfolio System are two very practical applications of *APL* at J. Ray McDermott. While containing many completely modern, state-of-the-art capabilities, these systems are used for important production financial work in our company.

*Randy Robinson is currently section manager, corporate applications, in J. Ray McDermott's Operations Research Department. In this capacity, he carries out analytical studies and develops advanced computer systems for corporate management. Many of the management support systems developed by Robinson and his colleagues have been implemented on STSC's APL*PLUS Service. Previously, as an independent financial consultant, and earlier as director of the research division at the Bank Administration Institute, he had extensive experience in financial analysis based on quantitative methods.*

*Robinson completed undergraduate and graduate work at the Massachusetts Institute of Technology, earning his master's and Ph.D. from the Sloan School of Management. Between periods of study for his two graduate degrees, he served a tour of active duty in the U.S. Navy.*

Patrick P. Gehl

# Marketing Management Applications

STSC, Inc., provides computing services—collectively known as the *APL\*PLUS* Service—to meet the needs of modern business. Because we in the STSC Marketing Department have our own business needs, we are avid customers of the service we sell. We use the service for virtually every management reporting and planning function. These include preparing budgets and tracking results, monitoring sales territories, ranking salespeople and sales offices, determining pricing strategies, evaluating promotional activities, and consolidating results through branch and regional levels. Let's examine a few of these functions to see what the resulting reports look like and to discuss how they are used.

## Planning Reports

Planning for field marketing means putting together a budget for each fiscal year. This is an online activity that allows each branch manager to enter his forecast for revenues and expenses. The regional managers and vice presidents then consolidate for their respective areas.

These first results always find the revenues too low and the expenses too high. However, since the programs are online and each manager can use *APL* to model his different strategies, we can iterate to an agreed-upon solution within one or two weeks. The budgeting system, when used in conjunction with MAILBOX (STSC's Electronic Message Processing System), provides instantaneous communications and feedback. The budgeting activity normally takes companies months, not weeks, to accomplish. However, the power of *APL* and the manager's ability to use it online make planning a standard and quick, yet flexible, process.

Figure 1 shows the details of a fictitious, but typical, branch office budget report. With our budget in place, we launch into a new fiscal year and begin to use systems written in *APL* to generate reports of the results.

## Monthly Operating Statements

Monthly operating statements are used by the marketing managers and myself to compare the year-to-date actuals to the plan or budget. In addition to containing very current information, the reports are very timely and readily accessible. They are available within ten working days of the beginning of each month and, since they are online, we can obtain them at any branch office in the world (or, in fact, at any location that provides a terminal and network access to the system). It should be pointed out that the STSC Accounting

STSC BUDGETING  --  FY 1975
SUMMARY BY COST CENTER                              1/31/75

COST CENTER:  999   HILLDALE

| DESCRIPTION | JUN | JUL | AUG | SEP | OCT | NOV | DEC | . . . | TOTAL |
|---|---|---|---|---|---|---|---|---|---|
| HEADCOUNT | 10.0 | 10.0 | 10.0 | 11.0 | 11.0 | 11.0 | 11.0 | . . . | |
| CAPITAL EXPENDITURES | 6000 | 0 | 0 | 6000 | 0 | 0 | 0 | . . . | 12000 |

**REVENUES**

| | JUN | JUL | AUG | SEP | OCT | NOV | DEC | . . . | TOTAL |
|---|---|---|---|---|---|---|---|---|---|
| APL SERVICES | 178000 | 177000 | 136000 | 124000 | 128000 | 145000 | 146000 | . . . | 1909000 |
| ●APL SERVICES | 0 | 0 | 0 | 0 | 0 | 5850 | 10450 | . . . | 71100 |
| BATCH SERVICES | 1000 | 1000 | 1000 | 1000 | 1000 | 1000 | 1000 | . . . | 12000 |
| VM CENTER SERVICES | 4000 | 4000 | 4000 | 4000 | 4000 | 4000 | 4000 | | 48000 |
| PROGRAMMING | 2000 | 2000 | 3000 | 3000 | 3000 | 4000 | 4000 | | 46000 |
| CONSULTING | 1000 | 1000 | 2000 | 2000 | 1000 | 1000 | 1000 | | 14000 |
| MANUALS | 50 | 50 | 50 | 50 | 50 | 50 | 50 | | 600 |
| MISCELLANEOUS | 200 | 200 | 200 | 200 | 200 | 200 | 200 | | 2400 |
| TOTAL REVENUES | 186250 | 185250 | 146250 | 134250 | 137250 | 155250 | 156250 | | 2032000 |
| ●UPDATED REVENUES | 186250 | 185250 | 146250 | 134250 | 137250 | 161100 | 166700 | . . . | 2103100 |

**EXPENSES**

| | JUN | JUL | AUG | SEP | OCT | NOV | DEC | . . . | TOTAL |
|---|---|---|---|---|---|---|---|---|---|
| SALARIES - MANAGERS | 2917 | 2917 | 2917 | 4473 | 4473 | 4473 | 4473 | . . . | 49008 |
| SALARIES - PROFESSIO | 11931 | 11931 | 12038 | 12038 | 12038 | 12038 | 12038 | . . . | 144698 |
| SALARIES - CLERICAL | 1075 | 1075 | 1075 | 1075 | 1075 | 1075 | 1075 | . . . | 12900 |
| COMMISSION PLAN | 1747 | 1743 | 4819 | 2148 | 2338 | 6534 | 3245 | | 47973 |
| FICA | 1009 | 1027 | 876 | 836 | 726 | 633 | 599 | | 12726 |
| FUTA | 14 | 10 | 10 | 13 | 12 | 11 | 10 | | 508 |
| SUI | 59 | 166 | 49 | 52 | 443 | 424 | 334 | | 3820 |
| GROUP INSURANCE | 750 | 750 | 750 | 825 | 825 | 825 | 825 | | 9675 |
| RETIREMENT PLAN | 707 | 707 | 834 | 790 | 797 | 965 | 834 | | 10186 |
| OVERNIGHT | 1050 | 1050 | 1050 | 1050 | 1050 | 1050 | 1050 | | 12600 |
| LOCAL | 820 | 820 | 820 | 820 | 820 | 820 | 820 | | 9840 |
| BOOKS/PUBLICATIONS | 100 | 0 | 0 | 0 | 0 | 0 | 0 | | 100 |
| SPACE RENT | 3219 | 3219 | 3219 | 3219 | 3219 | 3219 | 3219 | | 38628 |
| UTILITIES | 100 | 100 | 100 | 100 | 100 | 100 | 100 | | 1200 |
| AMORT - LEASE IMPTS | 200 | 200 | 200 | 200 | 200 | 200 | 200 | | 2400 |
| TELEPHONES | 1600 | 1600 | 1600 | 1600 | 1600 | 1600 | 1600 | | 19200 |
| POSTAGE AND DELIVERY | 150 | 150 | 150 | 150 | 150 | 150 | 150 | | 1800 |
| STATIONERY,PRINTING, | 250 | 250 | 250 | 250 | 250 | 250 | 250 | | 3000 |
| COPYING | 120 | 120 | 120 | 120 | 120 | 120 | 120 | | 1440 |
| EQUIPMENT REPAIR AND | 25 | 25 | 25 | 25 | 25 | 25 | 25 | | 300 |
| DEPRECIATION - OFFIC | 100 | 100 | 100 | 100 | 100 | 100 | 100 | | 1200 |
| OTHER | 50 | 50 | 50 | 50 | 50 | 50 | 50 | | 600 |
| DUES AND SUBSCRIPTIO | 25 | 25 | 25 | 25 | 25 | 25 | 25 | | 300 |
| TERMINAL RENT | 1350 | 1350 | 1350 | 1350 | 1350 | 1350 | 1350 | | 16200 |
| TERMINAL DEPRECIATIO | 185 | 185 | 185 | 185 | 185 | 185 | 185 | | 2220 |
| TOTAL EXPENSES | 29553 | 29570 | 32612 | 31494 | 31971 | 36222 | 32677 | . . . | 402522 |

| | JUN | JUL | AUG | SEP | OCT | NOV | DEC | . . . | TOTAL |
|---|---|---|---|---|---|---|---|---|---|
| PERFORMANCE | 156697 | 155680 | 113638 | 102756 | 105279 | 119028 | 123573 | . . . | 1629478 |
| ●UPDATED PERFORMANCE | 156697 | 155680 | 113638 | 102756 | 105279 | 124878 | 134023 | . . . | 1700578 |
| CUMULATIVE PERF. | 156697 | 312377 | 426015 | 528771 | 634050 | 753078 | 876651 | . . . | |
| ●UPDATED CUM. PERF. | 156697 | 312377 | 426015 | 528771 | 634050 | 758928 | 892951 | . . . | |
| EXP./REV. (o/o) | 15.9 | 16.0 | 22.3 | 23.5 | 23.3 | 23.3 | 20.9 | . . . | 19.8 |
| ●UPDATED EXP./REV. o/o | 15.9 | 16.0 | 22.3 | 23.5 | 23.3 | 22.5 | 19.6 | . . . | 19.1 |
| TOT. COMPENSATION | 17670 | 17666 | 20849 | 19734 | 19924 | 24120 | 20831 | . . . | 254579 |
| ●UPDATED TOT. COMP. | 17670 | 17666 | 20849 | 19734 | 19924 | 24120 | 20831 | . . . | 254579 |
| COMP./REV. (o/o) | 9.5 | 9.5 | 14.3 | 14.7 | 14.5 | 15.5 | 13.3 | . . . | 12.5 |
| ●UPDATED COMP./REV. | 9.5 | 9.5 | 14.3 | 14.7 | 14.5 | 15.0 | 12.5 | . . . | 12.1 |

**Figure 1—Typical Branch Office Budget**

Department requires ten working days to close the books; in fact, online operating statements that are 90 percent accurate are available within four to five working days.

Operating statements are available on the territory level and can be consolidated to a branch, regional, or company level using programs furnished by the STSC Accounting Department. An example of such a report is given in Figure 2.

```
C.C. 999      HILLDALE                    STSC, INC.
MONTH ENDED   6/30/75                 OPERATING STATEMENT                        RUN DATE:   7/31/75

                              CURRENT MONTH                        YEAR TO DATE
                     PC REV   ACTUAL      PLAN    VARIANCE    PC REV   ACTUAL      PLAN    VARIANCE
REVENUES
  APL SERVICES        96.5    234,589   155,000    79,589      93.4  1,370,614 1,189,000   181,614
  BATCH SERVICES       2.5      6,184     5,000     1,184       1.6     24,177    40,000   ⁻15,823
  PROGRAMMING AND CONSULTIN·  0.9  2,200  5,000   ⁻2,800       4.8     70,430    35,000    35,430
  OTHER REVENUES       0.0         95       250      ⁻155       0.1      1,572     2,000      ⁻428
    SUBTOTAL          100.0    243,068   165,250    77,818     100 0  1,466,793 1,266,000   200,793
  NORMALIZE REVENUE ADJ.  0.0      0         0         0       0.0          0         0         0
    TOTAL            100.0    243,068   165,250    77,818     100.0  1,466,793 1,266,000   200,793

EXPENSES
  SALARIES            10.7     26,022    20,950    ⁻5,072      11.1    163,051   161,744    ⁻1,307
  PAYROLL TAXES        0.8      1,975     1,645      ⁻330       0.6      8,253     8,958       705
  FRINGE BENEFITS      0.8      2,009     1,663      ⁻346       0.7     10,216    12,847     2,631
  TRAVEL               1.8      4,260     1,870    ⁻2,390       1.5     21,391    14,960    ⁻6,431
  RECRUITING           0.9      2,249         0    ⁻2,249       0.3      5,085         0    ⁻5,085
  OUTSIDE COMPENSATION 1.6      3,986         0    ⁻3,986       0.3      3,986         0    ⁻3,986
  EMPLOYEE TRAINING    0.1        202         0      ⁻202       0.1      1,385       100    ⁻1,285
  OFFICE SPACE         1.4      3,509     3,519        10       1.9     27,347    28,152       805
  TELEPHONES           0.8      1,946     1,600      ⁻346       1.0     14,307    12,800    ⁻1,507
  ADVERTISING AND PROMOTION 0.4 1,001        0    ⁻1,001       0.1      1,368         0    ⁻1,368
  OFFICE EXPENSES      0.5      1,168       695      ⁻473       0.4      5,865     5,560      ⁻305
  OTHER ADMINISTRATIVE 0.0         77        25       ⁻52       0.0        250       200       ⁻50
  TERMINALS            0.4      1,015     1,535       520       0.6      8,897    12,280     3,383
    SUBTOTAL          20.3     49,419    33,502   ⁻15,917      18.5    271,401   257,601   ⁻13,800
  NORMALIZE EXPENSE ADJ.  0.0      0         0         0       0.0          0         0         0
    TOTAL             20.3     49,419    33,502   ⁻15,917      18.5    271,401   257,601   ⁻13,800

NET BEFORE ALLOCATIONS  79.7  193,649   131,748    61,901      81.5  1,195,392 1,008,399   186,993

ALLOCATIONS
  CONNECT              9.8     23,806    23,806         0       9.8    144,171   144,171         0
  CPU                 22.1     53,698    53,698         0      21.4    313,524   313,524         0
  STORAGE              3.7      8,990     8,990         0       4.0     59,124    59,124         0
  RECEIVABLES COSTS    0.3        618       618         0       0.5      7,954     7,954         0
  MANPOWER             0.0          0         0         0       0.0        575       575         0
  EXPENSES             0.0          0         0         0       0.0          0         0         0
    TOTAL             35.8     87,112    87,112         0      35.7    524,198   524,198         0

PERFORMANCE            43.8    106,537    44,636    61,901      45.8    671,194   484,201   186,993
```

**Figure 2—A Sample Operating Statement**

## Monthly Ranking Report

The monthly ranking report (see Figure 3) is used to create a competitive atmosphere among the marketing people and branch offices. This is accomplished by ranking the salespeople by total dollar volumes for the current month and by ranking the sales offices by year-to-date revenues as percentages of their plans. In addition to creating the friendly competition I want, the report serves as a continued reminder to each marketing manager of his progress toward his yearly quota.

The monthly ranking report has proved to be a valuable tool for me over the years. Since the data is stored in matrix form, I can change the report format by simply sorting on different columns and providing the data as input to STSC's report generator, □*FMT*. For example, if I want to stress the selling of programming services for one or two quarters, I can sort the data on that column of the matrix and present the report ranked as such. If batch revenue was the emphasis, revenues would be sorted and ranked accordingly. Because *APL* is such a powerful programming language, and because the entire

7/31/75

*STSC, INC.*
*STANDINGS REPORT*
*JUN 1975*

*BY TERRITORY:*

| | | | APL/MISC | | BATCH | | VM | | CONSULTING | | CURRENT | > LAST MONTH | |
|---|---|---|---|---|---|---|---|---|---|---|---|---|---|
| | | | REV $ | RNK | REV $ | RNK | REV $ | RNK | REV $ | RNK | BILLING | P.C. | $ |
| 1 | 1248 | *GARY BOROSKY* | 94,583 | 1 | 2,998 | 2 | 51 | 6 | 6,117 | 4 | 103,749 | 21 | 30,457 |
| 2 | 1234 | *RAYMOND EDWARDS* | 67,398 | 3 | 2,093 | 6 | 143 | 5 | 1,504 | 8 | 71,138 | ‾12 | ‾25,041 |
| 3 | 1125 | *SIDNEY ANSELL* | 69,073 | 2 | 2,011 | 7 | 0 | 9 | 0 | 10 | 71,084 | *** | 71,084 |
| 4 | 1166 | *DICK LEE* | 54,514 | 4 | 2,927 | 3 | 0 | 10 | 8,145 | 3 | 65,586 | 4 | 4,954 |
| 5 | 1279 | *THOMAS RUSSELL* | 41,680 | 6 | 2,123 | 5 | 1,227 | 2 | 12,750 | 2 | 57,780 | 146 | 43,081 |
| 6 | 1291 | *RAYMOND PETRY* | 46,251 | 5 | 2,676 | 4 | 1,039 | 3 | 1,973 | 7 | 51,939 | 19 | 14,030 |
| 7 | 1263 | *STEVEN TABB* | 37,083 | 7 | 3,503 | 1 | 613 | 4 | 4,588 | 5 | 45,787 | 16 | 10,741 |
| 8 | 1393 | *RITA CRADDOCK* | 17,994 | 10 | 941 | 9 | 2,173 | 1 | 16,185 | 1 | 37,293 | 64 | 20,936 |
| 9 | 1313 | *WILLIAM GREEN* | 29,506 | 8 | 455 | 10 | 36 | 7 | 780 | 9 | 30,777 | 37 | 13,027 |
| 10 | 1322 | *NELLIE SWEENEY* | 26,557 | 9 | 1,253 | 8 | 36 | 8 | 2,500 | 6 | 30,346 | ‾9 | ‾6,137 |
| | | *TOTALS:* | 484,639 | | 20,980 | | 5,318 | | 54,542 | | 565,479 | 286 | 177,132 |

## Figure 3—Monthly Ranking Report

planning and control system is online, we experience a degree of flexibility not often seen in the business community.

## Research

The *APL\*PLUS* Service is used by the Marketing Department to conduct most of its research and development efforts. These efforts consist mainly of modeling the customer base to examine the effects of pricing strategies, measuring the dollar return on various promotional schemes, and tracking the sources of new business. In many of these activities, either raw *APL* or "throw away" code is used effectively.

In many cases marketing managers write their own *APL* programs to examine the effect of proposed activities on historical data. These programs are written online and are disposed of once the results are obtained. By having marketing managers use *APL* themselves to obtain these results, we avoid the time delays involved in submitting requests through a programming department.

One example of the results are graphic reports of the new business for a fiscal year. These reports are in the form of bar charts that describe revenue derived from various entry-level products, revenue derived from promotional sources, and the number of new customers by application area. Figure 4 illustrates one such bar chart.

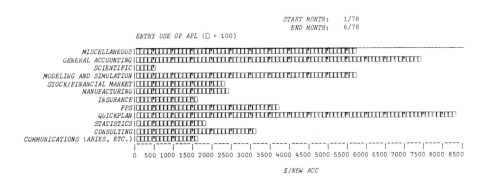

## Figure 4—Bar Chart of New Business Origins

## Summary

In summary, STSC's Marketing Department is an extensive user of *APL* and of the *APL*★*PLUS* Service. We run the various management functions using *APL* programs, and whenever possible we run the programs online. We take advantage of our ability to instantly access the system from locations throughout the world, our ability to update the marketing information file with timely data, and our ability to efficiently sort and display the information in a meaningful manner. This scheme has proven to be very effective for us, and we would recommend a similar system for each and every marketing organization, regardless of the type of product being offered.

*Patrick Gehl has been executive vice president of marketing for STSC since 1976 and a Member of the Board of Directors since STSC's inception in 1969. From 1969 to 1976, he served as vice president of marketing. Prior to joining STSC, Gehl organized and directed the first commercial APL time sharing service in the United States while employed by Marquardt Corporation.*

*Gehl is a graduate of Indiana State University and holds a Master's degree in physics from Purdue University.*

Ronald J. Bohm

# Magazine Distribution Management

The Circulation Management Decision System is used by Playboy Enterprises, Inc., to plan and monitor the newsstand distribution of *Playboy* magazine and *Oui* magazine. *Playboy* and *Oui* together have an audited monthly paid circulation of over 6.4 million copies, of which over 4 million are sold on newsstands in the United States, Canada, and Puerto Rico (for the six months ended June 1979). To understand why we need such an impressively named system to manage a seemingly mundane problem, you must first know a few things about the domestic magazine distribution system.

## The Distribution System

There are four links in the magazine distribution chain: the *publisher,* the *national distributor,* the *wholesaler,* and the *retailer* (see Figure 1). Most publishers, even those as large as Playboy Enterprises, Inc., prefer not to establish the inhouse organizations necessary to distribute their products widely. Instead, the publisher will sign a national distribution agreement for newsstand circulation with one of the 12-15 national distributors. For the services rendered by the national distributor, the publisher pays a commission on sales net of returned copies. Each wholesaler sells to all the retailers in his territory. Generally, each retailer deals with only one wholesaler. For example, if you were a retailer in Bethesda, Maryland, desiring to have certain magazines displayed on your counter, you would have to contact District News Company, Inc.

When the current issue is delivered to the retailer by the wholesaler, the wholesaler takes back the unsold copies of the prior issue. The wholesaler gives full credit to the retailer and passes the magazine covers of the unsold copies to the national distributor who, in turn, gives full credit to the wholesaler. The publisher, though, ultimately pays for all returns. Since the national distributor works on commission, he is motivated to minimize returns. But he assumes only the accounts receivable risk, not the returns risk.

The publisher's objectives are to:

- maximize sales
- minimize returns
- maximize market share.

But there are complications which make the distribution problem difficult to manage. For instance, advertising revenue is dependent on copy sales (see Figure 2). If a publisher reduces his print order to minimize returns, he may find he has sacrificed sales and endangered his advertising rate base (the minimum net sales as promised to advertisers). The conventional wisdom in this industry is "If you print more and display more, you'll sell more". The problem is to determine when the cost of putting an extra copy on display exceeds the expected revenue from the sale of that copy.

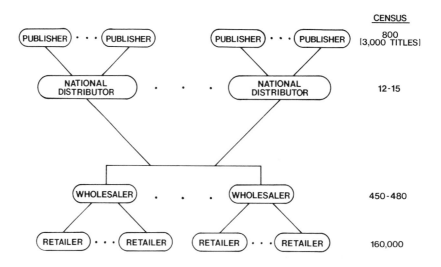

**Figure 1—Magazine Distribution Chain: US and Canada**

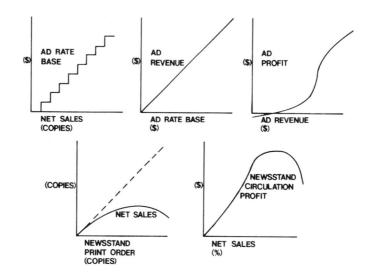

**Figure 2—Circulation, Advertising, and Profit Relationships**

Another complication in the distribution of magazines is the long delay between the off-sale date and the date the last return arrives (when the issue is "finalled"). By way of illustration, by the time we have final results on the April 1980 *Playboy*, we will be preparing the distribution for the November 1980 issue. That means the issue we are forecasting is seven periods out from the end of our history. I don't need to tell you what that does to forecasting accuracy. Some publishers are printing the Universal Product Code (UPC) on the cover to speed return processing. *Playboy*, however, considers the cover too important to its image to allow the use of the UPC.

Further complicating the problem is the recent increase in competition among wholesalers for retail accounts. When a retailer switches from one wholesaler to another, the history for both wholesalers no longer corresponds to the market we are modeling. Measures have to be taken to estimate the impact of the shift on the marketplace; and the history (and forecast) must be restated accordingly.

By no means have I listed all the complications, but in the interest of time, let's move on to a description of the Circulation Management Decision System.

## The Circulation Management Decision System

Proper management of the distribution of a national magazine requires that:

- For each issue, the optimal number of copies is printed.

- Each wholesaler has the same probability of selling all the magazines allotted to him.

To determine the proper print order, two forecasts are required. The first forecast is of the national demand for the issue being planned (top down). The second forecast is the sum of the wholesale forecasts for that issue (bottom up). Any number of techniques may be applied to the forecast of national demand. Therefore, I will dwell instead on the forecast of the wholesale demand.

For each magazine in the Circulation Management Decision System, we update monthly 475 demand models (one for each wholesale market). Consequently, we need a system that is efficient and self correcting. Using workspace $747 \ COSMIC$ on STSC's $APL \star PLUS$ System, we are able to account for seasonality, trends, and turnabouts in each market. We have modified the workspace to allow both linear and exponential curve fitting.

Each month we update the history with the sales for the most recently finalled issue. Before any information is introduced to the database, it is checked for reasonableness in two different ways (see Figure 3). In the first check we screen for unreasonable return percentages. That is, we define a range of acceptable return percentages, and those wholesalers whose return percentages fall outside of this range are investigated. In the second check we compare the reported sale with the forecasted sale. Any reported sale that falls outside the confidence limits of the forecast is also examined.

Once the data have been posted to the database, we make one final reasonableness check. If the model for a particular wholesaler is well conceived, the positive and negative forecast errors over time will cancel one another out. By looking at the running total of the forecast errors, we can determine if more recent sales are deviating from prior trends. In this way, the system signals the model's obsolescence and a new model is created.

The forecasting process (see Figure 4) begins with the generation of a market-by-market forecast, without considering the specific appeal of the issue being planned. We add to this "average issue" forecast when we expect the issue to be above average, and we subtract when we expect the issue to be below average. This is a highly subjective and rarely successful enterprise. Some issues succeed for reasons that escape us, while other issues, which we had expected to do very well, sell disappointingly.

To this adjusted forecast, we make market-by-market adjustments that reflect both changes in the marketplace and the local impact of the cover or content of the issue. By way of example, the September 1976 issue of *Playboy* had very strong sales in Washington, D.C., which some of us attribute to the pictorial on the girls of Washington.

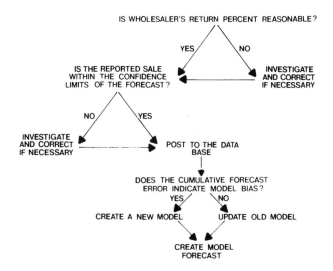

**Figure 3—Circulation Management Decision System: Data Filter**

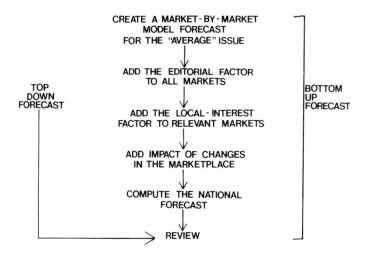

**Figure 4—The Forecasting Process**

After we have completed the forecasting process, we must then allocate the print run to the wholesalers. Once again, control is essential. We learned very early in this project that out of 475 mathematical models, a small proportion of them can be expected to yield unreasonable representations. To control against the distorting impact of these models, we impose limits on the models to prevent our monthly allocations from unwarranted volatility.

Once the allocation has been made, the wholesale allocations are reported by sales region and by state. The allocation is then recorded on tape and is shipped to the national distributor who must create the mailing labels to be forwarded to the bindery. When the wholesalers are notified of their allotments, they prepare allotments for their retail accounts.

## Monitoring the System

After the system had been programmed, we carried out two market experiments on three consecutive issues. The purpose of the first test was to see if, given no change in the print run for a set of experimental markets, we could achieve a lower return percentage than the control group. In the second experiment, we tested the hypothesis that we could use the system to help us lower the print order, thereby increasing efficiency, while not sacrificing sales volume. Both of these experiments were followed very closely. The results confirmed both hypotheses.

From that point, our strategy for the system has been to gradually increase the sales efficiency to the point where sales volume would be measurably affected. When we discover this critical efficiency level, we will then be in a position to analyze the tradeoffs between efficiency and profitability.

## Other Applications of the System

The Circulation Management Decision System has proven valuable in a number of other ways. Drawing on the database that was created for the purpose of performing allocations, we can now prepare the series of reports and analyses described below and graphically summarized in Figure 5.

|  | TYPE | MARKETS | TIME FRAME | RANKING | HISTOGRAMS |
|---|---|---|---|---|---|
| MARKET ANALYSIS | TREND | ANY SET | LAST 12 ISSUES | YES | YES |
|  | VARIANCE | ANY SET | LAST 12 ISSUES | YES | YES |
|  | EFFICIENCY | ANY SET | ANY ISSUES | YES | YES |
|  | SHARE | ANY SET | ANY ISSUES | NO | NO |
| MONTHLY REPORTING | ACTUAL VS. FORECAST | SALES REGION | PAST ISSUES | NO | NO |
|  | 12 ISSUE OUTLOOK | SALES REGION | FUTURE ISSUES | NO | NO |
| OTHER | DETAILED MARKET FACTSHEETS |  |  |  |  |
|  | ESTABLISHMENT OF OBJECTIVES |  |  |  |  |
|  | ANALYSIS OF MARKET EXPERIMENTS |  |  |  |  |
|  | CREATION OF STRATIFIED SAMPLES |  |  |  |  |

### Figure 5—Other Applications

- *Detailed Fact Sheets by Market:* Included on the fact sheets are the last six years of history, the forecast for the next twelve issues, a graph of the history, the forecast, and the confidence limits on the forecast.

- *Trend Analysis:* The twelve-issue history for each market. These ratios are then ranked and reported from worst to best. A histogram and summary statistics are provided.

- *Variance Analysis:* The standard error of the regression model is normalized by the average sales volume for the last twelve issues. These ratios are ranked and reported from worst to best. Histograms and summary statistics are also provided for this analysis.

- *Efficiency Analysis:* The net sales percentage can be computed for any period of time. The sales percentages are ranked and reported from worst to best. Histograms and summary statistics are also available.

- *Market Analysis:* For any period of time, we can analyze any region, edition, state, market, or set of markets with regard to its share of a given marketplace. For example, the salesman for a given region may want to know the issue-by-issue share of region sales for each market in his region.

- *Monthly Status Report:* The performance of each region is reported with the forecast for that region along with measures of trend and variance.

- *Establishment of Objectives and Evaluation of Performance:* The objectives for the sales force are based not on last year's sales volume, but on the forecasts made by the system for the next twelve issues. The system also assists management in setting objectives and monitoring performance regarding volatility of sales by market. For example, if a salesman can help a wholesaler reduce the volatility of his sales, the system can then improve its forecasts and thereby improve the sales efficiency for that market.

- *Analysis of Experiments:* Quite often, promotion campaigns are field tested in a number of markets before they are implemented nationally. The system is used to help in the random selection of a stratified sample. Once the promotion campaign has ended, the system can then be used to compare actual market shares for experimental and control markets with forecasted market shares. Significant differences in the forecast error between experimental and control markets are interpreted as being due to the promotional effort.

### Conclusion

The Circulation Management Decision System has come a long way in a very short time. What began as a special system to support a particular operational decision has blossomed into a multipurpose database system. In June 1977, STSC, Inc., was chosen as the vendor for the system, largely on the strength of its materials management system. In September 1977, the first test of the system commenced. From September until the following July, the system was gradually enhanced to reflect the idiosyncrasies of the magazine distribution system. Since April 1979 the system has been operating with very little change.

Our plans call for the expansion of the system to include demographic data, subscription data, and ABC (Audit Bureau of Circulations) data. The demographic and subscription data will help us measure our sales penetration of our target audience. The ABC data will help us identify markets where our share is weak. This information will help us to allocate our promotion dollars more productively.

*Ronald J. Bohm is a specialist in management science, holding master's and doctoral degrees in that field from the Massachusetts Institute of Technology. His undergraduate work was in mathematics. As director of management decision systems for Playboy Enterprises, Inc., he designs and implements decision models, management reporting schemes, and forecasts relating to book publishing, book clubs, licensing, merchandising, foreign editions, and overseas distribution.*

*Before joining Playboy in 1977, Bohm did consulting and special project analysis for a number of firms, including Knight Ridder Newspapers and Irving Trust Company of New York.*

**William M. Shaw**

# Computers Ain't Cool

It's no secret that consumer products companies spend billions annually on advertising and promotion. In 1980 alone, U.S. companies will spend in excess of $30 billion for promotion.

But there is a clear distinction between advertising and promotion. *Advertising* is nonpersonal communication in measured media (television, radio, print, outdoors) with clear sponsorship. *Promotion* is all other forms of company-sponsored communications apart from advertising and personal selling. Examples are

- trade shows/exhibits
- couponing (media, handout, in or on packages)
- sampling (at home, in store, in or on packages)
- premiums (self-liquidating or free)
- trade allowances.

Promotion also includes:

- sales and dealer incentives
- sweepstakes/contests
- refunds (coupons, cash, or product)
- cents-off packaging
- consumer education and demonstration activities
- rebates
- bonus packs
- point-of-purchase material

and not the least:

- direct mail.

While there is some overlap between advertising and promotion spending, expenditures for the latter have been growing at a faster rate—in fact, about twice as fast—as advertising.

One reason for such accelerated growth is the product management system that many companies have adopted. This system basically emphasizes the identity of brands, and rewards quick success. Since one of promotion's primary functions is to act as "an immediate consumer call to action", product managers are increasingly relying on promotions to complement advertising. The main reason for the growth in promotional spending, however, is that the consumer *does react*. In consumer products especially, consumers are offered a choice of many brands, some of which have few inherent distinctions. Promotion frequently produces strong economic incentives—especially today—to consumers to try, and buy, particular products.

This favorable consumer response to economic incentives is largely responsible for the huge growth in cents-off-couponing, which accounts for the majority of promotional dollars in the package goods industry. In 1978 the food and drug industries distributed an estimated 73 billion coupons; in 1979 the total exceeded 80 billion. In 1960 only 350 companies used coupons; in 1980 more than 1000 will.

As competition increases and inflation spurs prices, the average face value of coupons continues to climb. In 1971, the average face value was 10.2 cents, while in 1979 the figure was 16.8 cents. An average of 60 coupons per household were redeemed in 1978. Furthermore, the percent of households using coupons has increased from about 58 percent in 1971 to about 85 percent in 1979.

You might expect that well-established consumer products companies would use the most sophisticated means available to control and oversee promotional spending, especially since the economic effects on the company of such spending cannot be ignored. Surprisingly enough, many companies do *not* know:

- How much their industry spends on promotions.
- How much their primary competitors spend.
- How their competitors allocate that unknown sum.
- How much they themselves spend on promotions.
- How their own budget is allocated.
- What marketing objectives the individual promotions best serve.
- How various promotions interact.
- How their customers respond to promotions.

Too often, promotions are scheduled and tactics employed, simply because "that was what was done last year". Few companies have developed promotional principles to guide planning and ensure agreement with corporate objectives, though this practice is certainly increasing.

Since over $200 million is spent on promotion annually in the coffee industry, we in the Maxwell House Division make a concerted effort to plan and evaluate our promotional programs. The majority of our promotional budget is spent on couponing. Consequently, the planning and evaluation of couponing strategies seemed an ideal starting point for developing computerized information systems.

When we began the design of our system, we found numerous problems to consider in planning and evaluating couponing strategies. Unfortunately, we also found ourselves challenging an unexpected obstacle—the axiom among marketers that "computers ain't cool".

"Big deal", you may say, "don't I know that computers put a guy on the moon?" Sure, computers have been around for years, and they have tremendous capabilities, but *not* for the marketer. You see, a marketer is very much like a pilot who learned to fly in the old days—by the seat of his pants. The marketer and the pilot have other common attributes:

- They have complete and utter confidence in their own judgments.
- They are known for the high-risk fields they're in.
- As a result they enjoy a special privileged status.

A computer is too predictably perfect for them. It removes too much of the risk, and when the risk goes, so goes some of the mystique and most of the glamour.

Yet it is undeniable that only with computers can product managers organize and assimilate the multitude of data that affect consumer behavior and therefore have an impact on promotional planning. The following is only a sampling of the information a company might consider in comparing couponing strategies:

1. Method of distribution.
2. Audience reached by the coupon.
3. Area of the country.
4. Brand's retail availability.
5. Size of brand's consumer franchise.
6. Consumer's "need" for the product.
7. Product class size.
8. Competitive activity.
9. Stage in the product life cycle (i.e., new or established brand).
10. Degree of consumer brand loyalty.
11. Design and appeal of the coupon advertisement.
12. Discount offered by the coupon.
13. Face value of the coupon.

To elaborate on point 1, the method of distribution, here are some considerations relevant to most print media as vehicles for advertising and promotions (these should give you some idea why marketers flew by the seat of their pants):

| Types of Print Media | Considerations |
| --- | --- |
| Newspapers (regular) | Demographic selectivity |
| Newspapers (coop) | Lead-time requirements |
| Sunday supplements | Speed of redemption |
| Free-standing inserts | Ability to merchandise with the trade |
| Magazines (on-page) | Long-term benefits |
| Magazines (pop-up) | Editorial environment |
| Direct mail | Advertising value and image |

It becomes increasingly clear that only a computer can store all the vital information gleaned from continuous promotion, evaluation, and testing. Certainly the subjective evaluations, theories, and concepts to be tested, and the questions to be asked, remain in the control of the product manager. But the computer becomes an invaluable "product assistant" because of its ability to store and juggle virtually unlimited quantities of information.

Once the value of the computer is recognized, we begin to understand that computers can help us answer the most frequently asked marketing questions:

"Who spent how much on what, and what benefit resulted?" The next step is determining which system will best meet our needs; that is, which system will give us the answers we need quickly while offering us maximum flexibility to accommodate change.

A good system can sort through the result of past promotions to rank the effectiveness of those programs among different criteria. Based on actual past results, the system can instantly provide statistics affecting decisions about:

- type of premium or refund offer
- number of proofs of purchase or amount of money to require
- type of incentive to offer
- monetary value of the incentive
- duration of the offer
- methods of promoting the offer.

To give you an idea of the type of decisions we at Maxwell House must make, consider the following: Which of two promotional advertisements for a coffee would be more effective? One featuring a coupon alone, or one emphasizing a reuseable jar, but also offering a coupon of equal value.

Other things being equal, coupon redemption in advertising like this may be positively influenced from 2 to 20 percent depending on the promotional "overlay" (type of promotion featured in the advertisement) delivered with it. Other factors come into play, of course. For instance, if you violate a brand's premium principle, you may stunt normal consumer involvement or hurt brand image or long-term sales.

A computer can also assimilate geographically where a brand is spending its promotion dollars and where its volume is coming from. It can easily factor in which brand's sales it cannibalizes with each of its events and rank what vehicles work best alone or in combination to accomplish basic marketing objectives.

A computer can file away Diary Panel Data on different promotions' impact on a brand's user group. Heavy users react differently to a brand offer than a brand's light to occasional user, and you definitely need a different tactic if you are going after "ANTS" (aware non-triers, in marketing lexicon). Table 1 illustrates the practical information that the computer has provided.

We have accumulated an incredible amount of raw data on coupon redemption patterns.

To use this information effectively, we asked Scientific Time Sharing Corporation (now STSC, Inc.) to help us implement an *APL* application to track our promotional activities and those of our competitors. We built redemption tables based on historical observations. These tables predict quite accurately the percentage of coupons that will be redeemed, given a coupon value, geographic area, and type of media. With additional summary data about each planned promotional event, the system calculates the number of redemptions and the total cost of the promotion.

We can summarize events by brand, producing a "flow chart" of the overall plan for each brand. This greatly helps our budgeting process. We are also able to experiment with coupon values, investigating the cost effectiveness of changes in redemption rates and total costs. Using purchased data on competitive promotions, we can similarly analyze competitors' activities, and plan accordingly.

**Table 1 — Consumer Promotion Planning Guide**

| Technique | Primary impact | | |
|---|---|---|---|
| | Brand awareness | Attract new customers | Increase sales to present customers |
| Bonus packs | | | • |
| Cash refunds | | | |
|   Single purchase | | • | |
|   Multiple purchase | | | • |
| Contests/sweepstakes | • | | |
| Couponing | | | |
|   Media/mail | | • | |
|   In/on pack | | | • |
|   Multiple | | | • |
| Premiums | | | |
|   Single purchase | | • | |
|   Multiple purchase | | | • |
| Price-off | | | • |
| Sampling | | • | |

As computer novices, we were certainly "flying by the seats of our pants" in developing this tracking and planning system. Yet we found we could, by taking advantage of the flexibilities offered by *APL*, experiment with numerous data entry, reporting, and analysis techniques. We were overjoyed to discover our ability to answer unanticipated "what if" questions with little or no additional programming effort.

We have by no means finalized our computer-assisted planning efforts, but we are able to effectively use what we have, and we learn a little more at each step. Of course, there is always one more thing to consider when making strategic marketing decisions. So marketers will probably always be somewhat flying by the seats of their pants; but good computer systems will make them more durable pants.

*William M. Shaw joined General Foods Corporation in 1961. After progressing through the sales organization, he moved to Corporate Headquarters in 1966 as staff assistant and sales planning manager in the Desserts Division. In 1968 he was promoted to promotion planning manager for Kool-Aid and in 1970 to national promotion manager for Burger Chef.*

*Since 1975, Shaw has been promotion manager for the Maxwell House Division, which makes all General Foods coffee brands. His responsibilities include promotion planning, developments, execution, and evaluation as well as competitive tracking and long-range forecasting. Maxwell House is General Foods' largest division and the largest coffee company in the world.*

*Shaw holds B.S. and M.B.A. degrees from Northeastern University.*

William H. Bickford and Kenneth E. Golden

# Financial Reporting Systems:
# A Case Study

This paper discusses the design, implementation, and use of a financial reporting system for a multinational, multidivisional corporation. The corporation—Continental Diversified Operations (CDO)—sought to provide senior management with timely financial reports through automation of its manual reporting procedures.

Consultants from STSC, Inc. used the features and capabilities of STSC's Financial Planning System (FPS) to deliver a fully automated, conversational financial reporting system in two months' time—a full month ahead of schedule. The system has been running for over six months now and has met or exceeded all the goals set by the corporation.

The authors are indebted to Eugene R. Reilly, Director of Finance at CDO, for his invaluable assistance in preparing this paper.

## Background

CDO is one of five major operating groups belonging to the Continental Group, Inc., located in Stamford, Connecticut. Three divisions and over 20 plants make up CDO's operations. These plants and divisions are scattered over six countries: the United States, Canada, the Netherlands, Belgium, Germany, and Mexico. The plants report to their respective divisions, and the divisions report to corporate headquarters in Stamford.

Given the hierarchy of the reporting structure and the multinational aspects of the corporation, manual production of consolidated financial statements for senior management is a monumental and time-consuming task. Individual plant reports are prepared and submitted to divisional authorities who correct, consolidate, and forward the reports to corporate headquarters. At headquarters, the reports are again corrected and consolidated for senior management.

The financial reports consist of selected Profit and Loss and Balance Sheet items on both an actual and forecasted basis. Actual data, reflecting current operations, is submitted on a monthly basis. Forecast data is submitted on a weekly basis to provide monthly forecasts, and on a monthly basis to provide detailed quarterly forecasts.

Problems arise in the areas of currency conversion, report formats, timeliness, clerical errors, and management control. Many of the divisions use local currencies in their reports, thereby requiring currency conversion during consolidation of the reports. Various divisions use their own report formats, which means that extra effort is required to meld the various reports into one format for corporate reporting.

Because six countries are involved, the financial data does not arrive at the same time at corporate headquarters, which results in many delays in getting the final reports completed. Due to errors made at plant and divisional levels, the reports must be reviewed and corrected at divisional and corporate levels. All this review and correction consumes valuable time and effort. Given the multidivisional and multinational structure of the corporation, control over the periodic reporting of financial data is delegated to individuals below the corporate level, which results in some loss of control.

All these factors—currency, timeliness, report formats, clerical errors, and control—led CDO to seek an automated solution to its financial reporting needs.

## Solution

Since STSC, Inc., had previously implemented a successful general ledger product for CDO, STSC was invited to review the financial planning procedures and the reports, and to offer a possible solution that would overcome the shortcomings of the current manual operations. Initial discussions with the Director of Finance began in March 1979.

The financial planning and reporting system proposed by STSC consisted of:

- A capability to automatically convert all foreign currencies to U.S. dollars.

- An automated, conversational procedure to collect and verify data at the plant level.

- Exact duplicates of the report formats, as they were being manually produced.

- The ability to control access to data, at both plant and divisional levels.

- The ability to consolidate respective plant reports into one divisional report.

- The ability to consolidate divisional reports into one corporate report.

STSC was given the authority to develop an automated financial planning and reporting system in June 1979, and the system was delivered in August—a full month ahead of schedule. A major factor contributing to the early delivery was the general nature and flexibility of FPS. Built-in data entry, modeling, and report generator routines helped move systems development to a rapid conclusion.

After six months of use, the financial planning and reporting system developed by STSC is doing the job it was intended to do. All major goals have been met, and additional capabilities and savings have been realized. Some of the additional features are described below.

- *Automatic currency conversion.* Currency conversion is performed automatically, rather than manually. Currently, each plant enters its financial data using the local currency and specifies the rate of exchange to be used—the computer performs the tedious conversions.

- *Timely submission of reports; control over the reporting methodology; reduction in clerical time devoted to producing corporate reports; local access to the computer from all plant and divisional locations; computer-generated reports that need no retyping. Re-*

ports are available as soon as the data is entered. Under the manual system, data was either phoned or wired to the division and corporate offices. With the aid of the computer, data is entered only once, at the plant location, and all reports for all divisions and corporate headquarters can then be generated on request. Automation has reduced the time required to prepare and consolidate the reports, and deliver the finished reports to management.

- *Significant reduction in clerical errors.* The financial planning and reporting system has also significantly reduced clerical errors. Data is entered at only one location—the originating plant—where the people are most familiar with their particular set of numbers. Under the manual scheme, data was entered at the plant, again at the division for the divisional report to corporate headquarters, and again at corporate headquarters for the consolidation to senior management. This triple entry and handling of the same data was eliminated by the automated system.

Other standard features of FPS are now being studied and tested for incorporation into the corporate planning and analysis functions. These features are

- *Sensitivity Analysis,* which measures the impact of changes to, or fluctuations in, the data.

- *Value Seeking,* which searches for the value of a data element that will yield a desired report value.

- *Graphics,* which provides the ability to chart both data and report elements over time or against other data and report elements.

- *Risk Analysis,* which provides the ability to assign probability distributions to data elements and to measure their effects on key results.

CDO is very pleased with the financial planning and reporting system developed for them by STSC. The system has met their goals, which were to automate the manual procedures and to give senior management timely reports, and has additionally provided tighter control, cost reductions, and automatic currency conversion. The rapid implementation of systems such as this is made possible by the flexibility and power of STSC's Financial Planning System.

*Bill Bickford, currently branch manager of STSC's Westchester/Fairfield office, began his career with the company as a marketing representative. Working in three New York and New Jersey counties, he more than doubled revenues from his territory, accomplishing this through steady growth and the addition of five Fortune 500 companies as clients. He has broad experience in implementing and updating accounting systems, having worked for United Brands, Sybron Corporation, Harley-Davidson, Carborundum, and W. R. Grace.*

*Bickford received his bachelor's degree in accounting from the University of Idaho.*

*Ken Golden, who joined STSC in 1978, is a marketing representative in the company's Westchester/Fairfield office. His responsibilities include marketing*

*STSC products and services and designing, installing, and maintaining com-
puter-based systems for customers. Golden has over nine years' experience in
designing and supporting information systems. Before joining STSC, he worked
as a systems analyst with the San Francisco Police Department, as a senior
consultant with Planmetrics, Inc., and as a project manager with General
Foods Corporation.*

*Golden has a B.S.E. in electrical engineering from the University of Connecticut
and an M.B.A. in operations management from the University of California at
Berkeley.*

# Robert R. DeCloss

# Using *APL* for Construction Accounting

229 billion dollars! According to the United States Bureau of the Census *Construction Reports*, that is the total value of all types of new construction in 1979. (This amount is seasonally adjusted and annualized based on data through August 1979.) In 1972 the construction industry employed 4.1 million people in 921,000 companies.

As a businessman, I am intrigued by the sheer size of the construction industry. It is undeniably dynamic and exciting. We're all aware of the huge cranes hovering over immense steel frames, and we marvel as new buildings take form and are finally completed. Even the "hard hats" fill us with awe as they scurry across steel girders high in the air.

As exciting as the actual construction is to watch, the business side presents management with financial situations that require quick decisions to assure that particular ventures are profitable. For example:

- Government agencies and labor unions require frequent and accurate reporting of labor performed on each phase of each job.

- Weekly payrolls must be met promptly; delays can cause penalties that can impair or destroy the profitability of a job.

- So that management can determine the progress and profit of a job, all labor, materials, direct job expenses, equipment, inventories, and subcontractor fees must be established early.

The construction industry is complex and highly competitive. An accounting system for construction companies must be flexible enough to handle the weekly—even daily—changes required by government agencies, labor unions, management, and employees. It must be pertinent; that is, the data coming out of the system must be usable—not so detailed as to obscure its importance, but detailed enough to provide the right information to the right people at the right time. It must be easy to use. The requirements of the industry are intricate and numerous; time cannot be wasted trying to learn how to use a complicated accounting system. A system must be cost effective. The hours saved by personnel and the accuracy and completeness of the system all contribute to the cost effectiveness of a system. It must be secure; confidential data cannot get into the wrong hands. Finally, it must meet the particular needs of each company using it.

The accounting requirements of the construction industry are some of the most comprehensive of any industry. The most important functions that an accounting system for the construction industry must provide are

- payroll
- payables
- jobcost
- receivables
- equipment
- inventory
- general ledger.

The first three constitute an important trio. Payroll and payables feed the jobcost function to provide management with accurate and timely information. This information is used to determine profitability and progress on each job, problem areas on a job, and information useful for client billing and estimating future job bids.

## Payroll

Payroll must be able to handle the special accounting requirements of labor unions. Since each union negotiates its own contract, a payroll system must be able to meet the needs of several unions. For example, each union has different employee fringe benefits, such as insurance funds, apprenticeship/training funds, pension funds, welfare, contractor administrator funds, education funds, dues, and vacations.

To mention just a few of the possibilities, some unions require that employees get only straight vacation pay, while others require that the employees get overtime vacation pay. Most unions require subsistence pay for jobs beyond a certain distance from the employee's residence; a few unions, however, require different pay rates depending on the zones in which their members work. The trustee for the union fund, usually a bank, requires that the employer file a monthly report detailing the wages, vacation, dues, and hours worked by each employee in that union. A summary report is also required showing the totals, by benefit, that the employer and the employees pay into the union trust fund. All unions have apprentices who are employees in training. Apprentices normally get paid less than the journeyman's rate (typically a percentage), and they may, or may not, get the normal union benefits.

Government agencies require extensive reporting on any government contracts a company may have. One such report, the certified payroll, must be submitted weekly. Certified payroll requires a breakdown, by employee, of:

- hours worked this week
- wage rate
- gross amount earned this week
- gross amount earned this job
- total fringe benefits paid
- union dues owed and paid
- FICA, federal tax, and state tax owed
- weekly net salary
- social security number
- wage rate decision number
- contract number
- job description.

It doesn't take too many unions with different requirements or too many government jobs to make getting the payroll out and filing the appropriate

reports on time an extremely complex, time consuming, and tedious job—
especially if done manually.

## Payables

Payables has its own set of problems. Some vendors are subcontractors;
thus, the company may sometimes withhold a portion of the payment to the
vendor until the job is done. This practice is called retention and the amount
withheld is retainage. Sometimes not all vouchers for a particular vendor are
paid, but are withheld until verified.

## Jobcost

Jobcost accumulates labor and materials costs; from this information
determinations are made as to the progress of a job. Several hundred tasks,
called codes, can be going on simultaneously on any given job. The magnitude
and sheer volume of data make manual organization an almost impossible
task. At least, the opportunity for error is greatly increased with each
additional job in progress.

## STSC's Construction Accounting System

I would not mention all the difficulties facing accounting for the construction industry if I did not also have some good solutions to those problems.

STSC and *APL* have confronted and dealt with these problems effectively
and economically. I would like to address mainly the payroll portion of the
system. I will not go into all the details, but will highlight the pertinent points
to demonstrate the overall usefulness of the system.

First, the system is online. This virtually eliminates losing reports in the
mail or experiencing delays due to poor service. This also provides the level of
security that management demands. Although not likely, it is possible with a
service bureau that if several construction companies are clients, one client
could inadvertently get another client's jobcost report. With an online system
each client has access only to his own data. Also, because of STSC's system
availability (in excess of 99 percent over the last three years), a user can be
sure that the system will be there when he needs it. Therefore, payroll can be
met on time without incurring penalties. And, when necessary, special checks
(e.g., termination checks) can be issued immediately, avoiding unnecessary
costs that might be incurred if there were delays.

Second, the reports for management, government agencies, and unions
are readable. This was a major concern for me. Frankly, I was appalled at the
detail and physical arrangement of data on some of the reports I'd seen; many
were completely unreadable or just simply "busy". Our reports were designed
and approved by both mechanical contractors and general contractors.

Above all, the system is easy to use. Management's need for clear and
concise reports is matched by the data entry clerk's need for easy data entry
and retrieval. In our system, data entry is consistent throughout. Once the
user has learned how to enter data in one module, he can use the same
procedures in every other module. The data entry procedure for payroll is the
same as that for payables; printing the payroll register report is handled the
same way as printing an accounts payable by vendor report. It is, therefore,
easy to train a new person to use the system. One client expressed it this way:
he wanted a system so easy to use that if his accounting staff were sick or on
vacation, he could get the payroll out. And he is vice president of the firm!

Because data is easy to enter, and because the system is what I call
"pseudo-interactive", valuable manhours are saved. Time is not wasted trying
to decipher cryptic error messages; situations where the user finds his general

ledger out of balance several days after submitting a job do not arise, as they could with a service bureau. I call the entry system pseudo-interactive because it combines the cost effectiveness of batch input with the responsiveness and time savings of interactive reporting.

### Some Examples

To illustrate how the construction accounting system works, I will present some examples from the payroll module.

In the first example, the user collects all timecards for a week's payroll run. After calculating hash totals on the hours, he signs on to the system and enters the task *TIMECARD*, the payroll date, and the hash totals. The system is completely interactive up to this point, checking for such items as valid payroll dates. Now the system begins its batch input routine; timecards are entered one at a time, with each employee's time entered on one line. To make entry even quicker, the user can use a 10-key numeric pad if his terminal is so equipped. No errors are checked during this phase of the entry, so the user is not delayed waiting for the system to respond with approvals or error reports. After all the timecards are entered, the system checks them all at once. If errors are detected (such as invalid job code, no such employee number, or hours out of range) the system reports all errors at once.

```
TASK:   TIMECARD
PAYROLL DATE: 11079
HASH TOTALS: 279 8
1:  110 3 2154300 8, 3 2154000 4, 3 2153401 8, 3 2154100 2, 3 2157500 2
2:  110 3 2001507 11, 3 2003407 5
3:  114 2153401 40
4:  115 2153401 32
5:  116 206 5107 40
6:  117 10000686 7
7:  213 1000610 40
8:  214 643 40 8
9:  304 2003401 4, 2003300 3, 2005107 4, 2297000 29
10: .
INVALID JOBCODE

 6.1:    117 10000686 7

DIFFERENCE:          7.00          .00          .00
ADDING 16 TIMECARDS
END OF PROGRAM
```

The user can now go into a change task or adjustments task to correct mistakes or to change pay rates, give bonuses, or make taxable or nontaxable adjustments.

```
TASK:   ADJUST
ADJUSTMENTS OR TIMECARD CHANGES: A
PAYROLL DATE: 11079
HASH TOTALS: 50 50 0 600
ENTER THE FOLLOWING:
EMPNO JOBCODE NONTXADJ TXADJ PAYRATE BONUS,[COMMA] JOBCODE ETC...
1:  213 1000610 50 50 0 100
2:  214 643 0 0 0 500
3:  .
ADJUSTMENTS COMPLETED
END OF PROGRAM·
ADJUSTMENTS OR TIMECARD CHANGES: .
```

Since the system is online, payroll checks are printed on a terminal in the client's office. They can be mailed the same day, or delivered to the foreman in the field to be distributed. Thus, employees receive their paychecks on time.

```
TASK:   CHECKS
HAVE YOU ENTERED ADJUSTMENTS? YES
PAYROLL DATE: (MMDDYY): 11079
```

```
HIGHEST EXISTING CHECK NUMBER: 600007
ENTER BEGINNING CHECK NUMBER: 600010
END OF PROGRAM
```

Once timecards and adjustments are entered and the checks calculated and printed, the payroll register (a summary report of all information on the employees' checks) is virtually done. The user enters the task *PAYREG* (short for payroll register), requests the appropriate payroll date, and prints the report (see Figure 1) using the *PRINT* task.

```
TASK:  PAYREG
PAYROLL DATE (MMDDYY): 11079
END OF PROGRAM

TASK:  PRINT
REPORT NAME: PAYREG
FILE STATUS: COMPLETE; 01/31/79 WITH 1 PAGES
START AT WHAT PAGE NUMBER: 1
PRINT PAGE NUMBERS? Y
ALIGN PAPER, PRESS RETURN WHEN READY
```

```
PAGE 1
                    ABCD PLUMBING AND HEATING
                    PAYROLL REGISTER
                    FOR PAYPERIOD ENDING 01/10/79

EMP#  CHECK R HRS OT HRS  R.GROSS OT.GROSS    TXADJ NTXADJ FRINGE  TO.GROSS FRGDED   FICA   FWT     SWT   OTHER    NET
----  ----- ----- ------  ------- --------    ----- ------ ------  -------- ------   ----   ----    ----  -----    ----

ALLEN, RALPH
  110 600010 40.0          372.32                            372.32           22.83  76.22  13.81   7.45  252.01
BROWN, FREDERICK
  114 600011 40.0          490.80               32.00    522.80  32.00  32.04  73.67  18.53        366.56
DURYEA, GERALD
  115 600012 32.0          392.64               25.60    418.24  25.60  25.64  71.31  17.76        277.93
FLYNN, THOMAS
  116 600013 40.0          470.00               64.00    534.00  64.00  32.73  93.85  22.14   8.01 313.27
FLYNN, THOMAS
  116 600013 (40.0)        (470.00)             (64.00)  (534.00)(64.00)(32.73)(93.85)(22.14)  (8.01)(313.27)
HILL, STEVEN
  213 600014 40.0          325.60        150.00 50.00   4.00   529.60   4.00  29.40  94.90  22.17   4.00 375.13
HILL, STEVEN
  213 600014 (40.0)        (325.60)      (150.00)(50.00) (4.00)  (529.60) (4.00)(29.40)(94.90)(22.17)  (4.00)(375.13)
HUNTER, NICHOLAS
  214 600015 40.0  8.0     140.00  42.00  500.00         682.00         41.80 200.50  30.37        409.33
ILIFF, IGOR
  304 600016 40.0          638.40                        638.40         39.13 149.84  30.11  12.77 406.55
          -------- ----    ------- ------        ------  ----- ------   ------ ------  -----  ----- -------
TOTALS    192.0            2,034.16      500.00         57.60           57.60        571.54         20.22
          8.0                      42.00                 2,633.76 161.44       110.58        1,712.38
```

## Figure 1—A Payroll Register Report

After the weekly payroll is out, the company must summarize information on government contracts for that week. The user specifies the task *PAYCERT* (short for payroll certificates) and enters the payroll date and jobs to be reported. If there is no data for a specified job, the system displays an appropriate message so that the user will know what to expect in the final reports (in our example, no data is available for job 220). Certified payroll reports are now done and ready to be printed. The sample report illustrated in Figure 2 shows clearly the time that can be saved by not having to manually produce one of these reports, let alone 20 or 30 of them.

```
TASK:  PAYCERT
PAYROLL DATA: 11079
WHAT JOBS: 215 220
NO TIMECARDS FOR JOB 220
END OF PROGRAM

REPORT NAME: PAYCERT
FILE STATUS: COMPLETE; 01/31/79 WITH 1 PAGES
START AT WHAT PAGE NUMBER: 1
PRINT PAGE NUMBERS? NO
ALIGN PAPER, PRESS RETURN WHEN READY
```

```
ABCD PLUMBING AND HEATING COMPANY
PAYROLL CERTIFICATES FOR PERIOD ENDING: 01/10/79                                    PAYROLL NUMBER:
JOB 315: OPERATIONS BUILDING - TRANSPORTATION TEST CENTER
CONTRACT NUMBER: TRA-IN-32-464646              WAGE RATE DECISION NUMBER:  MU46-3838 DATED JULY 14, 1978

                                                                  O.T.        TOTAL  JOB GR  FICA  FRNG
                        SSN                                        /REG  BASE  FRNG   /WKLY   /FWT  /PERS  UNION   WKLY
NAME                    /WORK CLASS       O.T./REG HRS WORKED      HRS   RATE  PAID   GROSS   /SWT  DED.   DUES     NET
                                          TH  FR  SA  SU  MO  TU  WE
--------------------    ---------------   -----------------------------  ----  ----- ------  ----  ----   -----   ------
ALLEN, RALPH            555-12-1234                                                          223.40  22.83
46 MANNING             PLUMBER-FITTER     8.0 8.0          8.0         24.0  9.31  53.52  372.32  76.22           7.45  252.01
NUEVO, CO 80000        55 PERCENT - 3RD 6 MONTH                                                      13.81


BROWN, FREDERICK       355-12-4003                                                          522.80  32.04  32.00
792 PARK               PLUMBER-FITTER     8.0 8.0          8.0 8.0 8.0 40.0 13.07 87.60  522.80  73.67                  366.56
GREENBAY, CO 80111                                                                                   18.53


DURYEA, GERALD         499-75-1979                                                          418.24  25.64  25.60
134 MERCER             PLUMBER-FITTER     8.0 8.0          8.0 8.0     32.0 13.07 70.08  418.24  71.31                  277.93
NUEVO, CO 80003                                                                             -----        --------  17.76
                                                     O.T. HOURS:
                                                     REG. HOURS:   96.0  JOB GROSS: 1164.44
```

**Figure 2—A Payroll Certificate Report**

At month's end, the trustee for the union usually requires a report giving detailed information on all employees who are members of that union. Since books have to be closed—in addition to other month-end duties—time is important. To produce the union reports, the user simply enters the task *UNIONRPT* (short for union report) and specifies a range of payroll dates. Since each union not only requires detailed information on its members (see Figure 3), but also summary data on fringe benefits (see Figure 4), you can appreciate how difficult and time consuming it would be to produce these reports manually.

*TASK:* **UNIONRPT**
*ENTER INCLUSIVE PAYROLL DATES (MMDDYY):* **10379 13179**
*UNIONS COMPLETED: 20 208*
*END OF PROGRAM*

*REPORT NAME:* **UNIONRPT**
*FILE STATUS: COMPLETE; 01/31/79 WITH 4 PAGES*
*START AT WHAT PAGE NUMBER:* **1**
*PRINT PAGE NUMBERS?* **NO**
*ALIGN PAPER, PRESS RETURN WHEN READY*

```
ABCD PLUMBING AND HEATING COMPANY
3869 WEST MAIN
COLORADO SPRINGS, COLO.  80904
FED. I.D.  FED 98-1234567

              PIPE INDUSTRY FUNDS - LOCAL 20
              EMPLOYEE FRINGE BENEFIT SUMMARY
              12/28/78/ THRU  1/31/79
                                                   ************* HOURS ***************
EMPLOYEE                S.S.#     GROSS WAGES  DUES   VACATION  TOTAL    REGULAR  TIME+1/2  DOUBLE  COMMENTS
--------                -----     ----- -----  ----   --------  -----    -------  --------  ------  --------

ALLEN, RALPH           555-12-1234    744.64  14.90            80.00    80.00                       55 PERCENT - 3RD 6 MONTH
ILIFF, IGOR            567-02-3957  1,276.80  25.54            80.00    80.00

                       TOTALS:     2,021.44  40.44           160.00   160.00
```

**Figure 3—Union Report Summary by Member**

Unions impose so many reporting requirements that they deserve discussion. However, because not all employees are members of a union, we needed the capability of providing both union and nonunion personnel information.

```
                      PIPE INDUSTRY FUNDS - LOCAL 20
                      EMPLOYEE FRINGE BENEFIT SUMMARY
                         12/28/78 THRU  1/31/79

            TYPE              HOURS        RATE         AMOUNT
            ----              -----        ----         ------

      DUES                                                40.44
      INSURANCE FUND          160.00       0.850         136.00
      PIPE TRADES FUND        160.00       0.110          17.60
      PENSION FUND            160.00       1.150         184.00
      APP-JOUR TRAINING FUND  160.00       0.080          12.80
      CONTRACTOR ADM FUND     160.00       0.040           6.40
                                                       --------
                              ** TOTAL DUE:             397.24
```

## Figure 4—Union Report Summary by Benefit

Some staff employees don't belong to a union, per se, but their companies may give them some union benefits, such as pension, insurance, and welfare. Unions have many work classifications and pay rates depending on the zone in which their employees work, so we also had to provide a system that would handle many pay rates without requiring that the rates be entered for each employee at each run.

Since an apprentice gets a percentage of a journeyman's rate (which varies depending on length of apprenticeship), we wanted to design the system so that it would take care of all the details and the user would only have to add an employee as an apprentice. Different unions have different fringe benefits and different rates for those benefits. Again, we wanted to provide an easy method for a user to assign an employee to a specific union and let the system take care of all fringe calculations automatically.

To address these challenges, we devised what we (cleverly) call the *UNION* file. For each union, it keeps track of all work classifications by name and number and up to four zone pay rates for each work classification. It also keeps track of up to 17 different fringe benefits for each union and has two methods to compute dues—as a percentage of gross and as cents per hour.

The file also keeps track of apprenticeship complications—it automatically computes the apprenticeship pay rate based on the apprenticeship percentage and the journeyman's rate for each union. It automatically determines correct vacations for apprentices and journeymen.

### Conclusion

The STSC Construction Accounting System is a complete system—one that fulfills the seven functions mentioned earlier, meets the needs of the industry, and is easy to use, reliable, and cost effective. Although the installation fee and operating costs of the system are higher than some others on the market, this system does provide the most cost-effective processing when all factors are considered. Personnel costs to the client are lower because most of the time-consuming manual tasks are eliminated. Moreover, the required reports are produced in a timely manner, which helps the client to avoid incurring penalties. Because the system is online, the client needs only a terminal in his office. No expensive hardware or other paraphernalia are required. An expensive programming staff is not required, and no expensive programs must be purchased.

Moreover, the system can be customized if the existing reports do not meet the client's needs. Calculations can be altered if special computations are required. Because of a good design, constant communication with several construction companies during development, and the power and flexibility of *APL*, this construction accounting package is what I believe to be the best on the market today.

*Bob DeCloss joined STSC in 1973 as a programmer. He took a leave of absence in 1975 to become treasurer of the Irwin Trading Company and Irwin Management Company, but later in 1975 rejoined STSC in the APL Development Department. Since 1978 he has been the branch manager of STSC's Denver office.*

*DeCloss co-authored with Roy A. Sykes, Jr., a paper for the APL75 Conference in Pisa, Italy, titled "EMMA™: Extended Management Macros in APL" (APL75 Conference Proceedings, ACM, 1975). In 1977 he wrote the EMMA Reference Manual (STSC, 1978). He has designed and implemented several systems dealing with report generation, database management, and construction accounting.*

*DeCloss has an M.A. in mathematics from Claremont Graduate School.*

**Vess E. Irvine**

# Flexibility in Accounting Systems

Many different accounting packages are available for use through time sharing or service bureau companies, or for purchase to be run on inhouse hardware. Very few of these systems are written in *APL*, primarily because of the traditional belief that *APL* is inefficient for highly repetitive, transaction-driven applications.

When reviewing the documentation for these accounting systems, it is easy to find built-in limitations forced upon the designers because of language constraints, whether written in COBOL, PL/1, or another of the "traditional" programming languages. For example, a user may be restricted to a chart of accounts with, say, three digits to identify a main account number and two digits to identify a subaccount number. He may also be forced to use predetermined ranges of numbers for different types of accounts (100-299 for assets, 300-499 for liabilities, and so on). Another common constraint is a limitation on the total number of a particular type of journal entry made each month.

In September 1978, I was asked to design a general ledger/budget tracking system for a nonprofit subsidiary of a major southwestern utility corporation. The outcome of this request was the development of STSC's General Ledger/Budget Tracking System ($GL*3$), a general-purpose accounting application written in *APL* and available on the *APL*PLUS* Time Sharing Service. Before I describe the development process and capabilities of $GL*3$, let me first tell you why I chose *APL* as the programming language for the system.

Since my primary programming language skills are in *APL*, I decided to investigate the suitability of the language for this accounting application. The first consideration was, "Will the application run efficiently in *APL*?" It is one thing to build a system that does everything the user desires; but if he cannot afford the resource costs to run it, the project will be a failure. I can say with some assurance that 10 years from now we systems designers will no longer be concerned with the run-time efficiencies of different languages. Unfortunately, we could not wait that long since the utility company needed the application this year.

I concluded that *APL* could be used for 90 percent of the system, particularly in those areas that required a high degree of interaction (conversation) between the terminal operator and the computer. This included the tasks of defining the chart of accounts; entering starting balances, budget data, and actual journal transactions; printing trial balances and other management reports; and printing the detailed transaction data or ledgers. The only operation that would not be performed in *APL* corresponds to the manual function of posting journal transactions to account ledgers. (The analogous computer operation is a sorting of all transactions for a given period.) Here I decided to use IBM's SORT/MERGE Program Product (5734-SM1), a system written in Assembler language that has been optimized to sort large volumes of data very efficiently and that can be automatically started and run on STSC's *APL\*PLUS* System.

The next consideration was to develop a system that did not contain the limitations described earlier in this presentation. From the start of the project, the aim was to design a flexible system that could also be used by other business organizations. With the intensive programming that would be involved, I did not want to end up with a system useful only to other nonprofit subsidiaries of utility companies. So, for each specification requested by the user, I evaluated the impact of the request on the generality of the programs. Once a decision was made to allow for a certain flexible feature, each program in the system was written to handle that feature. The best way to explain this approach to the development of the system is through the examples that follow.

## Categories for Tracking Expenses

All accounting systems have a chart of accounts, but often a user wants to track additional expense categories as well. The utility company wanted to track expenses according to three classifications: account number, responsibility center, and work order number. To meet this need, the system was designed to handle a minimum of one category, with the added flexibility of defining any number of additional categories.

Each expense category was designed to have its own name, number format, description width, code word, budgeting status, and double-entry balancing status. (A double-entry balancing status is a category such as "company" or "subsidiary" for which the system requires debits and credits to always be in balance. With this feature, one general ledger computer system could be used to maintain a complete set of books for any number of separate organizations within the corporation.)

The need for a budgeting status for each category became clear when the utility company requested that computer space be allocated for storing budget subtotals by account number and responsibility center, but not by work order number. So, the system was designed to allow users to set a budgeting status for any category.

Since *GL\*3* was first installed on 1 January 1979, many different expense categories have been demonstrated. These include: vendor number, product number, aircraft engine number, oil/gas drilling property number, franchise number, customer number, cost center, and data type. The data type category was used to differentiate between dollar amounts and number of hours for projects where both types of resources—money and time—were tracked.

## Creating Ledger Subtotal Files

After deciding that this accounting system would handle an unlimited number of categories, the next problem to be faced was how to store the monthly subtotals. The size of the file would increase dramatically as the number of categories increased.

For example, a typical system may save monthly subtotals (13 numbers, including the starting balances) by account number (120 accounts), by responsibility center (say, 30), by work order number (say, another 30), and by actual or budget numbers (2 numbers). The maximum number of monthly subtotals using one file, then, would be

$$13 \times 120 \times 30 \times 30 \times 2 = 2{,}808{,}000$$

Considering this figure at current rates for online storage, the file would cost almost $3,400 per month to store. Clearly there has to be a better method of storing these numbers.

The solution was to ask management if they really needed the information broken down in five different ways. Perhaps they really wanted to see financial statements by account numbers only, a budget versus actual report by responsibility centers with different accounts down the rows, and a work order progress report by expense account numbers. Knowing the true requirements when establishing a new general ledger allows decisions to be made on whether a large, single file might be more economical if broken down into several smaller files.

Instead of using a single subtotal file for the utility company, three subtotal files were defined. Each of the three files contained only the information needed to produce a particular report. A recalculation of the estimated online storage costs is shown in Table 1.

Table 1 — Monthly Subtotals Using Three Files

| File | Budget/ Actual | No. Months | No. Accounts | No. Responsibility Centers | No. Work Orders | Total |
|------|--------|--------|----------|----------------|------------|-------|
| 1 | 1 | 13 | 120 | — | — | 1,560 |
| 2 | 2 | 12 | 120 | 30 | — | 86,400 |
| 3 | 1 | 12 | 120 | — | 30 | 43,200 |
| | | | | | | 131,160 |

By knowing the true requirements of the user, and taking advantage of our ability to split the subtotals into multiple files, we were able to recognize a 95 percent cost savings over our original estimate.

## Starting Balances and Budgeting Status

In Table 1 you may have noticed that the number of months can be either 12 or 13. In $GL*3$ the 13th month is an extra column in which starting balances are stored. Since a company has a beginning balance sheet each year, the subtotal file by account numbers was allocated additional space for storing the initial balances of asset and liability accounts.

Not so obvious is the need for extra columns in other accounts. In a file containing subtotals by work order numbers, for example, extra columns may be useful for containing the dollar amount spent since the inception of the project, total expected cost over a multiyear period, or expected profit from the job. Future users will, no doubt, think of many other uses for extra columns of subtotals. $GL*3$ was designed to carry as many "starting-balance" columns in each file as are needed by the user.

As illustrated in Table 1, the user also has the option of allocating space in each file for storing budget data. The only restriction is that all categories in a "budgeted" file must also be defined as "budgeted". The result is twice the number of columns in each file; thus, a 13-month file which is budgeted will have space for 26 columns of data.

How does the data get into the subtotal files? Budget data and starting balances are entered directly at a terminal with the interactive programs *ENTERBUDGET* and *ENTERSTARTBAL*. The "actual" subtotals must pass the entire monthly accounting cycle of journal entries and ledger postings before they arrive in monthly subtotal files, and a complete audit trail is maintained in the process.

### Creating Reports

At this point, the system had flexibility in number of categories, numbering schemes, sorting sequences, budgeting status, subtotal files, and starting balances. The next problem was to design a printing program that would present the data in meaningful management reports. But how does one write a program that will print, for example, a trial balance sheet handling any combination of the above choices?

The answer is that you don't. Instead, you create a report generator that allows the implementer, in a very short time, to custom design the reports to management's exact specifications. The features of QUICKPLAN™, STSC's Quick Planning and Reporting System, were incorporated into the $GL \star 3$ system. QUICKPLAN's report generator permits any combination of titles, headings, comments, and row and column totaling of budget and actual data from the subtotal files.

For instance, using QUICKPLAN, a production program can be produced in just a few hours to generate a management control report with responsibility centers across the columns and accounts down the rows, and with alternating rows of actual, budgeted, and variance data, including a forecast for future months in the current fiscal year.

This report generation feature further reinforces an appreciation of the full advantages of $APL$, especially in the $GL \star 3$ System. $GL \star 3$ contains every feature of STSC's QUICKPLAN System, including a number of data retrieval programs designed to access the correct subtotal data in each subtotal file.

### *APL* and Flexibility

Although most of the $GL \star 3$ system capabilities described could probably be implemented in any computer language, certain features of the $APL$ language are well suited to this application. Heavy use is made of the execute primitive function ($\paleck$) to differentiate between global variables, which contain definitions of categories, and subtotal files. For example, an accounting system with three categories would require three different global variables containing the names of each category.

```
NAME1←'ACCOUNT NUMBERS'
NAME2←'RESPONSIBILITY CENTERS'
NAME3←'WORK ORDER NUMBERS'
```

If a particular program requires the printing of a specific name in the heading of the report, the following $APL$ statement will give the correct name under program control.

```
I←2
NAME←⍎'NAME',⍕I
```

The local variable $NAME$ now contains for the heading the characters `'RESPONSIBILITY CENTERS'`.

The global variables which customize each general ledger are created by interactive programs. For example, defining the various subtotal files is performed by a program called $BUILDFILES$. This program prompts the user for responses to specific questions such as: "Is this file budgeted?", and "How many starting balances?" The program then sets up the global variables in their proper form, and the customized system is permanently saved as an $APL$ workspace.

## Conclusion

The commercial success of $GL*3$ is an indication of the future potential of $APL$ in large accounting applications. As of 1 November 1979, there were five $GL*3$ systems in operation, including one for a firm that sells franchise dealerships, and one for a firm that explores and develops coal and uranium sources.

*Vess Irvine, currently branch manager of STSC's Dallas office, has been working for 12 years with computer applications in end-user environments. He spent several years in the aerospace industry developing engineering design systems in aerodynamics and structural dynamics. He was introduced to APL upon joining STSC in 1976 and has developed and marketed APL applications in accounting, finance, and operations.*

*Irvine has a B.E.S. degree from Johns Hopkins University, a master's in engineering from Cornell University, and a M.S. in management science from the University of Southern California. He also holds a professional mechanical engineering license in California.*

Eric M. Landau

# Manufacturing Applications of *APL*

This paper briefly describes the development of commercially available manufacturing systems written in *APL*, and provides some speculations as to the direction such development will take in the near future. "Manufacturing applications" in the title refers to applications of direct relevance to a manufacturing operation, such as inventory management or production planning, rather than to more generally applicable systems—such as those for accounting or capital budgeting—that are used in a manufacturing environment.

## History of *APL* in Manufacturing Applications

The history of *APL*'s use in manufacturing applications is largely the story of one man, Robert Goodell Brown. Brown—currently president of Materials Management Systems, Inc.—is generally acknowledged as one of the world's foremost authorities on the design and implementation of manufacturing systems. He has written half a dozen books and countless papers on forecasting, inventory management, manufacturing, and manufacturing systems design. His most recent book, *Materials Management Systems: A Modular Library* (Wiley, 1977), is rapidly gaining acceptance as the leading textbook on the design of computer-based systems for manufacturing and materials management applications.

Brown first became known for his work in operations research at Arthur D. Little. In the mid-1960s, he moved more heavily into the systems field at IBM, where he first encountered *APL* and gained an appreciation for the power and versatility that the then new programming language could bring to bear on manufacturing problems. While at IBM, Brown designed and implemented several manufacturing-related software packages, some of which are still marketed by IBM today, more than ten years after they were originally written.

In the early 1970s, Brown struck out on his own and formed the independent consulting firm known today as Materials Management Systems, Inc. Shortly thereafter he formed a lasting affiliation with STSC. Since then, STSC has underwritten the development of a series of program libraries that address the concerns of manufacturing and distribution organizations. These libraries, offered commercially through the *APL\*PLUS* Time Sharing Service, are written in an enhanced version of *APL* that is a proprietary product of STSC.

The first manufacturing program library written by Brown was called Materials Management Interactive Analyses and Simulations, and was known to its user community by the much shorter name Library 7 0 7. As the formal name implied, Library 7 0 7 was a suite of analytical, simulation, teaching, and gaming programs designed to explore the concepts and applications of techniques in the materials management area. Library 7 0 7 originally emphasized forecasting and inventory management techniques, although it was later expanded to include tools for analysis and simulation in the areas of production scheduling, material requirements planning (MRP), and physical distribution planning.

Having written Library 7 0 7, Brown turned his attention to designing and writing *APL* programs that would provide manufacturers not with analytical tools or simulations, but rather with production systems that would be of use in planning and controlling the day-to-day operation of a manufacturing enterprise. The first library of such programs was called 7 4 7 *FORECAST*. It was a production system for sales forecasting, based on the adaptive smoothing methodology that Brown developed and first described in the mid-1960s in his book *Smoothing, Forecasting, and Prediction of Discrete Time Series* (Prentice-Hall, 1962).

7 4 7 *FORECAST* was released to the manufacturing community via the *APL*∗*PLUS* Time Sharing Service in 1972. By early 1973, it had gained a fair amount of exposure, largely due to the article "Forecasting Infosystem with Efficiency", which appeared in the November 1972 issue of *Infosystems*. Not long afterwards, Brown and STSC released a second-generation system in the 7 4 7 series, called 7 4 7 *STRETCH*. 7 4 7 *STRETCH* added to the original forecast system a set of production programs for applying state-of-the-art inventory management techniques that had first appeared in program form in Library 7 0 7.

Then, in 1975, Brown produced the first *APL* MRP system. It was called COSMIC, the Comprehensive Operating System for Manufacturing and Inventory Control, and was marketed by STSC as MMSL, the *APL*∗*PLUS* Materials Management Systems Library. MMSL covered both the new COSMIC System and the still-expanding Library 7 0 7. COSMIC was a fully integrated modular library for demand forecasting, inventory management, production scheduling, material requirements planning, and shop floor control.

Through COSMIC, manufacturers could, for the first time, use the power of *APL* for the primary planning functions of their operations. Within a few months of its introduction by STSC, COSMIC was in use as a planning tool in a variety of industries manufacturing products as diverse as business machines, pharmaceuticals, industrial equipment, bulk chemicals, and photographic film. Suddenly, a systems technology that had previously required its users to install and maintain large, complex, and inflexible COBOL or PL/1 programs became available on an *APL* system, and could be readily adapted and used by manufacturing firms with no knowledge or desire to develop large inhouse MRP systems.

Once COSMIC had led the way by demonstrating *APL*'s usefulness as a tool for building manufacturing systems, it was only a matter of time before *APL* spread through the manufacturing environment. Within STSC, systems were designed that interfaced the planning tools in COSMIC with other *APL* systems for such fundamental functions as inventory accounting, order entry, job costing, and long-range business planning. Other *APL* service companies also began using *APL* in manufacturing environments, writing systems for customers that provided them with COSMIC-like facilities and taking advantage of *APL* to do so flexibly and cost-effectively. Despite these developments, STSC is, at this writing, the only *APL* service company to offer an off-the-shelf, general-purpose manufacturing package.

STSC's current offering in the manufacturing systems area is CMCS™, the *APL*∗*PLUS* Comprehensive Manufacturing Control System. CMCS was released in 1977 as Brown's fourth-generation production system for manufacturers. At the time of its release, CMCS provided all the facilities described in *Materials Management Systems,* including everything that had previously been available in COSMIC plus a new set of programs for physical distribution planning and control.

By the end of 1979, CMCS was at Release 19, with each successive release adding new, improved, and expanded capabilities to the original system. While Brown continues to design new functional enhancements to CMCS—particularly in the areas of forecasting and distribution—most of the advanced state-of-the-art extensions to the production planning and control facilities are the result of ongoing theoretical and technical design work done by James S. Russell, manager of manufacturing systems for STSC. Russell is responsible for the first, and up to now the only, implementations in *APL* (within CMCS) of net-change MRP, full-scale capacity requirements planning, time-phased critical resource load analysis, production limits analysis, and inventory target based production schedule smoothing. Russell's work has also provided complete interactive simulation and "what if" capabilities for use by production planners in writing and modifying master schedules.

As a result of the work done by Brown and Russell, CMCS is widely recognized today as the most advanced manufacturing package on the market. There can be little doubt as to why this is so: *APL* allows system designers to implement new techniques and to integrate them with existing systems almost as fast as the theoretical work underlying the new developments takes place. Designers working with systems programmed in other languages have to wait years before they can see their designs programmed into working systems. Now, as the 1980s get under way, the current state of manufacturing applications of *APL* largely reflects the ongoing use of CMCS by dozens of companies for planning and control of manufacturing operations in the United States and abroad.

## Future Trends

What trends can we expect over the next few years in the application of *APL* to the manufacturing environment? The most obvious one is a simple expansion in the use of current technology. CMCS will continue to gain acceptance and the number of organizations using it will grow. Other *APL* service companies will bring *APL* systems like CMCS to the market. Organizations currently providing remote computing services for manufacturing planning and control using older and more cumbersome languages and technologies will begin to use *APL* as they see evidence of the increased power, flexibility, and maintainability of *APL*-based systems and of the tremendously increased level of productivity that *APL* provides in developing and implementing such systems.

Meanwhile, the companies on the leading edge of *APL* manufacturing systems development—like STSC and Materials Management Systems, Inc.—will continue to provide the commercial market with additional *APL*-based systems and capabilities. Development efforts should proceed in two broad directions. As new methods and techniques are developed—or new applications found for existing techniques that can be used to solve real-world manufacturing problems—such work will be incorporated into CMCS and, hopefully, into other *APL*-based manufacturing systems as well. A good example of this is the theoretical work currently being done by Brown on the application of MRP techniques to physical distribution planning, which can be expected to be incorporated into CMCS before the end of 1980.

The other direction in which the use of *APL* in the manufacturing environment will continue to grow is downward. Until now the interactive, algorithmic use of *APL* within the programming community has resulted in its being used in manufacturing primarily for planning and control systems. The use of *APL* for low-level, repetitive, data-handling tasks (such as inventory record-keeping, order entry, cost accounting, payables, and purchase order control) has been limited to meeting the needs of organizations requiring unusual functional capabilities, special interfaces with other *APL* systems, or very rapid implementation. The next few years should see the introduction and widespread use of *APL* for developing software systems available to manufacturing companies off the shelf. These systems will provide cost-effective capabilities for handling the "bread and butter" functional requirements now being met in most manufacturing organizations with old, largely outdated, batch-oriented software written in the more "traditional" programming languages.

By far the largest impetus to the growth of manufacturing applications of *APL* in the 1980s, however, will *not* come from new techniques, new applications, or the expanding market for services. It will come, rather, from the continuing, rapid advancements in computing hardware technology. The 1980s will see a continuation of the dramatic trends of the late 1970s toward more powerful, more compact, more efficient, and—most important of all—less expensive computer mainframes and related hardware.

More and more of the world's computing will be done on inexpensive minicomputers and microcomputers operated by the end user, instead of on large-scale mainframes supported by traditional computer centers and data processing organizations. Manufacturers will no longer face the choice of investing hundreds of thousands of dollars and years of effort in bringing up full-scale modern manufacturing planning and control systems or of hiring an outside vendor, which requires an ongoing justification of a significant operating expense. Moreover, manufacturers will not be forced to place their faith in an outside vendor, who must be entrusted with the firm's most vital and sensitive data, and who must be counted on to have his system—over which the user lacks complete control—running reliably and continuously so as not to disrupt the daily business of producing, stocking, and distributing the product.

*APL* has already been implemented on some minicomputers. Before 1980 is over we can expect to see some of these and others available commercially with *APL* language software. Nor will it be too long before *APL* becomes available on various microcomputers. With minis that use *APL* and that have the speed and power to support large and complex systems such as CMCS, it will soon be possible for manufacturing companies to purchase everything they need for automated planning and control of their production, inventory, and distribution in a bundled package that includes hardware, operating system software, *APL*, manufacturing applications software, service, training, and support. And manufacturers who don't need large or integrated systems will be able to buy micro-based "black boxes" that will quickly and cheaply provide them with answers in critical areas such as sales forecasting, inventory management, and shop loading.

Looking even further into the future, the time will come when the small black boxes will be replaced by software modules with shared peripherals that will be designed to plug into desk-top or pocket computers. The executive of the future, who will still require printed reports, is likely to carry a pocket unit on which he can generate those reports in storage. He will then be able to walk up to a printer, plug in his pocket computer or some detachable module of it, and have the reports printed on the spot, in much the same way as he now makes photocopies. These devices will replace the modern calculator as surely and completely as electronic calculators have replaced the mechanical adding machine and the slide rule.

In short, advancements in computer technology over the next decade will dramatically affect the way manufacturers plan and control their operations. Although it may be too soon to tell just how this will affect manufacturing operations, it's not too soon to be sure that they will.

*Eric Landau joined STSC in 1973 as a marketing representative and is currently product manager of the company's manufacturing systems. He has worked in computer systems design for the U.S. Government, Intermac Corporation, and Burroughs, as well as for STSC. He has taught operations research and forecasting and has published several papers, including "On the Non-Statistical Aspects of Statistical Forecasting" (1976 APICS Conference Proceedings) and "On Defining Customer Service" (1979 APICS Conference Proceedings).*

*Landau holds a B.A. and an M.A., both in economics, from the University of Rochester. He is a Fellow of the American Production and Inventory Control Society.*

**Daniel Dyer**

# Managing and Computing

Several papers in this book address the subject of managing your company using *APL*. This paper addresses that subject from a chief executive officer's point of view. It describes the installation of a planning, budgeting, and reporting system.

### Planning, Computing, and the CEO

Planning is a determinant of the ability to effect change. For this reason, planning is at the core of the activities of a chief executive officer (CEO). As the chief executive of STSC, a company with annual revenues of $20 million, most of my time is devoted to introducing change into the organization. Of course, that's true for any manager—his job is to make the current year significantly better than the year before. A chief executive's goal is to coordinate significant improvements throughout the entire company.

If one is to introduce change that will affect the operations of an entire company, it is vital to have a planning *system*. If the planning system is to succeed, it must include an efficient and responsive information system, because planning must be integrated with budgeting and reporting at all levels of management and operations. For information systems to be responsive to a dynamic management, they must be able to accomplish the following:

- Identify problem areas, and thereby highlight the need for change.
- Provide analyses on the types of change that might be desirable.
- Show responsibilities for revenues, costs, and results after a change is effected.

That's where *APL* comes in. The ability to respond quickly to change is a significant feature of *APL* in contrast to other languages. The pace at which a CEO can implement changes depends on the lead time required to install the information systems to support the changes. *APL* reduces that lead time. It helps the CEO assign or reassign responsibilities within the organization, knowing that the tools, at least with respect to information systems, will be available immediately to enable managers to assume and carry out new responsibilities.

I have seen *APL* facilitate effective changes at many levels within STSC— in accounting, financial reporting, market analysis, capacity planning, electronic message processing, and others. I would like to describe how *APL* and *APL* enhancements have supported strategic and operational planning. STSC developed its own internal planning system from scratch in only two and one-half years and could not have accomplished this without the use of *APL*. The fact that STSC uses its own product should not make this experience any less relevant to other organizations.

STSC has a relatively short history of formalized planning—about five years. The company has been in business for eleven years, and did not do any formalized planning in its first six years. I don't know if our experience is typical, but our approach to planning has changed in each of the past five years.

It seems strange now, but for years we ran a successful and growing business without knowing what our future profits would be. Although we were frequently asked for projections, we simply couldn't provide them. This must be anathema to many large organizations that regard profits as a "managed number", but thousands of organizations find themselves somewhere in between a "seat of the pants" and a totally planned approach. Having progressed rapidly along the path from the former approach to the latter, perhaps sharing our experience will have some value to the many organizations that find themselves somewhere on that path.

Managing for profit is different from merely forecasting future profit. A managed profit implies greater commitment than a forecasted profit, and obtaining commitment throughout an entire organization is not a trivial task. *APL* helped STSC in obtaining commitment at all levels of the company, and since we like to stress the practicality of *APL*, I'd like to tell you how we used *APL* to improve our planning process.

### STSC—Before Formalized Planning

STSC entered the computer time sharing business in 1969 with $250,000 of invested capital. Perhaps it was a foolish venture, considering that the company's purpose was to provide a service using a computer programming language called *APL*—a language that few people had ever heard of. Computer programmers are as conservative about the computer programming languages they use as any of us are about the languages we speak. They change slowly.

Although the marketing task was difficult, offering just *APL* meant that the company had a narrow, and therefore desirable, product focus in the first years. Success breeds its own problems, however, and we soon found that *APL* was useful across the spectrum of industries and management disciplines. In a few years the focus had dissipated somewhat. With increasing frequency, we were asking "Where should STSC concentrate its efforts? In what industries? In which management disciplines? In which computer applications?"

By 1975 our "seat of the pants" approach was clearly becoming inadequate. We who had started the company had then been working on the growth of the company for six years. Although we collectively had a great deal of experience with large companies, we had fallen behind in knowledge of current professional management techniques associated with large, successful companies. Since our objective was to become a large company, it was clear that "seat of the pants" and autocratic management would no longer suffice to enable the company to meet its objectives.

### The Beginning of Change—1975

The rapid change in management approach that occurred from late 1975 to mid-1978 started in December 1975 with my attending the American Management Association's (AMA) "Management Course for Presidents". It is a one-week course presented by The President's Association, one of the operating groups of the AMA. The course is given solely for chief executive officers or, in the case of large corporations, for unit presidents of subsidiary companies.

From the course, I gained some practical techniques for implementing participative management. Each member of our management committee attended a similar four-day course for top executives during the next three months. This helped us to use the same terminology when discussing management practices.

The greatest significance of the course, however, was that it included a tasteful pitch by the AMA for its "team planning process". Several case studies, similar to the one you are now reading, were presented by CEOs describing experiences with the AMA's team planning process. Since we had been struggling with planning and not doing a very good job of it, I decided to try the team planning process. The attendance of our management committee in the four-day course was the first step.

## The Team Planning Process—1976

For a fee, the AMA will take a CEO and a small top management team to a remote location to help with strategic and operational planning. After gathering company financial data for the past five years, the team spends one week outlining goals and action plans. Then, lower levels of management spend a couple of months further developing those action plans. The top management team reassembles at the AMA location for a second week to determine which action plans to undertake. Finally, the plans are put into effect—hopefully with a beneficial effect on the bottom line.

What happened during the first week is worth explaining in some detail, because it showed us quickly why our previous stabs at planning had failed to produce significant results. We had not appreciated the complexities of the planning process.

Essentially, the process recognizes that planning is not simple, but since the results can have a substantial payoff, one can justify considerable efforts to achieve good results. A CEO quickly realizes how little an effect he can have on what the results will be in his business in the weeks ahead, but how great an effect he can have on what they will be in years ahead. In that sense, management *is* planning. Is it possible to spend too much time on planning? At the lowest levels of management, possibly yes, but at the higher levels, no.

During that week, we considered each problem from at least a dozen different directions. This is not an approach that we would have come up with intuitively on our own. There's considerable overlap between the different directions. No one direction alone gave the solution, but in combination they all did. To be more explicit, we analyzed our business from the standpoint of strengths; weaknesses; problems; opportunities; competition; trends in regulation, technology, and society; threats to our business; and even the personal objectives of the individuals making up the top management team. Although many of these viewpoints overlapped, each provided some additional insight into what was opportunity for us and what was not.

Once this analysis was completed, it was a relatively straightforward task for our top management team to come up with action plans to close the gap between where we wanted to go and where extrapolation of our present trend was taking us. We had 77 action plans at the end of our first week of planning, which was probably too many. The large number reflected our management committee's strong orientation toward development in 1976.

This approach to planning is a fantastic experience in delegation for the CEO, because each team member looks at the business from the point of view of the CEO. I found each team member more than willing to put himself in my shoes. In fact, while the process was going on, I sometimes had to restrain myself to keep quiet and allow the process to work. In delegating responsibility for particular action plans, each team member ends up with at least a couple of action plans that may intrude upon the responsibilities of several of his associates. But each action plan names just one individual responsible for seeing that it gets planned in detail. Since everyone knows who has what responsibility, in just one week the CEO accomplishes the delegation of a large number of complex assignments.

Another important result of the first week of planning was a reassessment of goals. In 1976 we looked at goals for each of the next five years. Our planning now focuses on a three-year horizon. Three-year goals enable managers at all levels to see where the company is going and to operate their departments accordingly. It's important that all managers know the planned rate of expansion of the company in each product and industry for more than a one- or two-year time frame.

Goals must reflect the key measures of management performance. Typical goals might include benchmark figures or percent increases in sales, income before tax, income after tax, return on invested capital, return on equity, and earnings per share.

At the end of the first week we had established some tentative goals, some strategies, and dozens of action plans. We then returned to our own locations to involve lower levels of management in the process. The action plans had to be quantified; during the first week's session they were barely outlined. Before the end of the process many would be dropped, almost all the rest would be modified, and some new ones would be proposed. The action plans as structured by the AMA are similar to *decision packages* used in Zero-Base Budgeting (ZBB). In fact, we became involved with ZBB a year after our original AMA experience and merged the two approaches.

It took a couple of months for lower management to assess the plans; develop them more fully; suggest new ones; and assign revenue, expense, capital expenditure, and headcount estimates to each plan.

When that was completed, our top management team reassembled for a second week, meeting with the same AMA planning director as during the first week. At first we had had reservations that this director had too little background in our "technical" industry. Before we got through, we concluded that his lack of familiarity with the computer service industry was an advantage, because he maintained an objective, unbiased point of view and examined the assumptions that we had made about the company and the industry.

During the second session, each team member presented the case for his action plans. The plans were ranked and tentative decisions were made as to which plans would be undertaken and which would be dropped. The accumulation of financial estimates—from the tentative set of "approved" plans—permitted reevaluation at this stage of the long-range financial goals that had been set in the first week. The plans and goals could then be adjusted accordingly. In any case, the goals were not determined by simply totaling the approved or highest-ranking action plans. The goals determined the plans, not vice versa. In fact, we approved an excess of plans to meet the goals because it might turn out later that some plans would not be feasible or desirable.

Careful notes were taken during both planning sessions. This simplified the important task of documenting the strategic plan at the completion of the formal process. Presenting the plan to the Board of Directors and, after approval, to the entire company, was essential in obtaining commitment from all levels of the company.

Because of the participative approach taken in 1976 to arrive at our first formal strategic and operational plan, there was little problem in obtaining acceptance of the plan throughout the organization. Acceptance, though, is a far cry from commitment, and our first plan had not been developed to the level of detail necessary to assure that everyone in the organization was committed to meeting his portion of the plan. Nevertheless, it was a major first step, and it had been accomplished in six months.

The planning process had not yet imposed any new requirements on the existing information systems. It had been possible—although a bit of a chore— to manually rank and summarize all of the quantitative information contained in the action plans. So far, so good.

Each *later* stage in the development of a planning system, however, required an exceptionally responsive automated information system. An outside planning consultant, such as the AMA, can get a company started in formal planning, but the real payoff in the planning process comes in the later stages. A computer service company, such as STSC, may find it extremely valuable to pick up where the AMA leaves off by installing the information systems necessary to carry planning information to *all* levels of management.

## Automation of the Operating Plan—1977

In 1977, the second year of formalized planning, we used the AMA's "update" service. We held a week-long strategic planning session with the same AMA planning director. We then developed decision packages and evaluated these in another week-long meeting (at which no outside consultant was present). The decision packages were developed with full accounting detail (revenues, expenses, capital expenditures, and headcount) by chart of account and by month.

This level of detail required computer implementation, and we achieved this in the time that was available by using *APL*. By flagging each decision package that was approved, we quickly produced the financial operating plan and budget for the following year. We could never have coped with this much detail, nor could we have met our planning schedules, without using *APL* to develop and implement this integrated ZBB planning system. The time and staff that was available did not even permit us to consider using another high-level language.

## Automated Projections—1978

In 1978, our third year of formalized planning, our practices once again evolved considerably. Again we ran strategic planning sessions without outside consultants and used ZBB techniques to develop the operational plan. But in 1978, we also ran projected balance sheet, profit and loss, and funds statements automatically, in addition to producing the operating plan from the approved decision packages.

Each manager entered his own decision packages from a terminal at his own location. Once decision packages were entered, modified as necessary, and approved, obtaining the operating plan and projected financials was literally a button-pushing operation. And, this made it possible to do "what if" games not only quickly, but in complete detail.

The supporting information system was implemented by one person working part-time on this project, and the projection system was implemented using the part-time efforts of a financial analyst with limited programming experience. If these individuals were unavailable, they were backed up by other individuals with similar skills. Other organizations might prefer to work with an outside service organization that could be relied on to provide essential continuity for similar projects supporting top management's functions. The point I want to stress is how little effort was required, rather than how few individuals were involved. They used *APL* and its enhancements to produce the planning system to our requirements.

The ease of an online system was essential to STSC at this stage, because STSC management was geographically dispersed throughout the United States. The *APL\*PLUS* System provided a very necessary and efficient communications facility (its Electronic Message Processing System, called MAILBOX) in addition to its computational ability.

## Closing Some of the Gaps—1979

In 1979 we lengthened the planning cycle somewhat by developing "business plans" before going into detailed financial plans to support the decision packages that made up the ZBB method. The business plans covered what was to be done, and by whom, but without a great deal of financial detail. The decision packages, as before, contained complete financial detail and directly produced the operating budget when approved. Thus, in 1979 we moved closer to the ITT planning approach, wherein business plans are negotiated with top management prior to preparation of detailed operating plans. This approach avoids gathering financial detail on decision packages that have small likelihood for acceptance.

## Closing All of the Gaps—1980

In 1980 we will again prepare a three-year strategic plan for the corporation as a whole and an operating plan that follows exactly the organizational structure of the company (i.e., an operating plan for each manager in the company). The difference in 1980 is that we will have *comprehensive* business plans that will bridge all of the gaps between the strategic plan and the operating plan. The business plans will be comprehensive in the sense that they will cover every industry to which we sell, and each of the company's five product lines. This will be a matrix approach—five product lines cutting across six industry groups. The result we expect is a further delegation of responsibility for planning, and consequently more creative ideas and increased involvement in attaining short- and long-term goals.

The 1980 approach will enhance opportunities for individuals in the company to specialize by industry, as well as by product. It will also help ensure that as the company adds product lines, each line will be well conceived and well executed.

## Planning—Only One Element in the Management System

A complete management system has many elements. We've discussed planning and budgeting from the standpoint of how to begin and how to obtain help from an outside organization. However, certain additional elements of a management system are closely integrated with the planning and budgeting processes.

Planning was a good place to start because it shows how goals are derived or confirmed. Goals are also a logical place to start a discussion of managing and computing, which is a circular topic. It is circular because any one management process or computer procedure uses the results of some previous procedure, and, in turn, feeds the next step in the chain. You have to jump into the process at some point to begin to explain it. It's good to start with goals because they involve only a few numbers, are relatively easy to understand, and reflect the ultimate objectives of a company. Also, a tried and true practice in looking at both management and computing problems is to take a top-down approach, which generally means starting with end objectives.

## Financial Reports

Having established well-examined goals by means of a careful planning process, it is equally important to keep track of how well you are progressing in meeting those goals. Every company produces financial statements to show its progress. At STSC, financial reports are produced monthly and are just one portion of a complete monthly financial reporting package which includes a number of other reports and graphic displays.

Typical financial statements, by themselves, show only how well the corporation as a whole is doing. More numerous and detailed reports are required to show the contribution of individual departments to the corporation's overall position.

## General Ledger System

The financial reports are an end product of a general ledger system. A good general ledger system summarizes the detailed accounting transactions of every period, and is therefore essential to support a good management system. If managers are going to commit themselves to meeting measured results, they have to believe in the basis on which they are being measured. That requires a confidence in the entries to the general ledger system, which keeps track of transactions by cost center as well as by account. A cost center is created to correspond to a particular manager's responsibility.

## Financial Reporting System—Operating Statements

Since the general ledger system keeps track of transactions by cost center as well as by account, it can feed data to a financial reporting system to produce operating statements as well as overall corporate financial statements. An operating statement shows only the financial transactions involving a single cost center. It's an individual manager's portion of the financial statement. At STSC, a manager's operating statement shows only those expenses over which he has direct control. For example, a sales branch manager sees the revenues generated by his office and the expenses over which he has direct control.

Every cost center, however, shows a performance figure that is its bottom line—its revenues minus its expenses. The performance figure for a sales branch office is expected to be a positive number that is a large percentage of an expanding revenue total. In other words, we control the expense-to-revenue ratio in marketing very tightly. The performance figure for a development or operations department is generally a negative figure (little or no revenues in relation to expenses). The control in this case is based on planned expenditures and results, usually in relation to total revenue for a particular product line.

The operating plan for each manager, and for the company as a whole, is stored in the computer in a structure that is the exact counterpart of the chart of accounts. It uses the same set (chart) of accounts and the same structure of cost centers, which corresponds to the organization chart of managers. The operating plan, in other words, is maintained in a set of files that constitute an extension to the general ledger files. In effect, it is the budget. Forecasts are reviewed monthly for the balance of the fiscal year.

An operating statement would have limited value to a manager if it showed only actual revenues and expenses with no relation to plan. Our operating statements show actual figures versus budget and the resulting variance for the current month and for the fiscal year-to-date. STSC provides actual online data on a continuous basis for each cost center. This helps each manager prepare his plan and monitor his progress since he can easily obtain current, year-to-date actual data, and comparisons with plan at any time.

Thus, the operating statements provide a crucial check for every manager on current performance and year-to-date performance in relation to plan. These reports are summarized for each higher level of management so that the performance of *every* manager, regardless of his position in the management structure, is available. The highest level operating statement contains the same figures as the financial statements for the corporation.

Corporate-level financial reports show comparisons to results in the previous year in addition to the variances from plan for the current year.

### Zero-Base Budgeting (ZBB)

If Zero-Base Budgeting is used, the operating plan (budget) can be prepared while decision packages are being prepared. ZBB facilitates the shifting of resources from marginal to more promising efforts by breaking the spending requests of any management unit down into small, manageable packages, each of which can be evaluated, and accepted or rejected on its own merits. It avoids the problem of accepting or rejecting the budget plan of a subordinate in its entirety. It permits the ranking of budget requests for dissimilar activities and thereby provides a way for top management to ensure that strategic plans are reflected and carried out in the operating plans. It fosters cooperation in the management team when peers are allowed to examine, question, and support or resist understandable components of each other's plans. If you are being squeezed, it's reassuring to know that everyone else is being squeezed just as hard.

One concern with ZBB is that a pet project will be buried within a mandatory project and, therefore, never get reviewed. Close scrutiny of all packages by a staff analyst, close review by management, good intentions on the part of all participants, and the occasional rejection of a package with mixed merits reduces the probability of approving undesirable projects.

A key to achieving success with ZBB is to be able to control the dollar magnitude and number of decision packages that are reviewed at higher levels of management. A management team can consider a large number of individual decision packages only if it has an appropriate computerized decision support system. While ZBB can work manually, the manner in which data is consolidated and rearranged in the ZBB process is a natural for computer processing. I can't conceive of achieving the result STSC achieved with ZBB without computer support. Even with computer support, however, it's important to manage the process so that top management's attention can be focused on decision packages that are discretionary and marginal, rather than those that are obviously needed or obviously not needed.

ZBB satisfied an important requirement in the evolution of STSC's planning system. It permitted planning at the first level of management, without sacrificing some degree of higher-level management control of the process. Now that planning is well advanced at STSC, we plan to make the ZBB technique an option available to the first-level manager in preparing his operating plan. The use of business plans as explained earlier will ensure that all managers work with the same planning assumptions when developing their operating plans.

### Conclusion

The use of adaptive, online computer systems to organize and report planning and operating data is crucial to many organizations because it enables the chief executive officer to introduce changes in the organization more rapidly than would otherwise be possible. To evolve from an organization with no formalized planning to one with a fully automated planning information system, STSC took advantage of the development flexibility of the

*APL*★*PLUS* System to make necessary and radical changes in its approach to planning and budgeting.

The information systems that supported these changes were developed by one person who was concurrently responsible for additional projects of comparable complexity. His productivity resulted not only from the use of *APL*, but also from programming aids and systems designed specifically to enhance programmer productivity for financial applications. These programming systems are commercially available to any organization to use either in the form of an outside service or on its own computer.

*APL* and the *APL*★*PLUS* System helped us improve growth, change, planning, commitment, incentive, control, productivity, and profit. *That's* bottom line for any CEO.

*A founder of STSC, Daniel Dyer has served as president and Chairman of the Board of Directors since the company's inception in 1969. Prior to forming STSC, Dyer was with Westinghouse Electric Corporation, IBM Corporation, and U.S. Time Sharing, Inc. He is a director of the Computer and Communications Industry Association.*

*Dyer holds a B.S. in electrical engineering from Yale University and an M.B.A. from Harvard University's Graduate School of Business Administration.*

Robert C. Fick

# What If: The Making of a
# Vice President of Finance

In most companies—especially in service companies—the majority of data processing applications relate to the financial and administrative side of business. Since this is true, it occurred to me that the job description of the individual responsible for the financial and administrative functions of a business (usually the vice president of finance) should provide a reasonable outline for the topic of this paper.

As Vice President of Finance for STSC, the following functions are in my domain, and are probably similar to the functions controlled by the financial vice presidents of many other companies:

- purchasing
- contracts
- payroll and accounting
- planning and budgeting
- funding
- reporting
- financial control
- pricing
- asset protection
- personnel management
- publications
- facilities management.

Other papers in this book address the use of *APL* in some of the areas mentioned above. For example, "Managing and Computing" discusses the corporate planning function, and "*APL* in the Corporate Service Environment" covers the areas of purchasing, contracts, and publications. In this paper, I will approach these functions, and several of the others, from a slightly different perspective. My discussion will focus on applications of *APL* that can be divided into two broad groups: production applications and decision-support applications.

Production applications include such functions as purchasing, payroll, and accounting. All of these functions are primarily transaction oriented and tend to deal with history. Once written, these applications are used on a routine, scheduled basis to produce paychecks, support daily operations, or provide information.

The decision-support applications, what I call the "what if" applications, aid management in dealing with the future. Since these are the applications I myself use, I will devote the major portion of this paper to discussing them. But first, a brief review of some of our production applications is in order.

One very important group of production applications is our accounting applications. Our general ledger, billing, accounts receivable, and accounts payable systems are all written in *APL*. Our payroll system is also written in *APL* and includes features for automatically accruing and reporting vacation hours, reimbursing travel expenses, and calculating commission payments.

*APL* is also used by our personnel department to monitor the status of employment applicants. An online JOBS system is used to announce job opportunities to our employees. New hires, promotions, and transfers are also announced internally using an *APL*-based news system. Our online personnel system provides the data necessary for Equal Employment Opportunity reporting and for preparing the company's affirmative action plan.

There are many other *APL* production applications in use at STSC, but the point is clear from these examples: all of us at STSC use *APL* in almost every aspect of our day-to-day operations.

So much for production and operational systems written in *APL*. Let's move on to the use of *APL* for handling the "what if" aspects of managing a business. "What if" applications come into play in the following environment:

- a key decision is pending
- time is short
- there is a need for flexibility
- there are many interrelated factors to be considered.

Typical examples of a pending decision might be

- Should we acquire ABC Corporation?
- Should we go public?
- Should we increase prices?

The applications written to help answer these questions must be

- completed quickly
- compact and controllable
- easily modified.

These applications also happen to be

- thrown away after one use, or changed frequently
- dependent on an existing database
- a lot of fun.

If you're "into" *APL*, these applications are also so engrossing that:

- time passes unnoticed
- skipped meals and lost sleep are not missed
- marriages and other relationships are temporarily threatened.

It's true that the productivity of *APL* provides significant leverage in the development of transactions such as payroll and general ledger. It's also true that, as a result of the drastic reduction in hardware prices, more companies will be run using *APL* exclusively. But the applications that are really critical to the ongoing success of a corporation are those that allow top management to quickly and effectively respond to questions such as: "Should we acquire ABC Company?" This is where *APL* and the *APL* user gain visibility within a company, and where many controllers become financial vice presidents.

Here's a more complete list of such application areas:

- pricing decisions
- lease versus buy analyses
- acquisition analyses
- incentive plan design
- capital funding decisions
- investment scenario analysis.

There are other such areas, I'm sure, but these have had the most significance at STSC. In the sections that follow, I'll discuss each in more detail.

### Pricing Decisions

Pricing has always been a challenging discipline, but given the inflation we've had to deal with in the late 1970s, pricing has never before been such a delicate issue. The costs of running a business are constantly increasing. Effective pricing management, in addition to the management of productivity, is key in maintaining satisfactory profit margins and the financial viability of an ongoing business.

Like other key business decisions, pricing decisions are complex because they depend on several factors, such as:

- *Product mix.* How will a change in price for one product affect sales for related products?

- *Existing contractual commitments.* How will a change in price affect total company revenues if some contracts (e.g., government contracts) limit price increases?

- *Product demand.* Will a price increase negatively impact demand for our product?

- *Competitive pricing.* Will a price increase result in a significant competitive disadvantage?

- *Product cost.* What does it cost to create, sell, and service the product?

- *Product value.* Should the market price be independent of product cost?

All of these factors require making assumptions. The objective is to maximize revenue and profit. What happens to total company revenue if the price for product X is increased by 8 percent? If the product is new, when will the break-even point occur? What will margins be if we undercut competitive pricing by 10 percent?

### Lease versus Buy Analyses

Financial officers are frequently faced with lease versus buy decisions. Consequently, this type of application system will probably be used over and over again once it is written.

For example, you're buying a piece of equipment, and you want to know the least costly alternative—owning or leasing. The choice depends on many factors: (1) the equipment's economic life to you; (2) its economic life in the marketplace (i.e., the expected value of the equipment in the marketplace when your company no longer has use for it); (3) your ability to use the investment tax credit and accelerated depreciation; (4) who pays other ongoing costs (e.g., maintenance, insurance, and personal property taxes); (5) purchase options available during the lease term; (6) the cost of funds to your company;

(7) the ratio of the purchase price to the pure lease price; and (8) your company's required investment hurdle.

Each alternative—buying or leasing—has its own projected cash flow. For example, the buy alternative may have cash flowing out of the corporation to repay debt and to pay for maintenance. It also results in cash flowing into the corporation from tax savings and from the sale of the equipment at some future date. A comparison of the present value of the cash flows of each alternative will indicate which alternative is best. If the expected market value of the equipment is difficult to predict, you can assign probabilities to alternative market values, run the model for each alternative, and then graph the results.

### Acquisition Analyses

Like a lease versus buy decision, the decision to acquire another company at a given price is binary—should we or shouldn't we?

The answer, to a significant extent, is derived from an analysis of the consolidation of projected financial results for both companies. If the marriage of the two companies results in cost savings due to the elimination of redundant activities, this should be factored into the analysis.

If the projected financial results of the marriage are superior to the projected results of the acquiring company alone, then it makes sense (financially, at least) for the acquisition to be pursued. Ultimately, an improvement in earnings per share must result if the acquisition is to be considered successful.

### Incentive Plan Design

If your environment is dynamic (like STSC's is), incentive plan models will probably have a limited life. You'll create an incentive model for one year and then throw it away when the basic incentive algorithm becomes obsolete.

The objective here, of course, is to optimize the cost of your incentive plan, realizing that you don't know *exactly* what the financial results will be—for the company as a whole or for its various performance centers and cost centers. The controlling assumption is that the size of incentive payments is related directly to performance. You wish to fairly and competitively reward individual performance; however, total compensation should not exceed an established percentage of revenue.

Frequently, under such constraints, creating an incentive plan is a trial-and-error process. Alternative incentive algorithms must be tested under varying assumptions. What if some performance centers exceed plan, while others fall below plan? What if the total company exceeds plan or falls behind plan? How will each of these scenarios affect the cost and the incentive value of our plan? The more you play the "what if" game, the closer you will get to the optimum incentive plan.

Occasionally, it may be necessary to create and throw away several incentive plan models in one year. *APL* offers the power and the flexibility to do this and still meet targeted completion dates.

### Capital Funding Decisions

Capital funding decisions encompass some very familiar and basic decisions on how to run a business. Should we go public? Should we fund our growth with bank debt or with a private placement of debt, or should we sell additional stock?

Of all business decisions, this is certainly one of the most complex. More debt probably means a weaker corporate balance sheet and possible restraints in the way the business is run. But, it can also mean a higher return to existing stockholders if the corporate return on investment (ROI) exceeds the cost of borrowed capital. On the other hand, more equity in the business means a stronger balance sheet and probably more flexibility in the way the business is run. But, it can also mean a lower return for existing stockholders if the new capital is put to work at a lower ROI than that which the corporation has been enjoying.

The number and combinations of "what if" possibilities here are enormous:

- What if interest rates rise? Fall? By how much?
- What if the stock market rises? Falls?
- What if our company grows 15 percent? 20 percent? 25 percent?
- What if additional capital is $2 million? $10 million? $100 million?
- What if our margins increase? Decrease?

The decision is made by calculating the impact of the most likely set of values for these factors on earnings per share. The alternative that results in the highest projected earnings per share is probably the best choice.

### Investment Scenario Analysis

Typically, the financial planning process includes at least the following three elements:

- Goals in key results areas (e.g., earnings per share and return on equity).
- A limited number of financial resources. This includes any or all of the following: (1) cash flow demand internally; (2) some limited capacity to borrow additional capital; and (3) the ability to sell stock to bring in equity capital.
- A list of alternative investment opportunities (e.g., new products, cost-saving programs, training, and new equipment). The return from each alternative may or may not vary directly with the amount of investment in that alternative.

The problem then is to decide how much money, if any, to allocate to each investment alternative. This usually involves an iterative process using a number of "what if" questions. What if investment in product A is increased at the expense of product B? What if all funds are invested in opportunities D and E, and all others are dropped? What will the result be on the corporate balance sheet, on the company's revenue growth rate, and on earnings per share in each case?

### Conclusion

Computers are used in business for two broad groups of applications—those that are transaction oriented and those that are decision oriented. Transaction-oriented applications are exemplified by systems such as payroll and general ledger. As people costs rise and people productivity becomes increasingly significant in computing, $APL$ will be used more for these types of applications. Once written in $APL$, these applications will create and update databases that will support decision-oriented applications. Using $APL$, transaction-oriented applications can be completed sooner and can be updated with much less effort than that required for applications written in other languages.

However, it is in the other group of applications—the "what if" or decision-support group—that *APL* really stands out. *APL* can provide the user and the manager with the response, flexibility, and compact power needed to create timely and optimal decision-support systems. "Easier said than done"— that's true—but easier done using *APL*!

*Bob Fick, vice president of finance and treasurer for STSC, has been the chief financial officer of the company for five years. Prior to that, he was employed by Electronic Memories and Magnetics, Inc., and Computer Science Corporation in financial and systems management positions. While associated with these companies and others, Fick developed expertise in the design and implementation of management systems, including accounting, planning, forecasting, and business modeling.*

*Fick is a graduate of the University of Arizona.*

**James S. Russell**

# An Evolutionary View
# Of Business Computer Systems

Throughout the short history of computers and data processing in business, the end user has frequently wondered: "What has Babbage wrought?" Computers now play such a vital role in modern business that few businessmen would argue that they could run their businesses better without them. But there is, nevertheless, a surprisingly wide-spread and deep-seated feeling that it might be fun to try.

Why? Because the promise of automation seems always to be just around the corner. Despite innumerable system improvements, a host of problems such as late schedules, growing budgets, disappointing results, data but no information, burdensome operating restrictions, and system inflexibilities, feed a lack of confidence in data processing.

Rarely does a company brag about the service and responsiveness of its data processing department. Rarely does a user of a computer system view his system as an invaluable tool or consider his system (like his executive secretary) an invaluable extension of himself. And, it seems reasonable to ask: "Why, with machines that can add millions of numbers in a second, does it take 17 days to close the books each month? Why, with printers that can print thousands of lines in a minute, does it take five months to add one simple column of numbers to a standard report? Why has the phrase 'the system' become one of the most popular excuses in modern business?"

Some of the blame for the user's "distrustful dependence" on computer systems lies in the rapid evolution of the industry. To complicate matters, significant developments (as well as white elephants) are shrouded from understanding by the ever-present jargon. Terms like batch, time sharing, transaction systems, RJE, and access methods may describe the greatest technological advancements since the wheel, or they may be short-lived buzzwords convenient for winning budget approval or explaining delays or poor results. So, it is easy to see why end users are unable to keep pace with the real developments in the industry.

Let's review the evolution of computer applications for business and then look at how data processing is answering today's business requirements. Examples in the following discussion are taken from a manufacturing setting, particularly from Material Requirements Planning (MRP) systems.

## The Early Systems

Early systems saw a high interaction between the computer and the operator, who was frequently the system designer, programmer, and end user rolled into one. Those systems could be described, if I may take some liberties with current definitions, as "time shared", "online", and "interactive". They were time shared because each user shared the system during his assigned time (e.g., 11:30 P.M. to 3:00 A.M.), online in the sense that the primary input and output devices (card reader, line printer, and console typewriter) were connected to the computer, and interactive because the operator interacted directly with his program via the console typewriter.

Interactions between the computer and the "systagramerator" (systems analyst/programmer/operator) were often identical to interactions still used today, such as "please enter..." and "do you want to...". However, this was of concern primarily to the operator, who generally was the only one interactively involved with an application.

For end users who were not "systagramerators", the interface with the computer system was—as it continues to be today for the majority of inhouse applications—"batch".

## The Batch Mode

Batch has been characterized a number of ways (usually unkindly). The essence of a batch environment might be described as follows.

The user's opportunities to enter input into the system occur at prescheduled times. *All* input, including updates, requests, and corrections, must be complete by the input "deadline". Each deadline is fixed with little regard to when questions need to be answered, when significant events take place, or when needs for change are recognized.

A batch system's output is typically:

- late (most of the time)
- outdated before received (all of the time)
- full of data that is *not* needed
- missing data that *is* needed
- delivered in six carbon copies, all of which, while barely legible, can mysteriously manage to turn fingers and clothing a remarkable black.

Furthermore, users who prepare input and review subsequent output frequently find that:

- Some input didn't "take" (whatever that means).
- Some of the batch input transactions conflicted, resulting in completely strange, unexpected, and incomprehensible output.
- In spite of "foolproof", expensive, and elaborate features—such as key verification, data checks, batch balances, control logs, check digits, and serialized input—some transactions did not survive the translation from input to output.
- At least one critical input transaction was invalid, and scores of subsequent transactions were rejected as a result.

To relate the impact of a batch mode on manufacturing applications, perhaps some MRP background will help. Using a master schedule at the product level, an MRP system "explodes" material requirements to calculate two main types of information:

- The quantity of material necessary to build a product and its components.
- The date at which all components and material must be available to meet final demand without delaying production.

For example, to meet the build schedule for a product, the first step yields material requirements at the next lower level of the bill of material structure—usually various assembly level items. To meet the requirements for the assembly level items, a build schedule for those items must be developed. That build schedule in turn creates material demands at a subassembly level. The process continues, filtering down through multiple assembly, subassembly, fabricated part, purchased item, and raw material levels, until the production and replenishment schedules at all levels are complete.

But in a typical batch MRP system, a significant schedule change at one level may not be felt throughout the product structure for several weeks. The direct subordinates of the rescheduled item are the subjects of a flurry of "recommended order action" notices. Unfortunately, it will be next week before the planner has his first chance to heed or disregard those recommendations. Meanwhile—so as not to interrupt the batch MRP run—the "system" has to assume that the recommendations will *not* be followed, and continues planning the lower levels based on the original (and still current) orders that were recommended for change. When the order actions are implemented next week, a new cycle starts with recommended changes to the next lower levels.

It's easy to see that with an $n$-level product it will take $n$ weeks to see the impact of one change at all levels. When the change finally does filter down to the lowest level (and the suppliers respond that they cannot deliver to the earlier schedule), the exercise may have been for naught. Since the world doesn't stand still for $n$ weeks, and since other, often conflicting, changes are filtering down at the same time, it's not surprising that the system is always out of date (that means wrong!) and not too useful.

There are two other characteristics of a batch MRP environment:

- *The "Long Weekend"*. Due to the volume of data required and, in part, to the "chained file" approach of the MRP system, the typical "weekend" processing usually begins with a Thursday second-shift cutoff, but nevertheless runs through Tuesday.

- *The "Short Work Week"*. After input is prepared (keypunched, verified, etc.), the inevitable rerun made, and output printed, decollated, and distributed, the manufacturing staff often has only a few days to react to last Tuesday's output before preparing input for this Thursday.

In a batch environment, a manufacturing planner simply does not have the tools necessary to create and maintain a complete and workable total production and replenishment plan. He cannot see the impact at all levels of a proposed change. He cannot test alternate schedules. He cannot determine if he can, or must, increase the availability of subordinate material or if he has to instead reduce demand at the product level. So the batch production plan becomes just a wish list that is impossible to meet.

If I've created the impression that batch is a terrible operating mode inflicted on users by data processing departments, let me speak in defense of the latter. If it is any consolation, batch is just as cumbersome and unwelcome to data processing professionals as it is to users. As constant computer users, systems and programming staffs suffer the same problems many times over as the end users. The plight of the production planner is similar to that of a COBOL programmer who must code his programs on coding sheets, have them keypunched, submit the deck for a compile (if lucky, overnight), and start a multiweek sequence of "fix it a bit today", "compile it tonight", "fix it a bit more tomorrow", and so on.

Worse yet, not only do programmers have to cope with the same system and problems, but they have to work harder to develop applications that actually run in a batch mode. For example:

- Because a batch application has no immediate access to a user, questionable or incorrect input can't be corrected on the spot. The best alternative a programmer has, then, is to design and implement reject error listings, suspense files, error audit trails, and numerous other subapplications and provisions that may mean something to the programmer, but almost certainly detract from, obscure, and delay the primary applications to the user.

- Having lost the natural "first come, first served" sequence of input transactions, the designer must implement a strategy to presort and process input in some artificial sequence, and try to foresee those transactions that might conflict with others. For example, must "adds" be done before "deletes"? What happens if there are two conflicting "change" transactions?

- Not knowing how output will be used, the only logical strategy is to try and answer all possible questions. Hence, batch designers helped contribute to the popular implication of "report"—pages and pages of "data" (not quite information) that try to provide answers to any potential questions.

## Multiprogramming

With the advent of multiprogramming systems, batch was still batch, but at least more than one batch process could occupy the computer at a time. Multiprogramming greatly increased the usage of the computer equipment and made the job of scheduling in the data processing center considerably easier. Programmers loved it, because they now had a chance to get more than one compile or test run per day. Program decks were simply added to the system input queue and, with luck, processed that day. A lucky programmer could see his errors and maybe start a second or third round of corrections on the same day.

But to the application user, the advantages of multiprogramming were mostly lost. Production planners still had an "end of second-shift Thursday" batch input cutoff, and the output reports from the weekend runs were no more likely than before to be available until Tuesday morning. The increased programmer productivity was an indirect benefit. Now urgent bug fixes—like those to the stock status system, which would occasionally "lose" a complete part entry from the inventory master tape file—could be completed in only 4 or 5 months, instead of the usual 9 to 12 months.

## The Isolation of the Computer

As computer usage and demand grew (and with it data processing organizations, staffs, and budgets), a growth in control, formality, procedures, and standardization was a necessary reaction to the horror stories of bad runs, lost input, or general data processing foulups. One early effect was the elimination of the "systagramerator" and the complete separation of the user and the computer. System interaction via the console typewriter was eliminated and either replaced with input decks or "run-book" documents, with a professional computer operator provided to type the responses to the friendly "do you want to..." and "please enter..." messages. The computer room was locked, and lines started to form in front of the new glass-windowed input/output (I/O) counters. The demand for magnetic scheduling boards took off!

## Early Time Sharing

The academic community was the first to use time sharing as a way to side step the I/O window. The key to time sharing was the discovery that a simple teletype device, a length of twisted-pair wire, and a lot of help from a tricky operating system could replace the card reader, the console typewriter, and the line printer. Best of all, the combination effectively bypassed the queues at the I/O window and greatly reduced the need for schedulers, magnetic scheduling boards, keypunch departments, expediters, operators—in other words, all the layers that had separated the users from the computer.

The magic time sharing operating system seemed to do everything. By allocating its attention, in millisecond time slices, to all users, each had the illusion of a dedicated system. By some accounts, the effect was almost a step backward to the days in which each user hunched over the computer console during his assigned block of time. But the users loved it!

As the use of time sharing applications grew, there were some strange developments. Some were due to the languages (primarily BASIC) available in early time sharing. Others were just the normal triumph of bad luck over poor planning.

BASIC, with its limited I/O ability, encouraged the type of "conversational" dialog that system designers had found so cute on the console terminal. The dialog inevitably started with "hello, I'm..." or "welcome to..." and continued with as many "do you want to..." and "please enter..." queries as were required to collect operating parameters and set run options for the application in use.

The style was further encouraged because time sharing applications were impressive to demonstrate. To enhance demonstrations, the conversational interactions and the detailed prompts frequently reflected the level of prompting required by a novice user. On first viewing, the typical application, with its messages, prompts, and guidance, was amazing! On second viewing, the interaction was comforting and helped the user. During the third through the fifth uses of an application, the messages and prompts were tolerable. But from then on, a frequent user of the system began to hate the dull chatter of the teletype that kept him from getting to the "answer" part of the application.

Instead of "conversational", "interrogational" might be a better word to describe a BASIC time sharing application. Unlike a conversation between equals, the dialog between the system and the user is normally limited to questions and answers with the system playing the role of the interrogator. There was not much relief for the user who didn't want to answer some questions, who wanted to answer them in a convenient order, or who knew (from using the system umpteen times) all the answers and really didn't want to watch all the old questions print out one at a time at 10 characters-per-second.

However, early BASIC gave a programmer controlled interaction with the BASIC text editor. While he was entering and updating his program, he was in charge; he took the initiative and really directed the activities of the computer system. To change a line, he typed a line number and the new line; the order in which he made his changes was entirely up to him.

The programmers, though, were not inclined to pass this flexibility or control on to the end users. It's unlikely that BASIC would have ever enjoyed much popularity if the BASIC editor (used by a programmer to enter his BASIC program) had interacted in the same interrogational mode that the programmers inflicted on their users. For example, how would you like to write a basic program in this manner:

```
HELLO! WELCOME TO BASIC
YOU HAVE YOUR CHOICE OF ADDING NEW PROGRAM LINES,
CHANGING EXISTING LINES, LISTING YOUR PROGRAM,
OR RUNNING YOUR PROGRAM.
PLEASE ENTER YOUR REQUEST
(1=ADD,2=CHANGE,3=LIST,4=RUN)? 1
YOU HAVE ASKED TO ADD LINES TO YOUR PROGRAM,
IS THAT CORRECT (1-YES,2=NO)? 1
```

```
GOOD.   PLEASE ENTER THE LINE YOU WISH TO ADD
(THE LAST WAS 30)? 40
NOW PLEASE ENTER LINE 40? LET A = 2+2
LINE 40 ADDED.
PLEASE ENTER YOUR REQUEST (1=ADD. . .
```

Ridiculous? Yes, but not much more than many of the early application programs written in BASIC for time sharing.

Another peculiarity of early time sharing applications was that they suffered from what I call "application omnipotence", or "application arrogance". Because the terminal appeared to be a dedicated computer, because the programmer was usually the operator and the user, and because BASIC did not include provisions to share common program modules, to communicate between users, to share files, or to cleanly jump from one program to the next, the applications became insular and ad hoc. There were no provisions to recognize the existence of more than one user, no way for a user to interact with more than one application in the same session, and no way to share data or files among simultaneous users or to coordinate the activities of simultaneous cooperating users.

Instead, once the command RUN was typed, a BASIC program became omnipotent—it took control of the terminal and retained that control until the process was done. It was, in fact, almost a batch process. Though the user could exercise some control over the process (when the designer thought to ask the user for input), the application was always in one of two states—running or not running. And while the user's imaginary, dedicated computer (represented by the terminal) was running one application, no other application could start until the current one had finished. The user was almost back in the world of batch.

Another characteristic of early time sharing applications was the dual role of the first programmer/user. The programmer knew his audience—himself. As a result, the programmer/user had faith in his ability to reply correctly to each prompt. Thus the need for input checks and edits in the programs was slight, and programs were written that trusted the validity and reasonableness of user responses.

Perhaps the new user who replied YES to the query

```
PLEASE SELECT ACTIVITY (1=ADD,2=CHANGE,3=DELETE)?
```

deserved to generate a program error and get an octal dump on his teletype. But the poor user who received the prompt:

```
PLEASE ENTER GAMMA COEFFICIENT?
```

and was unaware that only the value of pi or the reciprocal of the natural log of $8E^-17$ would keep the program from aborting, was sure to be in a lot of trouble.

As time sharing usage grew, it encountered more problems:

- The number of potential users exceeded the number of programmers willing to learn BASIC. Applications written for personal use started to be used, and misused, by users other than the original designer.

- The number of users exceeded the number of available teletypes, and it became necessary to start scheduling terminal time—sometimes using a magnetic scheduling board!

- The number of people wanting answers from time shared applications exceeded the number of people willing to sit at the keyboard, and secretaries and typists were drafted to fill the new role of "operator".

There were some early manufacturing/MRP systems implemented in the time sharing mode. But, for the most part, they:

- Were conversational (interrogational) and cumbersome to operate.

- Recognized only the mode in which a single user at a single terminal interacts with a single application, so they could not provide simultaneous access.

- Were ill equipped to handle input errors, were not forgiving, and frequently had no restart provisions—a complete session's or day's work could be lost due to a system failure.

## Online Query Systems

In spite of the time sharing trend in the academic community, data processing staffs in industry had successfully avoided a move to time sharing. They had argued that they would lose control, and the discipline and standards that had been painfully established to avoid some of the early "systagramerator" abuses of computers would be lost. They had some good points, and those arguments, coupled with the fact that there were few aspiring BASIC programmers in industry, kept time sharing systems out of the inhouse data processing departments.

Data processing staffs, though unwilling to learn BASIC and be their own programmers, were also unwilling to remain isolated from the resources of their computers. Because batch was still not an acceptable solution to many business needs, data processing staffs finally decided that online access was worth a try. Purchase orders were written for terminals, controllers, more core and disk storage, and assorted strange boxes that held the key (according to the data processing staff) to bringing the power of the computer to everybody's fingertips.

In most cases it didn't work out quite that well. New terminals were delivered, but sat unused for months (except for occasional visits by programmers), waiting for "final system checkout". Changes and fixes to existing systems were slow or nonexistent because everybody was working on the online system implementation and check out. Computer capacity was scarce, because the online system folks needed more and more test time, and, for some reason, the online system didn't quite fit with the normal batch work or was too inclined to crash the system.

When the users were finally given first tentative access to the new terminals, they were disappointed to find that:

- The "power of the computer at their fingertips" was available only from 10:00 A.M. to 1:00 P.M. (due to the conflicts with batch work).

- The system usually didn't make it through that schedule without at least two or three crashes.

- Most of the online time was spent with the "system unavailable" message lit.

The hot topic of conversation became the state of the system, and the greeting "good morning" was replaced with "systems up!" or "systems down!".

The worst part was that even when the system was up, it didn't do much. It seemed that with all the work of reconfiguring the batch computer, adding remote access devices and controllers, and worrying about access methods, protocols, and message interfaces, nobody had any time to rethink the applications in terms of an online environment. Instead, the approach was to add the ability to retrieve and format data from batch report files. The terminal operator could request a part number status display, but the information that was displayed was the same data that was previously available on printed batch reports. The display still represented the Thursday second-shift cutoff, was still not available until Tuesday of the following week, and was completely static! All that time, effort, and money, and the most tangible improvement was that your fingers no longer turned black (at least, not between 10:00 A.M. and 1:00 P.M.)!

## Online Input

The data processing staffs assured the users: "Don't worry, we have crossed the threshold, and invested in the future; it is only a matter of time until online input is available". So the users waited (inevitably longer than originally scheduled) and one day, sure enough, online input arrived.

But the bad news—in more than a few cases, online input was a disappointment. Just as online output had only created a substitute for the high-speed printer and report distribution section of the data processing operations department (or would have, had the terminals been available longer than from 10:00 A.M. to 1:00 P.M.), the online input capability seemed to only create a substitute for the keypunch department. The input transactions that Production Planning had painfully inscribed on input forms were now typed at the terminal keyboard. And the worst part—the transaction input didn't do anything but sit there until after second-shift Thursday when the update (still a batch process) was started!

## Online Update

Progress, while at times too slow, was inevitable, and there are now inhouse systems in industry that do more than just display static report files or collect batch input data. Some systems now allow online update of the master files and generate status reports from the same master files. Now a user can enter a request to change a standard cost field, immediately display the master file data for that item, and see the change.

While that represents a step forward, it isn't enough. The user still doesn't have the power of a computer at his fingertips. Keeping the master files current and up to date is important—it's the tidy and good and clean thing to do, by all means. But, except in all but a few "electric blackboard" applications, it is *not* the main objective of the computer system.

For example, in the case of a manufacturing/MRP system, changing the schedule date or expected quantity of a work order in the master file is one thing—seeing the impact of that change on subordinate materials, department workloads, and projected stock balances is quite another. If the impact of a change is not seen until the next regularly scheduled update run, the user still does not have the access he needs to the capabilities of the computer.

## Transaction Systems

A transaction environment addresses the needs of application service to multiple online terminals distributed throughout the departments of a business. The characteristics of a transaction-oriented system are somewhat different from those of a conventional time sharing environment in two major respects:

- Multiple users share one or several common applications. The application programs provide simultaneous service to, and coordinate the activities of, all users.
- The users are not programmers or proficient terminal operators, but instead are performing "line" functions, using the terminals

for inquiries and activity-recording tasks related to those functions.

The concept of a transaction-oriented system is an important and powerful one, particularly in support of activity-level systems that can be best served by direct computer access. First, the transaction concept forces system designers to think in terms of real-world activities, events, and information needs, and eliminates a preoccupation with card layouts, batch report formats, and job streams. Second, the transaction-oriented approach creates an environment in which the system designer can (but, unfortunately, doesn't automatically) create a dynamic, online system that can react to real-world events as they occur.

There is a tendency to evaluate online system capabilities using time as a basis. A daily batch run can be justified on the basis of: "A turnaround time of 24 hours is fine. I can live with data that is as much as one day old; ergo, I don't need an online system." However, time is the wrong measure. Just as I don't expect an airlne to sell me a seat based on how many seats were available last Thursday, I cannot ask a stock clerk to locate a receipt based on where it was yesterday, or decide the availability of stock to fill a miscellaneous withdrawal request based on last week's production requirements for that material. Data that is not current is not correct. There may be degrees of being "up to date", from "totally obsolete" to "almost current", but right versus wrong is a binary decision!

A serious problem with many transaction systems relates to their performance. To avoid "race conditions" and conflicts between simultaneous users, many transaction systems adopt a strategy of staging the terminal requests and passing them one at a time to a single copy of an application program that services each request in turn. Because the resulting application activities cannot be overlapped, the capacities of these systems can be severely limited. If the application has more than a trivial amount of work to do, and if there are more than a few users contending for service, the pessimistic queuing theory predictions of service level are demonstrated, and response times increase exponentially as additional terminals are added.

## Conclusion

Perhaps as important as a list of the points I have been trying to make is a list of those that, although they might have been implied, I was not trying to make. First, my intent is not to criticize data processing staffs. It's easy, in retrospect, to point to examples of poor systems design and poor systems, but it is important to consider the technology that was available when systems were designed. Data processing is one field in which it is frequently necessary to do something "wrong" several times before a "right" way begins to emerge. The main lesson is that progress is being made, and so to adhere to yesterday's capabilities in an attempt to protect an "investment" in old systems is a sure way to deny yourself the fruits of that progress.

A second nonpoint: I have not been trying to claim that some modes of operation are good and others bad. All have uses for which they are appropriate. But there are applications for which each is completely inappropriate, and a mismatch between need and available operating modes can be disastrous. There are two points to be made here:

1. Make sure your systems designers have the ability and technological capability to deliver applications in the best and most effective mode to meet the need.

2. Don't be content struggling with a system that suffers from misapplied technology—insist that it be changed to address your real requirements. Those requirements *can* be met.

While it may be hard to predict when a system will suffer from misapplied technology, it is easy to diagnose when you see it. Some symptoms are

- The system is cumbersome and difficult to use.

- You have little or no control over what the system does. Instead you find that you have to sit back while it does something for (to) you.

- You find your system is more of a burden than a tool.

The last point that I wasn't trying to make was that you should fire any systems designers that fail to develop logical, completely human-engineered systems. I would also strongly recommend that you don't spend a great deal of time looking for perfect systems designers—or even perfect systems. If there were a perfect system designer, he would know that there is no perfect system (because that implies a static, unchanging need), so he would just design systems that support and accept change. Finally, as you encounter systems that are inflexible and cannot be changed, replace them and learn to avoid whatever technology may have led to the original inflexibility.

This paper should reveal my own bias regarding the contribution that *APL* can make to the solution of everyday business data processing challenges. That bias, which was developed after more than ten years in a batch COBOL data processing environment, is simply that *APL* represents a "better idea". *APL* systems in general and STSC's *APL*\**PLUS* System in particular have created an environment in which:

- A choice of operating modes is available—batch where appropriate, interactive when needed, transaction-oriented as required.

- The actual program implementation becomes a relatively small element of the total system development job. Consequently, mistakes can be corrected, and poor design decisions can be changed without losing major investments in program development.

- Users can be brought closer to computer resources, and computer systems can become the vital and responsive tools that they should be.

*Jim Russell is currently manager of manufacturing systems at STSC. He has accumulated twenty years experience in the computer and data processing field, primarily in developing and installing manufacturing systems. Before joining STSC, he held positions as data processing manager and manager of manufacturing industry systems with SCM and Control Data.*

*In addition to being a Fellow of APICS (the American Production and Inventory Control Society), Russell has earned the title of Certified Data Processor from the Data Processing Management Association.*

**Jack R. Becker**

# Development of the STSC Accounting System

When STSC first started business in 1969, only the invoicing of customers was computerized—a natural outgrowth of obtaining *APL* resource usage data as a modest matrix in a workspace. Now, ten years later, all our billing, accounting, marketing, and financial reports are produced by *APL* systems.

Maintaining the earliest system and producing invoices for a monthly billing of about $13,000 was a part-time job requiring only one to two days of work each month. Now, three full time people are required to maintain the combined billing/accounting systems and to produce invoices for more than $1.3 million per month. A 100-fold increase in revenue and a vastly expanded system have required only a 30-fold increase in man-hours of support.

This paper will briefly outline the growth of our accounting system, showing how *APL* simplified development along the way. It will also show how *APL* helps us maintain the current system of closely interrelated accounting and billing modules. Particular attention will be given to the updating of outgrown modules and to the addition of new capabilities.

## Design of the System

The basis of the first version of our accounting system was the hand system we were using at the time. The new computerized system contained four basic modules:

1. *General Ledger.* This provided a breakdown of amounts by cost center and a grouping of cost centers into regions. The only financial reports produced initially were trial balances, balance sheets, and profit and loss statements.

2. *Accounts Receivable.* Provision was made to assign payments to individual invoices. Aging and customer statement reports were also provided. Invoice data was obtained directly from the billing system and posted automatically by the sales journal.

3. *Accounts Payable.* This was essentially a mirror image of the accounts receivable module. Aging of payables and vendor statements were available. Payables journals produced checks automatically.

4. *Employees/Payroll.* This module maintained payroll and employee expense data. The first version of the payroll journal did not calculate payroll deductions—these had to be supplied as input. (At the time the first version was produced there were few employees, and work on the accounting system was still a part-

time job. Production of a complete module was postponed because of the need to provide programming support for marketing.) Paychecks were produced automatically by the payroll journal.

Many of the features built into that first version of the system survive in the current version:

1. Data is entered through "journal" programs which are similar to the journals of a hand system. Each run of a journal program produces a formatted journal sheet containing all the data entered at the terminal. All the journal programs that require input from the terminal have the same logical flow. They check data for consistency and require input of control totals.

2. Modules interface with the general ledger on the transaction level. In some cases, data from a single journal run is summarized before posting to the general ledger (e.g., sales data is summarized by revenue type and cost center, removing the customer detail), but data from separate journal runs is always distinct.

   The interface at the transaction level provides several benefits. The subsidiary modules are always in balance with their respective general ledger accounts. Closing for the month is a very simple operation; profit/loss is posted to the appropriate general ledger account and the data files are flagged so that no further entries for the month will be accepted. A side benefit, not consciously planned, has proved very useful. If a manager questions any of his expenses for a given month, we can easily supply the transaction items that made up the total for his cost center.

3. A consequence of the transaction-level interface is that many of the subsidiary modules are interdependent. For example, the cash disbursements journal of the accounts payable module also accesses and can alter data in the employee/payroll module (payment of employee expenses, expense advances).

4. Each module has a dataset associated with it. This dataset may contain one or more *APL*PLUS* System files. A given file is always tied to the same tie number, and the tie number is always included in the code as a literal constant.

## Updating the System

As STSC grew, updates to the accounting system were inevitable. Changes have been made to incorporate new features of the *APL*PLUS* System and to provide expanded modules when the old versions were outgrown. The employee/payroll module has been recoded twice; accounts receivable and accounts payable modules have each been recoded once. While expanded report capabilities have been added to the general ledger, the basic design of that module (the data structure) has not yet been changed.

When a module is updated, the major effort is put into the redesign of the data structure. We start by discussing the module with those who use it directly and with those who use the reports generated by it. The old data structure is examined to determine if any data items are no longer necessary. The result of these discussions is a "wish list" for features of the new module. Design of the new data structure then proceeds. Items no longer needed are dropped; new data items are included to support as many of the "wish list" features as possible. Data may be included for which there are no current requests if it seems likely they may be useful in the future. This is a difficult judgment to make and sometimes data is provided for which we never generate a use. We attempt to err on the side of including too much data rather than not enough.

Finally, we design free space in the data structure at every level. This procedure has often allowed us to make significant additions to a module without having to redesign the dataset.

After we determine the structure of a new dataset, we search the entire accounting system for all references to the old module. With nearly 80 workspaces in the system, this search could be a difficult task were it not for the design feature of including file tie numbers as literal constants in the code and for the string searching capabilities of *APL*. Character representations of the functions of all workspaces are maintained in document files, and a master directory is kept relating these files to the workspaces. The search function is only 12 lines long and locates all occurrences in the system of a given character string in less than ten minutes.

Copies are made of all workspaces that reference the module being changed and these are then altered to reference the new dataset. As a special precaution, the new data file is given a name different from that of the old file, and a different tie number is used. If a reference is overlooked, it would at worst result in a *FILE NAME ERROR* or *FILE TIE ERROR*; there would be no chance of storing garbage in the new file.

After all the coding changes have been made, a function is written to convert data for the module from the old file structure to the new. The new file is created on a test number and any other data files needed to test the new module are also copied to the number. All workspaces are then carefully tested.

Once testing is completed, installation of the new module is quite simple: the new data file is transferred to the "live" system and all new workspaces moved to the "live" library. Rarely does this take more than an hour to complete. It is normally done late in the afternoon when the system is not needed by the Accounting Department. If the operating procedures are not changed, the users need not be aware of the update.

A look at the last revamp of our employee/payroll module will help to put all of the above in perspective. The entire job, including complete file structure and user documentation, required about three months of work, sandwiched between a number of other major projects over an eight-month period. All the coding, testing, and documentation was done by one person. Shortly after the system was installed, we had to add a voluntary deduction for the United Fund. However, we had left room for additional voluntary deductions in the data structure. Addition of this feature (coding, testing, documentation, and installation) required less than one week of work.

## Adding New Modules

When adding new modules to the system, the procedure is much the same as that for updating an existing module. The job is somewhat simpler in that an existing feature does not have to be researched and its performance duplicated. After the data structure is defined for a new module, subfunctions are written to create the data from other accounting system datasets. These functions are then inserted in the appropriate workspaces and the dataset for the new module is created. Sections of the module that provide reports using the new data may be written before the module is installed or may be produced at a later time. Typically, some reporting capabilities are provided at the beginning, and more are added as users become familiar with the new module and begin requesting additional capabilities.

This points out one of the major benefits of *APL*: coding is so concise, and development of systems so rapid, that improvements to systems can be provided when they are needed. Report generators can be produced quickly; if they do not exactly hit the mark, they can usually be changed readily. This allows systems to grow and respond to current needs rather than to needs that are six months or a year old.

I would like to outline briefly an actual addition to our accounting system to amplify the dynamics of this procedure. Early in 1974 the call for some online means of determining historical customer usage was coming so loudly from so many directions that it had to be answered. A very simple dataset was defined—*HISTDATA*. This was an *APL\*PLUS* System file, organized by customer. For each customer there was a table of data, one row for each month. Columns of the table included:

- Date
- Invoice Number
- Territory Number
- *APL* Resources Used (Connect, CPU, Storage)
- Amount Billed

All data needed for this file was available for the current month in the billing system. A function was written to transfer this data from the billing system dataset to the new *HISTDATA* file. The function was inserted in the sales journal program. Since this journal had to be run once a month to transfer invoice data from the billing system to the accounting system, *HISTDATA* was assured of automatic updating each month. Design and implementation of this much of the system took about two weeks. It was installed as soon as it had been tested so that it was able to gather data while the interrogation portion of the system was designed.

Already in place was a system that allowed marketing representatives to obtain monthly statements of their territories' performance. The routines that obtained customer usage data were added to this system, and controls were provided so that a marketing representative could obtain data only for his own customers. This completed the installation of the system, which supplied customer histories for almost two years before additional capabilities were needed.

By 1976 large customers were increasingly being serviced by more than one representative. The secondary representatives had no way to obtain historical data on their portion of the account. Non-*APL* billings (batch and consulting) were now significant and these were not included in the history file. Credits and adjustments were also lacking. *HISTDATA* was clearly no longer adequate, yet it did produce very useful resource usage data.

We decided to retain *HISTDATA* and to generate a totally new module with a new dataset—*REVENUES*. This dataset contained all transactions involving revenue accounts. The following data fields were included for each transaction:

- Date
- Journal Reference Number
- Territory Number
- State Number
- Customer Number
- Invoice Number
- General Ledger Account Number
- Amount
- Entry Description

This dataset was first used to produce improved monthly territory reports. The reports could now include all revenues for a given territory and could be broken down by revenue type. Transfers and adjustments could be determined from the entry description and journal reference code. The territory reports were now complete, accurate, and fully automated.

The structure of the new dataset suggested a number of new applications. As the amount of data in the file grew, these applications were produced. Analysis of revenue by state was automated. A monthly ranking of customers by total revenues was produced. However, the major benefit of the *REVENUES* dataset is not in the formalized reports we produce using it; rather, it is in the ability it gives us to respond to questions like:

Who were the top 20 accounts in 1977 and what is their billing history for the last two years?

Can I see a plot of *APL* sales, batch, and consulting revenues (each separate) for the last three years?

What have allowances been as a percentage of total revenues over the last two years?

The *REVENUES* file was developed using an *EMMA*™ file structure. *EMMA*, which stands for Extended Management Macros in *APL*, is a proprietary data management tool developed by STSC to simplify, standardize, and extend the user's ability to manage large amounts of data. Because the *REVENUES* file has an *EMMA* structure, accessing the data is very simple. Answers to any of the previous questions can be obtained with no more than half an hour's work, unless a fancy formatted report is needed. In that case it might take two hours.

Early in 1979 a design flaw in *REVENUES* was encountered. Revenues could not be tied reliably to cost centers. Territory numbers were related to cost centers, but that relationship could change with time and no history was being maintained. A replacement data structure was defined called *REVDATA*, which contained all the data in *REVENUES* plus two new fields:

Cost Center

City Code

This change, which required about two weeks of work, allowed us to break down revenues by city as well as by cost center.

## Maintenance of the System

Because the accounting system is so large and contains so many interrelated modules, good documentation is vital to its survival. The system has grown according to need; we did not begin with a design specification for the entire system, nor for any of the individual modules. However, the data structures are always formally documented before coding begins on a module. As key utilities are produced, their functions and methods of use are carefully documented. As each user workspace is completed, a formal user document is produced, outlining all the features and giving detailed usage instructions for each.

This documentation is maintained online by a system we developed specifically for the accounting system. The documentation system keeps track of the workspace location of all user-accessible functions. Documentation may be added or altered by any of the programmers working on the system. The system maintains a record of all updates and provides a facility by which updates can be printed. This allows us to always maintain up-to-date printed documentation.

A second documentation system keeps character representations of the functions on file. This system also keeps track of updates, allowing all programmers to maintain up-to-date listings of the functions in the system. It also provides a means of searching the entire system for a specific function or for occurrences of any portion of code.

Our programming staff is split between two locations. I work in Los Angeles, California, and the other two programmers work in Bethesda, Maryland. We maintain a complete set of printed documentation at each location. Development or maintenance work can then take place at either location. The documentation system, coupled with the use of STSC's Electronic Message Processing System, make communication by long distance phone rarely necessary. When calls are required because of a critical problem, the duplicate sets of printed documentation provide the means of getting to the heart of the problem very quickly.

## Summary

The conciseness and flexibility of *APL* are the factors that have made production of our accounting system possible. Without *APL* the system could never have grown fast enough to keep pace with our changing needs over the last ten years. *APL* has also made it possible for us to accomplish the work with an amazingly small staff. Though the system is enormously complex, it is still possible for one person to have a good overview of the design of the entire system. I don't think that would be possible with any other programming language.

Our decision to make the modules interrelated and always in phase with one another has proved to be beneficial. A new application can acquire data from any dataset without the implementer having to be concerned with the status of the dataset; it is always current.

The keynote of our system is its flexibility—its ability to respond quickly to new requirements both small and large. Even when a need is not fully defined, it is feasible, in terms of the effort expended, to try many different approaches over time, iterating toward a satisfactory result. *APL* has freed us from the drudgery of producing mountains of code and has allowed us to turn our energies to the concern of what information our system provides and can be made to provide.

*Jack Becker, manager of accounting applications for STSC, has been with the company for more than ten years, having joined STSC shortly after its formation. He is currently responsible for the design and implementation of accounting and billing systems. Prior to coming to STSC, he had ten years' experience in scientific programming for the aerospace industry and, with Patrick Gehl, helped establish the first commercial APL time sharing service in the United States.*

*Becker has a bachelor's degree in physics from Occidental College.*

Marilyn J. Pritchard

# *APL* in the Corporate Service Environment

Before preparing this presentation, I asked the individuals responsible for the various areas in STSC's Corporate Services how they use the *APL\*PLUS* Time Sharing System, and in particular *APL*, to run their departments. They each came up with a half-dozen or more ways in which the system has become an integral part of their daily operations. In the space allotted here, I will describe those that have the greatest benefit.

Corporate Services comprises the areas of publications, word processing, contracts, legal and SEC matters, pricing, purchasing, general office services, and policy development. Much of the work in these administrative areas requires a large amount of accurate recordkeeping, text processing, and quick storage and retrieval of information. Therefore, many of our uses of the system involve the maintenance of small-to-medium size databases.

### MAILBOX Service—The Most Important Tool

Perhaps the most important need we have in Corporate Services is to communicate efficiently and cost-effectively with people in other STSC locations in the United States and Europe. The most important tool for doing this is our Electronic Message Processing System, called MAILBOX. Besides serving as a means to broadcast to other STSC people news of important events, changes in policies and procedures, and so on, MAILBOX is especially valuable to Corporate Services personnel in routinely carrying out their responsibilities.

In the Purchasing Department, MAILBOX is used by STSC employees to submit requisitions for goods and services and, in turn, is used by Purchasing to confirm or to request any necessary clarifications to those requisitions. Managers of the cost centers being charged for the order are often carbon-copied on such messages in lieu of waiting for their specific approval. Purchasing also uses MAILBOX to disseminate important information quickly, such as impending price increases for widely used items like computer printout paper, terminal ribbons, and printwheels. By keeping MAILBOX messages on file, Purchasing can retrieve any previous correspondence and information on a particular requisition.

With MAILBOX, the Contracts Department corresponds with field marketing personnel several times a day regarding contract terms, rates, and other customer and billing information. The contracts administrator notifies marketing representatives of contract expiration dates and of accounts approaching dollar limits on purchase orders. Using MAILBOX in these situations is less expensive than using the telephone, and provides written backup for the transaction, which is kept in the customer's file.

One area of Office Services—the Mailroom—relies heavily on MAILBOX to receive and acknowledge requests from branch offices for publications, terminal paper and ribbons, and other office supplies. Since some vendors (for example, the telephone company and an office supply firm) are also users of MAILBOX, our Office Services staff can message these vendors directly with telephone additions and changes and routine office supply orders.

## Address Management System—Another Commonly Used Tool

Next to MAILBOX, the application most commonly used by Corporate Services is the *APL*\**PLUS* Address Management System, called ADDRESS. Having one central database divisible by 50 or so attributes (such as "customer", "vendor", "employee", "stockholder", and "media") simplifies updating such information, affords flexibility in retrieving information, and avoids duplication of effort in maintaining information that is useful to various groups in different locations in the company.

Routinely, Corporate Services uses ADDRESS to prepare labels for sending purchase orders to vendors, notifying customers of new services or price changes, and sending material to other STSC offices. With the fileprint and special formatting capabilities of ADDRESS, we are able to produce a computer printout of more than 20,000 labels in a format that can be processed automatically by Cheshire® mailing equipment. We do this for bulk mailings like the STSC newsletter, the corporate brochure, and the seminar schedule.

In the following sections, I will relate several more specialized ways in which some departments in Corporate Services use the *APL*\**PLUS* System.

## Purchasing

Purchasing has set up an online "tickler" system which tracks a multitude of distinct tasks that require action at a later date. Their system stores an unlimited number of items with associated dates and priority levels. Later, they can revise the text of any item, reschedule any item without recopying it, and alter any priority settings. Items are held until the specified date, and then displayed in priority order.

*APL* allows Purchasing to perform extensive calculations easily. For example, a photocopier vendor recently presented the purchasing agent with nine different pricing plans for placing various photocopiers in STSC branch offices. Within a few minutes, the purchasing agent translated the nine plans into a one-line *APL* function which took the monthly volume of copies in each office (already known) and produced the monthly cost for each office under the plan. Prior to that, the vendor's salesman had suggested that he return for the information in a week or two!

One of Purchasing's responsibilities is to evaluate new terminals on the market. Being able to use *APL* greatly simplifies this process. By typing only a dozen or so characters, it is possible to produce pages of data to test a specific feature or pinpoint a possible weakness. For example, experience has shown that the expression `50 130ρ'`*`ABCDEFGHI`*`!'` is a good test of a terminal's overstrike capability, and `500 1ρ⍳500` is a good indication of its ability to handle short lines.

Several small databases are also maintained online by Purchasing. These include a file containing purchase order numbers and the date each needs to be renewed; an inventory file of terminals identifying who has each and its last reported condition; and a file of employees who have Day-Timer calendars containing the style, size, and refill date so that they can be reordered automatically.

Purchasing has also set up a workspace of *APL* programs for the Office Services staff to maintain an up-to-date directory of employees at the corporate headquarters office located in Bethesda, Maryland. Employee names and their MAILBOX codes and telephone extensions can be easily added, changed, or deleted. Car license plate numbers are also recorded for monitoring the restricted parking.

### Contracts

Many of the programs and databases used by the Contracts Department involve customer account and billing information and are also used by the Accounting Department. One workspace contains programs that list all the marketing representatives assigned to a specific branch office as well as all the customer accounts assigned to any specific marketing representative.

Another workspace is used by marketing representatives to assign new account numbers to customers. In response to prompts, a marketing representative enters information about a customer—name, address, billing rates and their effective dates, name of person to notify if contract changes occur, customer's primary product or service, marketing data on how the customer first learned of STSC, and what the firm's initial use of the system will be. After a marketing representative assigns an account, Contracts reads the information and enters it into the online billing system via other programs, thus establishing the customer as a billable account.

To maintain accurate customer records, Contracts must update information in the billing system, so there are programs to change customer names and addresses, delete or cancel accounts, lock or unlock accounts, change purchase order numbers, change rates or billable status, change service levels, and move user numbers from one account to another.

As part of its contract compliance responsibility, Contracts maintains an online file of accounts with expiration dates and maximum or minimum dollar or resource limits, and updates this file as contract renewals or changes are received. Information in this file includes cumulative monthly amounts billed against each account. Contracts reviews this file regularly and notifies appropriate marketing personnel of the status of any account nearing its limit.

When a request has been received for cancellation of an account, Contracts can access online month-to-date computer usage data to identify any subsequent usage. A file of stored tapes maintained by the Computing Center can also be accessed by Contracts to determine whether a particular customer has tapes in storage at the time of cancellation.

When review of an account's billing status is required (for example, at contract renewal time), Contracts can access an accounts receivable file and run programs to produce an aging or complete statement of account. Contracts then advises the marketing representative of the customer's billing status so that he can notify the customer.

It is important for STSC, both in developing its marketing plan for new services and in meeting its public reporting requirements, to know the percentage of revenue derived from specific industries. To help in this effort, Contracts assigns a Standard Industrial Classification (SIC) code to each new customer based on the information supplied by the customer when the account is initially set up. SIC codes are entered into the billing system, allowing us to determine revenue percentage by industry over any period of time.

### Word Processing

STSC's Word Processing Department prepares a wide variety of printed material, including proposals and contracts, SEC reports, form letters, technical papers, some user documentation, and internal publications like the Employee Manual. On the average, the department's two operators turn out 500 pages of material per month.

Instead of using more conventional word processing equipment, like Vydec or Wang, the operators use SCRIPT, a text formatting system developed by the Department of Computer Services at the University of Waterloo, and the CMS (Conversational Monitoring System) Editor. Both facilities are offered on STSC's *APL∗PLUS* VM Service. Using a large application system like SCRIPT has several important advantages over a more conventional approach: more sophisticated and extensive editing capabilities, shared files, security, simple archiving procedures, high-speed printing, and the flexibility to process large documents as well as small ones. All of this can be accomplished without developing new software or hardware interfaces.

The word processing operators enter and edit text via video-display terminals and print drafts of large documents on a high-speed line printer in the STSC Computing Center. To print letters and other small documents and to run final camera-ready copy, they keep two hard-copy terminals (one 30-characters-per-second, and the other 120-characters-per-second) finely tuned to their strict quality specifications.

Perhaps the most important benefit to us in using SCRIPT is that text files can be shared. Several people in different locations can work on one file, simultaneously or not. Because of this, someone 3000 miles away can review portions of a file at his terminal, while other portions of the text are being revised at headquarters. Obviously, this saves untold amounts of time and reduces shipping and related charges.

Other advantages of using an online text processing system will be covered in the next section as we look at how the Publications Department uses the *APL∗PLUS* System to prepare most of STSC's technical publications.

### Publications

The Publications Department mainly comprises technical writers and publications assistants who are responsible for producing technical publications distributed outside the company to customers and prospects. Technical writers originate the material or edit material that has already been written by others using old-fashioned tools like pen, pencil, or typewriter. Publications assistants then take over and enter the text online.

Like the word processing operators, the publications assistants use video-display terminals to enter and edit text. However, instead of using SCRIPT on the VM System, they use an editing and composition system called COMPOSE on the *APL∗PLUS* OS/MVT System. (COMPOSE and SCRIPT have similar capabilities, and it is mostly for historical reasons that Publications uses COMPOSE.)

The benefits of using an online text processor are the usual ones: the entire text of a document needs to be typed only once, an entire document can be searched for certain text strings and changes or replacements can be made throughout the document; different output media can be used such as video-display or hard-copy terminals, high-speed line printers, or tape; and access to the text can be tightly controlled by specifying who can read or change it.

All of STSC's major publications are now being photocomposed rather than having their camera-ready copy produced on a terminal or line printer using the *APLFULL* print train (with roman and *APL* type fonts). For preparing manuals that are to be photocomposed, publications assistants use another text processor, which is upwardly compatible with COMPOSE and simulates the way the text will be produced in final, photocomposed form. Besides text entry and editing, the photocomposition system has extensive error-checking features, can produce a table of contents automatically, has the ability to format typesetter input for the line printer in interim drafts, and interfaces with an offsite photocomposition service for actual production. Our manuals are usually typeset on one pass through the photocomposer!

The photocomposition system also includes a semi-automatic indexing system. The author builds a database of ideas from the manual, and a typeset index is generated automatically from the database. Other features of the photocomposition system include headings and footings (specified only once), two-level headings, standard table formats, and a wide choice of typefaces. Perhaps most importantly, the system has automatic page-makeup capabilities.

A more technical advantage of having the $APL*PLUS$ Time Sharing System available is exemplified by the part-time efforts of a technical writer in producing a volume of custom software for the department over the past two years. In other computing environments, this part-time effort might have required a full-time programmer.

For example, we recently were faced with the large and tedious job of designing our standard table formats for photocomposing tabular material, trying to anticipate all of the table formats we would ever need. Instead of designing the tables manually, we wrote an artificial intelligence program in *APL* that did the whole job automatically. The program was designed and implemented by a technical writer in three days, while we estimate that developing a similar program in, say, COBOL would have required about a month. Furthermore, because of the ease of developing, testing, and installing an *APL* program, the Publications staff often modifies existing programs or develops new ones within hours, or even minutes, of the time a need is perceived.

The Publications staff uses a wide variety of application programs in their work. Writing all of these programs in *APL* gives them a consistent, comfortable protocol that does not scare nontechnical staffers away from learning new applications. In addition, *APL*'s interactive, forgiving nature saves the staff a lot of time. People can teach themselves, get immediate feedback, and progress at their own speed. When an error occurs, a few keyboard entries from a publications assistant or from a helper summoned to the scene usually suffice to fix the problem and allow an operator to pick up work from the point of the error.

Deferred Execution, one feature of STSC's Automatic Control of Execution (ACE) facility, has automated the routine aspects of document production and moved text processing runs to non-prime time when customer usage is lighter.

The Publications production supervisor uses other programs that the staff has developed to perform routine calculations like estimating costs of all printing jobs. Having different printing and paper costs for various printing methods online, she can enter data such as the number of pages in a publication and quickly determine the most cost-effective printing method and the optimum number of copies to print.

The production supervisor also maintains an online publications inventory system. Each month, branch offices enter the number of copies of each publication they have in stock. The system compiles the data and reports the stock levels (grand totals or totals by branch) of all publications distributed by STSC. The production supervisor also uses STSC's internal news system (similar to our customer news system available in workspace 1 *NEWS*) to announce the arrival of new publications, their prices, and the schedule of delivery to branch offices.

## Conclusion

Surprisingly enough, although it has taken several pages to relate the most beneficial ways we in Corporate Services use *APL* and the *APL★PLUS* Service, I have actually omitted many more that we have come to take for granted. As we have grown, we have automated those jobs that were most repetitive and tedious, those that were most important to meeting commitments to customers, and those that could be done with the staff programming resources on hand at the time.

There are, however, additional applications where use of *APL* could simplify our work by automating more tasks and integrating them with existing programs. An online requisition and purchase order system and an online contract compliance system are only two examples of operations that would benefit by complete, cohesive automation of remaining manual procedures. With our continued growth, *APL* will serve as a valuable tool in producing these more comprehensive systems for our own internal use.

*Marilyn Pritchard holds two degrees in mathematics from Purdue University, a B.S. and an M.S. While teaching mathematics at Syracuse University, she took programming courses and then began work as a programmer/analyst at IBM Federal Systems Division in Gaithersburg, Maryland, and later at the Syracuse University Computing Center.*

*Since joining STSC in 1973, Pritchard has worked as publications editor, APL system librarian, and manager of publications. In December 1978 she was promoted to her current position as director of corporate services, where she is in charge of purchasing, contracts and other legal matters, pricing, publications, facilities management, policy development, internal controls, and general administrative support services. In July 1979, she was elected assistant secretary of the corporation.*

*Pritchard is a member of the Association for Computing Machinery. From 1976 to 1979 she was editor of APL* Quote Quad, *the principal technical journal serving the APL community; in 1979 she was elected Secretary-Treasurer of STAPL, the APL special-interest group within ACM.*

John W. Myrna

# Electronic Mail

Probably no technology is currently receiving more coverage in business publications than electronic mail. To many, electronic mail is still a futuristic concept. At STSC, it is a fact of life. Over the past ten years, it has become the lifeblood of our corporate communications system, and it is a very important factor in our sustained growth rate of 25 to 35 percent annually. This paper discusses the reasons electronic mail concepts are so important in today's business; describes the attributes of STSC's Electronic Message Processing System, called MAILBOX; and, finally, looks at the economic benefits of installing such a system.

### Today's Business Environment

In today's business environment, there is no pressure more critical than that of inflation. The dollars available to us today have less value than they did yesterday, and we can be assured that tomorrow they will be still less valuable. Inflation is making it continually more difficult to achieve the level of profitability we would like for our organizations. We must make a greater number of critical decisions in shorter periods of time than ever before. We must find ways for improving overall productivity while controlling the cost of doing business.

In most organizations, the cost of doing business is labor intensive. In fact, it is very common to find that labor costs represent 80 to 85 percent of the total cost of doing business (see note 1). However, this also means that labor costs represent a major area of opportunity for reducing costs.

Years ago, American industry recognized the opportunity for increasing the productivity of the blue-collar labor force. By applying new technologies and supporting blue-collar workers with capital equipment, the cost of blue-collar labor has been decreased. Very recently, we have seen a similar process begin to affect the clerical labor force with the application of technologies such as word processing.

In spite of these advances, office costs now account for 50 percent of the total cost of doing business (where before they were 20 to 30 percent), and they are rising at an annual rate of about 20 percent. Office costs are not only for clerical workers, but for the very expensive professional and managerial labor force.

In fact, 77 percent of the total office costs in the average business today are associated with professionals and managers. Yet, in most organizations, the capital equipment available to support this particularly expensive segment of the labor force is limited to a telephone, a dictating machine, and possibly a calculator. Expanding and improving this support holds immense potential for increasing managerial and professional productivity and for reducing operating costs. Booz-Allen Hamilton projects that within ten years office systems advancements could save American businesses more than 60 percent of the amount they currently spend for their entire professional-managerial labor force.

Before considering how to improve the productivity of managers and professionals, it is important to understand their role. A manager's role may be defined as follows: to gather information; to use that information to manage his decision process; and then, after making the decision, to disseminate information so that appropriate actions and plans can be executed. If we agree on that definition, then we also agree that the *flow of information* to and from the manager must have a very significant impact on his productivity and, correspondingly, on the expenses associated with the managerial labor force.

This concept is supported by Henry Mintzberg in *The Nature of Managerial Work* (see note 2). Figure 1 shows the percentage of time the typical manager spends each day in five major activity categories and the percentage of the day's significant activities achieved within each of these categories. The figure makes it apparent that the typical manager spends 78 percent of his time in mostly verbal activities relating to information gathering or dissemination—that is, on the telephone or in meetings of one kind or another. A significant portion of his remaining time—that allocated to desk work—is spent on paperwork. These are also information flow activities.

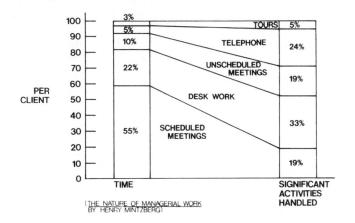

**Figure 1—Management Time and Activity Analysis**

Mintzberg's findings suggest that meetings are extremely inefficient and that the telephone represents the most efficient medium available to the manager. On the other hand, a recent study published in *Fortune Magazine* (see note 3), shows managers throughout the country identifying the telephone as the top time waster. The second and third factors they named as contributing to their inefficiencies were also related to communications—memos and meetings.

There are several reasons for telephone-related inefficiencies. We are all aware of the frustration of trying to reach someone by telephone. On the average, we will have to make four calls before we reach the person we want. Because telephone communication is verbal and impermanent, its quality will only be as good as our concentration and memory of the moment. And of course no phone call is complete without the necessary social amenities. Finally, if we are attempting to telephone across time zones, we introduce an additional set of complexities. If we want to communicate between the east and west coasts, the "window" available for verbal communications during business hours is no greater than five hours, including lunchtime. If either party takes an extended lunch, or if our friend on the west coast arrives at the office a little late, that five-hour window can quickly be reduced to nothing.

Memos solve, or at least relieve, problems of organization and retention, but they introduce other limitations. Most managers feel that only 25 percent of the information they receive through memos is relevant. A high percentage of the information required by management is of a time-sensitive nature; for this kind of material, the 11-step process required to generate a memo and get it from one desk to another is too slow. As for meetings, inefficiencies associated with them have to do largely with insufficient planning and structuring and, to some extent, communications issues.

What the managers in the *Fortune* study are saying is that communications—which is nothing more than information flow—is a vital part of their ability to function productively, but that conventional means of communications leave much to be desired. It was a similar feeling that gave rise to the development of STSC's MAILBOX System some ten years ago.

## The MAILBOX System

MAILBOX moves information electronically. Direct interaction with a computer—via an interactive terminal—replaces dictation, handwritten drafts, typewriters, and, in many cases, secretaries. Every MAILBOX user has access to a terminal. The user may choose to use the terminal himself or to have his secretary operate it. It has been STSC's experience that the typical manager or professional prefers to use the terminal himself.

The MAILBOX user simply types into the terminal to receive and send "mail". MAILBOX is easy to learn. Working with a concise set of commands, most users master MAILBOX within a matter of days. To check his incoming mail, the user types the word *PREVIEW*. The system responds by displaying the number of messages pending and the identification codes of their respective senders. To read some or all of these messages, the user specifies the level of confidentiality and enters the word *PRINT* (he also has the option of signing off and reading his mail at another time); the system then prints all of the messages he requested.

To send a message, the user simply types the command *SEND*. The system responds by prompting for the names of the recipients. When this information is entered, the system prompts for the text to be sent. After typing in the text, the user initiates the action to send the message. With this, the message is registered in our system in Bethesda, Maryland, and is *immediately available* for its recipients to read—whether they are in Omaha, Nebraska, or Paris, France.

The MAILBOX System automatically provides each message with a date, timestamp, sender identification, and a unique serial number. In addition, simple "actions" typed in by the sender make it possible to classify the message by level of confidentiality (personal, confidential, or nonconfidential) and to specify distribution. The message sender can "carbon copy" as many people as he likes, using regular carbon copies (which all recipients will be aware of) or blind copies (which will be visible only to those so copied). A message can also be designated "urgent", in which case it will be displayed before all other pending messages at the recipient's terminal. Figure 2 illustrates a sample MAILBOX message.

```
[1] CONFIDENTIAL
NO. 1234567   SENT  5 MAR 1980  18.55.24
FROM DDW
TO    EXEC
CC    BAS KMK JEAN DEK

RE:  AGENDA FOR EXECUTIVE COMMITTEE MEETING
     MONDAY, 10 MARCH 1980

HERE IS THE UPDATED AGENDA FOR OUR EXEC. COMMITTEE MEETING
NEXT MONDAY AFTERNOON.  PLEASE LET ME HAVE ANY FURTHER COMMENTS
OR ADDITIONS BY DAY AFTER TOMORROW AT THE LATEST.

1.  VICE PRESIDENT-FINANCE WILL GIVE FINANCIAL REPORTS FOR
    LAST MONTH.
2.  PROPOSED CHANGE IN EMPLOYEE STOCK PURCHASE PLAN:  REDUCE
    REQUIREMENTS FOR ELIGIBILITY FROM TWO YEARS TO ONE.
3.  ESTABLISH SCHEDULE FOR DEVELOPING OPERATING PLAN FOR FY 81.
4.  TENTATIVE PRICING FOR PROGRAMMING AND CONSULTING, VM SERVICE.

THANKS.  /DAVID

P.S.  YOU'LL NOTICE THAT ITEM 5, SAN DIEGO ACQUISITION, HAS BEEN
      DELETED.  WE'LL DISCUSS THIS AT APRIL MEETING.   /D
```

**Figure 2—Sample MAILBOX Message**

As can be seen, a MAILBOX message looks very much like a memo. However, unlike a memo, it is available immediately upon creation by the sender. Because MAILBOX is so direct, dispensing with a number of intermediary persons and processes, it eliminates the costs and delays associated with conventional memo distribution. Because the message is in machine-readable form, it may be automatically filed, indexed, retrieved, or printed. In addition, the recipient of a message may forward it to someone else without retyping anything except its serial number. If he likes, he may extend the message or add a footnote.

Most executives will agree that their time seems to belong to everyone but themselves. MAILBOX is a significant factor in putting executives and other participants more in control of their own time. The receiver of a message is not interrupted by the sender. Nor does the sender waste valuable time making call after call to reach the receiver. Messages are sent and received at the convenience of both sender and receiver, in total privacy, and in a cost-effective and timely manner.

MAILBOX also has the advantage of being enormously secure—so much so that at STSC we use it to communicate such highly confidential information as payroll changes. Every user has an established password that is known only by him. Furthermore, MAILBOX provides three possible levels of message confidentiality. When a user checks his mail, the system automatically prompts him for the level of confidentiality he wishes to see. The user who finds someone looking over his shoulder would probably ask only for his nonconfidential mail. However, if he were in his office alone, he would likely ask for all mail, including personal. The system will immediately respond by printing out all mail up to and including the confidentiality level designated by the user.

With MAILBOX, a manager or professional is no longer tied to his office for information access or secretarial support. With today's lightweight terminals, office conveniences and communications are extended to any place where there is a telephone—home, hotel room, or customer's office. If a MAILBOX user expects not to be reading MAILBOX messages for any period of time (e.g., when he's on vacation) he may put a "note" to that effect in the system so that anyone sending him a message will be aware that it will not be received immediately. He can also choose to have mail automatically forwarded to someone else for action during his absence. Upon his return, the accumulated messages provide a chronologically ordered account of activities that have taken place during his absence.

The immediacy of MAILBOX makes possible the completion of *written* work across great geographic distances in time frames that would be simply inconceivable using conventional communications. For instance, one recent Wednesday afternoon the project director at STSC's Paris affiliate found himself "stuck" on a proposal that was due on a client's desk before the close of business on Thursday. Before the proposal could be completed, more technical information was required—information that was not available in Paris.

So, at 2:00 P.M. Paris time, the project director sent a message stating his need to the vice president of international in New York. The vice president read it with his Wednesday morning mail and found that he was able to provide only part of the missing information. This he sent right away in a return message to Paris; at the same time he forwarded the original query along with a note of his own to the technical vice president in Bethesda.

The technical vice president in turn identified a technical expert on his staff who could come up with the information still needed. The technical expert worked out of STSC's San Francisco office. By noon Eastern Standard Time, a message was on its way to San Francisco.

The San Francisco staffer was consulting at a client's location and did not see the message until lunchtime, when he checked his mail from a terminal in the client's office. He then spent the afternoon working up the rather complicated technical data required. By the time he was done, it was 7:00 P.M. in San Francisco and the middle of the night in Paris—useless to place a trans-Atlantic call. But the San Francisco man sat down at his terminal and sent the information to Paris via a MAILBOX message, with copies to the technical vice president in Bethesda and the vice president of international in New York.

By the time the anxious project director reached his office in Paris the next morning at 7:30, all the information he needed was waiting. Within four hours it was written into the proposal. An hour later the completed proposal was sitting on the client's desk—well before the deadline and less than 24 hours after the project director's original MAILBOX message was sent.

We have found within STSC that MAILBOX has considerably improved the effectiveness of our meetings; it has also enabled us to reinforce our commitment to participative management, despite the fact that we have key managers headquartered at great geographical distances from one another. MAILBOX speeds up scheduling of meetings. It allows agenda items to be entered quickly and easily, and it facilitates discussion and agreement on the items from widely scattered participants. An agenda can also be changed at the last minute, with the knowledge of everyone involved. In effect, MAILBOX generates the positive dynamics of a meeting before the meeting takes place.

It is easy to envision applications that could only be handled with electronic mail techniques like those of MAILBOX. Group messages are a good example. MAILBOX groups are made up of users that have something in common. For example, a group named *MKTG* might hold address codes of persons with a special interest or expertise in matters relating to marketing. A single message addressed to *MKTG* will automatically go to all members of that group, whether there are 20 or 200 of them.

Imagine another hypothetical group identified as *INSAP* (for insurance applications). One of its members is John Jones, a customer representative who is having difficulty with an installation for a large insurance company. He wishes he could consult with other company representatives working in the same field, but he doesn't actually know who all of them are or which ones would be most helpful. By sending one message to *INSAP*, he has instant access to everyone in the company who's doing anything with insurance. We can see that this kind of communications capability can be immensely useful in terms of quality customer service.

### Economic Benefits

Several studies have recently been completed regarding patterns in electronic mail use. The results are significant to anyone interested in using this technology. It is clear from these studies that MAILBOX directly affects the area of greatest expense and greatest opportunity within most organizations today: 70 to 80 percent of MAILBOX use is by management and professional people. It is much more than a clerical tool.

The typical daily volume for each user is 5 to 10 messages sent and 10 to 15 messages received. Owens-Corning Fiberglass recently completed a study indicating that each message handled in an electronic mail system saves them roughly $4.72 over any other communications method. Multiply this saving by a per user daily message volume of 15 to 25 messages. It is easy to see that in a company with, say, 200 MAILBOX users, very substantial dollar benefits can be realized from the use of electronic mail.

There are other direct cost savings: telephone costs go down and memo generations will typically drop by approximately 15 percent. These are among the results of a recent survey of some 600 users of electronic mail conducted by Yankee Group Consultants. The increased productivity that one can expect with MAILBOX is evident in the survey finding that 20 percent of electronic mail use occurs outside business hours. In other words, the manager or professional is able to significantly extend the hours in which he can actively receive and send information.

Probably the most striking of all of the survey results is the last one. The profile of user response indicates that productivity increases typically range from 5 to 15 percent, with 8 percent as the norm. That factor alone would represent a 200 percent return on investment for a MAILBOX user.

### Conclusion

Can the use of an electronic message service help your organization? Aside from the direct cost savings and convenience it offers, a system like MAILBOX can more than justify itself solely on the grounds of its potential for improving managerial effectiveness. If a company can provide its managers and professionals with better information—or more timely information—on which to base their important decisions in today's intense business environment, the payoff can be very significant. Its impact can be felt in such vital areas as span of control, cash flow, sales productivity, or on any number of other elements important to the profitability of the organization.

While the cost of managerial and professional labor has been escalating at an extremely rapid rate, the unit cost of electronic communications, computer processing, and computer storage is at an all-time low. Thus, the option of applying these technologies has never been more reasonable.

The Appendix that follows contains technical information on STSC's MAILBOX System. Our own experience has been that electronic mail has substantially improved our profitability. We believe we are not unique.

### Appendix—Technical Notes on MAILBOX

The *APL\*PLUS* Message Processing System is the fourth major system STSC designed for communications between its customers and employees.

Evolving from a very primitive system, the various generations of MAILBOX have been in continuous use by employees and customers since January 1970. Since the current system was installed in July 1974, there have been 1.25 million messages sent. The current average traffic is about 35,000 messages per month.

MAILBOX is a message-oriented computer conferencing system. The package consists of a text editor, message posting and access functions, and a set of standard cover functions for private message handling. The system is designed so that individual users can tailor their use of the system to:

- allow private text management
- allow alternate sources of text (e.g., function listings, plots, text from manuals, and tables)
- allow control of messages to form conferences (e.g., capacity planning group, new feature testing, and technical review)
- allow the running of contests (e.g., name a new computer system or name a new product).

Computer conferencing is more a state of mind than a particular technology. While the MAILBOX may lack some of the formal cosmetics that characterize today's computer conferencing, it is computer conferencing nonetheless. It is the use of shared files, remote terminal equipment, and telecommunications networks to facilitate group communications where face-to-face contact is either not possible or less desirable. Ten years of continuous use have produced a very stable and valuable tool.

### System Environment

Because MAILBOX was implemented with the *APL*∗*PLUS* Service, there were major parts of the system already available:

1. The Time Sharing System
   - support for multiple users
   - support for multiple systems (production and experimental)
   - support for a variety of terminals
   - an existing telecommunications network.

2. The *APL* Programming Language
   - general purpose
   - good interactive interface
   - powerful language facilities to manipulate character vectors.

3. The *APL*∗*PLUS* File System
   - good language (*APL*) interface, completely integrated
   - standard, high-level, logical support—the application program does *not* worry about disk management, physical record size, or buffering; file recovery and daily file backup are an automatic part of the service.
   - *designed* for file sharing applications—every file has a file access matrix that controls 14 types of access per user; there are 16,383 different ways to specify access; system-level queuing commands "hold" a file during critical updates.

## Design Characteristics

There were three goals:

1. Security

   - no one can read any one else's mail—not through system crash; not through user prying; not even if he is the MAILBOX steward
   - once a message is posted, the system will never lose it
   - messages can be read only by the recipient.

2. Flexibility

   - easy to use—the system is self documenting; two prompt levels are provided: brief prompts for frequent users and more detailed prompts for infrequent users less familiar with the system
   - easy to customize—functions are modular; easy access to other text sources is provided
   - detailed documentation is provided.

3. Efficiency

   - advanced $APL$ coding techniques are used to select algorithms that are most efficient.

The system consists of one shared file and three workspaces. The file contains directories of users, directories of messages pending, control tables for the file, and messages. The user workspace $BOX$ contains a small text entry and editing system, $BOX$ posting and access functions, and interactive cover functions to send and print messages. The steward workspace $ENROLL$ adds, deletes, or changes enrollees. The steward workspace $MAINT$ provides file maintenance, automatic spooling, message purges, statistics, and creation of a new MAILBOX.

## Implementation Problems

1. There were no language constraints. $APL$ is quite up to this type of problem.

2. The amount of user memory available in a workspace at the time MAILBOX was first implemented (64 kilobytes) was a major constraint. This was solved by using one directory and "packing" data tightly; keeping functions on file and moving a copy into the workspace when needed; printing warning messages as users approached the end of available storage; and increasing the workspace size.

3. The design goal of extreme reliability and security taxed the design because it required extensive testing for breaks in execution during critical sections; the use of special features to seal the package and "hide" function names from view; verifying the message header with the user number *after* retrieving it from file, but before printing; and designing the steward function so that it can't find the file passnumber even during initialization.

4. The File System interlocks are such that there are no *absolute* holds—code must check and check again to ensure that file updates are synchronized.

## Doing It Better

In general the current system serves its purpose well. Most of the ideas for improving it are either extensions to the current system or have to do with new time sharing features for major new facilities.

*Notes*

1.  This and much of the other data presented in this paper derive from a study conducted by William H. Wood, an independent consultant.

2.  H. Mintzberg, *The Nature of Managerial Work* (Harper and Row, 1973).

3.  *Fortune Magazine*, 6 November 1978.

*John Myrna joined STSC in 1971 as manager of operations; in this position he organized STSC's Computing Center and nationwide communications network. He was subsequently promoted to manager of communications in 1973, director of development and design in 1975, director of development in 1977, and to his current position as vice president of development in 1979.*

*Myrna directs STSC's Operations Group and is a member of its Executive Committee and Technical Management Committee. He is responsible for the production and delivery of computing and telecommunications services and for the development of new applications, products, system features, and technologies.*

*Myrna holds a B.S.E.E. degree from the New Jersey Institute of Technology and an M.S.E.E. degree from Montana State University.*

**Judson G. Rosebush**

# Business Graphics

This paper describes the *VISIONS* Business Graphics System, developed by Digital Effects Inc., and available for use on STSC's *APL*PLUS* Service. *VISIONS* facilitates the design and generation of graphic displays, including multiple-line word formats (text charts), and line, bar, and pie graphs. The Business Graphics System uses consistent conversational behavior and common code.

The use of *APL* primitives for computer graphics notation has received some attention in recent years (see notes 1 through 6); however, design efforts toward large, integrated systems have concentrated mostly on task-specific or device-specific single workspaces (e.g., a workspace to plot line graphs on a Tektronix Plotter).

The *VISIONS* Business Graphics System gives any user a flexible method of generating a wide variety of graphs and textual formats—quickly, accurately, and efficiently—on a device of arbitrary description. Each graphics system within *VISIONS* (e.g., *TEXT*, *PIEGRAPH*, *LINEGRAPH*, and *BARGRAPH*) embodies uniform design considerations and features, at the user level and at the implementation level. The balance of this paper describes the construction of the system, its basic features, and use. Digital Effects suspects its work is not unique to the area of graphics, and encourages further discussion in the larger *APL* community regarding topics such as general arrays, dialog rules, and manipulation of functions in and out of workspaces.

I wish to thank the following people who contributed to the design of *VISIONS*: Steve Bartels, David Cox, C. Robert Hoffman, Donald Leich, Jan Prins, and David Schnebele.

## System Overview

Each of the graphics systems consists of a shell of application primitives that use the *VISIONS NUCLEUS*, a database management system called *VFILE*, and a defined set of user interaction rules, called *DIALOG*. The application systems may be used interactively, off-the-shelf, or the application primitives may be incorporated by a programmer into any *APL* environment with unique data access methods, customized front ends, or automated processes. The application primitives—as well as the functions in *NUCLEUS*, *VFILE*, and *DIALOG*—are well defined and documented online.

The *VISIONS NUCLEUS* consists of primitives for generalized graphic manipulation and display. A more detailed explanation of the basic concepts of the *VISIONS NUCLEUS* may be found in "*VISIONS*: A Computer Graphics Notation" (see note 6).

The *VFILE* system enters data and related descriptive information and stores it in a tree-structured file, much like a general array. An interactive application called *FILE* helps users enter, list, copy, delete, and rename data of all types and shapes. Data is identified by a complex name composed of data identifiers, separated by delimiters. For example, a file may be named *EXCHANGE.DATA.STOCK*. A name may be used to describe either a single piece of data, or many pieces of similar data. For example, *EXCHANGE.DATE.STOCK* might specify the closing information for a specific stock on a certain day, while *EXCHANGE.DATE* might specify the closings for all stocks on a single day, and *EXCHANGE..STOCK*, all daily closings for a single stock on file. More details are available in the *VISIONS User Manual* (see note 7).

The *DIALOG* facility solicits and evaluates user input by issuing question prompts, accepting and validating the user's responses, and storing the results in variables. These variables may then be used by functions of the application systems. *DIALOG* features include prompting, unified response rules, optional defaults, optional validity checking for ranges or choices, conditional prompting, implicit commands, error trapping, "help" messages, and abort pathways. Automated processes—including command expressions that may be saved for future use—may be implemented using a "type-ahead" feature of *DIALOG* in conversational mode, or directly as input to an *APL* function.

The *VISIONS* Business Graphics System is device-independent, so that output may be directed to printers, plotters, video-display terminals, or film recorders of any manufacturer. Color or black and white displays are possible, and vector as well as raster displays are supported. Additional systems exist for enrolling users, tailoring prompts, measuring usage, and installing and maintaining systems.

**Operation**

*VISIONS*, when used in an interactive mode, is managed by a master driver function that queries for system selection and, upon response, gathers the appropriate functions into a workspace. Each graphics application, such as *BARGRAPH* or *PIEGRAPH*, may contain a latent expression; this is executed and transfers control to a specific function. When one task is complete, such as the display of charts or graphs, control returns to the driver function, application-dependent code is purged from the workspace, and the user is again prompted to select a system. The master driver of *VISIONS* is actually a general-purpose utility and might be used for applications unrelated to graphics.

Following are a few examples of *VISIONS*. The first example demonstrates the *PIEGRAPH* system.

```
      )LOAD 4876000 VISIONS
SAVED  . . .
SYSTEM}PIEGRAPH
DATA ID}EXAMPLE.PIEGRAPH
FONTNAME}MACHINEB
CHANGE DEFAULT COLORS? N
ONE LINE TITLE}PROFIT CENTERS
TITLE COLOR} (RETURN)
PULL OUT SLICES? 2
2 IS NOT A VALID CHOICE
PULL OUT SLICES? Y
SLICE TO PULL: 2
AMOUNT OF PULL: .6
SLICE TO PULL: (RETURN)
ROUTE}DISPLAY
DISPLAY}TEK4662
```

This sequence creates the pie graph shown in Figure 1, using data stored in the file *EXAMPLE.PIEGRAPH.*

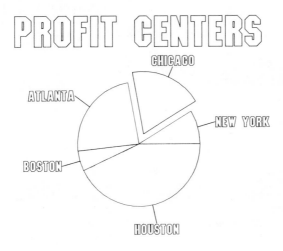

**Figure 1—A Sample Pie Graph**

The following sequence creates a bar graph (Figure 2) and includes several uses of *?* to view available options.

```
SYSTEM}?
FILE
TEXT
LINEGRAPH
BARGRAPH
PIEGRAPH
SYSTEM}BARGRAPH
DATA ID}EXAMPLE.LINEGRAPH
FONTNAME}HELVETICA
CHANGE DEFAULT COLORS? N
ONE LINE TITLE}TESTGRAPH
TITLE COLORS} (RETURN)
BARWIDTH: ?
1 VALUE REQUIRED
MIN AND MAX (ONE ROW PER VALUE): DEFAULTS ARE LAST COLUMN
    0              1               0.8
BARWIDTH: (RETURN)
BARGROUP WIDTH: (RETURN)
ROUTE}DIS
DISPLAY}?
VALID CHOICES ARE: (DEFAULT IS FIRST ROW)
TEK4013
TEK4027
SD4020
TEK4662
FR80
HP7221
DIABLO
DICOMED
AJ832
SOLTEC
TEK4025
DISPLAY}HP7221
```

In this example some questions were answered by pressing the RETURN key, resulting in automatic use of the default value. On monochrome displays, all colors are displayed in a single color.

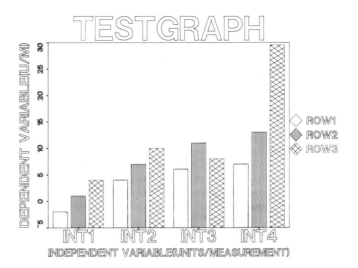

**Figure 2—Bar Graph Format**

The following sequence produces the same graph as Figure 2, but uses the type-ahead mode. The insertion of double slashes ( / / ) in an entry string substitutes for pressing RETURN.

```
SYSTEM}BARGRAPH
DATA ID}EXAMPLE.LINEGRAPH HELVETICA //
ONE LINE TITLE}TESTGRAPH // // // // //
ROUTE}DIS HP7221
```

The above examples use previously stored data. The following example shows how a new file is created, and illustrates some of *VISIONS'* prompting features.

```
SYSTEM}FILE
ACTIVITY}?
VALID CHOICES ARE: (DEFAULT IS FIRST ROW)
COPY
RENAME
TYPE
DIRECTORY
DELETE
ENTER
HELP
LIBRARY
SHARE
}ENTER
ENTER NAME OF INDEPENDENT VARIABLE}YEARS
ENTER NAME OF MEASUREMENT UNITS} (RETURN)
NUMBER OF INTERVALS OR CATEGORIES IN YEARS: 3
DO YOU WISH TO LABEL EACH INTERVAL? Y
LABEL1}1980
LABEL2}1981
LABEL3}1982
ENTER NAME OF DEPENDENT VARIABLE}REVENUE BY DISTRICT
ENTER NAME OF MEASUREMENT UNIT}000,000
NUMBER OF ROWS IN REVENUE BY DISTRICT: 3
DO YOU WISH TO LABEL EACH ROW? Y
LABEL1}EASTERN
LABEL2}MIDWEST
LABEL3}WESTERN
```

```
ENTER 3 ROWS WITH 3 COLUMNS EACH. SEPARATE VALUES WITH COMMAS.
ROW1: 3.45
3.45 IS 1 ITEMS, NEED 3
ROW1: 3.45,4.55,5.24
ROW2: 1.09
1.09 IS 1 ITEMS, NEED 3
ROW2: 1.09,1.44,1.78
ROW3: 2.55,3.00,3.44
OUTPUT DATA ID}DIST.FORCAST3
```

This data is now stored under *DATA ID 'DIST.FORCAST3'* and is used to generate Figure 3.

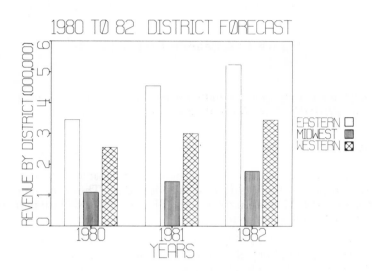

**Figure 3—A Sample Bar Graph**

The following sequence uses the *TEXT* system to create a chart of text (see Figure 4). The ? prompt is used again to reflect the help feature.

```
SYSTEM}TEXT
FONTNAME}?
VALID CHOICES ARE: (DEFAULT IS FIRST ROW)
MACHINEB
HELVETICA
CALCOMP
FONTNAME} (RETURN)
TEXT STRING}STSC
TEXT STRING}PRESENTS
TEXT STRING}BUSINESS GRAPHICS
TEXT STRING} (RETURN)
LEADING: (RETURN)
LETTER SPACING: ?
1 VALUE REQUIRED
MIN AND MAX (ONE ROW PER VALUE): DEFAULTS ARE LAST COLUMN
     0               1                 0.2
LETTER SPACING: (RETURN)
JUSTIFICATION}?
VALID CHOICES ARE: (DEFAULT IS FIRST ROW)
CENTER
LEFT
RIGHT
JUSTIFICATION} (RETURN)
OVERALL COLOR} (RETURN)
HIGHLIGHT LINES OR WORDS} (RETURN)
```

```
OVERRIDE AUTOMATIC SCALING? (RETURN)
ROUTE}DIS
DISPLAY}SOLTEC
```

**Figure 4—A Sample Text Graphic**

For additional examples or explanation of the operation of *VISIONS*, refer to the *VISIONS User Manual* (see note 7).

## Conclusion

The components and features of the conversational Business Graphics System can support many different applications. The problems involved include not only graphic manipulation and display, but also data management, user interaction, and system operation.

We continue to find *APL* a superior notation for the description and manipulation of graphic objects; we suspect the widespread work on general arrays (see notes 8 through 11) will encourage even more use of *APL* in computer graphics. Our investigation of the user interaction issue shows many attempts to formalize conversational style (see note 12; also workspace 6 *INPUT* on the *APL*\**PLUS* System); we wonder if there exists an algebra in the domain of responses to a prompt? Finally, we wonder if the language requires a built-in method for constructing a task from one or more groups of functions (see note 13) and then transferring control to that task.

*Notes*

1.  S. Baron, S. Bartels, and G. Martin, *Programmes Graphiques APL Pour Terminal Tektronix 4013*, (Compagnie Internationale de Services en Informatique, 1974).

2.  D. Galbraith, "Primitive Functions for Graphics in *APL*", APL *Quote Quad*, (Volume 7, Issue 2, Summer 1976).

3.  A. J. Rose, *Sketch*, (STSC, 1973).

4.  *Sharp APL Graphics*, (I.P. Sharp Associates, 1978).

5.  *IBM 5100 APL Graphpak*, (IBM Corporation, 1978).

6.  J. G. Rosebush, "*VISIONS*: A Computer Graphics Notation", APL79 *Conference Proceedings*, (Association for Computing Machinery, 1979).

7.  *VISIONS Business Graphics System User Manual and Reference Guide*, (Digital Effects Inc., 1979).

8.  T. More, "The Nested Rectangular Array as a Model of Data", APL79 *Conference Proceedings*, (Association for Computing Machinery, 1979).

9.  W. Gull and M. Jenkins, "Recursive Data Structures in *APL*", *Communications of the ACM*, (Association for Computing Machinery, Volume 22, Number 2, February 1979).

10.  R. A. Smith, "A Programming Technique for Non-Rectangular Data", *APL79 Conference Proceedings*, (Association for Computing Machinery, 1979).

11.  A. Hassitt and L. E. Lyon, "Array Theory in an *APL* Environment", *APL79 Conference Proceedings*, (Association for Computing Machinery, 1979).

12.  J. Sigle and J. Howland, "Structured Development of Menu-Driven Application Systems", *APL79 Conference Proceedings*, (Association for Computing Machinery, 1979).

13.  S. D. Crossley and G. R. Streeter, "An Overlay Method for the Effective Organization of *APL* Systems", *APL79 Conference Proceedings*, (Association for Computing Machinery, 1979).

*Judson Rosebush is president of Digital Effects Inc., a New York-based firm that specializes in computer animation systems and that produces film and video tape for television and motion pictures. Rosebush is also a practicing computer artist who has exhibited drawings and film in North America, Europe, and Japan. His primary software package, VISIONS, has been widely used by programmers and designers requiring three-dimensional color graphics capabilities. Rosebush has published several technical papers and has written for mass circulation media such as* Rolling Stone *and* The Village Voice.

*Rosebush holds a B.A. in art history from the College of Wooster in Ohio and an M.S. in television/radio from Syracuse University. He is a member of the Association for Computing Machinery.*

Part 3

# The Core of *APL*

**Jak Eskinazi**

# User-to-Application Interface:
# A Command Processor Approach

The designer of large systems is challenged by many different design criteria:

- database design
- security of programs and data
- designing and building utility programs that simplify programming and ease subsequent application maintenance.

This list is by no means complete. The seasoned $APL$ user knows that these topics are closely interrelated and that they invariably have wrinkles peculiar to each application.

Many of these topics are covered in other papers presented in this book. In this paper, I will describe a flexible and adaptable "command language processor". The focal point of the discussion will be the user interface (or "front end") for a hospital financial planning system that was designed and implemented in cooperation with end users and other analysts.

The term "command language processor" sounds quite formidable, but the reader should not be intimidated by such flowery terminology. There really is nothing new about it. It simply describes a mechanism that allows end users to interact with a suite of preprogrammed functions. The simpler applications, or those targeted to $APL$ users, may access programs using built-in $APL$ system features. A sequence of $)LOAD$ commands followed by function calls with or without arguments is the simplest form of a command processor.

Many applications have been designed in this manner and many more will be written in the future. However, it has been my experience that the real world is quite naive about data processing in general and about $APL$ in particular. Consider a data entry clerk entering what appears to be a valid command in immediate execution mode and being admonished with a $SYNTAX$ $ERROR$. The cause of the error may be very simple (e.g., the user forgot to load the right workspace), but the naive user's reaction can be quite traumatic.

When designing applications, regardless of the language used for the actual implementation, we designers are obliged to deliver a human-engineered system that makes the user's life simple. It should respond in everyday language, isolate the user from the actual computer mechanics, and protect the user and especially the data and programs from inadvertent errors or vicious attempts to breach security.

Briefly, our system is a financial model designed specifically for a hospital. Hospital financial management uses basic financial planning and modeling techniques. However, hospital services is a highly regulated industry; consequently, many reporting and reimbursement algorithms are required. Third-party payors such as Medicare, Medicaid, and Blue Cross typically reimburse hospitals on the basis of very stringent cost-based regulations; they may even require different cost-allocation algorithms when overhead is distributed. Our model performs these required computations so that the financial analysts can obtain true reimbursement figures from early budget preparation through the end of their fiscal year, when actual reports are filed with the proper agencies.

In the fall of 1979, we had fifteen users and handled the local regulations of four or five states.

## Our Design Requirements

In designing the hospital financial planning system, we set the following requirements:

- Our target user population would be composed of chief financial executives and hospital administrators.

- Typically our users would not be *APL*'ers. In fact, they would not care about the actual language used to implement their financial model.

- Our users have a jargon all their own. They talk about cost reimbursement, allocations, the bottom line, and so on. Since they are comfortable with those terms, we felt compelled to abide by them and to minimize the introduction of new terms.

- Most of our users either had never used a terminal or had mixed emotions about computers. Yes, they knew that the computer was a very useful tool but they did not like the tortuous mechanical contortions needed to obtain an answer. We wanted to reduce the "computerese" chore to simply dialing a number and signing on.

- Our target environment would be very volatile and variety would be the rule rather than the exception. Certain features or reports would be very meaningful to one user, but meaningless to another. We needed a simple mechanism to add and remove commands on a per-user basis.

- The model would be complex enough to warrant isolating the user from the actual programs and data. Catastrophic errors had to be prevented.

- The system should be easy for the newcomer to use, a system that could almost teach the user how it behaved and what options were available. Yet, we wanted a way to short-circuit long prompting sequences for the more seasoned user who knew exactly what had to be done and how to get there.

- We were psychologically opposed to "menu" prompting and felt that it would be impractical with an expected vocabulary of more than 300 commands. Our main objections to this technique were that it slows down user interaction by displaying the options in each prompt and that it becomes quite boring once the user is familiar with the system.

- The mechanism should allow the user to progress down a certain path and then abort the whole thing at any point before data was actually altered. This is a very important feature where the system is so rich that it is easy to pick the wrong path.

Certain limitations and requirements were also imposed by the internal design of the system:

- We wanted to handle 15 to 30 distinct workspaces and to automate workspace switching so that it would be transparent to the user. (It should be noted that extremely large workspaces would not help. Most of our workspaces provide different kinds of working environments and would still be segregated for maintenance and security reasons.)

- We needed a table-driven system that could be changed without reprogramming.

- We desired a mechanism that would let us easily phase new commands into the mainstream of the application. We would prerelease new commands to a selected and willing set of test users until we were certain that they were sturdy enough for public release.

- We needed a way to predefine and execute frequently used sequences of commands. This feature would allow sensitivity runs where a model element is changed, the affected section of the model is recomputed, and certain results are recorded. The process would be repeated for a whole set of input variables before a final report was generated.

- We wanted to make a set of maintenance and stewardship utilities available to ourselves through the same mechanism, and yet be sure that end users could never see or access them.

This paper covers two modules that were developed to address these needs. The *command processor* handles most user input involved with the selection and the execution of user commands. The *system supervisor* manages the programs and allows implementers and production code to "call" functions by name without worrying about the support environment they require or their actual location in the system.

## The Command Processor

Some of our problems could be quickly addressed and solved.

System access was simplified and computer mechanics were reduced to a bare minimum by adopting a design that always signs the user off with $)CONTINUE$. The $\Box LX$ in the $CONTINUE$ workspace places the user under control, and in interaction with, the command processor at sign-on. After dialing through the STSC network, the user enters only one line of magic:

    $\circ APLC$)1234567:$LOCK$

A nice side effect of keeping the user under program control is tremendously enhanced security and data integrity. The user cannot access programs and data from outside the system.

The ability to abort any given sequence was achieved by recognizing the word $QUIT$ in all our auxiliary prompters and immediately returning control to the topmost level of the command processor. The keys to this feature are STSC's Exception Handling Facility (which allows $APL$ programs to react automatically to errors and certain other events that can occur during execution) and our ability to retain program control if the user presses the BREAK or ATTN key. We opted to interpret the BREAK or ATTN signal as a request to "quit" while processing. Actual interrupt handling in critical computation-bound sections is subtle and beyond the scope of this paper, but pressing BREAK or ATTN invariably results in a return to the topmost system prompt.

Two features make the command processor easy to learn:

- At any point the keyword *HELP* can be entered by the user. It results in the display of a detailed description of the available options and of their effects. One of our pending projects is to cross-index these *HELP* messages to the user's manual such that the user would also be directed to the section containing detailed discussion and examples.

- An even shorter version of *HELP* can be obtained by simply pressing the RETURN key (entering an empty line) while in the command processor. In this case, the user is simply given a list of options currently available to him. Because we used mnemonic command names, pressing RETURN usually answers questions such as "Is the command spelled *ALSTATS* or *ALLOCSTATS*?"

These features are by far the simplest to address and implement. We still have the problem of naming and managing hundreds of commands. The brute-force approach would be to concoct a unique mnemonic name for each command and leave it at that. We did not consider it as an option. Instead, we made hierarchical lists of commands.

### The Prompt Matrix

The user would need to enter data, delete data, print reports, set parameters, add new departments, change department definitions, and so on. Some of the obvious action verbs are *ADD*, *CHANGE*, *DELETE*, *INPUT*, *PRINT*, *SET*, and the like.

Simply specifying that entry is to be performed is not sufficient; one must also specify what is to be entered. If you were to take a real application and analyze its user-accessible features, you would quickly realize that the command structure can be defined as a tree structure. An example of part of a command structure appears in Figure 1. This is but a small and simplified section of our real structure, but it suffices to explain how the command processor interacts with the user.

The commands shown in Figure 1 are arranged very much like a reporting or departmental structure, with the indents identifying the parent-subordinate relationship.

When the command processor is entered, it simply prints a double colon (::) and waits for the user to enter a command. At this point, the user may enter any of the top-level commands. For instance, Figure 1 indicates that *ADD* and *CHANGE* are two of the top-level commands. If the user enters *CHANGE*, the next prompt he will see will be *CHANGE OPTION*::, since he is not at the lowest possible level of the prompt structure. Now, assume that the user enters *DEPARTMENT*. The next prompt will be *CHANGE DEPARTMENT OPTION*::. When the user ultimately enters *ID*, reaching one of the lowest-level prompts in the chosen path, the command processor causes an *APL* function to execute and service the request.

Thus, the user may simply walk the prompts in a way that is conceptually similar to walking a tree until he reaches a leaf. Of course, the commands do not need to be entered in the tedious manner just described. The user could have entered *CHANGE DEPARTMENT ID* directly and achieved the same result. In fact, barring errors, the processor will accept multiple words at any level and pick them up one at a time as it walks down the hierarchy. These concepts are illustrated in the examples that follow.

```
ADD
....
CHANGE
  BUDGET
    ALLOCATION
      METHOD
      SEQUENCE
      STATISTICS
    EXPENSES
    REVENUES
    SENSITIVITY
    SPREAD
      CODES
      DEFINITIONS
      NAMES
  DEPARTMENT
    ID
    NAME
    MANAGER
    WORKLOAD
  USER
    NAME
    PROFILE
DELETE
INPUT
PRINT
SET
....
```

**Figure 1—A Part of the Command Structure**

```
:: CHANGE
CHANGE OPTION:: (RETURN)        User enters an empty line.
CHANGE OPTIONS ARE:
     BUDGET   DEPARTMENT   USER
```

```
CHANGE OPTION:: DEPARTMENT
CHANGE DEPARTMENT OPTION:: ID
```

At this point the command is fully described and the service routine takes over.

The next examples illustrate use of the *QUIT* option and how the processor reacts to unknown commands.

```
:: CHANGE DEPARTMENT
CHANGE DEPARTMENT OPTION:: QUIT
SEQUENCE ABORTED

:: CHANGE BUDGET SPRAED CODES
IGNORED ENTRIES: SPRAED CODES
(UNKNOWN COMMAND)

CHANGE BUDGET OPTION:: SPREAD CODES
```

Interaction with the command processor can be further shortened because the full words need not be entered. Provided enough letters of each word are entered to differentiate the entry from other valid entries at that level, the prompter will recognize them and act accordingly. For instance, the last example could have been as terse as *CH BUD SPR C*. If the user entry is so short that more than one match is found, the function will print the message *'UNABLE TO DIFFERENTIATE FROM:'*, followed by the words leading to the ambiguity. The message *'PLEASE BE MORE SPECIFIC'* is then displayed. Entries following the ambiguous word are ignored, as shown in the following example.

```
:: CH BUD SPR
CHANGE BUDGET SPREAD OPTION:: QUIT
SEQUENCE ABORTED.

:: CH BUD S C
UNABLE TO DIFFERENTIATE FROM:
     SENSITIVITY   SPREAD
PLEASE BE MORE SPECIFIC.
IGNORED ENTRIES:  S C

CHANGE BUDGET OPTION:: SP C
```

The command processor is actually driven by a character matrix almost identical to that shown in Figure 1. The only difference is that all top-level prompts are left justified and that lower-level prompts are successively indented by a single space instead of the two spaces used for clarity in the figure. As can be seen, this matrix contains all the necessary information to drive and control the behavior of the command processor as far as the user is concerned.

## The Executable Handler Matrix

Up to this point, we have alluded to the fact that the command processor takes some action when a leaf is reached, but we have not gone into the actual details. It turns out that the mechanism is a simple execute (⚙) of a predetermined string of characters. Figure 2 shows the original commands in Figure 1 and the accompanying executable statements for the change option and its subordinates. We refer to these statements as executable "handlers".

Thus, if the user enters the command *CHANGE BUDGET SPREAD DEFINITIONS*, the function named *CHSPDEFS* is executed to service the request. That function performs the desired task and drops back into the command processor. The user is then presented with another double colon and is free to enter another command.

```
PROMPTS                  HANDLERS

ADD
....                     ....
CHANGE                   HELP 58
  BUDGET                 HELP 76
    ALLOCATION           HELP 82
      METHOD             CHBALMETH
      SEQUENCE           CHBALSEQ
      STATISTICS         CHBALSTATS
    EXPENSES             CHBEXP
    REVENUES             CHBREV
    SENSITIVITY          CHBSENSDEF
    SPREAD               HELP 109
      CODES              CHSPCODES
      DEFINITIONS        CHSPDEFS
      NAMES              CHSPNAM
  DEPARTMENT             HELP 101
    ID                   CHDEPID
    NAME                 CHDEPNAM
    MANAGER              CHDEPMGR
    WORKLOAD             CHDEPWKLD
  USER                   HELP 111
    NAME                 CHUSERNAM
    PROFILE              CHUSERPROF
DELETE                   ....
....                     ....
INPUT
PRINT
SET
....
```

**Figure 2—Association between Commands and Handlers**

The process is very simple, and it is incredibly easy to use and maintain. A steward need only maintain two matrices in order to change the command structure, add new commands, or discard old ones. Of course, the service routines must still be written. We still have not found a way out of that chore.

Based on the description so far, one may suspect that the executable handlers for top and intermediate options are never executed and are superfluous. They are not. Indeed, the command processor executes service routines only when a leaf is reached, but the handlers for the other levels are used by the *HELP* option. Whenever a user enters *HELP*, the handler at that level is executed. In our case, these refer to a function *HELP* that reads a text component from a file containing appropriate *HELP* messages.

The concepts described above are easily implemented in a simple dyadic function that takes the command matrix as one argument, the handler matrix as the other argument, and thereby controls an application that fits in a single workspace.

## The Behavior and Access Control Matrix

A few more problems still need to be addressed:

- For consistency, we wanted to let the user supply data to the service routine via the command processor if desired. For example, if spread code *S*10 is to be altered, a construction like *CHANGE BUDGET SPREAD DEFINITION S*10 would be allowed. The command processor would not know the meaning of the data element $S10$, but it could conceivably pass this information along to the service routine in the form of a right argument.

- We needed a way to make different commands available to different users, based on their needs and stewardship status.

Figure 3 contains the same example as that in Figure 2, but a Boolean matrix that provides behavior and access restriction information to the command processor has been added.

| | | | | ACCESS | | | MODULES | PROFILE |
|---|---|---|---|---|---|---|---|---|
| | | | | *BOOLEAN MATRIX* | | | | |
| *PROMPTS* | *HANDLERS* | *SUP* | *ARG* | *PRV* | *SP* | *OPN* | *1 2 3 4 0* | *1 2 3 4 5 0* |
| *ADD* | | | | | | | | |
| .... | .... | | | | | | | |
| *CHANGE* | *HELP 58* | | | | | 1 | 11 | 1 |
| *BUDGET* | *HELP 76* | | | | | 1 | 1 1 | 1 |
| *ALLOCATION* | *HELP 82* | | | | | 1 | 1 | 1 1 |
| *METHOD* | *CHBALMETH* | | | | | 1 | 1 | 1 1 |
| *SEQUENCE* | *CHBALSEQ* | | | | | 1 | 1 | 1 1 |
| *STATISTICS* | *CHBALSTATS* | | | | | 1 | 1 | 1 1 |
| *EXPENSES* | *CHBEXP* | | | | | 1 | 1 | 1 |
| *REVENUES* | *CHBREV* | | | | | 1 | 1 | 1 |
| *SENSITIVITY* | ♣*CHBSENSDEF* | 1 | | | | 1 | 1 | 1 |
| *SPREAD* | *HELP 109* | | | | | 1 | 11 | 1 |
| *CODES* | ♣*CHSPCODES* | 1 | 1 | | | 1 | 11 | 1 |
| *DEFINITIONS* | ♣*CHSPDEFS* | 1 | 1 | | | 1 | 11 | 1 |
| *NAMES* | ♣*CHSPNAM* | 1 | | | | 1 | 11 | 1 |
| *DEPARTMENT* | *HELP 101* | | | | | 1 | 1 | 1 |
| *ID* | *CHDEPID* | | 1 | | | 1 | 1 | 1 |
| *NAME* | *CHDEPNAM* | | 1 | | | 1 | 1 | 1 |
| *MANAGER* | *CHDEPMGR* | | 1 | | | 1 | 1 | 1 |
| *WORKLOAD* | *CHDEPWKLD* | | 1 | 1 | 1 | | 1 | 1 |
| *USER* | *HELP 111* | | | 1 | | | 1 | 1 |
| *NAME* | ♣*CHUSERNAM* | 1 | 1 | 1 | | | 1 | 1 |
| *PROFILE* | ♣*CHUSERPROF* | 1 | 1 | 1 | | | 1 | 1 |
| *DELETE* | ..... | | | | | | | |
| *INPUT* | | | | | | | | |
| *SET* | | | | | | | | |
| .... | | | | | | | | |

## Figure 3—The Behavior and Access Control Matrix

The first column of the Boolean matrix is entitled *SUP* and it indicates whether or not the handler is to be handed over to the system supervisor for execution. (The supervisor and its features will be described later.)

- If the bit is set, the service routine is not resident in the same workspace and the supervisor must find and execute it in such a fashion that control returns to the command processor. The execute (♣) in front of the handlers having this bit set is a supervisor command. It is not an *APL* statement that is executed directly.

- If the bit is not set, the service routine is workspace resident and a simple execute (♣) is adequate.

The second column of the behavior matrix, entitled *ARG*, indicates whether or not the service routine expects an argument.

- If the bit is set and the user provides data tokens beyond those required by the command processor, the extra tokens are passed to the service routine as a character right argument. The mechanism is such that this argument is carried along even if the supervisor is involved and a workspace switch occurs.

- If the bit is set but the user does not provide extraneous information, the service routine is given an empty vector as its argument. Typically, in our service routines, this is a trigger to prompt for the required data or, if appropriate, to assume a default value.

- If the bit is not set and the user provides extraneous tokens, they are "ignored" and the service routine is invoked.

- If the bit is not set and the user does not provide extra data, the service routine is simply called with no right argument.

The discussion so far has made no assumption about the size or length of the commands except that the prompt matrix, the handler matrix, and the behavior control matrix must have the same number of rows. The command processor's behavior is controlled by the relative position and indent of the prompts. This implies that it would be quite simple to disallow commands simply by compressing the matrices to remove rows that are not of interest. This concept gave us the key to controlling access to the commands based on the individual user's requirements and conscious actions.

This command screening process is described in the remaining columns of the behavior and access matrix, which are segregated into the $ACCESS$ section, the $MODULES$ section, and the $PROFILE$ section. The access section deals with command screening based on security related tests. The module section deals with tests related to the operating environment parameters that are under each user's control. The profile section deals with screens based on an internal description of the user. The user profile is derived from the user's geographic location and can only be altered by stewards.

The data contained in the behavior and access matrix is used to develop a dynamic mask that is applied to the prompt and handler matrices before the command processor uses them to prompt for and recognize commands. Any command that the user should not use is compressed out of the matrices. If a set of commands is not present, there is no way for the processor to recognize them. This masking technique also paves the way to allowing the system stewards or privileged users to use maintenance utilities that are invisible to production users. Similarly, new features can be released to a selected subset of users known as "secondary privs".

- The $PRV$ (privileged) column indicates that the command is only available to system stewards whose user identifications are contained in a special list. These commands are not available to other users. All of our stewardship commands, including the one used to alter the control matrices, and all new features still under development have this bit set.

- The $SP$ (secondary privileged) column indicates that the command is only available to users whose user identifications appear in the secondary priv list. These are typically users who understand the model very well and who have volunteered to be guinea pigs for testing new features.

- The $OPN$ (open) column contains an access bit that is automatically generated and set by our maintenance utility if the other two restrictions are not in force.

- The $MODULES$ column contains bits that indicate which modules must be active before the command is made available to the user. Modules are logical subsets of the entire model. Modules may be selectively activated or deactivated by the user to control the source and level of detail of the base data. Note that in some circumstances more than one module may be specified for a command. This indicates that the command is available if any of the specified modules is active. The last module bit (0 in Figure 3) is the "module-doesn't-matter" bit; it is set automatically by our utilities if access to the command does not depend on which modules are active.

The *PROFILE* column contains a set of identifying tags that are attached to each user at the time that the user is installed in the system. Each profile number has a certain meaning. Some indicate the state in which the user operates (this is handy when dealing with local regulations, tax algorithms, or reporting requirements). Others may indicate the user's level of training (e.g., he has been trained to define and run sensitivity analyses properly). Profile 0 is the "user-profile-doesn't-matter" bit; it is automatically set if the command is not given any user profile restrictions.

In the general case, the bits described above can have any meaning whatsoever that applies to the system under consideration. The command processor only uses these bits to determine if a command is available. Actual column assignments are the system designer's prerogative.

In our particular example (Figure 3), the logic to generate the mask would be as follows:

1. Pick up the open access bit and the privileged or secondary privileged bit, if appropriate to this user. Or-reduce ($\vee$/) these to obtain the access mask.

2. Similarly, get the module-doesn't-matter bit and other module columns applicable to the user. Or-reduce these to obtain the module mask.

3. Do the same for the user profile bits.

4. And-reduce ($\wedge$/) all three resultant bits to obtain a preliminary selection mask.

The availability of intermediate commands is determined by a fairly complex procedure. Their availability is based strictly on the availability of their subordinates. Thus, it is necessary to:

5. Reset the selection bit locations for the top and intermediate prompts. That is, only retain the bits for the leaves of the command tree.

6. Use partition function techniques, specifically or-sub-reduce, to walk up the prompt tree to identify the prompts that should be retained. A prompt is retained if any of its subordinates are retained.

7. Apply this final mask to the prompter and handler matrices to select the subset applicable to the user, given his present environment and profile.

## The System Supervisor

A system as complex as a comprehensive financial management model requires extensive bookkeeping, tracking, security, and handshake and restart mechanisms. In our case, the collection of programs that handles most of these tasks is known as the supervisor.

Some of the supervisor's duties include:

- Ensuring that files are properly tied at all times.

- Taking care of automatic updates to user files and performing routine maintenance chores at sign-on.

- Providing a restart mechanism to handle the inevitable line drops as well as the occasional hardware failures.

- Providing a simple and consistent method for trapping internal errors and hard *APL* errors such that the problem is logged and reported to the stewards before the user is softly shut down with an explanatory message.

- Providing a way to catalog functions that reside in a file or in workspaces so that they can be invoked by name.

- Last but not least, handling workspace chaining and complex "job streams" automatically.

In the remainder of this paper, we will address only these last two aspects of the supervisor.

The function catalog is an integral part of the supervisor and is usually accessed only through a function called *SUPER*. The entry for each function in the catalog consists of the function's name, a file pointer, a workspace address, and a workspace list.

- The *function name* is encoded and represented by a single value in a floating-point vector. This directory has no duplicate entries.

- The *file pointer* parallels the function name directory and contains each function's file address. A positive entry indicates that the character representation of the function will be found in that component of the file, while a zero entry indicates that the function is workspace resident. An element with a zero entry in this list must have a positive entry in the workspace address vector. An element with positive entries may or may not have a nonzero workspace address. Both are well-defined situations.

- The *workspace address* indicates whether or not the function must be executed in a specific workspace and, if so, which workspace. A zero entry indicates that the function is file resident and executable in any environment. A positive entry indicates that the function must be executed in a specific workspace and points to the name of this workspace in the workspace list. The function may actually reside either in the said workspace or on the file; the determining factor is the function residence pointer.

- The *workspace list* is a character matrix in which each row contains a workspace name. By convention, the first row contains the name of the main workspace that contains the command processor.

A few examples may help clarify how the function catalog is used. Let us assume that the workspace list looks like the following matrix (the user numbers and extra spaces have been elided):

```
PROMPTER
DATAEDIT
ALLOCATION
MAINT
```

A hypothetical function catalog could then look like this (note that function names would be encoded into floating-point numbers in an actual function catalog):

| FUNCTION NAME | FILE POINTER | WORKSPACE ADDRESS | INTERPRETATION |
|---|---|---|---|
| *SUPFNS* | 83 | 0 | *SUPFNS* resides in file component 83 and can be executed in any workspace. |
| *ADDGRP* | 0 | 2 | *ADDGRP* resides in workspace *DATAEDIT* and can be executed only there. |
| *MGMTPREP* | 96 | 3 | *MGMTPREP* resides in file component 96 and must be executed in workspace *ALLOCATION*. |

The supervisor uses this function catalog to link between workspaces and to access functions residing on files. The catalog also enables a calling function to request execution of another function without worrying about the other function's true location.

*SUPER* accepts commands in two different ways.

- Immediately as a right argument.

- Indirectly via a file-resident execution buffer. The importance of this feature will become evident as we discuss stacked sets of commands.

## The Supervisor Commands

♠ *Execute the function that immediately follows.* The name of the function is assumed to be the characters between the ♠ and the first blank encountered in the statement.

- If the function is file resident and requires no special environment, it is brought in and executed.

- If the function is file resident and the workspace in which it must be executed is not the one at hand, a "quietload" ($\Box QLOAD$) of the required workspace is performed before the function is brought in from file.

- If the function resides in a different workspace, that workspace is quietloaded.

In any event, any and all characters after the first blank in the statement are passed to the function at the time of the call, as if they were a right argument. For example:

```
SUPER '♠CHSPNAM'
SUPER '♠CHSPCODES USERDATA'
```

→ *Fetch the function from the file.* The function is brought into the workspace, but not executed. All characters after the first blank in the statement are disregarded.

↑ *Quietload another workspace.* Two variants are recognized. A statement like ↑*ALLOCATION* means "quietload the workspace *ALLOCATION*". A statement like ↑1 means "quietload the first workspace in *WSLIST*" and is typically used whenever a user enters the word *QUIT* in response to any prompt in the system. This has the effect of immediately returning control to the command processor. In all cases where *SUPER* is forced to quietload another workspace, it does so only after taking the remaining unexecuted job stream and depositing it in the execution buffer. This is also true of loads implied through a ♠ command.

It should be noted that our users never interact directly with the supervisor by using these commands. Instead, the supervisor is given arguments by cover functions. For instance, suppose the command processor receives a "change budget spread codes" command with a declared handler of

⍋*CHSPCODES* and the supervisor bit is set (as shown in Figure 3). When the prompter detects this particular command, it will call *SUPER* with the argument '⍋*CHSPCODES*' to service the request. This kind of clean interfacing and division of responsibilities allow for a much simpler command processor design. The command processor need not be concerned with the mechanics that may be required to execute a service function. These tasks are delegated to the supervisor and the command processor only worries about accepting and matching user commands.

The supervisor is also capable of accepting a stream of multiple commands at once and executing them in sequence. The diamond statement separator (◇) is used to separate commands. For example,

*SUPER* '⍋*SUPFNS* ◇↑3 ◇→*CHARIN* ◇→*IGET* ◇→*IPUT* ◇→*PUT* ◇*MGMTCAL* ◇↑7890 *PROMPTER*'

is a job stream that executes functions, fetches others, and swaps workspaces. Once the primitives are known, most job streams are as readable as this one.

Typically such complex job streams are generated when the user requests a report that requires execution of the model. In that case, the job stream is composed of the model elements (functions) that must be executed to generate the desired report. (This particular mechanism is described in detail in another paper entitled "A Data Management Technique Using a Graph Structure", which appears elsewhere in this book.)

In the last example, note that the statement *MGMTCAL* contains no supervisor command. These types of statements are executed directly in the workspace that happens to be active. They are assumed to be executable by *SUPER* without error.

The assumption made in this example is that all of the workspaces loaded contain the statement *SUPER* '' in their latent expressions. When executed with an empty argument, *SUPER* checks the execution buffer that is maintained on file. If commands are found there, *SUPER* processes those commands. If a command requires a workspace swap, the unexecuted portion of the command is written back into the execution buffer before the new workspace is quietloaded. This mechanism provides continuity in moving from workspace to workspace.

*SUPER* is reentrant and can always be called upon to perform a task even if the caller is executing as part of a job stream. No limitations are imposed on the level of nesting. When *SUPER* is called with an argument, the commands in the argument are executed directly without affecting a job stream in progress, provided the new commands do not require swapping workspaces.

For instance, if the user wants to send a MAILBOX (STSC's Electronic Message Processing System) message to another user or to a steward, the command processor will execute *SUPER* '⍋*MBSEND*'. The supervisor then switches to the proper workspace (if necessary), fetches *MBSEND* from file (if necessary), and then executes it. However, *MBSEND* requires two subfunctions: *TEXTEDIT*, which is a text collector/editor, and *XMIT*, which ultimately transmits the edited message. Both of these functions are file resident. *MBSEND* has been called by the supervisor, and it in turn executes *SUPER* '→*MBSEND*◇→*XMIT*' to install its subfunctions in the workspace. This is an example of a reentrant call to *SUPER* that does not cause a quietload.

If a quietload must be executed, the balance of the command stream is deposited in the execution buffer, so that the new job stream overwrites the original one. For instance, still using our MAILBOX example, suppose that the user typed a message and then changed his mind and typed *QUIT*. All of our input processors recognize this keyword and execute *SUPER* '↑1' which, in this case, is a reentrant call that requires a quietload. The effect is to empty the execution buffer and to immediately return to the command processor.

The practice of aborting any unfinished job stream in the execution buffer when a workspace is swapped has proved useful in this particular application. Such a drastic action is not, however, required by the workspace-chaining technique in general. The supervisor could, for example, modify the existing job stream instead of simply overwriting it.

As you can see, the concept of the supervisor is just about as simple as that of the command processor. This elegant simplicity should not, however, disguise the power and flexibility that is gained by the implementers. Isolated from purely process-oriented chores, the implementer can operate at a higher conceptual plateau that is much closer to the real problem-solving environment.

## Conclusion

Both the command processor and the supervisor described here are stand-alone subsystems that can be used independently. However, even a loose coupling between them produces a structure and programming environment that is quite flexible and an implementer's delight. One can start with a modest set of user commands and add new ones, including stewardship utilities, as the need arises.

While space and the proprietary nature of the code does not allow me to publish the actual programs, the following statistics should give you a feel for the modest size of these functions and the size of the system they have been able to manage with ease.

- The command processor is 18 lines of code and occupies 1808 bytes. It uses five small, general-purpose utilities that occupy another 828 bytes.

- Development of the user mask at sign-on is by far the most complex operation. That particular function is 11 lines long and occupies 824 bytes.

- The main supervisor function that handles the commands described here (as well as some error-trapping features) is 23 lines long and occupies 2008 bytes.

- We have 630 prompts, and the most complex path is presently four levels deep.

- The whole system is estimated to have 1100 unique functions, 720 of which are main functions known to and managed by the supervisor. The other functions are for support operations and for other modules such as a data manager and a report generator.

- The supervisor manages 18 different workspaces.

Readers interested in another aspect of this model—and the way we generate job streams to control the model logic—may want to refer to a paper entitled "A Data Management Technique Using a Graph Structure", which also appears in this book.

My intent in presenting this paper is to share some ideas that worked well for me and that increased my productivity as well as the quality of a large system. These concepts are transportable and applicable to a variety of systems. I hope that I have sparked some interest in implementers to adapt these ideas to their particular needs.

*Jak Eskinazi joined STSC in 1974 and is currently a small systems analyst, involved in planning and marketing small systems software. He previously held positions with STSC as a marketing representative, applications consultant, and applications consultant manager. Major projects he has worked on include the Hospital Financial Management System and the Moebs Remote Order-Entry System.*

*Eskinazi has a B.A. in chemistry and a Ph.D. in education, both from Syracuse University.*

**Jack S. Reynolds**

# Data Sharing
# In Large Application Systems

When designing large application systems that involve the sharing of data (i.e., more than one person has access to the same data), there are many questions that need to be asked and answered. The questions generally revolve around one key question: "How sophisticated do you wish to be about the control of data sharing?" Any level of control you want can be provided. There are, however, costs (programming costs and ongoing operational costs) associated with each control implemented. There are also risks (usually the likelihood of unauthorized access to the data and the possibility of file damage) associated with each control not implemented. The design process consists of weighing the estimated costs against the possible risks, and developing a compromise that satisfies specific requirements.

The first part of this paper discusses several general questions about application design. These questions are of a background nature; the answers are used primarily to help evaluate the costs and risks associated with various controls. The second part of the paper discusses specific controls that can be implemented, and indicates how to evaluate the costs and risks associated with these controls. And finally, the third part of the paper discusses how the various controls associated with data sharing relate to other areas of large application design.

## General Questions

There are several general questions that are important to ask and answer before design begins. Unfortunately, the questions are often left unasked and therefore there is no standard answer. Each designer and implementer has his own answers which may be in conflict with others' answers. Even in the case of a single designer, if the questions are not asked, a wrong answer may be assumed and the design can become needlessly complex.

As an example, the designer may believe the data to be highly confidential and, therefore, design the system with elaborate controls over data security. In fact, the data may not be highly confidential, so many or all of the controls designed into the system could be eliminated, thus saving a lot of programming time and expense.

It is a good idea for the designers to have a well-established consensus about what problem the application will solve, who will use the system, how the system will be used, and in what environment the system will be written and used.

1.  The Nature of the Application

What is the nature of the application? It is important to know how the application will be used. A general ledger application that will be reviewed by auditors needs to have tight control over the quality of the data right down to the penny, so there is a need to have tight control over the interaction among the different users. For example, since the confidentiality of the data in the general ledger is likely not to be very high, many users will have access. It could be disastrous if one person deleted the transaction detail before the books had been closed for that month.

On the other hand, a long-range planning system might be dealing in millions of dollars, and discrepancies in the input data of several thousand dollars might not be very significant. The results of the system are projected operating results of the corporation five years from now that are dependent upon the selection of one of several possible paths. In this application, the quality of the data needs to be good only at a very gross level, and tight controls are probably not necessary. The output reports, however, represent the basis for making key decisions, and access to them should probably be very tightly controlled.

These examples illustrate three questions that need to be asked about the nature of the application:

*   *How confidential is the data?* The confidentiality or sensitivity of the data ranges from nonconfidential (such as data that is part of the public domain) to very confidential or personal (such as personnel or payroll data). There is, of course, an entire range of varying degrees of confidentiality lying between these two extremes. Even though the data may be considered nonconfidential when looked at in small amounts, care should be taken to evaluate the importance of having the data available on a computer. The power of the computer makes it possible to aggregate the nonconfidential data into highly confidential analyses and summaries.

*   *How good does the data have to be?* It is also necessary to consider the importance of data integrity. The old kitchen axiom "too many cooks spoil the broth" applies to the world of data processing as well. Too many people entering, editing, and displaying the same data can spoil the data. Fortunately, it is possible to control this, but first you should determine if it is really necessary.

*   *What procedures are involved in running the application?* Are there any normal operating procedures that could be affected by having more than one person using the system? For example, in a general ledger application a trial balance must be run before closing the books for a month, and the books must be closed for a month before transaction detail for that month can be erased. With more than one person using the system, the chances of these events happening out of sequence are greatly increased. Another example is a budgeting system where each division is given access to the database to enter and edit their requested budget. After all divisional budgets have been entered, no more entry or editing is allowed while the divisional budgets are consolidated into a corporate budget. Decisions are made at this time about which expenses to authorize. After the final decisions are made, the individual divisions are again given access to the database, but only to display their final, revised budget. In both of these examples, it is necessary that the events happen in the proper order. Safeguards can be programmed into the system, or you can rely upon the staff to make certain that events proceed in the correct sequence.

## 2. The Users

Who are the users of the system? What classes or types of users are needed? These may include, for example, data entry clerks who only enter and edit the data, analysts who are allowed to display the reports, and a system steward who controls all aspects of the system such as adding a new user or installing a new program. What sort of people will be filling these roles? Are they naive users or sophisticated programmers?

In many design areas the answers to these questions will allow you to make the proper decisions in regard to which controls to implement. For example, it is probably unnecessary to build in a lot of controls to prohibit the data entry clerks from examining the data when they lack the necessary programming skills to get at the data. It might, however, be necessary to implement procedural controls to protect the integrity of the data.

## 3. The Environment

Another important consideration is the environment in which the system will be written and used. In particular:

- *Are there any enhancements to the programming language that can reduce the amount of programming required?* Since you are programming in *APL*, you will want to know what features are available with the implementation you are using. The most important question here is that of files. Do you have a file system that allows the sharing of data? Without such a file system, it is almost impossible to write a shared application. This failing can be circumvented to a certain extent if there is a way to execute system commands (e.g., )*SAVE* and )*COPY*) under program control. If you do have such a file system, find out what features are provided to control data sharing. For example, the *APL*∗*PLUS* File Subsystem (see note 1) provides three features that facilitate the sharing of data. The file access matrix makes it possible to allow very specialized types of access. File "holds" allow the programmer to avoid race conditions that result when two or more people are trying to update the same file at the same time. And finally, the file component information provides help in designing an audit trail. An example of another feature, available on some *APL* systems, is the ability to make programs uninterruptable. This allows the programmer to avoid worrying about what happens when a program is halted and what local variables may be available for inspection.

- *What procedures are followed at the computing center and your office that could affect your design?* Standard operating procedures at the computing center can greatly influence your design. It would probably be unnecessary to design tight controls over the security of the data if the security at the computing center is below the level that you require. It would also be unnecessary to provide these controls if printouts are left lying around the office, or if users share sign-on and file passwords. Another example is that of backup. Does the computing center back up your data? How often? The answer to this question can help determine the consequences of your data becoming damaged. It can also influence your design of an audit trail that will help recovery, if it becomes necessary.

The above discussions only touch upon some of the many questions that can and should be asked. There will, no doubt, be several concerns unique to your particular environment. You should take the time and effort to fully understand the environment in which you will be working before going on to design the specific controls that will make your system successful.

## Specific Areas of Control

This section discusses several specific areas of control that can be programmed into a system. The specific controls discussed relate to security, data integrity, simultaneous access, and an audit trail. Finally, a method of designing and implementing a system that facilitates the use of controls in all of the above areas is briefly discussed.

### 1.  Security

Security is frequently the most important control to implement. It relates to the prevention of unauthorized use of the data. Because the controls implemented for security purposes often indicate what a particular user is and is not allowed to do with data, these controls are also very closely related to those used to protect the integrity of the data.

For example, in a general ledger application, you may give data entry clerks access to post (append) transactions to the file, but not to print (read) the summary reports (e.g., balance sheet and income statement). Other users should be allowed to print these reports, but not to post transactions. There might be other functions (e.g., dropping transaction detail for months that have been closed) reserved for a single person designated as the system steward.

Another example is a personnel system. Each record in this system might contain the following information for one employee: employee number, name, address, manager, salary, age, race, and sex. Because of the highly confidential and sensitive nature of this data, it is essential to have strict controls. For example, several people could be given access to employee number, name, and address; managers could be given access to the salary information only for those employees reporting to them; the corporate salary administrator could be given access to salary information for all employees; and the equal employment opportunity officer could be given access to summary reports showing race, sex, age, and salary, but no detail information.

A simple method of controlling the access involves giving all users unlimited access to all of the programs and data, and simply telling them what they can and cannot do. This will work very well if your users are naive. If, however, your users are sophisticated, this technique provides no real control. Yet, it can still be a viable option if the data is nonconfidential. The advantage of this technique is that no special programming is required.

Another slightly more restrictive approach is to provide unlimited access to the data, but control access to the programs. This assumes that the data will be accessed through programs that are provided by the application programmer. Again, the system is not protected against the sophisticated user who can get at the data directly, but is protected against a naive user inadvertently doing something he shouldn't. The implementation of such a design is usually only slightly more difficult than the first approach. You must spend the time and effort to make certain that each user is provided with exactly the programs he should have. One easy way of doing this is to put a validation program at the beginning of each user-level program. An example of such a program is shown below.

```
      ∇  VALIDATE
[1]      →((1↑⎕AI)∈VALIDΔUSERS)ρ0
[2]      ⎕←'*** YOU DO NOT HAVE ACCESS TO THIS PROGRAM.'  ◇ →
      ∇
```

A much more elaborate and secure method of accomplishing this is described in the paper "User-to-Application Interface: A Command Processor Approach", which is presented elsewhere in this book.

Another, more powerful method of control is available on those systems that have shared file systems with some sort of file access control. Use of this facility makes it impossible for the clerk who has been denied read access to the general ledger file to read data from the file. Indeed, the program will stop with a *FILE ACCESS ERROR*. This method usually requires some careful examination of the problem, and most likely requires some additional programming or a rethinking of the file structure. The reason for this is that although the posting of data in the general ledger application is essentially an appending process, what usually is done is not only an append, but the updating of one or more directories (read, catenate, and replace). The only way around this is to give the clerk both read and replace access in addition to append access. A sophisticated user will quickly find his way around this. Rather than granting this sort of access, the directories can be put in separate files, and the user granted append access to the transaction file, and read/replace access only to the directory file. This works nicely in simple situations, but in most situations makes the file structure needlessly complex.

The three methods of access control mentioned so far (i.e., tell the users what they can do, restrict access to the programs, and set file access controls) provide increasing levels of control over the use of the data, with a corresponding reduction in the possibility of a security violation. All of the methods are good for preventing naive users from accessing the wrong data. None of them, however, will prevent a sophisticated and sufficiently motivated user from getting at some of the data (except perhaps by using file access controls and being very careful with the file design). The nice thing about all of these approaches is that they are relatively easy to implement since they require very little additional programming. If the nature of your application is such that the possible risks inherent in these approaches is not a problem, there is no need to use more control.

A final method providing a great deal of security involves using locked *APL* programs to control access to files (possibly involving passnumbers). For example, a person that is allowed to look only at the first two fields of a record might be given a locked function that looks as follows:

```
      ∇ R←READ COMP
[1]     R←2↑□FREAD 1,COMP,123456789
      ∇
```

Because access to the file is through locked functions, even sophisticated users cannot get at the data without using the functions provided. Therefore, they will be able to perform only those activities for which they are authorized. If security is a major concern, this is probably the way to go. However, the extra programming associated with providing this type of control is usually high because of the necessity to examine every line of code, thinking about areas where a security violation could occur. If many types of access are required (such as in the personnel system example), maintaining and updating the system can become a major task. It is also wise to take the time to reexamine the file structure since the choice of a different file structure could make these controls much easier to implement.

2. Data Integrity

As already mentioned, the problem of protecting the integrity of the data is very closely related to the problem of security already discussed. Indeed, the possibility of damage is greatly reduced simply by controlling access to the data.

The only additional controls that might need to be implemented are controls to ensure that certain key events happen in the proper sequence. This is easily accomplished by granting all users access to a file that contains a set of status flags. For example, in the general ledger application, one flag could be used to hold the value of the last month closed. The program that closes the books for a month would have to increment this flag when the job was completed. The program for dropping transactions for closed months, then, would ask for the month through which transactions should be dropped, compare this against the flag, and either continue (if the month has been closed) or stop. A simple function demonstrating this technique is shown below.

```
      ∇ CHECKMONTH MONTH
[1]     →(MONTH≤LASTΔMONTHΔCLOSED)ρ0
[2]     □←'*** BOOKS CLOSED ONLY THROUGH MONTH ',▼LASTΔMONTHΔCLOSED ◊ →
      ∇
```

Such checks and controls are usually fairly easy to implement. It can, however, take a lot of time in the design process to make certain that all the necessary checks flow together and that they are properly located in the system. Thought should also be given to the possible necessity for overriding these controls when the normal flow of events shouldn't be followed.

### 3. Simultaneous Access

Allowing users to access the data simultaneously presents even more possibilities for damaging the data. A "race condition" results when two or more users try to update the same file at the same time. The final result depends on the sequence in which the different users are serviced by the *APL* system.

As an illustration of this condition, consider once again the example of the personnel system database. What happens when one user tries to update an employee's salary while another user tries to update the same employee's age? Suppose each user reads the employee's record into his active workspace and makes his respective change. Then both attempt to replace the record into the database at the same time. The final result will depend upon the order in which the file replacements are made. In one case, the record will show a new age and the old salary, while in the other case, the record will show the new salary and the old age. Clearly this situation needs to be anticipated.

One easy way to avoid this problem is to prohibit simultaneous use of the files. This is easily accomplished on systems that provide two methods of file access: access for exclusive use and access for shared use. If all programs are written using exclusive access, then race conditions will not occur. Another way around the problem is available on systems that provide some mechanism for temporarily holding a file (i.e., preventing other users from using the file until it is released). The program for updating the record can then be written as: hold file, read record, change field, replace record, and release file.

It is important to realize that there are problems with both of these methods if you are also providing your users with the ability to restart their programs after a line drop. Suppose the first user reads in a personnel record and changes the salary field, but is dropped before replacing the record in the database. Before the first user has a chance to sign on again, a second user signs on and completes an update to the employee's age. Finally, the first user signs on again, restarts the program, and completes his update. The change to the employee's age made by the second user is then erased. This problem can be avoided by a careful examination of the programs to determine where a restart procedure should continue from the point of suspension, and where it should "back up" before continuing.

Status flags (discussed earlier in conjunction with preventing file damage) provide a more positive method of controlling simultaneous access. They also help to avoid the problems resulting from restarting programs. To implement status flags, the program updating the file should set an "update in progress" flag before starting the update, and should reset the flag when the update is completed. Before setting the flag, the program should check to see if the flag has already been set by another user and, if so, should not allow the update to proceed.

Fortunately, the only situation where simultaneous access is a major problem is with simultaneous updating. Two users printing a report at the same time does not cause a problem. If a report is printed at the same time that an update is in progress, the report may be incorrect (and it may be desirable to prevent this from happening), but at least there is no danger of file damage.

Allowing simultaneous access can be very costly in terms of programming time because of the need to consider all possible user interactions that can occur. Because many of the situations rarely occur, they are often overlooked. Designers realize this fact and, therefore, spend a lot of time convincing themselves that they have indeed considered all possibilities.

## 4. Audit Trail

The final area of control is that of providing an audit trail. Essentially, an audit trail indicates *who* did *what* to the files, and *when*. In many applications, audit trails are used only to help track down problems. In such a situation, a good audit trail is invaluable. But an audit trail can also provide useful information about how the system is being used. If some information indicating execution costs is included, the audit trail can help to indicate areas where improvements can be made to help reduce costs.

Implementing an audit trail is usually not too difficult. In fact, some *APL* file systems provide information on each file record indicating who last changed the record and when the record was changed. In many applications, this information is sufficient. This has the wonderful advantage of not requiring any additional programming. A more detailed audit trail can also be provided by recording all activity in a separate file. Even this approach is fairly easy to implement. However, if the volume of activity is large, the audit trail file can become very expensive to store. In this case, procedures and programs should be developed for dumping this data when it is no longer needed.

## 5. Remote Service

The final part of this section presents an approach for designing and implementing systems called *remote service* (see note 2). Remote service differs from the traditional approach of "self-service", where user programs read and update the system files directly. In remote service, a master task—constantly running on a separate user number—does all reading and updating of the main system files. User programs communicate requests to this task through an auxiliary request file, and then wait for responses through an auxiliary response file. This approach provides advantages in all the areas of control discussed in this paper. Some key advantages follow:

- *Security*. The users only have append access to the request file, read access to the response file, and no access at all to the main system files. The master task determines which requests are allowable and which should not be processed because of a security problem.

- *Data Integrity*. Because users do not have direct access to the main system files, the possibility of damaging the data is greatly reduced.

- *Simultaneous Access*. Because all requests for a file update are appended to a request file and are processed sequentially by the master task, race conditions cannot occur.

- *Audit Trail*. The request file can be used as an audit trail.

There are clearly additional advantages to this approach in other areas of system design (e.g., restart procedures and maintenance). But, this approach may not be suitable for all applications, and it may require that the programmer learn new programming techniques. However, when the approach is suitable, its advantages can easily compensate for the time spent in learning.

## Relationship to Other Design Areas

As already indicated, the controls used to manage data sharing are highly interrelated to other areas of large application design. This final section describes a few of the interrelationships with respect to restart procedures and crash recovery, maintenance and update, and designing a file structure.

Restartability in a system forces the designers into considerations of simultaneous access. The status flags used to prevent simultaneous updating of the files are very useful in determining how to recover from a system crash. For example, if none of the status flags are set, recovery is probably unnecessary since nothing critical was interrupted. If a flag is set, you've got a starting place for further determination of any necessary recovery actions. A good audit trail can also aid in the recovery procedure by indicating what was done just prior to a crash. Further, an audit trail can eliminate the reentry of numerous transactions if the files must be backed up to a previous state.

Maintenance of a system is generally made more difficult with each control implemented. This is simply because each additional control means more lines of code and more code to maintain. Also, whenever a control requires the use of locked functions, it becomes necessary to maintain two copies of the programs (one locked copy available to the users and one unlocked copy unavailable to the users). When actually performing a program update, care must be taken to avoid impacting the users. The status flags discussed in relation to simultaneous access can be used to determine when to perform program updates.

Designing a good file structure is probably the key to a good overall design. In fact, every area of control discussed in this paper has an impact upon the file design. In the case of security, establishing who should have access to what data helps to determine the content of the files. For example, if some users are allowed access to summary data, but not to detail data, it may be best to have two files. One file would contain only detail data, while the other file would contain only summary data. Those users who are allowed access only to summary data would then be given access only to the summary file.

In the case of data integrity and simultaneous access, the status flags used are stored on files and, therefore, must be considered in the file design. With simultaneous access, thought should be given to structuring the files so as to reduce the possible occurrences of race conditions. Finally, in the case of audit trails, if you plan to take advantage of the audit information provided by the file system you need to make certain that the file is structured so this information is meaningful. Audit trails are often maintained in separate files.

## Conclusions

The design and implementation of a large application system can be a formidable task. The control of data sharing is only one of the many aspects that must be considered. This paper has discussed key areas where the control of data sharing is possible. In each area, methods for implementing the controls have been indicated and evaluated.

*Notes*

1. L. M. Breed, *APL\*PLUS File Subsystem Instruction Manual*, (STSC, 1971).

2. D. A. Link and M. W. Gardner, "Deferred Execution: An 'ACE' of an Application", *APL79 Conference Proceedings*, (ACM, 1979).

*Jack Reynolds is currently an applications consultant manager in STSC's Boston office. Before joining STSC, he was with IBM where he learned APL and developed expertise in a variety of database design and data storage and retrieval techniques. Recently he completed installation of a portfolio management package for an insurance company, and he is currently directing development of an inventory cost accounting system for a national manufacturing firm.*

*Reynolds holds a B.A. in mathematics from Dartmouth College.*

Charles E. Yates

# Maintenance Systems

In users' and programmers' attempts to quickly obtain "working" systems, it is not surprising that features of a system that will not be apparent immediately, but may be strongly influential in the future, are pushed to the background during program development and design. This is somewhat ironic, as features that are ignored during development may in fact have a large impact on the usefulness and extendibility of a system in the near future.

More specifically, the set of files, programs, and variables that constitute the solution to a problem (*application*)—coupled with the set of interrelated ideas, procedures, and flow that describe the interactions (*system*)—frequently fall short of addressing ancillary problems such as:

- Updating and maintaining programs without affecting users.
- Providing for alternate programs for specific users.
- Tracking program modifications.
- Allowing the user to revert to using a previous set of code.
- Providing for prerelease testing of new or modified programs.

In many cases "end-runs" are devised from necessity, such as doing the maintenance in off-hours, providing special workspaces, or copying programs from other workspaces for an individual user. This approach may be acceptable for a system serving few users, but when additional users are added the system may deteriorate rapidly.

Users, especially those who are not data processing professionals, prefer to operate in an environment of stability and control. Furthermore, users, and system stewards or maintainers, particularly dislike calling or being called at 3:00 A.M. because a program is not working, and find it even more annoying if the program worked fine the last time.

A maintenance system will help alleviate some of these problems and can be devised for most any application system. It can coordinate multiple maintainers, shield users from ongoing maintenance and development activity, and provide an organized basis for library updates and consistency.

## When Are Maintenance Systems Required

Definite candidates for maintenance systems are applications that service more than one or two users, contain more than 100 programs, span more than three workspaces, or must be updated frequently. As the user community grows, so does the likelihood that changes will be needed to meet individual requirements. The task of implementing those changes becomes more and more formidable. A maintenance system will help assure orderly change and growth without disruptions. Increasing numbers of programs—especially specialized programs—add to the burden of the maintenance programmer. Frequent updates to those programs, which must be communicated to the users, force the steward to seek some scheme other than $)LOAD, )COPY$, and $)SAVE$ to accomplish this task. Figure 1 shows a progression from a simple application with no maintenance system to a more complex application and maintenance system.

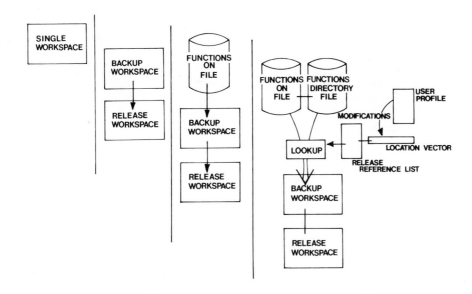

**Figure 1—Progression of Maintenance Systems**

## Requisite Conditions

One requisite for instituting a maintenance scheme is adherence to good programming standards, such as program consistency and modularity of design. These features should assure that unrelated programs in different workspaces will not have the same name, and that individual programs can be replaced by updated ones without impairing routines interfacing with them.

Another requisite is the ability to maintain functions-on-file, which are pulled into workspaces as needed. This allows the system to be configured by specific "user profiles" that define the variation of the program to be used for each user. This idea will be discussed in more detail later.

STSC's Comprehensive Manufacturing Control System (CMCS™) consists of over 2800 programs, including numerous versions of most. To demonstrate the features of a large maintenance system, the scheme devised for coordinating the maintenance, update, and program release activities of CMCS will now be briefly described.

## Structure and Procedures of CMCS's Maintenance System

Figure 2 is a visual representation that will aid discussion of CMCS's maintenance system. An application is made up of many programs; these programs may be imagined as lying sequentially next to each other on a shelf. Each program in an application may be thought of as beginning in *version* one, which lies at the bottom of each stack. As time progresses and the application evolves, many programs may change. These changes can reflect simple bug fixes, new developments, format changes, and so forth.

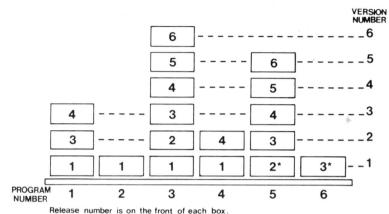

Release number is on the front of each box.
*Programs 5 and 6 were not created until releases 2 and 3 respectively.

**Figure 2—A "Shelf" of Application Programs**

If a maintainer can create a new version of a program (to be placed on top of the appropriate stack) without impairing the operation of the previous versions (beneath it in the stack), then he can test enhancements and new developments and fix bugs before releasing a new version to users. When he creates the new version, the maintainer specifies whether it is a special version for a particular user or group, or for general use.

Each unique program name is referenced by a serially assigned number. The combination of this reference number and the version number denotes a specific program stored on the file. As existing programs are modified to create new versions, they retain the same program number, but advance in version number.

When the maintainer has finished modifying and testing a new version he makes a *release* to the system. A release may be thought of as the latest version of each program in the application system, or, using the shelf analogy, as placing a marker (denoting the release number) on the top member of each changed stack. As such, a release constitutes a set of programs that become the "new standard" as of one point in time. Unless otherwise specified, the default version each user then begins to use is this new standard.

A unique program-names list and a numeric location vector constitute the Release Reference List. In the program number position of the numeric vector, the Library index (functions-on-file component number) of the "standard" is stored (see Figure 3). This reference list is stored in a central place and is keyed by release number. The creation of this reference list and the running of a workspace update utility (to bring new copies of utilities, if required, into each workspace) constitute the "release".

A "user profile" identifies which versions of which programs a user wishes to use. It is commonly stored in the database. It may specify special versions of programs, or indicate that the default will suffice. It consists of a release number if other than the latest release is to be used, or 0 if the latest release is to be used. To identify overrides, it also contains a mapping of the alternate program number and that program's Library index. The alternate version

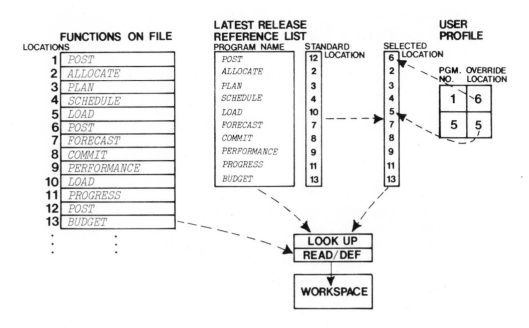

**Figure 3—Defining the Desired Release**

number (to determine the Library index) is usually communicated from the steward to the user for subsequent lookup and selection of the alternate to be placed in the user profile. A lookup in a directory file is required to determine the Library index from the program name and version number. This is provided by a program that also allows the user to display and modify his profile. For instance, at any time the user has the option of reverting to a previous release or version by simply selecting the previous number and storing it in his profile.

Whenever a program is requested by a user, it is brought into the workspace from a file so that it can be executed. This is done either by trapping a *VALUE ERROR* exception or through the use of small cover functions, either of which call a lookup utility. This lookup utility uses the Release Reference List for the release selected in the "user profile", modified by any variations identified. Each program uses the lookup utility to identify and call its own required subroutines.

If a user encounters a problem during execution, the maintainer may correct the problem in the program on file "in place" or create a "new version" (to be made available in the next release) to make the desired correction. He may allow the user to access the updated program prior to its official release, so the routine may be rerun. A program that has destroyed data, however, may have to be completed manually by the steward rather than being rerun by the user after the correction is made.

Information on every program is stored in a function directory file, which is an *EMMA*™ file (see *Extended Management Macros in APL*, STSC, 1977). As the first version of a program is filed, a maintenance routine gathers information from the file and makes some "next function" assignments. The function directory keeps track of:

- program name
- program number (serially assigned to unique program names)
- version number
- library index (component number in the file)
- who last changed the program
- when the program was last changed
- status (tested or untested)
- workspace map (in which workspaces can this program be referred to)
- encoded program name (for sorting)
- release number (0 if special, or the release number it is scheduled for)
- whether the program is workspace resident (when a release is made, is it to be installed in the workspace).

Using a functions-on-file maintenance routine, a programmer can create new versions of programs from existing ones. This routine looks in the function directory file for the latest standard version of the program specified, pulls the program into the workspace for editing, and files it in a new slot. The function directory maintenance routine assigns the next available version number to this new program and gathers the information necessary for tracking the evolution of the program as well as for reference and lookup or search.

An existing version is edited using another maintenance routine. A specific program name and version number must be specified to use this routine. When used on released programs, this routine may impact the production system. Therefore, its use should be confined to prerelease functions.

As each new program or version is edited or added to the file, the maintainer briefly explains what changes were made, and why, and the directory is updated. Through file holds and reservations, maintenance tasks can be shared by multiple, simultaneous maintainers.

Once a new program or version has been filed, it is available for prerelease testing. All the maintainer need do is "select" the appropriate version of the program and store it in his user profile; henceforth that new version will be used whenever a reference is made to the program name. This gives the maintainer the ability to run tests on prerelease programs in their natural environments.

## Features

In addition to location information, the fields of the function directory file provide the basis for searching. Each field may be used in relational tests or in combination with retrieval functions for displaying specific information. Some examples of questions that might be asked are

- Who last changed a program?
- Which programs have been changed since last week?
- Which programs have not been tested?

Using a string-search program ($SEARCHFILE$) in combination with some test and retrieval utilities (see Figure 4), the maintainer can perform text matches against the program file, as in the following example:

```
(LIB OF THOSEWITH NAME EQ 'UPDATE') SEARCHFILE '⎕FREAD'
```

This statement displays the lines of programs on file whose names are *UPDATE* and in which the string ⎕*FREAD* appears.

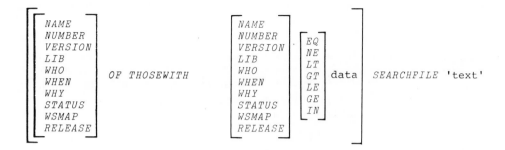

**Figure 4—Test and Retrieval Utilities**

The previous example works in the following manner:

- The expression *NAME EQ 'UPDATE'* tests the directory field called *NAME* for any programs with the name *'UPDATE'* (this yields a Boolean result).

- *THOSEWITH* translates the Boolean result into directory indexes.

- *LIB OF* retrieves the contents of the Library index field for those indexes.

- The result is fed to *SEARCHFILE*, which searches each of those functions for the string ⎕*FREAD* and displays all lines containing that string.

Any test statement used provides for selective searching of the program file. Variables can be used to reference field numbers (e.g., *NAME* may have the value 1).

Since the programs are brought in from a file, rather than residing in workspaces (with the exception of a few utilities), the maintenance task is easily coordinated, and it is no longer necessary to be "signed on to the right user number" or to worry about accounting for multiple copies of workspaces. File access and maintenance utilities and procedures govern the update process.

Each time a program is updated, a description is stored that explains what changes were made and why, when they were made, and by whom. This provides a clean audit trail so that others need not spend time making the same update or fixing the same problem. This information may also be printed on listings to show the evolution of a program.

Combining the directory file searching capabilities with the program search for a particular string allows the maintainer to make faster and more accurate mass updates to programs. This is often useful; for example, when replacing all bare file reads with cover functions, or when replacing fixed tie numbers with consistently named variables.

## Conclusion

Updates and enhancements are necessary to keep a system viable, but they must be implemented without interrupting ongoing computer use. New features that will benefit all users should be easily extendible, but special modifications should be feasible without disrupting other users.

Special user requests for particular operations should not necessarily imply change for "all or none". The ability to grant such requests, with little or no modification to documentation and no undesirable impact on other users, adds to the user's sense of individuality and to his confidence in the system. It also makes life easier for the system steward.

The use of functions-on-file and a maintenance system add a great deal of flexibility and utility to most large systems. These features allow maintainers to work normal schedules, make changes without affecting users, and devote attention to users' individual needs. The maintainer can easily leave a clean trail for others to follow. The user feels secure knowing he can "fall back" on programs that "worked the last time", as well as move ahead in an orderly manner.

*Chuck Yates joined STSC in 1973 and is currently manager of application development for STSC's Comprehensive Manufacturing Control System (CMCS™). In this capacity, he is responsible for CMCS maintenance and development and for customer installations and support.*

*Yates has more than eight years of experience as an APL programmer, designing and implementing custom applications for scheduling, operations planning, and information systems. In 1977 he began specializing in manufacturing systems and has since been instrumental in developing many of the CMCS features. He has also taught APL courses for STSC personnel and customers.*

Ralph L. Fox, Jr.

# Design Considerations of a Financial Planning System

STSC's *APL*PLUS* Financial Planning System (FPS) is a comprehensive software product for financial modeling, planning, reporting, and analysis. This paper will examine some of the design decisions and trade-offs that occurred during the development of FPS. The more comprehensive a software package, the more numerous, diverse, and occasionally conflicting the criteria are in both initial and subsequent stages of development. Therefore, a close look at the design decisions in implementing FPS can be a valuable aid for other software developers. First, a brief description of FPS is in order.

### FPS: An Overview

STSC's Financial Planning System consists of two interacting parts: a common library of FPS workspaces and a user-created database. The database contains the types of information described below.

- Input data:

    financial time series

    ratios and parameters

    names and other character text

    application-specific data structures.

- Processing definitions:

    models

    merges and consolidations

    sensitivity analysis sessions

    value-seeking and optimization sessions

    risk analysis sessions.

- Output results:

    financial time series

    summary measures of performance.

- Display definitions:

    report definitions

    tabulation definitions.

The FPS workspaces contain:

- Maintenance programs to create, modify, summarize, and dispose of databases.
- Conversational and nonconversational programs to enter input data.
- Conversational programs to enter processing and display definitions.
- Nonconversational data management programs that make up the modeling language.
- An extensive library of specialized financial, forecasting, and statistical routines to supplement the modeling language.
- A flexible report generator.
- Programs to plot and analyze model results.
- Miscellaneous programs to provide system documentation, orientation, and assistance.

The initial installation and development of a software product such as FPS might typically follow these steps (though the user's needs might be satisfied at some intermediate point):

*Installation of the initial system:* A demonstration system is installed with the standard FPS conversational modules for system creation, data input, model calculation, and report generation. Simplifying assumptions are made to get a general idea of the system.

*Enhancements and customization:* The revelations of the initial system lead to a formulation of more detailed relationships and more complicated calculations, and the system begins to be modified. For example, the report production process might be customized by including application-specific prompting or by modifying some of the standard formats.

*Familiarity:* The routine operations of the system are turned over to a less technical person for whom custom data input and checking programs are written.

*Growth:* Use of the system spreads to other departments, so a custom utility for system generation and maintenance is provided.

*Integration:* The application stabilizes and is "systematized"; that is, the customized pieces are sewn together to produce the ultimate system written in the user's terms and reflecting his environment.

FPS was designed to be particularly easy to implement and use with the above scenario in mind. Given the ease of installation of FPS, the swiftness with which one application proceeds to total systematization is frequently limited only by the speed with which the user and his organization become accustomed to the system and its capabilities.

## Design Considerations

The primary requirements of the FPS design were (1) it had to have an extensive "financial modeling language" that would compete aggressively in the financial software marketplace, and (2) it had to provide for a variety of financial analyses, but it had to be "easy to use" in order to appeal to naive as well as sophisticated users. To satisfy these requirements, the following characteristics were set as goals throughout the development of FPS:

- comprehensive technical capabilities
- ease of use
- modularity
- operating alternatives

- execution efficiencies
- flexibility/adaptability.

As might be expected, the interaction of these goals necessarily resulted in compromises. Moreover, there were additional considerations because FPS was to be offered in a time sharing environment. The following discussion will share some insights about how FPS evolved, taking into consideration these goals.

### Comprehensive Technical Capabilities

The first builders of FPS recognized that the most important task facing a financial analyst is the construction and application of meaningful and accurate financial models. Therefore, they established a bias toward computational prowess in FPS. *APL* was the natural choice for the "host" language of the FPS system because of its inherent powers. Not only were statistical, forecasting, and analytical routines easily programmed into FPS, but they were implemented in the style most appropriate for each technique.

By programming FPS in *APL*, sophisticated routines for sensitivity analysis, value seeking, optimization modeling, risk analysis, simultaneous equations solution, and consolidations were quickly made available to users in a library of stand-alone routines, or as capabilities that could be switched on and off as needed. Furthermore, the power of *APL* was always available to any person, from end user to system developer, to use at any point in the system.

### Ease of Use

Most financial modeling packages claim to be "easy to use", but realistic financial models must simulate extremely complex relationships. A real danger is that "ease-of-use" demands might impose simplistic rigidities upon the models, making it difficult to construct an accurate and valid model acceptable to the end user.

Using the sophistication of *APL*, valid, comprehensive modeling systems can be designed and enhanced easily, thereby avoiding the pitfalls of implementing a limited structure and limited vocabulary with a "messy", general-purpose language. Yet, with only very basic knowledge, a relatively naive user can learn and apply independent sections of FPS sequentially, mastering and fine-tuning the most basic and crucial parts first, while allowing the standard FPS modules to handle the rest.

### Modularity

Espousing modularity in software applications is nothing revolutionary, but the course of FPS development has convinced us that modularity is intimately tied to a system's ease of use. Nevertheless, customers have suggested that the FPS modules be systematized with a program which, at the end of one task, would prompt the user for the next task to be performed. To do this would detract from many of the benefits derived from modularity. In fact, we have found, through experience, that modifications to the individual modules of FPS systems are best made before the modules are tied into the user's application.

### Operating Alternatives

The initial implementation of FPS had a mixture of operating modes. There were conversational sections (prompted input) and nonconversational sections (programs requiring arguments and producing explicit results). For example, model creation was originally implemented as a nonconversational activity because it was usually unique to each user, almost always underwent change, and would have taken extensive resources to implement in a conversational fashion. Report production, on the other hand, was implemented as a conversational process because it was simpler to implement and the initial developers were able to conceive how it could satisfy most users' needs, provided it was capable of modification.

However, as FPS evolved, nonconversational alternatives were offered for original conversational segments and vice versa. Now a user can often choose between being prompted for model logic or programming his own models. He can define a report "noisily" or "quietly", and he has a choice of several options when invoking the report generator. These modifications were made possible by several years of familiarity with customers' needs, as well as several years of *APL*PLUS* System development (e.g., STSC's proprietary Exception Handling Facility, which allows *APL* programs to react automatically to execution errors). It became possible to offer some standard modeling capabilities as the difficult implementation tasks became less intractable. Furthermore, users seemed to develop a taste for much more sophisticated features than were originally envisioned, so some segments, such as the report generator, have been undergoing continual enhancement.

An application is initially implemented based on expected later modes of operation. However, should circumstances or needs change, the application should be designed to accommodate modifications with relative ease. That is, a conversational piece should be constructed with cleanly specified interfaces and special-purpose data management programs. Conversely, a nonconversational piece should include a consistent set of single-purpose programs upon which a flexible front end can be based.

### Execution Efficiencies

Execution efficiencies were built into FPS in numerous ways. For example, offering alternate modes of operation, such as conversational or nonconversational, helped improve performance and contributed to ease-of-use. Programs reacting to state settings before performing specific tasks were naturally more efficient than general-purpose routines that had to handle all cases. Other efficiencies in FPS were achieved using the following tools and techniques:

- The power of *APL* for parallel processing of entire data arrays. Numerous "naturally looping" algorithms are replaced by sophisticated nonlooping *APL* expressions.

- Meticulous data-blocking techniques within the modeling language.

- Switchable error checking, so that once a model has been debugged, it can execute without validity checks.

- Alternate algorithms and methodologies (looping versus nonlooping, for example) selected in reaction to the shape of the problem.

- An alternate report generator that sacrifices some standard frills to do bulk formatting.

However, some execution efficiencies may infringe on certain user-oriented features or require more expertise on the part of a user. For example, a system that does not check for errors is more efficient than one that does. But the user must either be more familiar with the system or willing to risk changing the model or entering incorrect data without being monitored by the system. Or he might have to refer more often to documentation to learn program syntax and arguments, rather than depending on prompts or "help" messages.

## Flexibility/Adaptability

As comprehensive as a financial modeling system may be, it must allow for customization, when necessary, to meet specific user needs. Numerous "hooks" are interspersed throughout FPS for this purpose. They are switches, variables, or programs placed at points in the system where a user might want access to the internal workings. Ample documentation is crucial at these points, so a user knows the possibilities and can achieve the desired results. An example of a hook is found in the FPS report generator, which will pause to execute programs defined by the user. Such programs might print special text, temporarily modify formats or decorations, or change the structure of the report.

These hooks may, but do not necessarily, affect the efficiency of FPS. For example, a hook may offer the user the option of inserting either an extremely efficient, special-purpose data retrieval program or a real "grinder".

## Time Sharing Considerations

Additional impact on the design of FPS came from the fact that FPS currently is a time sharing product, residing in a common library on the $APL*PLUS$ System. The problem is not that a particular application might have multiple users sharing the database and doing simultaneous updates; those situations are infrequent, and are solved in the underlying structure of the $APL*PLUS$ File Subsystem. The difficult task is to deliver enhancements and upgrades to users who may save a $MODEL$, or occasionally an $INPUT$ or $REPORT$, workspace in their private libraries.

Though FPS enhancements are designed to be upwardly compatible, it is important to give the user the option of *not* receiving a program update that would overwrite a customized version of the original program. For example, a French user might replace the FPS utility program in which all "yes" or "no" responses are made; an update to the system should not automatically destroy those efforts. Some update-related features of FPS are described below.

- Workspace identification and timestamp are saved in each workspace.

- A program is provided to examine the workspace identification and determine any differences between program lists for that workspace and the related common library workspace.

- A program is provided to examine the workspace identification and timestamp and perform any necessary redefinitions of programs from an FPS maintenance file.

- A program-on-file system is provided for the larger, enhancement-prone programs, where each call to the program results in its being defined from an always-current version on an FPS maintenance file. (For execution efficiency, the heavily used programs of the modeling language are workspace resident.)

- A program called $START$ is included in each workspace to establish all global variables and otherwise initialize the workspace. For workspaces apt to be saved in private libraries, $START$ is actually on an FPS file where system stewards keep it up-to-date.

- Version tracking is provided in the database structure so that the underlying file architecture can be enhanced.

- An online documentation system is maintained, which reads program descriptions from a file and reflects the most current program improvements.

- Online workspace cross references and program tree displays are provided.

These update and version-tracking tools do not affect the technical capabilities of the system and are generally independent of efficiency considerations. The benefits that accrue in terms of use, confidence, reliability, and appeal of the system greatly aid the promotion and acceptance of this time sharing application.

*Ralph Fox, currently manager of STSC's Financial Planning Development Group, has been with the company for over four years. He is responsible for the engineering and continuing enhancement of STSC's Financial Planning System (FPS). He is also the developer of a maintenance system that permits the documentation and continual upgrade of the 30 FPS workspaces.*

*Fox holds an A.B. in mathematics from Boston College, and an M.S. and M.Phil. also in mathematics from Yale University. Prior to coming to STSC, Fox was on the mathematics faculty at Fairfield University. He is a member of the Society for Industrial and Applied Mathematics.*

Gary A. Bergquist

# QUICKPLAN Design Considerations

This paper reviews the considerations underlying the design and implementation of QUICKPLAN™, STSC's Quick Planning and Reporting System, and looks at certain QUICKPLAN features that are the result of these considerations.

## Why QUICKPLAN?

QUICKPLAN was designed to help business users construct financial plans and reports—quickly, simply, and cost-effectively. Its specific aim was to automate financial spreadsheet planning and reporting.

During the last two decades, the sophistication of financial planning and modeling techniques has increased dramatically. Nevertheless, the backbone of financial planning remains the "spreadsheet" (the vertically and horizontally lined sheets of paper used by accounting managers and financial analysts), the sharp pencil, and the desk-top calculator. Typically, spreadsheet planning is not complex. Time frames are clearly specified (e.g., the 12 months of the next fiscal year). Line items are well defined and understood (e.g., a subset of the company's chart of accounts). Calculations rarely get more complex than addition, subtraction, ratios, and percent changes. Typical examples of spreadsheet planning are budgeting and long-range planning.

Although this kind of planning is not complex, it can be tedious. It is common in spreadsheet planning for the analyst to go through several versions, changing numbers and recalculating totals and other summary figures. The purpose of QUICKPLAN is to make life easier for the analyst by automatically performing the calculations and retyping the spreadsheet. Freed from the drudgery, the analyst can concentrate instead on analyzing end results and asking meaningful "what if" questions.

Figure 1 shows a typical QUICKPLAN report. The report was defined by the following calculation instructions:

```
     ∇ CALC
[1]    1000 LEQ LADD 1100 THRU 1500
[2]    2000 LEQ LADD 2100 2200
[3]    3000 LEQ LADD 1000 2000
[4]    3 CEQ CPCT 2 1
     ∇
```

and the following print instructions:

```
      ∇ REPORT
[1]     FIELDS 30 10 10 10
[2]     TITLES 1 2 3 ,S
[3]     HEADINGS 0 1 2 3
[4]     COMMENT 'ASSETS'
[5]     COMMENT 'CURRENT ASSETS:'
[6]     LINES (1100 THRU 1500),U,1000,D
[7]     COMMENT 'FIXED ASSETS:'
[8]     LINES 2100 2200 ,U,2000,S,3000,D,B
[9]     COMMENT '(NOTE: 1977 FIGURES ARE UNAUDITED.)'
      ∇
```

```
                        GARSDEN CORPORATION
                     COMPARATIVE BALANCE SHEET
                          (1976 - 1977)


                                                           °/°
                                       1976      1977    INCREASE
                ASSETS
                CURRENT ASSETS:
        1100    CASH                  $3,449    $3,793     9.97
        1200    SECURITIES              246       264      7.32
        1300    RECEIVABLES           6,829     7,539     10.40
        1400    INVENTORY            12,623    13,671      8.30
        1500    PREPAID EXPENSE         379       417     10.03
                                    -------   -------    -----

        1000    TOTAL CURRENT ASSETS $23,526   $25,684    9.17
                                    =======   =======    =====

                FIXED ASSETS:
        2100    PROPERTY, PLT, ∈ EQMT. $31,525  $34,380    9.06
        2200    (LESS DEPRECIATION)  (13,507)  (14,628)    8.30
                                    --------   --------   ----

        2000    TOTAL FIXED ASSETS   $18,018   $19,752    9.62

        3000    TOTAL ASSETS         $41,544   $45,436    9.37
                                    =======   =======    ====
        ---------------------------------------------------------
                (NOTE:  1977 FIGURES ARE UNAUDITED.)
```

## Figure 1—Typical QUICKPLAN Report

QUICKPLAN was *not* intended to provide sophisticated financial modeling capabilities. Such capabilities—automated sensitivity analysis, value seeking, solution of simultaneous equations, and Monte Carlo risk analysis—are available through financial modeling systems such as STSC's Financial Planning System (FPS).

What QUICKPLAN *was* designed to provide are the basic modeling capabilities required in typical spreadsheet applications. QUICKPLAN applications have the flexibility to grow in terms of time periods, line items, report complexity, and number of reports. The keys to this flexibility are QUICKPLAN's simplicity and practicality.

### Simplicity

QUICKPLAN assumes that its users are not necessarily experienced computer programmers. The system must enable such users to communicate easily with the computer; at the same time, they must give it enough information so that it can generate a spreadsheet plan or a report.

The QUICKPLAN user who must convey his plan specifications to the computer via a sequence of keystrokes is in a situation not unlike that of the financial executive who is out of town and must telephone to his secretary the instructions for a report he needs done within 24 hours. In both cases, the executive is forced to communicate all the necessary specifications without waving his hands or illustrating what he means on a piece of paper.

Time pressures force the executive specifying his report format by phone to be as concise as possible. This conciseness is necessary—even desirable, considering the value of managerial time—but it means that the secretary must work with less than complete information. Consequently, the report produced is likely not to be exactly what the executive wants and often must be redone, sometimes more than once. This means more effort and, above all, more time. Only if the executive can identify and communicate the needed changes clearly and quickly to the secretary and only if the secretary has nearly the patience and speed of a computer—only then is there a chance that the report will be done when needed.

QUICKPLAN allows the user to keep the conciseness that saves him so much time; an important design goal of the system is to allow the user to be as concise as possible when defining the calculations and report formatting for his spreadsheet plan. Specification must be simple. In general, highly repetitive specifications are defined via simple conversational programs, such as *ENTERLINES*. The following is a sample terminal session illustrating the use of *ENTERLINES*:

```
    ENTERLINES
RGS NAME:  CBS
ITEMS TO BE ENTERED - NAME, FORMAT, SCALE:   N
SEQUENTIAL?  YES
ENTER INCREMENT
☐:
    100

ENTER LINE NUMBER
☐:
    1100
1100 NAME:  CASH
1200 NAME:  SECURITIES
1300 NAME:  RECEIVABLES
1400 NAME:  INVENTORY
1500 NAME:  PREPAID INTEREST
1600 NAME:  END
MORE?  NO
LINE NAMES STORED
```

Less standard specifications are defined via flexible nonconversational commands. Some examples are

```
    FORMAT '-$'
    SCALE 1000
    3 CEQ CPCT 2 1
    NUMBERS OFF
```

What distinguishes QUICKPLAN is that it allows the user this simplicity and conciseness without exacting a high price in delayed results. When iterations are necessary, when the report must be run out again and again, the computer makes the process a great deal easier, faster, and more accurate. The report can be specified, changed, and run out in several versions—all in less than 24 hours.

### Practicality

To allow the user to be concise, QUICKPLAN must be practical. It must exercise common sense if the user has specified insufficient or contradictory information. Like the secretary who receives report specifications by phone, it must do the best it can with the information it has.

If a particular specification is unknown, QUICKPLAN will make a reasonable guess. Such guesses are known as *default assumptions*. For example, if the title for a report is specified but its horizontal positioning on the page is not specified, QUICKPLAN's assumption will be that the title should be centered. The primary advantage of using defaults is that it saves time. In defining a report, the user may swiftly specify the salient features without paying attention to the unimportant details. All features not specified take on default interpretations. Once the report is generated, the user can attend to any annoying details whose default settings may be inappropriate for the particular report.

The defaults assumed by QUICKPLAN are oriented toward spreadsheet planning and financial reporting needs. For example, unless specified otherwise:

- Titles will be centered.

- Negative numbers will be formatted in parentheses, for example, (58.00), rather than with a minus sign, for example, -58.00.

- Large numbers will be printed with commas, for example, 56,184,100.0, rather than without, for example, 56184100.0.

- Line names will be printed with line numbers, for example,

```
1100   CASH           $3,449      $3,793     9.97
1200   SECURITIES        246         264     7.32
```

When defining a report, the QUICKPLAN user has the choice of accepting standard default settings, such as the ones above, or of overriding them with his own special settings. Given this flexibility, the user may accidentally define a report whose details are logically inconsistent with each other. For example, the title may be wider than the report width; nonzero numbers may be divided by zero; formatted numbers (with commas, decimal points, and parentheses) may not fit in their specified field widths; or columns may be formatted differently from rows.

How are such discrepancies resolved? If the user has provided specifications which are contradictory, QUICKPLAN will *improvise*. It will use its financially oriented common sense to "best guess" the intent of the specifications and will act accordingly. The advantage of the improvisation is, again, to save time. The user need not worry about remaining consistent. When encountering an inconsistency, QUICKPLAN will not print out a cryptic diagnostic message and abruptly terminate, bringing the report to a halt. Rather, it will proceed to completion, doing the best it can with the specifications it has been supplied. Then, *if* QUICKPLAN's improvisations are inadequate, the user can correct his inconsistent specifications.

For example if specified column headings will not fit into specified field widths, as much of the heading as possible will be printed. In a field width of five, the heading

```
          o/o
       INCREASE
```

will become

```
          o/o
        INCRE
```

If special row and column formatting is specified, the column formatting will override the row formatting for numbers encompassed by both.

```
              6,829        7,539      10.40
             12,623       13,671       8.30
                379          417      10.03
Row ──────▶ $23,526      $25,684     │9.17│
                                      ▲
                                   Column
```

If you try to display titles that have not yet been defined, they will be printed as all-blank:

```
    TITLES 1 2 999 999 3
    ACME CORPORATION
COMPARATIVE BALANCE SHEET


      (1980 - 1981)
```

If a nonexistent line number is referenced during calculations, the line will be treated as if it did exist and contained all zeros:

```
      L 1100 9999 1200
3499      3793      9.97      52
   0         0         0       0
 246       264      7.32      95
```

If division by zero has been specified, zero will be returned as the result:

```
      25 2 60 DIV 5 0 6
5 0 10
```

If too few numbers are provided as input to a specified line, the last number provided will be replicated as necessary:

```
      1900 LEQ 25 26
      L 1900
25 26 26 26
```

## Conclusion

QUICKPLAN was designed to help the financial analyst do quick planning. To accomplish this objective, the attributes of simplicity and practicality were built into QUICKPLAN. The simplicity manifests itself in the conciseness of the user-QUICKPLAN interface, which is conversational or nonconversational, as appropriate. The practicality manifests itself in the system's capacity to compensate for inadequate or contradictory specifications by making default assumptions or by improvising.

The key advantage of QUICKPLAN is its simple and speedy user interface. The immense appeal of this feature has, at times, led users to apply QUICKPLAN to problems that should have been solved with some other tool. QUICKPLAN was developed for a limited, but very important financial purpose—spreadsheet planning and reporting. It is in these uses that QUICKPLAN finds its best and most powerful application, in them that it can grow and evolve to meet the needs of its users.

*Gary Bergquist—currently branch manager of STSC's Hartford, Connecticut, office—has been with the company for over five years. He started as an applications consultant in Houston, where he helped develop QUICKPLAN, STSC's Quick Planning and Reporting System. He also worked as a marketing representative in the Houston office before moving to Hartford.*

*Bergquist has a B.S. in management from the Massachusetts Institute of Technology.*

Jak Eskinazi

# A Data Management Technique Using a Graph Structure

While playing around with the embryonic concept and design alternatives for a large hospital financial planning system, we quickly identified a real need and a wish.

The need was to manage a large amount of data efficiently, both from the machine's and the implementer's points of view and in terms of flexibility, utility, and ease of use. If you have ever done serious work on large systems, you can appreciate our dilemma even at this early stage; the various aspects of this need always seem to be at odds with one another. Faster execution almost invariably dictates less flexibility and usually more workspace load.

We expected the final model to be quite large and we wanted to develop an intelligent mechanism that could determine which sections of the model needed to be reexecuted if a data element was changed. Typically, when data is changed in a model, the whole works must be rerun to obtain accurate reports. Our wish was embodied in my favorite battle cry: "There has got to be a better way (in this case, to control execution of a model)."

In this paper, I will attempt to share with you some of the avenues that were available to us and the way in which we solved our dilemma. With hindsight, things always seem simpler and results appear obvious. I hope that this paper will provide the hindsight. The object of the paper is to share a real and working solution to fairly general problems and to provide enough fine detail so that you can build upon these ideas and produce even more powerful or elegant solutions.

It is very difficult to describe isolated modules of a large system by themselves, especially when they complement and interact with one another. Toward the end of this paper you will find references to a "command processor" and a "supervisor". These two modules are independently described in a companion paper entitled "User-to-Application Interface: A Command Processor Approach", which is also published in this volume. You may wish to read that paper first to get a picture of the whole system and the way in which the modules interact through their interfaces.

## The Alternatives

When designing a database, the obvious choices available to the *APL* programmer are to use something that already exists, to write something from scratch, or to use the available file system (in our case, STSC's *APL∗PLUS* File Subsystem) in the raw with fixed component locations (e.g., all expenses are in component 1023). Each approach has its merits and shortcomings. Our process of discovery went something like this:

- Fundamentally, our system would be a single user system. This immediately removed concerns related to simultaneous data accesses. (With the advent of Detached and Deferred Execution, however, this early and apparently reasonable assumption proved wrong and we were forced to design interlocking mechanisms to prevent cross-talk between tasks.)

- In terms of size, our data elements would be fairly stable. Structural changes could occur, but would be rare.

- Like most financial models, time always seemed to be one of our data coordinates. This suggested that we could use STSC's Financial Planning System (FPS) in whole or in part. In addition, FPS's rich library of integrated financial routines could ease the development of the model logic itself.

- If all of our data could be represented in terms of line items and fields—such as expenses, revenues, and the like—STSC's *EMMA*™ Data Management System could be used. While *EMMA* does not provide any financial routines, it has proved an incredibly powerful tool in the hands of an *APL* programmer.

- We needed simulation capabilities that would allow users to make copies of the model to play "what if" games, without affecting the base data. *EMMA* layering techniques would address that need, nicely and cleanly.

- We expected the model to require large volumes of data as input as well as intermediate results. We had to plan for a database size in the range of 200,000 to 2 million bytes. This made the raw file approach less desirable and the FPS and *EMMA* solutions more palatable since they both offer features for managing large amounts of data.

The fly in the ointment did not show up until we started thinking about the data elements themselves. Our database would be constructed of model elements with widely varying shapes. Some arrays had two coordinates, along the lines of department by adjustment types. Others had three coordinates, as in departments by expense type by periods. The rank of our data elements also varied from vectors to three-coordinate arrays. In addition, the length of each coordinate was usually different (at the present time, we have defined 34 unique coordinate lengths). The complexity of this collection of matrices made a strictly rectangular solution, such as that provided by *EMMA*, totally impractical.

Need I say more? In the spirit of true *APL*'ers, we decided to implement our own flavor of a data management system that would address our particular needs.

## The Data Manager

Our data manager's primary charter is to let the model access the data as a conceptual array, regardless of its real physical location or makeup. The access method is very similar to the *APL* concepts of indexing and index assignment. The caller refers to the desired data element in the form of a data-array identifier and the planes, rows, and/or columns that must be fetched and brought into the workspace. Alternatively, the caller may specify a data array, coordinates, and data that must be deposited in those locations as if an indexed assignment were to be made.

We opted to identify data elements by unique numeric values and we adopted the term *nodes* to refer to them. The reason for the node nomenclature will become clear when we address our controlling structure.

Fundamentally, our file design is quite straightforward. The top portion of our data file is reserved for fixed directory locations and scratch-pad working storage. File components beyond a certain boundary are used for node storage. The directory into this area consists of two vectors: a main directory containing a list of node numbers, and a location pointer vector indicating the corresponding true physical locations of the data. Consider the following main directory and location pointer vectors:

```
MAINDIR←. . . 828 632 498 816 . . .
LOCPNTR←. . . 123 782 109 438 . . .
```

Node 498 would be found in *APL* file component number 109. Even this scheme is not new and resembles many GET/PUT databases that have been designed and used very successfully at this level of simplicity. However, we had to handle an added wrinkle: some of our nodes, especially the three-coordinate nodes, had a design limit of 312,000 bytes. We could not realistically expect to manipulate arrays even half this size in one chunk, regardless of workspace size. We needed to break up or *slice* nodes into consecutive file components of manageable size and design access utilities that would handle the boundary problems.

Typically, all models provide for a *simulation* or "what-if" capability that allows the user to model the effect of different assumptions (e.g., what would happen if inflation is 14 percent and sales are 10 percent lower than expected). Generally, simulations are performed on a copy of the base data in order not to compromise the contents of the original. Quite often a copy of the whole database is made for each simulation. Alternatively, using our two directories, *MAINDIR* and *LOCPNTR*, it is possible to make a copy of the variable data and to operate with a new set of directories pointing to it. While on the surface this option does not seem to offer any advantages over a duplicate database design, we will describe how we enhanced this simple idea. But first, let's formally describe our directories.

**The Directories**

After a few false starts, we settled on the following formal directory definitions:

*DND*

> This is the *directory* of *nodes* and is the main entry into the other pointers. Attempts to access data nodes which do not exist here cause various error conditions that are trapped and reported.

*COO*

> This contains the *coordinate* definitions. It is of same length as *DND* and contains data-node rank and size information in packed form. The generalized format is '*AAABBBCCC*' where

$\underline{A}$ ↔ length of the first coordinate.

$\underline{B}$ ↔ length of the second coordinate.

$\underline{C}$ ↔ length of the third coordinate.

If a coordinate does not apply to the array, its length must be set to 0. Some examples follow:

```
123000000 ↔ a 123-element vector.
 15056000 ↔ a 15-row, 56-column matrix.
  5103034 ↔ a 5-plane, 103-row, 34-column array.
```

*SDIR*

This is the simulation directory. The entry is a hash of the form *'JTFFFFFNN'* where

*J* ⟷ the coordinate to be sliced, if the need arises.

*T* ⟷ the node data type, defined as:

1  Boolean

2  character

3  integer

4  floating point.

*F* ⟷ the true data file component number, which contains the node or the lead component if the node is sliced. For sliced nodes, the "set" of components making up the node is sequential starting with this component.

*N* ⟷ the number of components (including the lead component in the set).

The sliced coordinate can be any one of the coordinates of the data array. For instance, a matrix can be sliced along the first coordinate, in which case a certain number of rows of the logical matrix are stored in a file component (see Figure 1). Alternatively, if a matrix is sliced along the second coordinate, vertical slices of the matrix (collections of columns) are stored in individual components (see Figure 2).

The selection of the sliced coordinate is very important and can affect data access times drastically. If a matrix is sliced along the first coordinate and most of the accesses manipulate whole rows (read or write), things are fine since all of a row is always found in a single file component. However, to access whole columns, *all* the file components in the set must be manipulated. The sliced coordinate should be selected such that cross-grained accesses are minimized.

The node data type is used to determine the size of each data element and to compute how many rows or columns of an array can be stored in a single file component in a way consistent with the value of the blocking factor *BLK*.

For example, an *SDIR* entry of 230005304 identifies an integer node sliced along the second coordinate and occupying the file components 53, 54, 55, and 56.

A file component and set length of 0 are valid, indicating that the node has been obliterated. Such entries may be found for any node in the main directories on file. These indicate nodes that are formally defined but that do not presently exist (i.e., they need to be recomputed by a certain process).

*USE*

This Boolean vector is of same length as *DND* and indicates whether or not the data identified in the corresponding element of *SDIR* is being used by another simulation. This global is generated at the time that *SDIR* is extracted, and it is then maintained in the workspace. Its use will be explained when the simulation mechanism is discussed.

*FREE*

A Boolean vector of length equal to the number of components in the file. It indicates which file components are *free* for reuse. When new data storage locations are needed, the data manager always attempts to fill gaps and holes instead of appending new components to the file. This pointer is used to quickly locate such unused components.

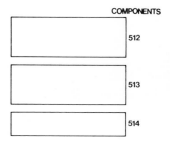

**Figure 1—Matrix Sliced Along First Coordinate**

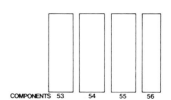

**Figure 2—Matrix Sliced Along Second Coordinate**

*SIM*

A pointer identifying which *sim*ulation is presently active. This variable identifies the set of directories that should be used at any given point in time.

*BLK*

The blocking factor, indicating the maximum file component size in bytes. The data manager slices nodes such that the size of a file component will never exceed this value.

This design does impose certain limitations. The major ones are listed below.

1. The data manager cannot handle files with more than 99999 components. If more than 99999 components exist, a *FILE INDEX ERROR* or *SYNTAX ERROR* will result.
2. It is assumed that no single node will ever need more than 99 components for storage.
3. Scalars (rank 0) or arrays of rank greater than 3 cannot be handled.

These limits are high enough, however, that they have not hindered us in any way.

Figure 3 shows an example of directory entries for two simulations. It would be useful to go through a few nodes in detail.

| | _____SIMULATION 0_____ | | | _____SIMULATION 1_____ | | |
|---|---|---|---|---|---|---|
| *DND* | ___COO___ | *USE* | ___SDIR___ | ___COO___ | *USE* | ___SDIR___ |
| 35 | 005 000 000 | 1 | 1 1 00190 01 | 005 000 000 | 1 | 1 1 00190 01 |
| 36 | 007 005 000 | 1 | 1 1 00216 01 | 007 005 000 | 1 | 1 1 00216 01 |
| 601 | 061 006 012 | 0 | 1 3 00393 04 | 061 006 012 | 0 | 1 3 00191 04 |
| 602 | 061 012 000 | 1 | 2 3 00153 01 | 061 012 000 | 1 | 1 3 00153 01 |
| 603 | 061 005 012 | 1 | 1 3 00137 04 | 061 005 012 | 1 | 1 3 00137 04 |
| 604 | 032 005 012 | 0 | 1 3 00167 02 | 040 005 012 | 0 | 1 3 00217 03 |
| 605 | 032 005 012 | 0 | 1 3 00000 00 | 032 005 002 | 0 | 1 3 00169 02 |
| 606 | 005 012 000 | 1 | 2 3 00184 01 | 005 012 000 | 1 | 2 3 00184 01 |
| 608 | 061 006 012 | 0 | 1 3 00408 04 | 061 006 012 | 0 | 1 3 00149 04 |

**Figure 3—Directory Entries for Two Simulations**

Node 36       is a matrix having 7 rows and 5 columns; the data is in use by another simulation. If necessary, the data could be sliced along the first coordinate. The node contains Boolean data and occupies file component 216 for both simulations.

Node 603       is a three-coordinate array having 61 planes, 5 rows, and 12 columns. The same data is being used by another simulation. The slice coordinate is 1; data type is integer; and the data can be found in file components 137, 138, 139, and 140.

Node 604       has a *USE* of 0, indicating that each simulation contains different data. The *SDIR* entries substantiate that fact. The data related to simulation 0 is located in components 167 and 168, while the data for simulation 1 is in components 217, 218, and 219. Another interesting thing about this node is that in simulation 0 it has 32 planes while in simulation 1 it has 40 (the user may be simulating the addition of eight cost centers).

Node 605

has an interesting $SDIR$ entry for simulation 0. The node has 32 planes, 5 rows, and 12 columns; it is not being shared with simulation 1; it will be sliced along the first coordinate; and it contains integers. However, it does not as yet exist (it resides in component 0 and requires no components for storage). This is an *invalid* node. Its contents must, at some point, be created by the model. Node validity will be discussed in detail in the section dealing with the graph structure.

## Handling Simulations

Another nice side effect of the $DND$, $COO$, and $SDIR$ pointer scheme is the neat and highly space-efficient way in which simulations are generated and maintained. In reality, these directories are matrices having one row per simulation. The first time a data access takes place, the appropriate rows (as indicated by $SIM$) are extracted and deposited in the workspace for use by subsequent data manager calls.

With our design, generating a new simulation turned out to be tantamount to making a duplicate entry in the three directories $DND$, $COO$, and $SDIR$. Note that we duplicate only the directories, not the data. The new simulation points to the same physical data locations as the source simulation.

Provided that data is accessed for read-only purposes, this situation is ideal. However, when data must be written back, we obviously cannot put it in the original locations since the nodes are being shared or are in use by another simulation. The $USE$ pointer, which is generated when the directories are materialized, provides a rapid way of identifying these nodes. On an update operation involving a shared node, our utilities would have to make a copy of the data before updating it and change the pointers in $SDIR$ as appropriate. That is exactly what happens. From that point on, further read references to that node will result in accessing the new location and all updates can be performed in place. Thus, our simulations share data as much as possible and duplicate storage only to the extent that they have truly different nodes.

Obviously, this complicates the logic of the update utilities (it does not affect read utilities) and costs more when a copy must be made. However, for a given simulation, a node will be copied only once in its lifetime and then only if absolutely necessary. In our environment, it turns out that the small extra CPU overhead is more than offset by the storage costs that would have been incurred if all the nodes were duplicated when a simulation was created.

The running code or the model proper is indifferent to simulations and the associated logic. These are handled entirely within the data manager and are transparent to the model, which simply reads and updates nodes by number. For all practical purposes, there is total isolation between simulations, a great boon to the analyst developing the model logic.

In nearly three years of existence, the data manager has never failed us in any way or breached the simulation wall.

## Data Manager Interface Functions

The right argument to the main data manager access functions can be a specially formed character vector or a numeric scalar. The character vector argument is a statement that must be well formed according to the following syntax rules:

1.  The leftmost entry is the node to be accessed; it is separated from the rest of the statement with a colon ( : ).

2.  The rest of the statement consists of executable expressions—one for each coordinate of the data node—that select specific parts of the array. The expressions produce either indices or Boolean selection vectors as appropriate. An elided expression has the same meaning as an elided index in $APL$. The expressions for each coordinate are separated by diamonds ($\Diamond$).

3.  The executable expressions may not refer to or make use of two-letter variables starting with a delta (i.e., $\Delta A$-$\Delta\Delta$). All internal labels are single-letter, underlined identifiers and are also not available for use in the executable statements.

4.  The caller should not make any assumptions about the order in which these expressions are executed. For instance, a specification like `'605: A∨B ◇ B←COLID≥MIN'` is bound to create problems since the first statement depends on the previous execution of the second statement. Among other things, the order of execution is dependent on the coordinate that is sliced, and it is best to treat it as if it were erratic and unpredictable.

5.  As long as the other rules are followed, embedded assignments are valid and may be used if so desired (for example, `'605: IND←B/ιρB ◇'`).

A numeric scalar right argument refers to the data node as a whole entity that is to be manipulated in its entirety, even if it has been internally sliced.

Four main access/update functions are supported:

$r \leftarrow BGET$ spec

Boolean get, a direct equivalent to the $APL$ compression operation. The shape of the result and the conformability rules are the same. Here are a few examples:

```
r ← BGET '345: BIT'          ↔ r ← BIT/VECTOR345
r ← BGET '605: ◇ BIT'        ↔ r ← BIT/[2] MATRIX605
r ← BGET '605: BIT ◇'        ↔ r ← BIT/[1] MATRIX605
r ← BGET '8023: BIT ◇ ◇ B'   ↔ r ← BIT/[1] B/[3] ARRAY8023
```

$r \leftarrow IGET$ spec

Indexed get, equivalent to an $APL$ indexing operation. The shape of the result adheres to the indexing rules of $APL$ and the same restrictions apply. Here are some examples with their $APL$ equivalents:

```
r ← IGET '345: IND'          ↔ r ← VECTOR345[IND]
r ← IGET '605: ROWS ◇ COLS'  ↔ r ← MATRIX605[ROWS;COLS]
r ← IGET '8023: ◇ ROWS ◇'    ↔ r ← ARRAY8023[;ROWS;]
```

$r \leftarrow data\ BPUT$ spec

Boolean put, with no direct $APL$ equivalent. It is used to perform assignments with Boolean index specifications. An example would be

```
data BPUT '605: R ◇ C'       ↔ MATRIX605[R/ιρR;C/ιρC]←data
```

$r \leftarrow data\ IPUT$ spec

Indexed put, the equivalent of an $APL$ indexed assignment. A few examples follow:

```
data IPUT '345: IND'         ↔ VECTOR345[IND]←data
data IPUT '605: ◇ COLS'      ↔ MATRIX605[;COLS]←data
data IPUT '8023: P ◇ R ◇ C'  ↔ ARRAY8023[P;R;C]←data
```

The logic followed by the retrieval functions is fairly simple and can be understood quite readily. However, the logic followed by the $PUT$ functions is quite complex and deserves more careful analysis. Four distinct cases are handled:

Case 1    Read existing data, do an indexed assignment, and replace the new data into the previous file locations.

Case 2    Read existing data, do an indexed assignment, but replace into free slots (i.e., make a copy on the way).

Case 3    The node does not exist. Create an empty node of the correct rank, size, and data type; index assign new values; and replace into free slots.

Case 4    The whole data array is supplied. Slice and replace into free slots.

The decision as to which algorithm should be used is based on a number of criteria:

1.   Is the node found in *DND* (i.e., known to the system)?

2.   Is the node already in the file (i.e., does it contain data)?

3.   Is the node shared with another simulation (in use)?

4.   Is the whole node to be changed?

These decisions can be arranged in a truth table, as shown in Table 1.

**Table 1 — Truth Table**

| In DND | In File | Use | Whole | Logic |
|---|---|---|---|---|
| Y | Y | Y | Y | Compute blocking, allocate new components, use Case 4. |
| Y | Y | Y | N | Allocate new components, use Case 2. |
| Y | Y | N | Y | Release slots presently in use, recompute blocking, allocate components, use Case 4. |
| Y | Y | N | N | Use Case 1. |
| Y | N | — | Y | Compute blocking, allocate components, use Case 4. |
| Y | N | — | N | Use Case 3. |
| N | — | — | — | Value Error. |

We also support a few other access functions that give us additional capabilities. These are

(*node,coord*) *DMCOMP bv*

Equivalent to a node compression operation that removes planes, rows, or columns that are no longer needed. The left argument is a two-element vector identifying the node to be manipulated and the compression coordinate. The right argument is a Boolean of the correct length. Once the operation is performed, the coordinate pointer *COO* is also appropriately modified.

        123 2 *DMCOMP BIT* ↔ *MATRIX*123←*BIT*/[2]*MATRIX*123

(*node,coord*) *DMEXP bv*

Very similar to *DMCOMP*, except that it performs an expansion operation. Its logic equivalent is

        123 1 *DMEXP BIT* ↔ *MATRIX*123←*BIT*\[1]*MATRIX*123

$r \leftarrow node \; DMSUM \; spec$

This function is dyadic and may or may not return an explicit result, depending on the manner in which it is called. As the name suggests, this is a data manager node-summing utility. The right argument may be numeric or character. A numeric right argument is expected to be a two-element vector. The first element indicates the node that should be summed and the second element indicates the coordinate along which the summation should be performed. This operation is equivalent to $APL$ plus-reduction $(+/)$. If the right argument is a character vector, it is assumed to be a data manager executable statement similar to the ones used with the main access utilities. In addition to those rules, $DMSUM$ imposes the following restrictions:

- An executable statement may be specified for one and only one coordinate.

- When the summation is performed, it will be done along the coordinate that contains the executable statement.

- Only the elements specified in the executable expression will participate in the summation.

The left argument of $DMSUM$ is expected to be a numeric scalar or an empty vector. A numeric scalar indicates that the results of the summation specified by the right argument are to be deposited in this node. It is the caller's responsibility to ensure compatibility between the result generated and the definition of the target node. If the left argument is empty, the results of the summation are returned to the workspace as the function's explicit result. Some examples follow:

```
r ←'' DMSUM 815 2        ↔  r ←+/[2] NODE815
r ←'' DMSUM '802: P ◇◇'  ↔  r ←+/[1] NODE802[P;;]
210 DMSUM 815 1          ↔  NODE218←+/[1] NODE815
218 DMSUM '802: ◇ R ◇'   ↔  NODE218←+/[2] NODE802[;R;]
```

The data manager and its utilities satisfied our data manipulation needs very cleanly and quite efficiently. Once implemented, it relieved us from the detailed chore of handling filed data and file directories. It also appreciably hastened the development of the model proper.

Our wish to find a smart mechanism to control the execution of the model logic still remained unsatisfied, however.

- We wanted a mechanism that would allow selective recomputation of model elements to save on processing time. For instance, if only data affecting Blue Cross were changed, we did not want to recompute Medicare and Medicaid deductions.

- From an implementer's point of view, our environment is very volatile in terms of relationship definitions and data content. Health care is highly regulated. Federal, state, and local regulations change frequently. We wanted to segment the model into smaller, more manageable pieces that would lend themselves to quick redefinition without having to recode a monolithic model.

- Being in a growth situation, we wanted a structure that would simplify the addition of new features or the deletion of those that were no longer in use.

- With the large number of model functions that were expected, we wanted to create an environment that would catalog our functions and quickly describe their interrelationships and interfaces in terms of the input and output data.

We addressed these needs almost by accident. It was a matter of being in the right frame of mind at the right time.

## The Tree/Graph Structure

While organizing the data manager nodes, we started writing documentation that would identify a model function (e.g., cost allocation) and we started listing its input and output nodes (e.g., the initial expenses, allocation sequence, allocation statistics, and so on produce the final expense and allocation detail nodes). These lists started looking like a tree where we were linking nodes in terms of predecessors and successors. A few years prior to this, I had seen an efficient and elegant solution to a departmental reporting structure handled as a tree and fully described as two integer vectors. I borrowed the idea and reworked it to describe the predecessor-successor relationships among our nodes. The only new concept was the definition and tracking of the model function that transformed the predecessor (input) nodes into the successor (output) nodes in a third vector. In other words, we not only identified the relationships but we also named the paths.

Once we had developed the tree structure, we found that it was not really a tree in the formal sense, but a *graph* (an *acyclic-directed graph*, to be specific). Still, we found that the terminology of trees seemed to describe what we were doing better than graph terms. We have, therefore, tended to use terms loosely and have applied tree and graph terms interchangeably.

Before defining and using our graph representation, we will describe a few terms and ease into the graph structure itself through an example.

## Glossary of Terms

Starting with the word "graph", this mechanism requires a good understanding of the terms that will be used to describe its various components. A clear understanding of the terminology involved is a prerequisite to understanding the concepts and structures that will be described in the rest of this paper. The terms will not be defined in alphabetical order, but in a sequence that will make them easier to understand.

### Graph or "Tree"

A graph is a formal definition of relationships between the various elements of a structure. It defines which elements are used to produce or arrive at another element. Conversely, a graph structure can be used to identify which elements are prerequisites to creating another element.

In our environment, each element is either a data object or a relationship between data objects. Relationships are in fact programs that manipulate data objects.

A departmental reporting structure is a graph with certain limitations imposed on the nature of the relationships. Loosely termed, this structure can also be called a "tree". The only restrictions we impose on our structure are that closed loops are not allowed and that relationships have a certain direction associated with them (i.e., inputs create outputs, outputs may not create inputs).

If you are not familiar with such graphs, it would be adequate to think of our structure as a tree. Because the tree concept is more useful in understanding relationships between elements, we use terms that apply to tree structures.

### Node

A node is a data element, identical in our case to a data manager node. The node nomenclature used by the data manager is identical to the nomenclature and numbering used in the graph.

*Task*

A task is a real *APL* function that performs operations on the contents of nodes. In the purest sense, tasks are paths that transform some nodes (input) into other nodes (output). At times the output may take the form of a report, but the definition still holds if paper is seen as a repository for results and data.

*Predecessors*

When used in conjunction with a task, a predecessor node is one of the inputs to the task. When used in conjunction with a node, a predecessor is one of the nodes required before the said node can be created. The term *immediate predecessor* refers to the direct input nodes to a task. The term may also be applied to a node to identify its "parents".

Starting with a node (or task), if we were to locate its immediate predecessors and all of their predecessors until we reached the highest level of nodes input by the user, we would have located *all predecessors*.

*Successors*

When used in conjunction with a task, a successor node is one of the outputs to the task. In the context of nodes, a successor is a node that depends on the contents of the node in question.

The term *immediate successor* identifies the direct outputs to a task (or node), without taking the relationships any further.

*All successors* to a task (or node) are all nodes that depend on its results directly or indirectly through the chain of relationships.

*Creating Task*

When a node is the result of operations and transformations performed on its predecessors, the function performing the operations is referred to as the node's creating task. In our environment, a node may not have more than one unique creating task. However, a node may have no creating task (top nodes input by the user), and different nodes may have the same creating task (multiple outputs).

*Top Nodes*

These nodes are the highest elements in the hierarchy and must be entered from a terminal. In tree terminology, all nodes that have no predecessors are top nodes. By definition, top nodes have no creating task unless the input processor used to manipulate them is considered to be part of the "tree".

*Intermediate Nodes*

These nodes have predecessors as well as successors. Intermediate nodes always have a creating task.

*Leaves*

Leaves are terminal nodes or the ultimate outputs. These nodes do not have successors.

*Walking*

This term is used to indicate that one is following one or more of the "tree" paths. One can *walk up* the "tree"; this indicates that one is starting from a leaf and locating all paths all the way up to top nodes. In this case, one keeps locating predecessors. *Walking down* refers to the reverse operation, where one starts with top nodes and identifies all successors.

*Node Validity*

The graph is simply a structure; it really is independent of true data content. However, in our environment, the graph uses the same nomenclature as the data manager, and the data manager has the task of tracking the data content of each node. The "tree-walking" utilities need to know if nodes are present (valid) or if their contents are outdated or not present (invalid). This is accomplished via the *DND* and *SDIR* vectors that are maintained by the data manager. This is the only interface between the data manager and the tree-like graph structure.

A node is valid if, and only if, the 100 residue of its *SDIR* entry is nonzero (i.e., it occupies file components). Otherwise the node is said to be invalid. In Figure 3 all nodes except node 605 for simulations 0 are valid.

*Levels*

The level of a node is defined as the number of tasks in the *longest* path that must be traveled from top nodes to arrive at it. All top nodes are assigned a level of 1. The level of all other nodes is computed from this point.

The level of a task is defined as the highest level of its immediate predecessors (input nodes). Levels are used by the "tree" walkers to properly sequence the predecessor task(s) that must be run to generate a report or a given node.

Formally, in a tree structure, all predecessors to a node exist exactly one level up. In our case, predecessors may be any node any number of levels up. We also allow paths to diverge and rejoin even if the length of each divergent path is different. These are the major differences between a tree and an acyclic-directed graph such as ours.

Figure 4 shows an example that may clarify some of the terms used.

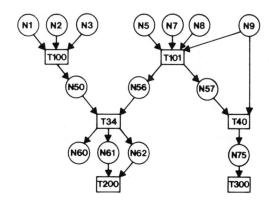

```
            Nodes: N1, N2, N3, N5, N7, N8, N9, N50,
                   N56, N57, N60, N61, N62, N75
       Top Nodes: N1, N2, N3, N5, N7, N8, N9
Intermediate Nodes: N50, N56, N57
   Leaves (Nodes): N60, N61, N62, N75
           Tasks: T100, T101, T34, T40, T200, T300
   Leaves (Tasks): T200, T300
Immediate Preds. to N75: N57, N9
All Predecessors to N75: N57, N9, N5, N7, N8
Immediate Successor to N9: N56, N57, N75
  All Successors to N9: N56, N57, N60, N61, N62, N75
Creating Task for N50: T100
```

**Figure 4—An Example of the Graph Structure**

**Definition of the Graph**

Our graph is represented by three integer vectors known as $PRED$, $TASK$, and $SUCC$. These three vectors are sufficient to thoroughly describe the structure.

The best way to describe the contents of the graph is to build it to represent the small example given in Figure 4. Let us look at task T101 and its immediate predecessors and successors. This task has four inputs and two outputs. Somehow we must be able to show these relationships. The way this is accomplished in our system is by listing each predecessor-task-successor triplet in corresponding elements of three vectors. For instance, this task would have the following entries in our three vectors:

```
PRED←    5    7    8    9    5    7    8    9
TASK←  101  101  101  101  101  101  101  101
SUCC←   56   56   56   56   57   57   57   57
```

Note that *all* unique input-output combinations are included in the representation and that each task requires as many entries as the product of the number of inputs and the number of outputs. This results in space inefficiencies, but we preferred to keep these definitions rather than increasing CPU costs and the complexity of the graph-related utilities.

The graph in the example would be represented as shown in Figure 5.

The relative positions of the triplets in the vectors are totally immaterial, and the tree is totally defined. For instance, to find the inputs to task 101, the algorithm would be

$$INPUTS←\ UNIQUE\ (TASK=101)/PRED$$

To find the outputs, we simply need:

$$OUTPUTS←\ UNIQUE\ (TASK=101)/SUCC$$

Top nodes are defined as not having predecessors. That is, any node appearing in the $PRED$ list but not appearing in the $SUCC$ list are top nodes:

$$TOP←\ UNIQUE\ (\sim PRED\epsilon SUCC)/PRED$$

By using, transforming, and combining these elementary operations, the graph can be walked in all directions to determine all parental relationships. Walks performed on this structure are quite reasonable and the required utilities are very simple to write.

The graph is an integral part of our system. In fact, with the exception of supervisory and maintenance tasks, it has the responsibility of identifying the function or functions that are needed to satisfy a user request, locating them, sequencing them, and ultimately causing their execution.

The graph is nothing more than a conceptual picture and a formal definition of the interplay between data elements and programs. It just happens that, if properly defined and used, it can free the user and the stewards from operational details involved with the running of a multitude of functions to achieve a desired end result.

At this stage it may be reasonable to ask what such a graph could contribute to a complex financial model. The answer lies in our fundamental, immovable, and ever present design specifications:

- The system should be user oriented and easy to use. Part of this design specification is satisfied by our command processor (see the paper entitled "User to Application Interface: A Command Processor Approach", which appears elsewhere in this book). Part of it is expanded in design specification two.

- Given a certain report that must be produced, the system should *automatically* execute the appropriate model segments if the

| PRED | TASK | SUCC |
|------|------|------|
| 1    | 100  | 50   |
| 2    | 100  | 50   |
| 3    | 100  | 50   |
| 5    | 101  | 56   |
| 5    | 101  | 57   |
| 7    | 101  | 56   |
| 7    | 101  | 57   |
| 8    | 101  | 56   |
| 8    | 101  | 57   |
| 9    | 101  | 56   |
| 9    | 101  | 57   |
| 50   | 34   | 60   |
| 56   | 34   | 60   |
| 50   | 34   | 61   |
| 56   | 34   | 61   |
| 50   | 34   | 62   |
| 56   | 34   | 62   |
| 9    | 40   | 75   |
| 57   | 40   | 75   |
| 61   | 200  | 9999 |
| 62   | 200  | 9999 |
| 75   | 300  | 9999 |

**Figure 5—Representation of the Graph Structure**

environment affecting the report has changed since the last time it was produced. The graph addresses this design specification.

Fundamentally, our users perform only two logical operations. They enter or modify data (e.g., revenues) or model parameters (e.g., allocation method and sequence) and ask for results in the form of reports. Our users should not be hampered by the model logic. Obviously, through training and documentation, they should be aware of the logic and data interrelationships, but at any given point in time—if they change some data or assumptions—they should be able to simply ask for a report without worrying about which tasks should be reexecuted. The graph fills the gap and provides us with the logic necessary to generate the required report from the changed data.

Our decision was to let our users change data at will. Changing data would simply flag successor nodes as being outdated or invalid, but would not force their recomputation. When you think about it, intermediate and leaf nodes need not be recomputed until a report requiring the affected intermediate data is requested.

Interacting with the graph can be summarized in two primitive operations:

1. When the user manipulates input data (top nodes in the tree-like graph) and subsequently files the changes, the system must identify all its successor nodes as being invalid (i.e., they must be recomputed).

2. When the user asks for a report, the system must determine the correct actions that must be taken to generate the predecessor nodes that feed data to the report.

## The Interface Functions

### INVALIDATE node

The argument to INVALIDATE is a list of nodes that have just been changed by some user action. Typically, these are top nodes that have been changed via the input processor. The function checks the nodes that are supplied and walks down the graph to identify all successor nodes that are related to the supplied argument. These successor nodes are located in the data manager directories and they are thrown away. That is, their SDIR entries are set to point to no component (trailing zeros) and all space previously occupied by these intermediate nodes is flagged as FREE. Thus, all nodes that are successors to the nodes being invalidated are thrown away and will have to be recomputed the next time the "tree" is walked up. Note that INVALIDATE does not affect the nodes given as arguments in any way, only their successors.

### TASKWALK tasks

This function expects as its right argument a set of report (leaf) tasks, such as T200 and T300 in our example. A quick check is made against the data manager directories to see if the immediate predecessor nodes are pointing to data file components (i.e., are they valid). The validity of all predecessors implies that the reports can be immediately generated. In this case, the function terminates and returns an empty explicit result.

If some of the nodes are not valid according to the data manager, the "tree" is walked up from the supplied task(s) to identify all predecessor nodes. The job stream that must be run to ensure the validity of these nodes is returned as a character vector. This vector is the argument that should be passed to our supervisor for execution to validate the nodes.

In the event that a walk is to be performed, the following logic is used:

1. The "tree" is walked up to identify all predecessor nodes that are prerequisites to the given report(s).

2. The data manager pointers are used to identify which one of these predecessor nodes may be invalid.

3. For all nodes that are found invalid in step 2, the creating task is identified and retrieved into a matrix. In effect, this matrix contains the functions that must be executed to create the desired nodes.

4. The tasks obtained in step 3 are sequenced in ascending order according to their level; only unique occurrences of each function are retained to ensure that each function is called only once. This list is then massaged into a job stream that is palatable to the supervisor and returned as the explicit result. The supervisor program can then reexecute the appropriate parts of the model, as directed by the result of *TASKWALK*.

Typically, *TASKWALK* is used when the user asks for reports through the *PRINT* command. The function that services this command simply validates the user-supplied report names, transforms them to their task numbers, calls *TASKWALK* to generate the prerequisite job stream (if any), catenates the true report function names to this job stream, and turns the whole thing over to the supervisor for execution.

Note that this logic does not necessarily reexecute the whole model. Only those tasks that are absolute prerequisites to the reports of interest are executed. All other paths are left in their original state of validity or invalidity.

To give you a feel for the size of our tree, here are a few interesting statistics:

- Our tree has 1978 entries in each vector.

- All told, we have 268 tasks; 108 of these are report (leaf) tasks. The others are intermediate tasks in the model logic.

- We presently support 381 unique nodes. Interestingly enough, 205 of these are input nodes.

- The longest path in the tree is 14 levels deep.

- *INVALIDATE* is 11 lines long and occupies 960 bytes.

- *TASKWALK* is 30 lines long and takes 3016 bytes. However, it should be noted that our version prompts the user for report codes and thoroughly validates the entries. Close to 20 lines are devoted to that necessary chore.

As can be seen from our interpretation and use, tree/graph structures are not very esoteric concepts. They are easily understood and useful in many cases.

For some reason, non-*APL*'ers and even certain accomplished users operate under the misconception that *APL* does not lend itself to graphs or trees and that they are too cumbersome and inefficient to use. In a small way, I hope that I have been able to dispel some of these misconceptions and that you will at least keep these concepts in your bag of tricks. They may come in handy and solve a problem when you least expect it.

*Jak Eskinazi joined STSC in 1974 and is currently a small systems analyst, involved in planning and marketing small systems software. He previously held positions with STSC as a marketing representative, applications consultant, and applications consultant manager. Major projects he has worked on include the Hospital Financial Management System and the Moebs Remote Order-Entry System.*

*Eskinazi has a B.A. in chemistry and a Ph.D. in education, both from Syracuse University.*

Paul A. Geller

# Writing Maintainable *APL* Programs

Maintainable programs, by being well structured and easy to read, are easy to repair and modify—so *what*? Indeed, why bother to write maintainable programs? After all, we set out to write programs which correctly solve problems. Because computer programmers are notorious optimists, we imagine that our programs will neither break down nor need modification. And yet, most professional programmers spend more time maintaining existing programs than writing new ones. We write maintainable programs to conserve the programmer's time and the program user's time, thereby conserving money. This paper discusses why and how to write maintainable *APL* programs.

### Why Write Maintainable *APL* Programs?

Simply stated, we write maintainable *APL* programs to save the programmer's time and the user's time. But why is program maintenance such a drain on the programmer's time?

Programmers make mistakes.

To disguise our mistakes, we call them "bugs", but they are mistakes by any name. We make mistakes because we don't fully understand the problem to be solved, or because we are pressed for time, or because we are careless. In any case, the error must be corrected. And while we dive into the heart of the program to perform surgery, the user sits in the waiting room hoping for the patient's speedy recovery.

Users make mistakes.

Not without their share of the blame, users too make mistakes. The common euphemism for the user's mistake is "specification change" (the specification is the description of what the program is supposed to do). Again, there are many reasons why specifications change. The most common reason is probably that the actual results of the program are not what the user imagined them to be. And again, surgery is required.

Many computer programs are orphans.

By the time some mistakes are discovered, the parent (programmer) is nowhere to be found (typically he or she has moved on to another project or job). So a foster programmer must nurture the ailing program and help bring the bloom of health back to its cheeks. To do this, the foster programmer must learn the idiosyncrasies of the child (program), and this can be a difficult task. Once again, the user waits.

Broken programs are difficult to fix.

Of course this isn't always true. Occasionally, a well-placed kick will fix an ailing television set, and sometimes it's that easy with computer programs. Happily, televisions usually have the same problems over and over. The owner learns to fix these problems, and the fix becomes a simple procedure. Unhappily, computer programs often seem capable of generating an endless variety of problems. And while we seek an endless variety of solutions, the user waits.

The program user has been waiting too long, and the programmer has wasted far too much valuable time. The next section is a guide to writing easily maintainable programs.

## How to Write Maintainable *APL* Programs

Three important factors that contribute to program maintainability are design, documentation, and style. The three sections that follow outline practices in each of these areas that will produce more easily maintainable programs.

1. Invest Time in Design.

The design for a computer program is like the blueprint for a house. The reason we hire architects to plan houses is not that carpenters (and masons, plumbers, electricians, etc.) are not skilled craftsmen; we hire architects because drawing the blueprint is a necessary first step in building a house. The blueprint ensures that all the parts fit properly. For example, we don't want the plumbing for the kitchen sink to wind up in the bedroom. The same is true for computer programs. Even the highly skilled programmer must begin with a good design. *Design before programming.*

To produce a good design, start with a brief overview of the problem to be solved. Work with the user to produce a written statement of the problem in one or two concise paragraphs. Make sure the user agrees with the problem statement, and make sure you understand it. Refer to this statement often during the design process to ensure that you solve the right problem. *Write a concise statement of the problem.*

As far as the user is concerned, the most important element of your solution is its output. Get a clear description (with examples) of the output needed. If a report is needed, get an actual sample from the user. If no sample is available (as in the case of a new report), have the user draw one. The sample should include all necessary details (titles, headings, etc.), and the numbers should be realistic. Refer to the problem statement to make sure that this output (which is exactly what your program will produce) meets the user's needs. *Get sample output.*

To produce output, your program probably requires input. List all input items and describe their characteristics. For numbers, determine acceptable upper and lower limits, whether they are whole or fractional, and so on. For characters, find out how many characters are allowed for each input item, and find out if an item must be one of a list of choices. For example, an input item might be store numbers, and the input might have to be one of a list of existing store numbers. In a case like this, you must also determine the source of the list of existing store numbers. *List and describe input items.*

To complete the picture of what the program will do, find out how the input items are processed to produce the desired output. That is, find out how each input item is used to produce the output. Some items may appear in the output just the way they were given; other items may not appear in the visible output, but still contribute in the processing. For example, some input items may be used in calculations, and while the results of the calculations appear in the output, the original input does not. After going through all of the input items, make sure you know how all of the output is produced. *Define how inputs are used to produce output.*

Now you've collected the problem statement, input items, process descriptions, and sample output. It's time to begin drawing the blueprint.

Inputs, calculation results, and sometimes output are stored in variables or files. These data structures are the working raw materials for the program. Structure the data to make the processing easy. For example, if a list of names is to be alphabetized, the names should probably be stored as a character matrix (one name per row) rather than as a character vector. The proof of this assertion is found by comparing the processing required for the two structures. It's relatively easy to reorder the rows of a matrix; it's not easy to reorder pieces of a vector (like names in a character vector). Consider all the processing requirements. If there are conflicting requirements (and there always are), order them by frequency or importance (the problem statement should be a helpful reference) and optimize your data structure designs for the most important processes. *Design and test the data structures.*

By now you're anxious to begin programming. Your fingers long for the familiar feel of your terminal keyboard, and you want to see tangible results of your efforts. The user is eager to try the new toy you are creating, and your manager scowls when he looks in to see that you are at your desk rather than at your terminal. Resist a little longer.

Before casting your design in the relative concrete of a computer program, review it with someone else. By now you are so engrossed in the problem that you may miss the forest for the trees. Gaining another programmer's point of view is a good way to improve your design. Your design can now reflect the experience of two programmers instead of one. And you may discover changes to the design that save programming time and result in a better final program. *Review your design with another programmer.*

Finally, you're ready to begin programming. Following the guidelines in Sections 2 and 3 will help you to write programs that are easy to read, debug, and modify.

The guidelines in the next two sections are excerpted from *Guidelines for Writing APL Applications* (STSC, 1979). They were written by the branch applications consultant managers at STSC. These people are experienced programmers who manage professional *APL* programmers. The guidelines were not developed in an academic atmosphere; they do not suggest idealized or untested practices. Rather, they reflect the collected wisdom of years of practical experience writing and maintaining *APL* programs.

2. Document thoroughly.

In workspaces:

- Every workspace has a *DESCRIBE* that tells what the workspace does and points to more detailed information.

- Every workspace has a *WSID* variable (a character vector containing the workspace identification in the same form returned by □*WSID*). In case a user saves a private version of the workspace, this variable identifies its origin.

- Workspaces built around public library workspaces such as STSC's Financial Planning System (FPS) include a comment in the autostarted function of the form: ⍝ *THIS WORKSPACE IS BUILT AROUND WORKSPACE '702 MODEL'*.

- In the autostarted function, document the source of any locked utility functions that are used (e.g., workspace 244 *EMMA* or workspace 901 *OUTPUT*).

In functions:

- Document the source of locked, stand-alone utility functions (like functions from workspace 6 *DATES* or 6 *SORT*) in the calling function.

- Comments must be accurate—they must agree with the code. When updating code or files, be sure to add, delete, or change function comments as needed.

- Comment unavoidably obscure statements.

- Function comments include descriptions of arguments and results.

- The first line of every function includes a comment telling what the function does.

- Document functions before coding them.

- Use function comments to describe *what* is being done, not how it's being done; clear code does not require a translation. For example, use:

  ```
  ⍝ ADD A NEW TRANSACTION
  ```

  rather than:
  ```
  ⍝ CATENATE A ROW TO THE BOTTOM OF THE MATRIX
  ```

- Include your suspicions about problem areas in function comments. For example:

  ```
  ⍝ THIS ALGORITHM WILL FAIL IF THERE ARE NO
    EMPLOYEES IN A DEPARTMENT
  ```

- Use appearance-oriented techniques to help make listings more readable. For example, isolate the code in the body of a loop by inserting a function line containing only a comment before and after the code.

3. Follow practices of good coding style.

   In workspaces:

   - Use a single function to tie all files so that it can be used in restarting as well as autostarting.

   - Name the function that ties the files *TIEFILES*.

   - Initialize and describe all variables global to the workspace in a function called *GLOBALS*.

   - Distinguish global variables by underlining.

   - Use as few global variables as possible. This means that data is passed via function arguments and results instead of globals; function identifiers that don't need to be global are localized.

   - *⎕LX* contains `'AUTOSTART'` or `'⍙ AUTOSTART'`.

   - Use naming conventions. For example, *TFILENAME* names a variable containing the file tie number of the file named in *FILENAME*.

   In functions:

   - Don't modify function arguments.

   - Assign the result variable only when ready to exit.

   - Write restartable function lines.

   - Name function results consistently.

   - Avoid ⎕ output unless immediately followed by ⎕ input.

- "Launder" input, especially before filing it.
- Replace repetitive expressions with calls to a common function.
- Write code in "building blocks" that can be independently tested.
- In general, write for clarity rather than efficiency. An algorithm that's fast today may not be fast tomorrow, but clearly written code is a joy forever.
- Limit nested parentheses to three levels.
- Don't embed constants that may change. Put them in global variables or in a file.
- Use tools like *RELABEL* or *ORDLOC* (both from workspace 11 *TOOLS*), or 901 *FCL* to clean up code.
- Code only after documenting.
- Don't use embedded assignments.
- Don't reinvent the wheel; use proprietary utility functions.
- Don't use modified versions of public library functions.
- Use meaningful identifier names except for temporary values; use and reuse single letter identifier names for them.
- Avoid reusing identifier names for new purposes.
- Avoid using confusing identifier names. Avoid similar adjacent characters (like 0 and *O*); avoid long identifier names that differ only in the last few characters.
- Keep error messages with the error-checking code.
- Write functions that can be listed comfortably on a single page.

Looping and branching:

- Always branch to line labels or zero.
- Keep label names within an application consistent.
- Use $L1$, $L2$, and so on or $\underline{A}$, $\underline{B}$, and so on to name line labels.
- Keep the normal flow downward, error handling to the right.
- Branch ahead except for loops and retries.
- Branch in a consistent fashion. (The most common forms are $\rightarrow B/A$, $\rightarrow A[B]$, $\rightarrow A\rho B$, and $\rightarrow A\downarrow B$.)
- Never use the bare (niladic) branch.
- Loop in a consistent fashion. Use a leading, rather than a trailing, test.

*Paul Geller earned a degree in computer-assisted literary analysis from Vassar College in 1974. In 1976 he joined STSC as a marketing representative, and two years later assumed his current position as a technical training specialist in STSC's Marketing Education Department.*

*As a technical training specialist, Geller is responsible for designing and implementing educational programs for STSC personnel. One such program, the Marketing Organization Development (MOD) program, is an innovative and highly successful two-week course for marketing representatives and applications consultants.* Guidelines for Writing *APL* Applications *(STSC, 1979), a by-*

*product of the MOD program, was compiled and edited by Geller and contains extensive checklists and advice for writing APL applications.*

Allen J. Rose

# Making *APL* Palatable

*APL* has been available on computers since the mid-1960s and by now most people who are active in computing have at least heard of it. Why isn't the whole world using it? To answer this question, we have to review *APL*'s history.

*APL* was originally developed by people with a scientific bent, and the early system facilities reflected this. There were no commercial formatting features, and data storage was severely limited. But *APL* did appeal to the scientific and academic communities as a "quick and dirty" way to get answers.

In the early days, most *APL* presentations were oriented toward the scientific community, and those few people from the world of business computing who saw it were horrified by its funny-looking symbols (and to a lesser extent, by the terse and intense presentation of many of the early promoters of *APL*). By 1970 both formatting facilities and files were developed on most *APL* time sharing services to make the language more tractable for commercial computing. Unfortunately, by this time *APL* had already developed a public reputation of "scientific only", so it was difficult to get people who had been turned off by early viewings to look at it again.

A small but discriminating group of business people did come to tolerate *APL* in the 1970s. Typically, this acceptance came when, out of desperation, they engaged some wild-eyed *APL*er to solve a critical business problem that probably would have gone unsolved without *APL*. Over the years, they tolerated the funny-looking symbols because *APL* got them results.

*APL* can continue to grow modestly by employing small, isolated cells of *APL* devotees to deliver results to harried managers who can't get them using more traditional techniques. But there is a better way for *APL* to grow and to benefit management much more fully than through the occasional "mission impossible".

People who have enough intelligence to use a hand calculator (this includes most managers) can learn to use *APL* productively for their own calculations. Likewise, for larger projects, they can gain enough understanding of how and why *APL* works to improve their statements of requirements to their staffs. However, most managers don't seem to want to learn *APL*, either out of fear, embarrassment, or lack of time. For those of us concerned with the future of *APL*, the challenge is to present the topic to a fundamentally uninterested, but potentially very influential, audience of our peers and management.

This paper discloses a technique for presenting *APL* in a tutorial style that has won the respect of many business people. While the presentation can be accomplished in less than an hour, it teaches enough *APL* to cope with at least 50 percent of the typical calculations needed to support business decisions. Moreover, performing these calculations in *APL* can result in a savings ratio of at least four to one over manual or calculator efforts.

Success in this presentation (or any other, for that matter) comes from keeping the audience's attention. Attention will wane if the presentation is dull. It will disappear should the audience miss any of the key points on which subsequent topics are built. Of course, the presentation will also suffer if it isn't organized to capitalize on the self-reinforcing effect of properly sequenced exposition.

The risk of a dull presentation can be minimized by presenting *APL* using an online terminal. Surprisingly, the quality of the visual image produced on the terminal isn't critical: it seems that the motion or sound of the terminal is what matters.

The most important aspects of the presentation are a logical progression of *APL* features and facilities (lavishly portrayed through easily understood examples), and a clean cutoff point to terminate the presentation. The examples don't have to be directly relevant to your audience's computational needs; indeed, if your examples hit too close to home, your listener may be distracted by the temptation to internally compare *his* concept of his problem with *yours*. Thus, it's better to select common examples that are likely to be understood by everyone, regardless of professional interests and backgrounds.

The goals of the presentation are to provide the audience with enough *APL* instruction to appreciate the use of array calculations (otherwise, there would be no advantage over BASIC or similar languages), and to show how easy it is to develop *APL* programs. This approximates the material covered in detail in Chapters 2, 3, 4, 7, and 10 of *APL: An Interactive Approach* (Wiley, 1976).

## Script for the Presentation

*Editors' Note:   The text that follows is meant to be used as a script by a speaker actually giving a presentation. Stage directions for the speaker are italicized.*

*Begin your presentation with the audience positioned so that they can see the printer or screen of the terminal. Show them the keyboard, or a picture of it such as that given in Figure 1.*

The keyboard we'll be using is very much like a typewriter keyboard, except for a few unfamiliar (or funny-looking) symbols, most of which we won't need for today's purposes.

The terminal can solve arithmetic problems much like a simple hand-held calculator, except that the "smarts" are not in the terminal itself, but rather in a central computer that is accessed by telephone. *Dial the access number and sign on.*

As I was saying, the terminal can be used much like a calculator:

Addition:

```
      5+2
7
```

Multiplication:

```
      5×2
10
```
*If the audience has computer experience, comment on the use of × rather than *.*

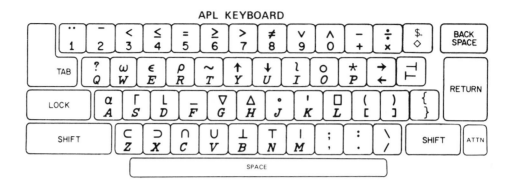

**Figure 1—An *APL* Keyboard**

Subtraction:

      **5−2**

3

      **2−5**

⁻3              *Comment on the symbols used for subtraction and negative numbers, if a question is raised.*

Division:

      **5÷2**

2.5

      **5÷7**

0.7142857143

Calculations are accurately made to 16 decimal places, although the default setting of the system is to print no more than 10 significant digits. That's easily changed. *(You can optionally demonstrate* $)DIGITS$ *here, but remember to set it back to* $10.)$

One of the most popular features of modern calculators is their ability to store one or a few constants that you're likely to use repeatedly in your calculations. That's usually done in calculators using a key labeled M (for memory) or STO (for store). Most computer languages have similar features, but on computers they are much richer—you can usually associate a mnemonic name with the data you're storing.

For example, if I needed the value 3.14159 repeatedly in calculations, I would give it some memorable name, like *PI*. Here's how you do it:

    *PI*←**3.14159**

The arrow symbol is what makes it happen. The symbol is called **store** or **assign**. Regardless of what you call it, what is important is that when you need that value again, you can get it simply by mentioning its name:

    *PI*+**10**

13.14159

      **2×***PI*

6.28318

Suppose you need the value 6.28318 for subsequent steps in your sequence of calculations. Quite simple—just think up a name for it and assign it:

    *TWICEPI*←**2×***PI*

Now observe the difference in the last two lines I typed. On the last line, I typed $2 \times PI$ and the computer didn't print an answer. However, on the line above it, I also typed $2 \times PI$ and the computer printed an answer. What is it that causes the computer to print an answer on the paper? Obviously, it depends on whether the arrow is there or not. Stated simply, if you calculate anything and tell the computer where to store the answer, the computer will store it and leave the paper unmarked. On the other hand, if you calculate something but don't tell *APL* where to put it, it will put the answer on the paper. And we've just learned how you control output in *APL*! Output happens if you don't give the answer a better place to go. It's just that simple.

Compare this (for those of you with prior computing experience) with how you learned to get output from other computing systems. It was a task of moderate difficulty to learn how to calculate the answers to your problems. But where were those answers? They were somewhere in the innards of the computer. You had to learn another task, equally difficult, but much more clerical in nature, to figure out how to print the answers. Many people who struggled through learning to print the answers from computers using systems other than *APL* are convinced that computers are tough to "talk to". However, we've just shown that computer output need not be any more difficult than producing an answer on a hand-held calculator.

If you forget what you've got stored away, there's a simple command that lists what is stored, in alphabetic order:

```
    )VARS
PI       TWICEPI
```

*VARS* stands for "variables", which is the proper name for stored data.

So far, we've discussed addition, subtraction, multiplication, and division, as well as how to get answers printed out. Surely, if that's all that's available, we'd be as well off using a hand-held calculator. How do we decide whether to do calculations on a computer or a calculator?

The deciding factor is not the complexity of the problem. The first time you solve any problem, you must go through it one step at a time, translating your thoughts into actions by pressing the keys of either your calculator or your computer terminal. But, if you have to go through those same steps repeatedly with different data, then you need more automation in your life. That means computers. In other words, the thing that decides whether a given set of calculations should be done on a calculator or a computer is somehow related to the amount of repetition that is inherent in the work.

Let's see how *APL* deals with repetition. Here is a trivial example. Suppose I'm running a store with only three products, and I have two weeks of sales volumes:

| | A | B | C |
|---|---|---|---|
| WEEK 1 | 9 | 7 | 8 |
| WEEK 2 | 3 | 4 | 5 |

We already know how to obtain the total sales by products:

```
    9+3
12
    7+4
11
    8+5
13
```

But it saves time to enter:

```
    9 7 8 + 3 4 5
12 11 13
```

and get all three answers at once. Here we see something that can't be done as easily on hand-held calculators (nor for that matter, on most computing systems). What did we do? We added the list (or **vector,** which is the proper name) consisting of the three numbers 9 7 8 to the corresponding list, or vector, 3 4 5. It's obvious that the computer performed pairwise additions. And don't think that we're stuck with vectors of only three numbers. We could just as easily have solved a problem involving 30 numbers, or 300, or 3000. The practical upper limit for how many numbers you can calculate in one vector is in the range of 10,000 to 20,000, but you can have as many vectors as your business problems require.

We'll be using this data over and over again, so let's assign them to variables:

```
    WEEK1←9 7 8
    WEEK2←3 4 5
    WEEK1+WEEK2
12 11 13
```

If we now wanted to save the total (so we could add to it in future weeks), we could enter:

```
    TOTAL←WEEK1+WEEK2
```

Let's add a twist to the problem. Suppose in week 2 we had sold 5 units of product A, 5 of B, and 5 of C. One way to get that answer is

```
    WEEK1+5 5 5
14 12 13
```

but having to count the appropriate number of 5's seems like a subhuman task, and indeed *APL* permits either of the following:

```
    WEEK1+5
14 12 13
    5+WEEK1
14 12 13
```

Let's abstract what we've learned so far. If you add two vectors together, they must have the same number of numbers. The result is a vector:

$$V \leftarrow V + V$$

If you add a single number to a vector (a single number is called a **scalar**), the scalar is repeated enough times to match the vector, and the result is again a vector:

$$V \leftarrow V + S$$
$$V \leftarrow S + V$$

And, of course, if you add two scalars together, as in our very first example $5+2$, you get a scalar result:

$$S \leftarrow S + S$$

This looks very promising for addition, but how about multiplication, subtraction, and division? For example, suppose the respective volumes sold for products A, B, and C were 9 7 8 and the unit costs for each were 3 4 5? The total costs are

```
    9 7 8×3 4 5
27 28 40
```

and the generalization is that any time you multiply two vectors with the same number of numbers, you get a vector containing the pairwise multiplications:

$$V \leftarrow V \times V$$

Now, let's take a great leap forward and replace the +'s and the ×'s in the above rules with the symbol **○**, where **○** means that you can use any of + − × ÷:

$$S \leftarrow S \circ S$$
$$V \leftarrow V \circ S$$
$$V \leftarrow V \circ S$$
$$V \leftarrow V \circ V$$

For example, if your starting inventory for each of the products A, B, and C is 20, how much is left after the first week's sales (9 7 8)?

```
    20-WEEK1
11  13  12
```

That's an example of scalar minus vector. *At this point pause, take a deep breath, and summarize.*

What have we got so far? We have:

1.  The ability to enter single data items (scalars) and store them with mnemonic names.

2.  The ability to enter lists (vectors) of data and store them with mnemonic names.

3.  The ability to calculate combinations of that stored data using addition, multiplication, subtraction, and division.

4.  The ability to store the results of those calculations for use in some subsequent step.

5.  Alternatively, the ability to **not** store the results, which will cause them to print on the paper or screen, where we can see them and make management decisions on the basis of what we see.

Reflect on these abilities. They make up around 80 percent of the useful calculations that most business people perform in a lifetime. After all, in our business lives we perform relatively simple, step-by-step calculations, but we certainly do them on vast quantities of numbers. So, if part of your life consists of taking a column of numbers, doing something to it, and making another column of numbers out of it (I myself have not been able to escape this activity entirely), then what we've learned so far will eliminate all the drudgery in those aspects of our business lives. And there are still a few more useful things I'd like you to know.

Lists of numbers are a popular and convenient way to store business data because much business information is naturally a series of numbers, such as a sequence of sales volumes for a product over many time periods, or the sales volumes of a sequence of products such as our A, B, and C. But suppose the data involves both time periods and different products? For instance, the two weeks of sales for the three products that we started with

|        | A | B | C |
|--------|---|---|---|
| WEEK 1 | 9 | 7 | 8 |
| WEEK 2 | 3 | 4 | 5 |

may be better thought of as a table with two rows and three columns, rather than as two distinct vectors. Moreover, suppose the data shown above is the sales report from our downtown store, while our suburban store has the following results:

|        | A | B | C |
|--------|---|---|---|
| WEEK 1 | 6 | 7 | 2 |
| WEEK 2 | 7 | 0 | 3 |

We'd probably want to consolidate the data for a corporate report:

|         | A  | B  | C  |
|---------|----|----|----|
| WEEK 1  | 15 | 14 | 10 |
| WEEK 2  | 10 | 4  | 8  |

This is how we put the data from the downtown store into a table:

*DOWNTOWN← 2 3 ρ 9 7 8 3 4 5*

The funny looking symbol ρ (rho) takes the data on its right and makes it into a table whose rows and columns are given by the data on the left (2 3). This is evident when we print the result.

```
    DOWNTOWN
9 7 8
3 4 5
```

Similarly, we enter the data from the other store:

```
    SUBURBAN← 2 3 ρ 6 7 2 7 0 3
    SUBURBAN
6 7 2
7 0 3
```

and the consolidation is done by simply entering:

```
    DOWNTOWN+SUBURBAN
15 14 10
10  4  8
```

In other words, just as two vectors of the same size can be added together, two tables of the same size and shape can be added.

$$T←T+T$$

The next example calculates the percentage of total sales that were made in the suburban store.

```
    100×SUBURBAN÷(DOWNTOWN+SUBURBAN)
40          50          20
70           0          37.5
```

Obviously, not only can tables be added to tables, but tables can be divided by tables, and tables can be multiplied by scalars. In fact, any of + − × ÷ can be used to perform calculations on tables. Here are all the generalizations we've made so far:

$$S←S∘S$$
$$V←V∘V \qquad V←S∘V \qquad V←V∘S$$
$$T←T∘T \qquad T←S∘T \qquad T←T∘S$$

The sales tables that we just used had to be entered into the computer by typing in each data item individually. However, there are certain types of tables that don't require each data item be entered. Consider this table of taxes:

| TAX TABLE |   | TAX RATES |     |     |
|-----------|---|-----------|-----|-----|
|           |   | .01       | .02 | .05 |
| COST      | 1 | .01       | .02 | .05 |
|           | 2 | .02       | .04 | .10 |
| OF        | 3 | .03       | .06 | .15 |
|           | 4 | .04       | .08 | .20 |
| ITEM      | 5 | .05       | .10 | .25 |

The fifteen numbers in the body of the table could be calculated by performing every possible multiplication of the numbers 1 2 3 4 5 with the numbers .01 .02 .05. In *APL* that is done as follows:

```
      1 2 3 4 5   ∘.×  .01 .02 .05
0.01                0.02              0.05
0.02                0.04              0.1
0.03                0.06              0.15
0.04                0.08              0.2
0.05                0.1               0.25
```

The symbols ∘. tell the computer to perform every possible combination of the operation (in our case, ×) using the numbers on the left and the numbers on the right. Calculations like this result in a table with as many rows as there are numbers on the left, and as many columns as there are numbers on the right. The calculations aren't restricted to multiplication, either. They can be any of + − × ÷, and the generalization is

$$T \leftarrow V \circ . \mathbf{o} V$$

There are many professional people who spend much of their working lives calculating entries in tables. While hardly anyone does that sort of work manually these days, most computer programming languages still require several lines of programming (using DO-loops or the equivalent to force the iteration) to get it done. In *APL*, however, it's a very direct and straightforward activity using ∘..

We've seen many useful things that can be done with our old friends + − × ÷, but is that all there is to arithmetic? There are several other arithmetic operations that are very useful in business calculations, but because of the way most of us were taught our arithmetic originally, we don't recognize them as such. I'm going to introduce two of them now; time doesn't permit covering them all.

The two operations are called maximum and minimum, and their symbols are ⌈ and ⌊. They work much like addition or multiplication in that they compute a scalar answer based on combining two scalar numbers, one to the left and one to the right. Instead of resulting in a sum or a product, however, they result in the larger of the two numbers (for ⌈) and the smaller of the two numbers (for ⌊).

```
      2+5
7
      2×5
10
      2⌈5
5
      2⌊5
2
```

Just like + − × ÷, ⌈ and ⌊ can be used in the formulas we've covered wherever **o** appears. For example, suppose five people entered a bar with a floor show. The first person consumes $3.00 worth of refreshments, the second person drinks $10.00 worth, the third person doesn't have anything, the fourth person orders a $2.50 drink, and the last person has a $3.50 drink. On the way out, they learned that there was a $3.00 minimum charge for each. How much did they each pay?

The respective bills are $3.00, $10.00, $3.00, $3.00, and $3.50. That's trivial to do by hand, but how do you tell a computer to do it?

```
      3⌈10 3 0 2.5 3.5
10 3 3 3 3.5
```

The formal business terminology for a situation like this is "minimum order size", and it is a very common business calculation.

Here is another example. For 1980, your Social Security withholding will be computed as 6.13 percent of the lesser of your 1980 salary or $25,900. In *APL*, it's expressed as:

```
      .0613 × SALARY ⌊ 25900
```

So far we have seen operations that work on pairs of numbers, or that produce new vectors or tables by pairing up other vectors or tables. A different class of calculations involves adding up all the numbers in a vector, or multiplying all the numbers in a vector. For instance, suppose we wanted to know the total bill of all five barflies in the previous example. First, we store the vector of individual debts as $X$:

```
X←3⌈10 3 0 2.5 3.5
X
10 3 3 3 3.5
```

Mathematicians have a notation for obtaining the sum over $X$. It looks like this:

$$\sum_{i=1}^{n} x_i$$

and it has always seemed like a lot of pompous notation for such a simple concept. *APL*'s notation for the sum over $X$ is both shorter and more graphic:

```
+/X
22.5
```

You can think of *APL* performing the work this way:

```
10 + 3 + 3 + 3 + 3.5
```

As you can see, the + is inserted between adjacent numbers in the vector. Of course, you aren't restricted to additions—any of the members of the family $+ \; - \; \times \; \div \; \lceil \; \lfloor$ can be used. The generalization is

$$S←\circ/V$$

Other useful examples of this operation, called **reduction,** are

```
⌈/X          The largest value in X.
10

⌊/X          The smallest value in X.
3

(⌈/X)-(⌊/X)      The difference between the largest and
7                the smallest value, called the range.
```

When dealing with tables of data, sometimes you need to sum across and sometimes you need to sum down. Summing across a table uses the same notation as summing over a vector:

```
+/DOWNTOWN
24 12
```

while summing down is signified by placing a bar (−) through the slash (/).

```
+⌿DOWNTOWN
12 11 13
```

The generalizations are

$$V←\circ/T$$
$$V←\circ⌿T$$

Now that we know how to obtain sums, let's see how we can calculate averages. Everyone knows this is done by adding the numbers together and dividing that sum by the number of numbers that were added. However, it is not a trivial task to calculate an average using most computing systems. In fact, the example of calculating the ordinary arithmetic average is often the first significant example chosen by authors of computer textbooks. In most computer languages it requires simultaneous considerations of such advanced concepts as storage allocation, input, output, initialization, and looping. But in *APL* it is simply expressed as $(+/V)÷\rho V$. The symbol $\rho$ used in this context gives the number of numbers in the following data. For our previous example of the bar bills:

```
        X
10  3  3  3  3.5
        ρX
5
        (+/X)÷ρX
4.5
```

As brief as the above solution is, it is a bore to have to type in those characters repeatedly if you have many sets of numbers to average. And that's where computer programming comes on the scene. What we want to do is to have the computer retain (memorize) the rule, or algorithm, for how to compute an average. Then we can later refer to it by a mnemonic shorthand whenever we need to find an average, much as we used *PI* to stand for the value 3.14159.

We tell *APL* that we're starting to enter a program by typing the character del (∇) followed by a template, or pattern, of the new program. In our example, we'll call the program AVG and enter it like this:

```
        ∇  R←AVG  V
[1]
```

The computer replies with [ 1 ], indicating that we are in the process of entering a program, and it's now time to enter the first line of the program.

```
[1]     R←(+/V)÷ρV
[2]
```

The computer replies with [ 2 ], waiting for the next line of instruction. But there isn't anything else to do in this program, so we type ∇, which completes program entry:

```
[2]     ∇
```

We can now use the new program:

```
        ANS←AVG  X
        ANS
4.5
```

It worked, but how does it do it? When we typed the line *ANS←AVG  X*, what was at that time in *X* (10  3  3  3  3.5) was transferred to *V* inside the program. Then the average of those values was calculated on line [ 1 ] and the result was placed in *R*. When the program finished, what was in *R* was transferred to *ANS*. Then (on the next line) we displayed *ANS*. Thus, just as the operation ∘.× can be used wherever it is needed in your solution of problems, the new program *AVG* can be used wherever and whenever you need to calculate an average.

Programs can be much more complicated than the little one we just wrote to calculate an average. However, every *APL* program is built using exactly the same principles shown here. When compared to equivalent programs written in other programming languages, *APL* typically requires around one-fourth to one-tenth of the programming effort.

We've just spent about an hour introducing *APL*. If you are exhausted from the experience, I'm not surprised, because in that hour we've covered as many capabilities as it would take six to eight hours to master if we were talking about any language other than *APL*.

## Epilogue

Readers of this paper may be dismayed by the apparent naiveté of the presentation. However, this presentation has been given hundreds of times, and it invariably works. For people with no programming experience, it presents *APL* using a hand-held calculator as an analogy—a comparison that seems to scare no one. For people who are programming experts, the style of presentation is sufficiently different from most other programming language introductions to deter them from prematurely comparing *APL* with what they already know.

Indeed, its not until the last ten minutes that programming per se is discussed. By that time, the battle is won. All one needs to do is compare the program *AVG* with one written in a more familiar language such as FOR-TRAN, COBOL, or BASIC to be convinced.

*Allen Rose has been STSC's vice president/technical director and a Member of the Board of Directors since STSC's inception in 1969. From 1968 to 1969, Rose served as program administrator for APL in the Data Processing Division of IBM. From 1965 to 1968, as an IBM research staff member, he taught and promoted the use of APL within IBM and to its customers. Prior to that he was a research statistician for Procter and Gamble.*

*Rose is co-author of APL*: An Interactive Approach *(Wiley, 1976), a widely used APL textbook. He served as a national lecturer for the Association for Computing Machinery from 1974 to 1979, and is currently a speaker for the Data Processing Management Association.*

Edward R. Novicky and Arlene E. Ryan

# The Use of *APL*
# In Applied Econometric Analysis

*APL* is ideally suited to perform regression analysis, the principal tool of econometrics. With the increasing use of econometrics to anticipate the effects of economic change on businesses and the economy as a whole, the *APL* language is quickly becoming the programming ally of corporate, financial, government, and academic forecasters. In particular, the power of *APL* in econometrics lies in its inherent ability to do matrix algebra with ease.

In econometrics, the method of ordinary least squares (OLS) is perhaps the best known and most widely used technique of regression analysis. Given a set of observations, such as a time series on a particular variable, the econometrician is usually interested in examining how this variable is affected by movements of other variables, termed *independent* or *explanatory* variables. For example, business analysts might be concerned with how sales are influenced by the degree of competition and by expenditure outlays on advertising. The econometrician is furthermore interested in statistically testing the significance of the explanatory variables. A useful format for performing these analyses is that provided by matrix algebra.

The following section illustrates the compatibility of *APL* with matrix algebra in applying the OLS method. It is followed by a macroeconomic example that estimates the "marginal propensity to consume" of the U.S. economy.

### The General Mathematical Model

If $y$ is a linear function of the independent variables $x_1, x_2, \ldots, x_m$, plus the error term $e$, then the $i$th observation of $y$, denoted $y_i$, can be written as:

$$y_i = b_1 + b_2 x_{i2} + \ldots + b_m x_{im} + e_i$$

where the subscript $i$ refers to the $i$th observation, and $b_1, b_2, \ldots, b_m$ are the coefficients of the terms. If all $y$ observations are stacked into a column vector, the linear function can be expressed as illustrated in Figure 1, or in more compact matrix algebra notation as $y = XB + e$.

The objective of the ordinary least squares technique is to minimize the sum of the squares of the error terms $e$; that is, to fit a line (or plane, or $n$-space, depending on the number of variables) through the observations such that the summed squares of the differences between the predicted values of $y$ and the observed values of $y$ are minimal. The maximum likelihood estimate, or least squares estimate, is found by calculating the value of $\hat{B}$ (the vector of estimated coefficients) that minimizes the sum of the squared error terms ($e^2$).

$$\Sigma e^2 \quad = e'e \quad = (y - X\hat{B})'(y - X\hat{B})$$

$$
\begin{bmatrix} y_1 \\ y_2 \\ y_3 \\ \cdot \\ \cdot \\ \cdot \\ y_n \end{bmatrix} = \begin{bmatrix} 1 & x_{12} & x_{13} & \cdots & x_{1m} \\ 1 & x_{22} & x_{23} & \cdots & x_{2m} \\ 1 & x_{32} & x_{33} & \cdots & x_{3m} \\ \cdot & \cdot & \cdot & \cdot & \cdot \\ \cdot & \cdot & \cdot & \cdot & \cdot \\ \cdot & \cdot & \cdot & \cdot & \cdot \\ 1 & x_{n2} & x_{n3} & \cdots & x_{nm} \end{bmatrix} \begin{bmatrix} b_1 \\ b_2 \\ b_3 \\ \cdot \\ \cdot \\ \cdot \\ b_m \end{bmatrix} + \begin{bmatrix} e_1 \\ e_2 \\ e_3 \\ \cdot \\ \cdot \\ \cdot \\ e_n \end{bmatrix}
$$

**Figure 1—The Mathematical Model**

Applying the calculus to minimize the summed squared error terms, it can be shown that the estimated coefficients $\hat{B}$ can be computed as follows (see note 1):

$$\hat{B} = (X'X)^{-1}(X'y)$$

The applicability of *APL* to solving this problem can now be presented explicitly. *APL*'s facility in manipulating matrices is readily demonstrated. For example, to build a matrix X with $n$ rows and $m$ columns, the *APL* statement takes the form:

$$X \leftarrow (N,M) \ \rho \ (X \ data \ values \ in \ row \ sequence)$$

To build a column vector Y of $n$ values, one uses:

$$Y \leftarrow (N,1) \ \rho \ (Y \ data \ values, \ n \ of \ them)$$

The real power of *APL*, however, can be seen in its ability to solve matrix algebra problems directly. The *APL* notation that applies to this problem can be summarized as follows:

- $X'$ (the transpose of matrix X) is written $\lozenge X$.

- $XY$ (the product of matrices X and Y) is written as $X + . \times Y$.

- $X^{-1}$ (the inverse of matrix X) is written as $\boxplus X$.

Thus, we can apply *APL* to estimate $\hat{B}$ from the formula:

$$\hat{B} = (X'X)^{-1}(X'y)$$

simply by converting it into *APL*:

$$B \leftarrow (\boxplus((\lozenge X) + . \times X)) + . \times ((\lozenge X) + . \times Y)$$

The result $B$ is an $m$-element column vector whose elements are the estimated coefficients of the independent variables. As terse as this statement is, *APL* can express this least squares estimate in an even shorter form:

$$B \leftarrow Y \boxplus X$$

### Example—The Keynesian Consumption Function

The *APL* statements for solving the least squares estimate can now be applied to a macroeconomic problem—estimating the economy's "marginal propensity to consume".

One of the most common consumption functions in the economic literature is the Keynesian consumption function,

$$c = b_0 + b_1 yd$$

which states that the level of consumption purchasing $c$ that will occur in an economy is equal to some minimum level of purchasing $b_0$ that will occur even if there is no disposable income in the economy, plus some proportion $b_1$ of each addition to the economy's level of disposable income $yd$. The parameter $b_1$ is the *marginal propensity to consume*, the fraction of each additional amount of disposable income that will be spent for consumption purposes.

To estimate the parameters $b_0$ and $b_1$, we have extracted annual data for personal consumption and disposable income (in billions of real dollars) for the years 1960 through 1978. A scatter diagram of consumption versus income is shown in Figure 2. Intuitively, the objective of the OLS technique is to fit a regression line through the points to minimize the sum of the squared error terms, that is, the sum of the squares of the vertical distances between the regression line and the actual observations. In Figure 2, the vertical distance $e_i$ between the fitted line and the $i$th observation is the error term corresponding to that observation.

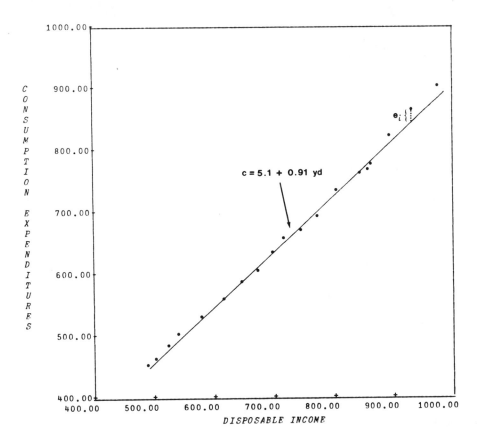

**Figure 2—Relationship between Consumption and Income**

In matrix notation, the problem of estimating $b_0$ and $b_1$ from the historical data can be expressed as shown in Figure 3. Alternatively, this expression can be written as $c = XB + e$.

$$
\begin{array}{cccc}
c & X & b & e \\
\begin{bmatrix}
452.988 \\
462.234 \\
482.863 \\
501.361 \\
528.686 \\
558.102 \\
586.062 \\
603.157 \\
633.410 \\
655.409 \\
668.909 \\
691.936 \\
733.021 \\
767.674 \\
760.695 \\
774.562 \\
820.564 \\
861.693 \\
900.771
\end{bmatrix}
& = &
\begin{bmatrix}
1 & 487.100 \\
1 & 500.725 \\
1 & 521.825 \\
1 & 539.075 \\
1 & 577.050 \\
1 & 612.575 \\
1 & 643.550 \\
1 & 669.825 \\
1 & 695.150 \\
1 & 712.700 \\
1 & 741.425 \\
1 & 769.275 \\
1 & 801.300 \\
1 & 854.525 \\
1 & 841.975 \\
1 & 859.675 \\
1 & 891.875 \\
1 & 929.400 \\
1 & 972.600
\end{bmatrix}
&
\begin{bmatrix}
b_0 \\
b_1
\end{bmatrix}
+
\begin{bmatrix}
e_1 \\
e_2 \\
e_3 \\
e_4 \\
\vdots \\
e_{19}
\end{bmatrix}
\end{array}
$$

**Figure 3—An Example of the Mathematical Model**

An analyst working at a terminal can solve this problem readily by entering the appropriate values and then executing the *APL* expression for the OLS estimate:

```
CONS ← 453 462 483 501 529 558 586 603 633 655 668 692
CONS ← CONS, 733 768 761 775 821 862 901
YD ← 487 501 522 539 577 613 644 670 695 713 741 769
YD ← YD, 801 855 842 860 892 929 973
X ← 1,[1.5] YD
```

The last statement constructed a two-column matrix $X$ where the first column is all 1 and the second column is the values in $YD$, as in Figure 3. Now the estimates of $b$ can be computed directly:

```
B ← CONS ⌹ X
B ⍝ DISPLAY THE ESTIMATED COEFFICIENTS:
5.08 0.91
```

The first element of $B$ is the minimum level of purchasing $b_0$, and the second element is the marginal propensity to consume, estimated to be 0.91 for the U.S. economy in the given time period.

## Conclusion

This simple example shows how the econometrician can develop his own *APL* programs for performing economic analysis. Besides the powerful facility offered by raw *APL*, economic analysts can also use econometric and statistical packages such as those available on STSC's *APL\*PLUS* System. These packages include tools for econometric modeling and forecasting. Interactive programs are provided for building models easily, and the estimation techniques include not only ordinary least squares, but also generalized least squares, two-stage least squares, principal components, and polynomial distributed lags.

Applications on the *APL\*PLUS* System provide tools for the analyst to create and use his own database via simple storage, retrieval, and update functions. National economic time series data—such as GNP, prices, employment, and industrial output—are available on the *APL\*PLUS* System from the Citibank Economic Database. International data is available through the International Financial Statistics (IFS) Database. User-specific data can be linked with these and other external data sources to formulate and test relationships between economic variables, and to construct economic models for analysis and forecasting.

*Notes*

1.  For complete details, see J. Johnston, *Econometric Methods* (New York: McGraw-Hill Book Company, 1972), chapter 5.

*Ed Novicky joined STSC in 1978 and is currently manager of economic systems in the company's Management Technology Division. He has extensive experience in the development and use of microeconomic and macroeconomic models to analyze economic issues and events. He is currently directing analyses for the Department of Energy related to assessing the economic impacts of the second national energy plan, including the analysis of the macroeconomic impacts of the President's 1979 energy message on domestic crude oil decontrol. He has also developed and used inter-industry, energy supply and demand, and macroeconomic models.*

*Novicky holds an M.B.A. in economic analysis from Cornell University.*

*Arlene E. Ryan is an economist with the Economic Systems Group of STSC's Management Technology Division. She has accumulated five years of experience in energy analysis, specializing in econometric modeling of energy supply and demand, OPEC pricing and production strategies, and solar market penetration. Ryan is currently involved in a project for the Office of Conservation and Solar Applications in the Department of Energy, analyzing investment and capital flows in the U.S. economy and their implications for energy investment.*

*Ryan received an M.A. degree from Georgetown University, where she specialized in mathematical economics and econometrics.*

**Ronald S. Karpf**

# Management Statistics
# With *APL*

*APL* is the most appropriate computer language for carrying out statistical analysis due to three aspects of the language that characterize and distinguish it from other computer languages. First, *APL* allows matrices or arrays as data elements. Next, the *APL* language contains a powerful set of (primitive) operators that manipulate arrays of data including not only basic linear algebraic operations, but also logical operators. Lastly, the interactive nature of *APL* is precisely suited to the iterative nature of statistical analysis. Thus, *APL* provides an atmosphere that reinforces and facilitates the proper performance of statistical analysis.

This paper is directed to managers who must solve statistical application problems. The basic message is that the best tool for solving such problems is *APL*. This is because of *APL*'s interactive nature and the kinds of data objects on which *APL* operates—characteristics that distinguish *APL* from all other languages.

The technical superiority of *APL* for statistical computing is easy to establish. The language of statistics is matrix algebra. In the *APL* language, matrices are basic data elements with a complete set of primitive operators to manipulate them. It is this capability to perform statistical computing in the language of statistics that makes *APL* so appropriate.

But more important than its technical advantages is the environment that *APL* provides for performing statistical analyses. The easy access to data and analysis routines that *APL* affords invariably leads to a real understanding of the information provided in a set of data. Such insight is the proper objective of statistical analysis.

The importance of the interactive nature of *APL* for statistical computing cannot be overemphasized. It removes the "black box" feeling that is associated with so many statistical packages. Statistical analysis is basically iterative in nature, and so the tools to undertake analysis must enhance this type of process. In this sense, *APL* advances the purposes of analysis, rather than hindering it as so many other languages do.

In the remainder of this presentation, I will indicate who should be using *APL* for statistical analysis, amplify the arguments for using *APL* and identify some of the basic *APL* resources for statistical analysis.

## Who Should Perform Statistical Analyses?

There is an incorrect notion that statistical analyses should be performed only by statisticians—at least, that the work called statistics should be performed only by someone in that profession. While this is true in some circumstances, such as basic research or the design of industrial experiments, it is not so in many of the day-to-day applications encountered by managers. Statistics touch our everday lives—they are used or calculated by many people on a daily basis.

Statistics are used and calculated routinely by everyone. For instance, we all have our own sets of personal probabilities that we somehow calculate, without even being aware that we do it. From them we decide on courses of action. Actions are based on subjective personal assessments of the probabilities of outcome. Successful outcomes are what we strive for.

Also, many of us have at one time or another tried to estimate gas mileage or cost per gallon. These are simple problems that most of us can carry out without thinking of them as statistics. But, if I presented the problem to you in terms of ratio estimators and homoscedasticity of variances, and told you to consult your family statistician for a solution, many of you would think I had gone too far.

What characterizes managerial and statistical applications? Basically, they are descriptive problems that require the processing of large amounts of information and the summarizing of that information into a smaller set of numbers that represent the relevant results. This smaller set of numbers, or statistics, must be able to impart information that can be easily understood by a variety of people. Often, important decisions will be made based on these results. Whereas computers can quickly process large masses of information, people cannot. They require statistics to summarize information.

Many managerial statistical applications can be adequately solved by managers—by those who understand the problems and the data and who are most concerned with solutions. All it requires is a positive attitude (rather than a fear of mountains of seemingly unrelated numbers), close proximity to the data, and the application of common sense.

This brings us to *APL*. The most appropriate tool available for total involvement with data and problem solving is the interactive *APL* language.

## Reasons for Using *APL* for Statistical Analysis

In this section, I would like to present some of the reasons for using *APL* for statistical analysis. Certainly, if we carefully choose the structure of the problems presented, any language can appear to be the proper medium in which to solve the problem. Consequently, I will not argue from a specific analytical viewpoint. Rather, the argument for *APL* is that for a rather large number of applications, it is the proper tool to use. Our presentation stresses those aspects of *APL* that facilitate analysis in a natural way.

An analysis can be thought of as comprising three separate steps:

- data preparation
- analysis
- presentation of results.

In each stage, *APL* has distinct advantages over other languages due to its interactive nature and the types of data items on which it operates. As such, these advantages are almost unique to *APL*.

The preparation of data for analysis is the total process of organizing and entering data into the computer. This includes data entry, editing, data verification, the handling of missing data, and the database design. Needless to say, incorrect implementation of the data will invalidate subsequent analyses, and poor database design can be an impediment to a smooth analysis.

The data entry facility of *APL* is probably the easiest to use of any programming language. The *APL* statement $X \leftarrow \square$ requests data input from the terminal and stores it into a data vector named $X$.

The natural organization of the raw information in statistics is a two-dimensional array—observations by variables. This organization is also natural to *APL*, since *APL* allows arrays as elements of the language. Also, *APL* has powerful operators that can be applied to such structures, paralleling theoretical functions in statistics, and data subset selection is easy using *APL* logical and compress operations. If the data is presented in character form, the symbolic operators of *APL* are useful.

The analysis of information is basically an iterative process during which reasonable procedures are applied to data to understand what the data implies. Analysis is characterized by striving to get to the essence of the information (for future decision making), the application of algorithmic procedures to the data, and basing present actions on previous answers.

The most frequently used statistical methodologies use one or more of the following statistics:

- means
- sums of squares
- ranks.

The strength of *APL* for statistical programming is derived partly from the ease with which these statistics can be written in *APL*. The mean of a vector of numbers $X$, for example, is simply represented as:

```
MEAN ← (+/X) ÷ ρX
```

Sums of squares are similarly easy to write. It is from these statistics that variance estimates, the keystone of statistics, are calculated. For instance, the variance of a vector $X$ is easily written as:

```
(+/(X-MEAN)*2) ÷ ρX
```

Analysis of variance statistics can similarly be coded by correctly choosing $X$ and *MEAN*.

Nonparametric procedures are coming into increasing use and prominence today, and are based on functions of the ranks, which are also easily written as:

```
X[⍋X]
```

One aspect of *APL* that, more than any other, makes it appropriate for statistical analysis is its interactive nature. Basically, *APL* gives you a large, incomprehensibly powerful calculator that can be used to perform operations as simple as adding two numbers, or as complicated as multivariate analytical procedures. In either case, the user is totally involved. The data is there for you to immediately examine, as are the results of an analysis. New ideas can be acted upon at once. Problems can be investigated. Thus, *APL* actually helps to create the proper environment in which to perform statistics. No other language achieves this as successfully as *APL*.

The last stage of an analysis is the presentation of results. It is a communications problem—we must communicate the knowledge gained during the analysis stage. In this regard, graphing and tabular techniques are very powerful in summarizing and easily relating the essential facts. Once again, powerful elements of the *APL* language and available software provides managers with the tools to generate the precise reports they require.

In summary, there are very powerful and compelling reasons for using *APL* for statistical application problems. When *APL*'s advantages are combined with preprogrammed algorithms for statistical analysis, graphing, and table generation, we have an arsenal of tools that cannot be matched by any other language.

### *APL* Resources for Statistical Analysis—How to Get Started

The organization of data is important in analysis. The manner in which the information is packaged should not get in the way of analyses. For statistical analysis, we generally conceptualize the dataset as a two-dimensional matrix with columns for variables and rows for individual observations. Many of the available *APL* functions for statistical analysis will require that the input data be organized in this manner.

The first set of workspaces you will want to investigate is in Library 2 on STSC's *APL\*PLUS* System; the workspaces are collectively referred to as *STATPAK* and were written by Professor W. K. Smillie. Working Memorandum Number 110, *STATPAK: An APL Statistical Package* (STSC, 1975), is available to explain how to use these workspaces.

*STATPAK* contains *APL* functions to perform many of the most frequently encountered statistical procedures, such as:

- Analysis of variance for simple balanced designs.
- Simple and multiple regression.
- Basic descriptive statistics.
- Histograms and two-way contingency tables.
- Correlation analysis.
- Residual analysis.

An example is provided by the function *DSTAT* in workspace 2 *STP*1. *DSTAT* calculates basic descriptive statistics for a vector of input data. A sample of statistics generated by *DSTAT* follows:

```
      X ← 65 63 67 64 68 62 70 66 68 67 69 71
      DSTAT X
SAMPLE SIZE             12
MAXIMUM                 71
MINIMUM                 62
RANGE                   9
MEAN                    66.66666667
VARIANCE                7.696969697
STANDARD DEVIATION      2.774342309
MEAN DEVIATION          2.222222222
MEDIAN                  67
MODE                    67    68
```

As simple as it is, *DSTAT* is an extraordinarily valuable tool in basic analysis. It summarizes and imparts a lot of information, and is easy to use. Other functions in the workspace are similarly useful and simple.

A second package of useful statistical software, IBM's *APL* Statistical Library (*STATLIB*), is available in Library 42 on STSC's *APL\*PLUS* VM System. This package duplicates and expands on the functions available in *STATPAK*. Between the two packages, you should find all of the methodological approaches you will require in application problems.

*STATLIB* contains functions for:

- Analysis of variance for balanced and unbalanced design.
- Simple and multiple regression.
- Nonlinear regression.
- Basic descriptive statistics.
- Analysis of covariance.
- Contingency table analysis.

- Acceptance sampling planning.
- Correlation analysis.

A nice aspect of the package is that many standard statistical tests are conveniently packaged as functions with annotated results.

Lastly, the remaining workspaces in Library 2 on STSC's *APL∗PLUS* System should be investigated. The functions in these workspaces, and those in workspace 10 *PLOT*, greatly facilitate the graphic presentation of results. They provide the capability for scatter plots, bar charts, time series charts, and so on. These methods of presentation are of prime importance for adequately communicating information.

The ultimate resource for analysis, though, is not contained in these workspaces, but rather in the combination of *APL* with common sense and native intelligence. The judicious use of these facilities and of preprogrammed software will lead to successful applications.

*Ron Karpf is currently a statistician with the Insurance Institute for Highway Safety. Prior to joining IIHS, he worked as a statistician with the Management Technology Division of STSC, Inc.*

*Karpf earned his Ph.D. in statistics from the American University. He is an active member of the Association for Computing Machinery, the American Statistical Association, and the American Association for the Advancement of Science.*

Christopher T. Stathes

# *APL* and Optimization Modeling

A true optimization process must determine the best possible answer to a given problem. Optimizing processes work with mathematical models that represent the real-world situation under study. These models allow for multiple solutions and the investigation of alternatives without impact on operations. The models also force critical analysis of the relationships that govern the situation or process being studied, often providing valuable insight in itself. Further, through the use of developed techniques, the models can be optimized.

Mathematical programming is a class of optimization modeling techniques that satisfy demanding requirements and that have proved efficient in determining the optimal solution to complex problems involving large numbers of possible activities and operating constraints. Mathematical programming provides the precise information required for evaluating competing processes, conflicting alternatives, and interacting activities, and is essential for analyzing economic tradeoffs.

The mathematical programming approach efficiently solves problems in which:

- A large number of feasible combinations of activities exist.

- It is possible to measure which solutions are better than others.

- There are many concurrent activities, some of which can substitute for others.

- Interactions between activities are multidimensional, and the activities compete for limited resources.

- Problems cannot be partitioned and solved piece by piece.

- Finding the *best* solution is more beneficial than finding just any feasible solution.

- "What if" questions about the optimal solution need to be investigated.

Mathematical programming algorithms determine the best obtainable solution that achieves a designated objective and satisfies all of the specified requirements and constraints. For example, the objectives might be to maximize productivity, minimize production costs, or minimize the number of product changeovers.

**Information for Better Management**

Planning the use of company resources—capital, people, time, equipment, materials, and facilities—is a complex task. The "right answer" must satisfy numerous and often conflicting constraints—constraints that are affected by capital limitations, plant configuration, distribution networks, market forecasts, product-mix requirements, warehouse capabilities, and company policies. To deal effectively with these complex business decisions, managers and planners are turning to the proven optimization technique of mathematical programming.

Usually the tradeoffs among the many possible answers are complex and multifaceted. Optimization models enable the decision maker to properly evaluate the countless alternatives and tradeoffs that often confuse and delay the decision process. Optimization modeling provides management with the precise information required to make the right business decision.

An effective optimization model must offer decision makers the ability to obtain answers quickly and in a form that is easily interpreted. STSC's Management Technology Division (MTD) has developed a user-oriented optimization modeling concept that has been used in the development and implementation of interactive systems that meet these requirements. Optimization models developed by MTD have provided the answers to difficult user problems including:

- How should available capital be allocated to investment opportunities?

- Where should manufacturing and distribution facilities be located, and how should they be sized?

- Where are the bottlenecks in the production/distribution system, and what is the payoff associated with removing such constraints?

- How should production be scheduled to minimize inventory costs while maintaining desired service levels?

- What are the effects of new technological processes on the overall production system?

- What is the most profitable mix of products?

- What are the economic impacts of governmental regulations regarding various environments?

- What is the proper allocation of shipments between a company-controlled truck fleet and common carriers?

- How should company-owned truck fleets be routed and scheduled?

- How can the effects of potential energy shortages be minimized?

- What is the best way to sequence and size manufacturing runs?

- How should an available staff be assigned—by location or task—to maximize the efficiency and utility of the organization?

- Where and when should new staff be assigned?

The range of problems that can be solved effectively by using optimization modeling is unusually broad. MTD has applied optimization modeling to help managers make the right decisions about investment strategies, materials management, capital budgeting, vehicle routing and scheduling, product mix, plant expansion, inventory control, cash management, machine loading, production scheduling, productivity problems, market forecasting, economic impacts, facility sizing and location, contingency planning, product distribution, energy price effects, network analysis, and resource allocation.

Except for the most trivial problems, optimization modeling requires the use of a computer to perform the optimizing calculations. To be optimized, the problem must be systematized for representation on the computer, and analysis must be performed using the results. More specifically, for a successful systematization and optimization, certain functions must be completed. First, a problem definition must be formulated. Second, data types and data sources must be defined. Next, the interfaces between the external data and user, and the internal model and system, must be defined.

These steps are followed by specification of the information and results to be produced by the analysis (often termed the "reports"). Then, program specifications are written and a choice of programming language is made. Finally, programming, testing, debugging, implementation (installation and solution of the actual problem), and analysis of the results are performed. System components must also be created to handle the tasks of data input, data storage, model generation, model solution, and reporting of results.

## User-Oriented Systems for Decision Makers

Until recently, the power and benefits of optimization modeling were available only to those managers with expertise in mathematics and data processing, as well as management. Now MTD has freed the decision maker from these technical restrictions by developing *user-oriented* modeling systems.

MTD designs modeling systems that can be used by the business analyst or manager without reliance on computer programmers or mathematicians. User interaction with the system is straightforward and requires no programming experience. This is because MTD constructs model-generator programs that accept problem-descriptive data in a context familiar to the user. The system then translates this information automatically into the correct mathematical representation of the problem. The resulting model—which defines the objectives of and restrictions on the problem under investigation—is then optimized using MPSX/370 (IBM's Mathematical Programming System Extended). Once the optimal solution is found, the modeling system uses a report writer built by MTD to translate the model's mathematical representation into a series of management-oriented reports using the format and terminology specified by the user.

MTD's modeling systems are effective management decision tools because many user-oriented capabilities have been incorporated into them:

- Communication with the modeling system is in a format and context familiar and comfortable to the user.

- The model is easily modified by the user through data changes. No reprogramming is required.

- The modeling system is data driven so that a whole class of models can be generated and solved without reformulation. This means that the user can specify additional variables (products, plants, warehouses, processes, vehicles, and investments) or revise constraints (limitations, capacities, requirements, demands, and policies) by changing only the data.

- The user need not be concerned with the mathematical considerations underlying the model structure, nor with the algorithms and computer techniques required to optimize his model.

- The modeling system presents the solution in terminology and context familiar to the user and appropriate for the kind of management decisions he wishes to make.

- The modeling system provides the capability to answer a wide range of "what if" questions without reformulation or reprogramming of the modeling system.

### Analyzing Sensitivity to Changing Conditions

The use of an optimization modeling system typically involves entering problem-specific data, computing the optimal solution, determining the optimal solution's sensitivity to change (by systematically computing alternative solutions based on changes to key data), and preparing management reports. The most powerful, and usually the most difficult, step in this process is analyzing the problem's sensitivity to change. In essence, the user determines how the optimal solution changes when specific assumptions or conditions change.

MTD-implemented modeling systems offer the ability to answer these important "what if" questions quickly and precisely. Frequently asked sensitivity questions include:

- What if product demand changes from that forecasted; how should production get back on course?
- What if a plant's production capacity is increased; what are the expected changes in product profitability?
- What if a new warehouse is added or an existing one expanded; how are distribution costs affected?
- What if the cost of capital changes or the inflation rate changes; how does the investment plan have to be changed?
- What if the price of certain raw materials increases dramatically; what are the best substitutes at each plant?
- What if a production or distribution facility is shut down; how should work be distributed?
- What if wage scales change; how can productivity be maintained?
- What if marketing runs a promotion for a product line; what costs will manufacturing incur in order to satisfy increased demand?
- What if a division is sold or a new subsidiary is bought; how will the rest of the operation be affected?
- What if energy prices continue to rise significantly; what are the benefits of new technological processes?
- What if service levels are revised; what will be the impact on costs?
- What if environmental regulations are relaxed or tightened; what will be the impact on productivity?
- What if competitors change product prices or marketing strategies; what is the best response?

It is not unusual for the user of a modeling system to make many sensitivity runs to gain insight on the true nature of the problem being solved. The already powerful sensitivity analysis capabilities available through the use of mathematical programming techniques have been enhanced significantly in the optimization modeling system implemented by MTD. Sophisticated, user-oriented features allow the decision maker to perform sensitivity analysis efficiently. In a typical MTD modeling system, sensitivity solutions can be determined for less than ten percent of the cost of obtaining the optimal solution. Such efficiency allows the user to rigorously test a proposed decision before its implementation.

When developing an optimization modeling system, a critical choice arises when the programming language for system implementation is selected. A well-suited language will facilitate system development and operation. All of the major programming languages have been used with varying degrees of success, and many proto-languages have been developed specifically for modeling and optimization. The key function of the language is to support logic that will serve as a bridge between data input and the representation of the model in a solvable form.

Criteria have been established for the selection of a programming language. The language should be flexible, modifiable, maintainable, efficient, and easy to use. The language should also have workable interfaces—as needed—with other file types, packages, and languages. Additionally, the language should provide for cost-effective development (productivity, implementation speed, and debugging time), and should allow for unambiguous modeling that accurately reflects both the model formulation and the data of the situation being studied.

*APL*, as a language and as an environment, answers the question of which language to select. Why *APL*? There are many reasons:

- Interactive data input serves to help the user create and modify the data for quick and efficient use. *APL* supports both vector- and matrix-oriented data structures which closely corresponds to the way most data is tabulated or thought of in the "real world" (i.e., groupings of like things).

- Data storage is dealt with through the component concept. Data files are manipulated as workspaces, which allows for efficient movement of vector and matrix files of data. *APL*, when properly used, gives the ability to dynamically vary the amount of data stored—to add, replace, and delete data elements, vectors, matrices, and files using file functions and other *APL∗PLUS* System features.

- During model generations, *APL* gives modeling systems tremendous power to do matrix-type operations. These tend to lie at the heart of most data manipulations in a modeling system. *APL* has the ability to handle data and name matrices concurrently and to do multiple-indexed referencing. *APL* also has the power to index submatrices, reshape vectors and matrices, and perform other operations that lead to the desired structure of the resultant matrix. Encoding and decoding operations are well handled in *APL*; conversion of literal information to the equivalent numeric values is straightforward. *APL* operators provide a powerful bit-manipulation capability; therefore the breadth of standard submatrix forms can be automatically constructed from short statements or functions.

- For generating model solutions, the *APL* notation is itself concise and powerful. This leads to rapid and efficient implementation of algorithms and heuristics when the optimizer is to be embedded within the system.

- Linkage to other languages and packages is made efficient through the use of shared variables to produce CMS files (under VM), or to retrieve files produced by other languages and packages. All these routines, programs, or packages can be called from *APL*. This means that all environmental changes are transparent to users of the modeling systems.

- Report writing is enhanced by the use of *APL* tools like STSC's
  □*FMT* report formatter. These tools facilitate the creation of
  formatted management reports.

## Conclusion

In summary, an effective optimization modeling system, coupled with a
language such as *APL* that facilitates system development and operation,
enables decision makers to enjoy the benefits of this comprehensive management tool.

*Chris Stathes joined STSC in 1978 and is currently manager of optimization
systems in the company's Management Technology Division. Through over
eight years' experience in technical consulting, he has acquired expertise in
numerous operations research and modeling applications, as well as in the
areas of economic analysis, optimization systems, database design, and data
storage and retrieval techniques. Currently, Stathes is developing operations
research applications, most notably for mathematical modeling systems.*

*Stathes has degrees from Cornell University and the Wharton School of
Finance and Commerce.*

Scott N. McAuley and James R. Nelson

# The Professional Programmer's Tool Kit

What powers does the expert programmer possess that allow him to build working systems in such a short time? Intuition? Analytical ability? Experience? These are three of the qualities that distinguish excellent programmers. However, none can be acquired overnight.

When we peer up an expert's sleeve we invariably discover something that *can* be acquired quickly by any programmer—a set of "tools" to increase productivity. A programmer working without tools to aid in the development, debugging, and documentation of systems should seem as incongruous as a plumber without a wrench or a carpenter without a hammer.

In this paper, we will describe the types of programming tools available to users of STSC's *APL\*PLUS* Service, and show advantages of using these tools at different stages of program development.

### Why Tools?

Behind all programming activity is a single driving force: the quick delivery of a working system to an end user. To accomplish this goal, it is desirable to minimize the time and resources spent on:

- developing the system
- running the system
- maintaining the system
- modifying the system.

Any technique that minimizes the time spent on system development and maintenance is an aid in quickly accomplishing the final objective. In this paper, we will describe the use of *APL* functions, which we call "tools", as aids to development and maintenance.

The programmer's tools serve the same purpose as the carpenter's tools—they are a means to an end, a way of doing otherwise difficult tasks with relative ease. These tools aid in accomplishing tasks that are common to many programmers; some tools are common to many applications (e.g., routines for file access, input, sorting, and reporting); some involve changes made to the elements of a system (editing the functions); and some are concerned with documenting the system (both as a development aid and in generating reference lists). In every case, the use of tools allows the programmer to concentrate on the real job—that of developing an efficient system quickly.

Programming tools can be divided into three main classes:

- Utilities, which accomplish routine tasks like entering, formatting, and manipulating data.
- Documentors, which display and analyze pieces of a system.
- Function fixers, which modify the elements of the system.

The sections that follow describe the general characteristics of each class of programming tools. The Appendix at the end of the paper lists some of the utilities, documentors, and function fixers available on STSC's *APL\*PLUS* System.

## Utilities

*Utilities* are functions that accomplish the routine tasks of an application. Since these tasks exist in many applications and their usefulness often overlaps sufficiently from application to application, generalized functions that perform routine tasks may be used. Often, it would not be difficult to construct working "custom" functions to accomplish these tasks for the application at hand. However, the time required to design, code, and document a set of functions for entry, sorting, data management, and date formatting is considerable—maybe as great as the effort required to deal with the "heart" of the application (i.e., that part of the application that is not generalized).

Utilities save the programmer time because they are prewritten, pretested, and predocumented. Their designers have generally done a thorough job in testing for "edge conditions" and optimizing for efficiency. What's more, many people use them, and their use promotes the standardization of techniques across applications and among different programmers. This in turn makes the learning process simpler for the new programmer who must maintain or enhance a system he did not write.

As an example, many of the applications written by STSC programmers use the *EMMA*™ Data Management System as a tool. *EMMA* is a system for maintaining large amounts of data. *EMMA* functions save programming and maintenance time. The maintenance programmer need only know that the system is *EMMA*-based to understand the mechanics of adding, sorting, and deleting data. And, he can take comfort in the knowledge that *EMMA* functions are robust and well documented.

## Documentors

*Documentors* have a dual purpose: to display in a convenient format the elements and interrelationships within a system, and to reduce testing and debugging time. Unlike utilities, these functions are rarely incorporated in user applications; nor is their design usually a simple matter.

For example, tools like STSC's Workspace Documentation Package (WSDOC) provide an "automatic" means of producing technical documentation. WSDOC can list definitions of all workspace elements and provide a complete cross-reference of these elements to answer the following questions:

Which functions are called by other functions?

Where are global variables used and where are they specified?

Which functions or variables are shadowed by others of the same name?

Documentors can also be put to use during the debugging and testing stage of a system. Tools like the function *SESHOW* in workspace 11 *WSSEARCH* can save a great deal of time in locating the occurrences of syntactic elements that aren't performing as expected. The function *DETVARS* in workspace 901 *UTIL* displays the contents of relevant variables. These documenting tools save time and reduce the effort required to find and list important information. Again, the programmer is free to concentrate on solving problems unique to the application at hand.

## Function Fixers

*Function fixers* are functions that are used to change the definitions of other functions. Function fixers allow the user to make significant alterations to other functions more quickly and easily than with function line editing. Function fixers are used in the following circumstances:

- To make the same change to many functions. For example, the functions *FNREPL* and *CHANGE* are used to change all occurrences of one function or variable name to another (e.g., *NAME*1 to *NAME*2).

- To make multiple changes within a function. For example, the function *FCL* can rename all labels in a function; the function *FNED* makes changes to subsets of lines in a function.

- To make changes that require substantial analysis. For example, the function *FCL* can localize variables; the functions *UNPAREN* and *BRKOUT* improve readability and restartability.

- To make a change to a function line that can't be changed any other way. For example, the function *FNED* edits lines of a function that are longer than the print width.

Humans tend to err when performing repetitive tasks; function fixers do not. Function fixers take advantage of the power of *APL* to use a list of functions as data and to manipulate these functions in the same manner that other programs manipulate data in applications. They perform repetitive tasks at great speed, without error.

## When Can Tools Be Used?

Tools are useful in designing, coding, and maintaining an application. Let's look at the benefits of using these tools during these three stages of programming.

- In the *design* stage, utilities can form a significant part of the overall design. Since they are predesigned, the programmer is free to concentrate on designing the unique, difficult parts of the system.

- In the *coding* stage, utilities save time since they are precoded and pretested. Also, documentors can be used to list and help debug parts of the system as the system is built. Function fixers allow the programmer to alter the system while it is being developed.

- In ongoing *maintenance*, documentors are used to locate problems and function fixers are used to resolve problems. Utilities help in two ways: their existence provides familiar ground for the maintenance programmer, and they are almost never the cause of errors themselves. Consequently, they simplify error diagnosis.

## Conclusion

Up the sleeve of the expert programmer are not magical powers, but rather a set of tools to speed programming tasks. These tools, like the mason's trowel or the surgeon's scalpel, are virtually indispensable. By handling common or repetitive tasks, tools allow the programmer to concentrate on the important task—that of quickly developing an efficient system.

## Appendix—Programming Tools on the *APL\*PLUS* System

Following are descriptions for the most widely used utilities, documentors, and function fixers available on STSC's *APL\*PLUS* System. More information can be obtained by loading the appropriate workspace and entering *DESCRIBE*.

| Utility | Description |
|---|---|
| *EMMA* | The *EMMA* Data Management System incorporates facilities for storing, manipulating, retrieving, and deleting data from a conceptual matrix stored in a file on the *APL\*PLUS* System. *EMMA* simplifies the design and documentation of file structures, the programming and testing of access mechanisms, and the implementation of changes in application scope or size. |
| FILESORT | The File Sort Facility is an *APL* interface to the IBM SORT/MERGE Program Product. FILESORT provides an efficient means of sorting large volumes of data contained in *APL\*PLUS* System files. |
| Input Manipulation | Workspace 6 *INPUT* contains functions that accept character input; numeric input; forced-choice input; bulk input; and combined character, numeric, and forced-choice input. |
| Sorting Arrays | Workspace 6 *SORT* contains utilities for grading, ranking, and sorting arrays. One group of functions handles numeric arrays as a collection of independent row vectors; a second group is used to grade, rank, and sort rows of a matrix relative to one another. |
| Partitioning Arrays | Workspace 6 *PARTFNS* contains user-defined functions that apply certain *APL* primitive functions independently to each partition of an array. |
| Date Manipulation | Workspace 6 *DATES* contains functions for converting, formatting, and verifying dates, and for performing miscellaneous manipulations on dates based on the Gregorian calendar. |
| Directing Output | Workspace 901 *OUTPUT* contains functions for directing output to a terminal, line printer, or high-speed data terminal (HSDTS). The workspace also contains functions for controlling paging, upper and lower margins, titles, and other aspects of formatted reports. |
| File Printing | Workspace 1 *FILEPRINT* contains functions that aid in submitting requests for files to be printed on a high-speed printer or at a high-speed data terminal (HSDTS). |

| | |
|---|---|
| Tab Setting | Workspace 14 *TABS* contains functions to establish and verify the horizontal tab stops on a variety of terminals. |
| Plotting | Workspace 10 *PLOT* contains a flexible set of programs for displaying data in graphic form. |

| *Documentor* | *Description* |
|---|---|
| WSDOC | Workspace 901 *WSDOC* contains functions to list the contents of a workspace—names and definitions of functions and variables, and extensive cross-reference reports. Output may be directed to a terminal or to a high-speed printer. |
| FILEDOC | Workspace 901 *FILEDOC* contains functions that produce a formatted list of *APL*PLUS* System files. Options allow listing of directory components of *EMMA* and QUICKPLAN™ files. |
| 901 *FL* | Workspace 901 *FL* contains the function *FL*, which produces a list of functions in the active workspace. The function also provides some cross-reference capabilities. |
| 11 *WSSEARCH* | This workspace contains functions that find and display character strings and syntactic elements in some or all functions in the active workspace. |
| 11 *TOOLS* | This workspace contains the function *FNIDS*, which searches a given function for identifiers belonging to certain categories (locals, labels, and so on). It also contains the function *XREF*, which displays a cross-reference for a given function. |
| 901 *UTIL* | This workspace contains the function *DETVARS*, which produces an abbreviated display of the values of some or all variables in the active workspace. |
| 901 *FDFNS* | This workspace contains the function *GL*, which produces a list of the names and definitions of functions, variables, and groups in the active workspace. |

| *Function Fixer* | *Description* |
|---|---|
| Editing | Workspaces 11 *FNED* and 11 *FLE* contain the functions *FNED* and *FLE*, respectively. These functions perform editing under program control and perform syntactic and nonsyntactic replacement on some or all function lines. They also edit lines that are too long for function line editing, or that contain embedded new-line characters. |

Localizing

The function *FCL* in workspace 901 *FCL* can localize identifiers referenced in a function. *FCL* can change the names of identifiers, sequentially rename labels, insert or strip diamond statement separators, strip comments, and list a function in one of several formats.

*CHANGE*

Workspace 901 *FDFNS* contains the function *CHANGE*, which replaces one or more syntactic elements in some or all functions in the workspace. Character constants and comments may optionally be included in changes.

11 *FNR*

The function *FNREPL* in workspace 11 *FNR* replaces a syntactic element in one or more functions in the active workspace.

11 *TOOLS*

Functions in this workspace remove embedded assignments, localize variables, alphabetize locals, sequentially rename labels, remove comments, and remove extra parentheses.

*Scott McAuley joined STSC in 1977 as a marketing representative and is currently an applications consultant in the company's Los Angeles office. Before joining STSC he spent a summer as a junior systems analyst for Sunkist Growers, Inc., and taught APL, accounting, and finance at the UCLA Graduate School of Management.*

*McAuley has a B.A. in economics from the University of California and an M.B.A. in accounting and finance from the UCLA Graduate School of Management.*

*Jim Nelson holds two degrees in mathematics from Michigan State University, a B.S. and an M.S. He worked for two and one-half years as an associate mathematician with the Upjohn Company, where he assisted in the inhouse installation of APLSV.*

*Nelson came to STSC in 1975 as an applications consultant. He designed and implemented a wide range of customized applications, including a worker's compensation cost control system, a billing system for mental health hospitals in Ventura County, California, and a long-range planning model for ARCO. In 1978 he assumed his current position as applications consultant manager in STSC's Los Angeles office. His responsibilities now include defining standards for APL programming style and managing APL software development efforts.*

John W. Myrna

# STSC's Design
# And Development Considerations

STSC's *APL\*PLUS* System is constantly being enhanced. There is never a shortage of ideas or proposals about possible features or systems that could be useful. How are these suggestions sorted out, and how does STSC implement those that are selected?

This paper discusses the main criteria used by STSC to evaluate new features proposed for design and implementation; it also discusses three additional considerations. The four essential questions are, therefore:

- What are the decision criteria?
- Who is the audience?
- How will the feature be used?
- What is the best medium for implementation?

Individuals involved in developing applications, as well as users, may find these considerations relevant to their own interests. STSC has recognized that a greater awareness of the underlying development criteria, as well as objectives, leads to more productive development, and produces results with improved consistency and quality.

## What Are the Decision Criteria?

Literally hundreds of enhancements to the *APL\*PLUS* System have been proposed over the past years. Just about every one of them could provide some useful capability. But there is no way that every proposal can be, or should be, implemented. Since development resources can implement only a small fraction of those suggestions, a careful selection process is important. Of course, the most fundamental criterion is the cost/benefit ratio of the development.

When estimating costs, all potential cost elements must be examined. Design and documentation are the major front-end costs, while ongoing user training and program maintenance are the major recurring costs. Coding a program typically accounts for only about 10 percent of the total cost.

Estimating benefits is more difficult than estimating costs. Asking users to estimate how much time they would save if they had a particular feature provides one measure of value and productivity. For enhancements that provide totally new solutions, an estimate of new revenues, deferred costs, or time and money savings helps indicate the value of the enhancement.

We attempt to verify that the cost is more than outweighed by the benefit before continuing the process. Naturally we always keep an eye open for "bargain enhancements"—features that have modest implementation costs, but that provide significant improvements in the system. Very few features, however, fall into that category. Furthermore, as problems and solutions are always dynamic, never static, it is never easy to predict costs or benefits accurately.

Usually features are *not* both "the answer to people's prayers" *and* easy to implement. Rather, they fall into either one of the following categories:

- They improve productivity by providing a better (quicker, cheaper, easier) method of accomplishing a task.

- They provide the first means for accomplishing a previously infeasible task.

Most proposals fall into the first category. When a large number of users are working on the same problems with the same applications, ideas for improving their productivity flow easily. Someone doing function editing, for example, can imagine many improvements that would save a few seconds every day. Examples of this type of enhancement that have been implemented are multiple line deletion, editing of longer lines, dot-comma editing, and most recently, semicolon editing.

Since enhancements of this type are, for the most part, incremental features to existing facilities, they are usually simple to implement, document, become familiar with, and use. However, because they are incremental and may not have been perceived as crucial enough to have been implemented initially, they also tend to add only a small increment of value. For one thing, they tend to address the needs of a relatively small set of users who perform the particular improved task frequently enough to appreciate nuances of design. Enhancements of this type are implemented when it is anticipated that many users will find them valuable, or when they are part of a larger enhancement or system currently planned.

The greatest value usually comes from the second category of enhancements. Reasonably enough, these enhancements generally involve substantial design, development, and implementation efforts, as well as documentation. Furthermore, since they address heretofore uncharted application areas, it takes longer to learn to master and use them. Examples of such enhancements are $\Box FMT$, report formatting, the $APL \star PLUS$ File System, and ACE (Automatic Control of Execution).

Because of the varying efforts and payoffs corresponding to both types of development, we attempt to balance the efforts devoted to implementing small, easy features with the efforts put toward more substantial developments addressing new applications.

A final criterion for judging a proposal is whether it is a special case of a more general problem. By stepping back to take a broader view, we may be able to solve a whole family of problems rather than only one specific case. One pitfall to avoid, however, is generalizing to the point of dismissing a problem by judging that it is a special case of a more general, unsolvable problem.

## Who Is the Audience?

It is reasonable to divide users into two broad categories: application users and professional programmers. Since the two groups impose different requirements on their computer usage, different system designs may be suitable depending on who will be using the system more frequently. The usage of a feature can be significantly reduced if its design is aimed at the wrong audience. If both groups have use for a new feature, but a compromise approach is taken in an attempt to meet the needs of both groups, utility for *both* groups may be reduced. On the other hand, a program that meets the needs of its audience will inspire program loyalty and continued use and development.

When designing for application users, designers keep in mind that these users are more knowledgeable about their particular tasks and applications than about $APL$ or even computers. Therefore, enhancements are purposely made more casual and less primitive; they tend to use free-form syntax, as in system commands. Applications specifically designed for end users also tend to neatly format results, have few edge conditions or side effects that might confound the user, and are more likely to be written in $APL$. These characteristics are aimed at removing unnecessary complexities from the application to make it easier for the user to understand and to use. However, they also tend to make the programs somewhat less flexible, and remove a degree of control from the user.

On the other hand, when designing for professional programmers, designers keep in mind that these users are technically trained and versed in software engineering and computing. Therefore, enhancements can be less casual and more primitive and can require explicit syntax. These programs offer more options, more control, and more flexibility than programs designed for application users only. However, they assume of the user, and indeed often require, a high degree of skill and technical knowledge about the program's content and workings.

Enhancements specifically designed for professional programmers tend to be programmatic (as in system functions), and might return results in forms suitable for further program manipulation. They may have edge conditions or side effects, and are more likely to be written in low-level languages for the sake of efficiency. These features are generally aimed at increasing a programmer's productivity and providing the facility for complete, explicit, and precise control of particular functions. Generally, the more control a user has, the greater the complexity offered by the facility.

### How Will the Feature Be Used?

Two characteristics of use have an impact on how a feature is designed: the expected frequency of its use and the amount of programming knowledge assumed of the average primary user. These characteristics are correlated to generally classify use, by feature, as one of the following three "styles": interactive casual, interactive programmatic, and noninteractive programmatic.

*Interactive casual* is characteristic of features (or parts of a feature) that are accessed infrequently. Ideal design will allow use without reference to a manual. Values returned, as well as diagnostic information, are usually displayed in an easily understood format. Examples of features tailored to this style of usage are system commands and application systems such as the 1 $NEWS$ Facility on the $APL*PLUS$ System.

*Interactive programmatic* usage is characterized by more frequent use of a feature or by enough use to warrant the effort of writing functions or an input script to automatically perform the frequently used task. Exceptional conditions, however, are still assumed to be handled casually by the user at the terminal. System functions that signal errors (e.g., $\Box XLOAD$) are representative of this style of usage.

The third type of usage is *noninteractive programmatic*. A program designed for this type of use is expected to handle any exceptional condition. System functions that return "error codes" (e.g., $\Box DEF$) are examples of features designed for this usage class.

Some enhancements, in fact, are developed specifically to convert application styles from the second to the third class, and back again. For example, $\Box ERROR$ can convert an error code into an exception, and $\Box ELX$ can convert an exception into an error code.

Enhancements, however, are used in all three styles at one time or another. STSC attempts, when it can, to serve more than one class of use when designing a new feature. A good example of this can be found in STSC's Deferred Execution Facility, which allows the automatic scheduling of $APL$ production tasks. All the casual, interactive user needs to do is load workspace 935 $DEFEX$ and enter $DEFER$. He will then be prompted for all other entries. $DEFER$ will accept times and dates in a variety of forms and will report on its progress in an understandable format. At the other end of the spectrum (noninteractive programmatic), Deferred Execution has self-contained primitive functions like $DFREQ$, which can be copied into a workspace and incorporated into any application. Results of these primitive functions are unformatted, but organized to simplify programmatic analysis.

### What Is the Best Medium for Implementation?

Select an implementation medium that best fits the needs of the user and the requirements of the new feature. The choices of media include $APL$ user-defined functions, "magic" functions ($APL$ user-defined functions that are installed as part of the language interpreter), auxiliary processors, system functions, and $APL$ language primitives. A general rule of thumb, however, is that the quicker the means of implementation, the less efficient the end result. The inverse, unfortunately, also tends to be true.

The choice of medium involves two separate, but generally interdependent, aspects: nature of access (e.g., $APL$ function call or shared-variable access to an auxiliary processor) and implementation approach (e.g., $APL$-coded magic function or PASCAL-coded system function). The examples that follow illustrate these aspects:

- Implement an auxiliary processor in Assembler language to access a collection of preexisting statistical programs written in FORTRAN.

- Implement $\Box DEFL$ in $APL$ and install it in $VS\ APL$ as a magic function to quickly provide users with the capability of this system function, while avoiding expensive implementation in Assembler language.

- Implement a database and reporting system like QUICKPLAN™ (STSC's Quick Planning and Reporting System) in $APL$ to allow individual customization.

- Implement the $APL*PLUS$ File System in Assembler language with access to system functions to support high volume and high efficiency shared use.

- Implement the utility functions in workspace 6 $INPUT$ in $APL$ as a working prototype for a future set of system functions.

- Implement the batch $APL$ Deferred Execution System in $APL$ to manage complexity and to allow the facility to be transported to other $APL$ time sharing systems.

### Conclusion

At STSC the development process involves selecting features with good cost/benefit ratios and carefully considering the audience and type of usage so that the feature will be implemented using the best media to meet the requirements of the user and the feature. But more than that, it is the process of careful planning and attention to detail. Care must be taken to avoid implementing an enhancement capriciously, or working a system into a corner. STSC wishes to maintain consistency with what has proved worthwhile in the past and to continue to be compatible with current *APL* implementations; however, STSC also strives to be at the forefront of development, leading the pack.

*John Myrna joined STSC in 1971 as manager of operations; in this position he organized STSC's Computing Center and nationwide communications network. He was subsequently promoted to manager of communications in 1973, director of development and design in 1975, director of development in 1977, and to his current position as vice president of development in 1979.*

*Myrna directs STSC's Operations Group and is a member of its Executive Committee and Technical Management Committee. He is responsible for the production and delivery of computing and telecommunications services and for the development of new applications, products, system features, and technologies.*

*Myrna holds a B.S.E.E. degree from the New Jersey Institute of Technology and an M.S.E.E. degree from Montana State University.*

**Robert A. Smith**

# Nested Arrays:
# The Tool for the Future

I find myself in the peculiar position of one who is "selling" *APL* to people already convinced of its value. Similar to carrying coals to Newcastle. However, what I'm selling promises to be as powerful compared to current *APL* as *APL* is compared to FORTRAN. It is an important new extension called "nested arrays". So, since new ideas require changes in one's thinking, some justification is needed before one undertakes the effort of understanding, much less accepting, these new *APL* tools.

Introducing nested arrays to *APL* programmers is similar to introducing *APL* to FORTRAN programmers. We use similar "sales" techniques:

"This new facility has more powerful data structures that adapt more naturally to the problems at hand."

"It also has a rich set of primitive functions and operators that are tailor-made to manipulate these new data structures."

"By using this facility, you will be more productive."

It does sound as though I'm talking about *APL* to a room full of FORTRAN programmers!

To be honest, though, the most important common statement is

"To take full advantage of this powerful new tool, you will have to change your way of thinking, even to the extent of unlearning some bad habits."

We've been saying this all along to programmers first learning *APL*; the same will apply to those of you when first learning about nested arrays.

Some of the unlearning may come easy. No longer will non-rectangular data have to be forced into rectangular structures. No more trying to fit round pegs into square holes!

Many data with which you now deal are non-rectangular. For example, the names of the months vary in length, yet are frequently stored in a 12-row matrix, with each name padded out to a common length. Typically, upon selecting a row from this matrix, the pad characters must be removed. Clearly, the pad characters are an artifact of the need for rectangularity, and as such contribute nothing to the use of the data. They only get in the way.

You can get an inkling of why a matrix might not be the best data structure for the names of the months when you consider that, of the two dimensions of this matrix, only one is used to access the data. In other words, the data has row significance, but no column significance. A much better structure for this data is a nested array, which is a 12-element vector whose scalars are the individual months' names. Of course, this representation isn't available in current *APL*, but it is with nested arrays.

        ***MONTHS***              *(Blanks are shown as 'o'.)*

*JANUARY*oo
*FEBRUARY*o
*MARCH*oooo
*APRIL*oooo
*MAY*oooooo
*JUNE*ooooo
*JULY*ooooo
*AUGUST*ooo
*SEPTEMBER*
*OCTOBER*oo
*NOVEMBER*o
*DECEMBER*o

        ***MONTHS*[3;]**          *The view along the rows has significance.*

*MARCH*oooo

        ***MONTHS*[;3]**          *The view along the columns does not.*

*NBRRYNLGPTVC*

The above example actually makes two important points. The first is that nested arrays allow a more natural representation of data; in particular, such artifacts as pad characters become unnecessary. The second is that, in fact, not all dimensions are of the same importance. This latter point leads to another piece of unlearning.

In current *APL*, we have only one level of dimension to exploit (the one obtained by the primitive function shape). Until now we have not considered the relative importance of dimensions; rather, all dimensions are at the same level. In a 12 by 9 matrix there is nothing to indicate the relative importance of the length 12 dimension from the one of length 9. With nested arrays, however, we can have multiple levels of dimension, and so their relative importance can be implied. It makes more sense, for example, to store the above set of months' names as a vector of vectors than as a matrix.

Be careful not to conclude that this distinction is made because of the non-rectangularity of the months' names. Rather, the distinction is based upon the inherent, relative importance of the dimensions. For example, consider appropriate data structures in which to store the three-letter abbreviations of the months' names. Certainly, one possibility is to use a 12 by 3 matrix. However, there is still no cohesion of the data along the columns; the values in no column of the data have any particular meaning. This suggests that a better data structure is a nested array which is a 12-element vector whose scalars are 3-element vectors (the abbreviations of the months' names)—again, a vector of vectors. Thus, instead of the length 12 and the length 3 dimensions appearing at the same level (as in a 12 by 3 matrix), they appear at different levels. The more important dimension of the two is on the outside; the less important on the inside.

### What Are Nested Arrays?

We've been talking about nested arrays in somewhat vague terms. The time has come to be a bit more precise. Simple arrays in *APL* are rectangular collections of scalars. At that level of description, nested arrays are no different. That is, a nested array is still an array as we know it. Where nested arrays differ from simple arrays is in their scalars. A scalar in a simple array is a single number or character, whereas a scalar in a nested array can be any array!

This may seem strange at first, but it represents a powerful extension. Transforming an array into a scalar can be thought of as akin to stepping back from a problem to get a better perspective. In both cases detail is subsumed, allowing you to see the larger aspects or structure.

Actually, those of you who have used the *APL\*PLUS* File Subsystem have been doing this all along. Think of an *APL* file as a vector whose scalars are arbitrary arrays. If we say that a simple array has a depth of zero, then a file has a depth of one. That is, in a simple array there is an outer structure (its shape), but no inner structure—all scalars are single, simple objects. However, in a file there is an outer structure (the file's length or number of components) and an inner structure (the shapes of the arrays in each component). Since an array always has an outer structure, depth is a measure of inner structure.

Now, generalize the structure of a file to allow the outer structure to be shaped arbitrarily (for example, as a matrix), and to allow the scalars (the components) themselves to be nested arrays. You can then begin to see the power and breadth of nested arrays.

Also, files store data of varying shapes and types (numeric or character). This data is placed in components without concern for the variations. That is, the file's information content is divided into two levels: the outer level is the distinction between component numbers, and the inner level is the distinction between values within a given component. This same division is offered by nested arrays, but in a richer way, through an arbitrary number of levels on which to make such distinctions.

So, a nested array is an array whose scalars may contain arrays themselves. Moreover, with such general structures, there is no longer any reason to bar numbers and characters from being contained in the same array. Consider the advantages of no longer having to segregate the numeric and character portions of a data record, or, perhaps better yet, no longer having to encode one data type in the other. Another happy bit of unlearning!

With nested arrays, the two types of data can be stored together without the user having to take any special action. While there are still no meaningful arithmetic computations to be performed on character data, there can be structural and/or content similarities between the two types which may encourage you to store them together in the same array. For example, an employee record might contain character information of the employee's name and address, and numeric information such as the date of hire and salary. This information can be joined together in one array (probably as a vector of arrays—some scalars, some vectors) and manipulated as one entity (for instance, stored in a single file component). However, don't get the impression that all the character data must be gathered together in one spot and all the numeric data in another. The two types can be interspersed in any manner, even as they might naturally appear.

## What Can We Do with Nested Arrays?

The availability of nested arrays opens whole new areas which become more feasible to address.

Let's expand upon the last example and build a nested array containing employee data. In the process, we'll introduce some of the primitives of nested arrays. By the way, as of this writing, the symbols used to represent these functions and operators have not been fixed, so don't take the ones used below as final.

An employee record might consist of the following items:

- name (character vector)
- address (character vector)

- date of hire (numeric scalar)
- salary (numeric scalar)

First we need to make each of these items into scalars, for which there is a primitive function called *enclose* (symbol ⊂). The enclosed scalars can be joined together into a four-element employee vector as follows:

    *EMP←(⊂NAME),(⊂ADDR),(⊂DOH),⊂SAL*

A collection of employees might form a department, which can be represented as either a vector of employee vectors, or as a four-column matrix, each row of which is an employee vector. The choice between the two is a matter of taste. Note that with the matrix form there is significance for both the row and column views. A row contains all data about a single employee; a column contains a single attribute (for instance, salary) about all employees. Let's use the matrix form. To append a new employee, we use the familiar:

    *DEPT←DEPT,[1] EMP*

Some simple inquiries about this department can be formulated such as:

Select the names and addresses of employees hired in 1980 or later:

    *(800101≤DEPT[;3])/DEPT[; 1 2]*

The above code fragment is quite straightforward, as it should be. A simple request should require a simple piece of code. What is important is how naturally these familiar functions apply to nested arrays.

To extract the name of an employee (say the third one in the matrix *DEPT*) we first index to that scalar (via *DEPT[3 ; 1]*), and then apply *disclose* (symbol ⊃) which is the inverse function to enclose:

    *⊃DEPT[3;1]*

The result is the simple character vector of the employee's name.

This nested array of employee data can be enlarged in several ways. One way is to add more outer structure, such as incorporating the department into a higher level of organizational structure, say, divisions. The divisions themselves might not have any higher-dimensional structure, so they would be collected together in a vector:

    *DIV←(⊂DEPT1),(⊂DEPT2), . . .*

The variable *DIV* is a vector of matrices. Now to find out how many employees are in each department of this division, we need another primitive, this time an operator. The key to the problem is in the word "each". We want to apply something to each item of *DIV*. This concept is already familiar to us with scalar functions. A description of the expression 2+*A* might be to add 2 to each scalar of *A*. In this case, we want to determine the shape, or size, of each item in *DIV*. To the rescue comes the *each* operator (symbol ¨), which applies its argument (a function) to each item of the data. For example, to determine the shape of each item of *DIV*, use

    ρ¨*DIV*

The idea of the each operator is that it makes its function argument into a scalar function. Hence, the derived function that results from applying the operator obeys the same rank- and shape-conformability rules as scalar functions. In particular, the rank and shape of the result in this case is identical to that of the argument. In general, when applying a function *f* to an array, the items of the result are obtained as follows:

1. Select a scalar from the array.
2. Disclose the result of step 1.
3. Apply the function *f* to the result of step 2.
4. Enclose the result of step 3.

In symbols, with $R \leftarrow f\ddot{\ } A$,

    R[I] ↔ ⊂f⊃A[I]

Note how disclose is used to peel away the scalar wrapping of $A[I]$. The function is applied to this uncovered array; the following enclose ensures that the result is a scalar. It is this interaction that enables the each operator to apply its function argument in the manner of a scalar function.

Back to the problem of determining the number of employees in each department, we first apply monadic shape to each item of $DIV$ using:

       ρ̈DIV
    12 4   6 4   20 4

There are 12 employees in the first department, 6 in the second, and 20 in the third. Note that the actual format for displaying this result has not yet been decided.

Since the each operator applied the shape function as a scalar function, the number of elements in the result is the same as the number of elements in $DIV$. The items of the result are themselves the enclose of the shape of the items of $DIV$. The items of $DIV$ are all four-column matrices, so the result is a vector of two-element vectors. In each two-element subvector, the first element is the number of rows (number of employees), the second is the number of columns (four).

From here, we can proceed in several ways to obtain just the first element (the number of employees) from each subvector. One way is to apply the each operator again, this time to the dyadic function reshape where we are reshaping each two-element subvector to a scalar. That code would be

       ''ρ̈ρ̈DIV
    12 6 20

## Conclusion

Let me recall my first impressions upon encountering $APL$. Perhaps you, too, had similar impressions. I recall thinking that something must be wrong, that there were things missing. It couldn't be as easy as it looked. Up to that point, programming had been a hard task. There were so many things to keep track of. So much work was necessary to accomplish anything. But that feeling wasn't present when I began programming in $APL$. To me, $APL$ represented a major step forward in programming.

Now that feeling of programming being difficult has returned. Certainly, the problems have gotten harder, but knowing about better tools like nested arrays sheds a different light on programming tasks. I see how to accomplish these tasks more easily using nested arrays.

Why do we need nested arrays? Because the programming tasks of the future are going to be harder. To address these more challenging tasks we must be prepared to accept new ideas, and to use new and better tools. Nested arrays are one of the $APL$ programmer's most powerful tools for the future.

*Bob Smith joined STSC in 1971 as a marketing representative and subsequently held the positions of regional marketing manager, director of systems, and applications analyst. In 1979 he assumed his current position as senior research associate. Smith has used APL since 1970 and has in-depth experience in all facets of the language. He has written numerous articles and manuals, and has designed and implemented several APL enhancements, applications, and systems. Smith is currently leading STSC's project to design and implement nested arrays.*

*Smith has a B.A. in mathematics from the University of Vermont and has completed graduate coursework in mathematics at the University of Maryland. He is a member of ACM and helped form the Washington, D.C., chapter of STAPL.*

**Carl M. Cheney and Scott N. McAuley**

# A Consumer's Guide to Choosing an *APL* Terminal

Much has been said about the language features and applications available on different computer systems running *APL*; in fact, many papers in this book deal with these things. If we are going to use *APL*, we also need another machine—a terminal to communicate with the computer. This paper is concerned with that "other" machine—the faithful *APL* terminal.

Finding the right *APL* terminal can be a difficult, expensive, frustrating, and time-consuming task. In this paper, we provide a guide for the consumer shopping for terminals. We offer some pointers on what to look for in an *APL* terminal, and we compare the features of some popular terminals. We have limited our discussion to "start-stop" devices capable of displaying *APL* characters; data storage devices, remote job-entry stations, synchronous terminals, and graphics devices are, therefore, not covered in this presentation.

We wish to thank David Michelson for his comments and information, Allen Rose for his encouragement and anecdotes, and Judy Syfers for her assistance in the research necessary to prepare this paper.

### What's So Special about *APL* Terminals?

*APL* is an interactive language, demanding close communications between the user and the system. Since this contact occurs through a terminal, the interface between user and terminal is important. Seemingly small factors can become important—just ask anyone who has discovered the location of the BREAK key by accidentally interrupting an executing program at a non-restartable point, or who has had to squint to discern the difference between the printed character sequences − / and = / in a function listing. The *APL* user typically is thinking analytically, and is in the process of solving a problem under some time pressure. The last thing he needs is a clumsy terminal.

So, what's important in an *APL* terminal? First, there's the keyboard. *APL* is both a computer language and a notation. As a notation, it uses graphic symbols not found on a traditional typewriter keyboard. For a terminal to properly display *APL* notation, all the characters shown in Table 1 must be available on the terminal.

Table 1 shows 140 distinct *APL* characters; however, only 94 printing characters are defined in the USASCII code used by most terminals (and only 88 in the IBM EBCDIC code). The need for additional characters is met by overstriking two characters. In fact, 52 of the characters in Table 1 are formed using overstrikes. These 52 overstruck characters are transmitted to and from the *APL* system as *three* distinct characters—the two characters to be overstruck, joined by a "backspace" character (for instance, the *APL* character ≠ is sent as /, BACKSPACE, and ⁻.

## Table 1—*APL* Notation

| | | |
|---|---|---|
| *$ DOLLAR-SIGN* | *≠ NOT-EQUAL* | *⊼ NAND* |
| *¢ CENT-SIGN* | *α ALPHA* | *⊽ NOR* |
| *[ LEFT BRACKET* | *ε EPSILON* | *⍝ LAMP* |
| *] RIGHT BRACKET* | *ι IOTA* | *⍋ GRADEUP* |
| *( LEFT PARENTHESIS* | *ρ RHO* | *⍒ GRADEDOWN* |
| *) RIGHT PARENTHESIS* | *ω OMEGA* | *⊖ ROTATE-MINUS* |
| *; SEMICOLON* | *, COMMA* | *⌿ SLASH-MINUS* |
| */ SLASH* | *! SHRIEK* | *⍀ BACKSLASH-MINUS* |
| *\ BACKSLASH* | *⌽ ROTATE* | *⌹ DOMINO* |
| *← LEFT ARROW* | *⊥ DECODE* | *▼ THORN* |
| *→ RIGHT ARROW* | *⊤ ENCODE* | *⍎ HYDRANT* |
| *¨ DIERESIS* | *○ CIRCLE* | *◇ DIAMOND* |
| *+ PLUS* | *? QUERY* | *⊣ RIGHT TACK* |
| *- MINUS* | *~ LOGICAL-NOT* | *⊢ LEFT TACK* |
| *× TIMES* | *↑ TAKE* | *} RIGHT BRACE* |
| *÷ DIVIDE* | *↓ DROP* | *{ LEFT BRACE* |
| *\* POWER* | *⊂ IMPLICATION* | *A - Z  ALPHABET* |
| *⌈ CEILING* | *⊃ REVERSE IMPLICATION* | *Δ DELTA* |
| *⌊ FLOOR* | *∩ INTERSECTION* | *A̲ - Z̲  UNDERSCORED ALPHA* |
| *| MODULUS* | *∪ UNION* | *Δ̲ DELTA-UNDERSCORED* |
| *∧ AND* | *_ UNDERSCORE* | *0̲ - 9  NUMERALS* |
| *∨ OR* | *⍉ TRANSPOSE* | *. PERIOD* |
| *< LESS-THAN* | *⌶ I-BEAM* | *⁻ NEGATIVE-SIGN* |
| *≤ LESS-THAN-OR-EQUAL* | *° NUL* | *' QUOTE* |
| *= EQUAL* | *⎕ QUAD* | *: COLON* |
| *≥ GREATER-THAN-OR-EQUAL* | *⍞ QUOTE-QUAD* | *∇ DEL* |
| *> GREATER-THAN* | *⍟ LOGARITHM* | *⍱ DEL-TILDE* |
| *Ø DANISH AND NORWEGIAN* | *Ä GERMAN A UMLAUT* | *Ö GERMAN O UMLAUT* |
| *Ü GERMAN U UMLAUT* | *£ BRITISH POUND* | *¥ JAPANESE YEN* |
| *Ñ SPANISH N TILDE* | | |

For a terminal to display an overstruck character, it must be capable of either

- displaying the first character, stopping, backspacing, and then displaying the second character, or

- accepting the three-character sequence containing the overstruck character as a "valid" overstrike and displaying its representation.

Because of the need to overstrike characters, *APL* terminals present a greater challenge to their designers and manufacturers than do terminals for "ordinary" computing or word processing. Compromises in design frequently lead to less-than-perfect performance; many of the features discussed later in this paper relate to the presence or absence of compromises.

## A Little *APL* History

When Kenneth Iverson wrote *A Programming Language* (Wiley, 1962), he probably gave little thought to how his notation would be displayed. A few years later, though, an *APL* group at the IBM Research Center realized the difficulty of setting "Iverson notation" in type for publication.

Legend has it the group paid a visit to an IBM typewriter factory in Lexington, Kentucky, in the mid-1960s and looked through available Selectric® type faces to see what might be used. They knew it was important to distinguish ordinary alphabetic characters from symbols used in *APL* notation; for example, to establish a clear difference between the alphabetic "T", "X", and "I" and the *APL* "encode" (⊤), "times" (×), and "modulus" (|). Consequently, they chose italic font for the *APL* alphabet. Upright numerals were chosen to distinguish "*O*" and "*I*" from "0" and "1". Of the 88 keys on the Selectric, 36 were used for the alphabet and numerals.

The group, suspecting that additional *APL* symbols might be added in the future, decided to use overstrikes to form some of the special symbols in Iverson's notation. These symbols were chosen from the character sets then available to align well when overstruck. A collection of 88 *APL* characters was made into a Selectric typesphere. Soon, this typesphere was used on the first *APL* terminal—the IBM 1050.

This character set remained the standard for *APL* terminals until the design of the Tektronix 4013 terminal. This machine had the capacity to generate characters in software, since it was fundamentally a graphic display device. The terminal could transmit six more characters than an IBM terminal, since it used the ASCII communications code. Its designers chose to add the six characters { } $ ◇ ⊣ and ⊢ to fill the gap (the $ and ◇ could be formed on the IBM terminal, but only as odd-looking overstrikes).

The mapping of *APL* symbols into the ASCII character set, as defined by Tektronix, was proposed as a standard by members of the *APL* Users Group and accepted by the *APL* Project of SHARE (an IBM users' group). It has since become the de facto standard of the *APL* terminal industry. This overlay standard is described in STSC Working Memorandum No. 105, *APL-ASCII: An ASCII Overlay Standard* (STSC, 1974), written by L. M. Breed.

Currently, there are about a dozen manufacturers of *APL* terminals and perhaps 30 distinct terminal models available. Manufacturers offer a wide range of features at a wide range of prices. Terminals can display output on a screen, on paper, or on both. Printing terminals can use plain or thermal-sensitive paper and can print using a typesphere, "daisy-wheel", or dot matrix. Terminals can display from 64 to 218 columns and can weigh from 10 to 150 pounds. Some have built-in graphics capabilities and some may connect directly to telephone receivers or telephone lines. And, depending on their capabilities, terminals can cost from $1500 to $13,000.

Nevertheless, the multiplicity of features available on *APL* terminals need not bewilder the buyer. Features vary greatly in importance depending on the intended use of the terminal. To help the prospective buyer in systematically evaluating the features of importance to him, we have organized our discussion around three classes of terminal features:

- Features of concern to all users.
- Features specific to printing or display terminals.
- Features specific to different types of use.

The sections that follow discuss these features in detail, and Tables 2 and 3 provide summary guides for printing and video-display terminals, respectively. The information in the tables was collected carefully and to the best of our knowledge is correct. Not all terminals and manufacturers are represented. Prices are current as of February 1980, and in some cases represent only one distributor of a product. Readers are asked to use this information as a representative guide to the features that are available and to determine for themselves the suitability of a terminal to their particular needs.

## Features of Concern to All Users

All *APL* terminal users will be concerned with these fundamental terminal capabilities:

- communications speeds and connection to the host computer
- entry and display features

## Table 2—Features of Video Display Terminals

| | Agile A155 | Anderson Jacobson 630 | Anderson Jacobson 832 | Computer Devices Inc., 1132 | Computer Transciever Systems Inc., Execuport 4000 | Computer Transciever Systems Inc., Execuport 4080 | Decriter LA 36 | Qume Sprint V | Tally T-1612 | Texas Instruments 745 | Texas Instruments 820 | Trendata 4000 | Diablo 1640 |
|---|---|---|---|---|---|---|---|---|---|---|---|---|---|
| Supports tabs? | Y | Y | Y | N | Y | Y | Y | Y | Y | Y | Y | Y | Y |
| Numeric keypad? | Y | N | Y | N | Y | Y | Y | Y | Y | N | Y | Y | Y |
| Speed range in characters per second | 30–120 | 10–30 | 10–30 | 10–30 | 10–30 | 10–30 | 10–30 | 10–120 | 30–960 | 10–30 | 10–960 | 10–30 | 10–960 |
| Programmable soft keys? | N | N | N | N | N | N | N | N | N | N | N | N | N |
| EIA accessory jack? | N | N | N | Y | Y | Y | N | N | N | N | N | N | N |
| Powers up with tabs set? | N | N | N | N | Y | Y | N | N | N | N | N | N | N |
| Modular phone connection? | N | N | N | Y | Y | Y | N | N | N | Y | N | N | N |
| Built in modem available? | N | Y | N | N | Y | Y | N | N | N | N | N | Y | N |
| Dials access number? | N | N | N | N | N | Y | N | N | Y | N | N | N | N |
| Pedestal? | Y | N | Y | N | N | N | Y | N | Y | N | N | N | N |
| Side tables? | N | N | Y | N | N | N | Y | N | Y | N | N | Y | Y |
| Maximum printing width | 158 | 140 | 158 | 132 | 136 | 80 | 132 | 158 | 132 | 80 | 132 | 158 | 158 |
| Repeat key? | Y | Y | N | Y | Y | Y | Y | Y | Y | N | N | Y | N |
| Selected repeating keys? | N | N | N | N | N | N | N | N | N | N | Y | N | N |
| All keys repeat? | Y | N | Y | N | Y | Y | N | N | Y | Y | Y | Y | Y |
| Suitable for programmer? | Y | Y | Y | Y | Y | Y | N | Y | Y | Y | Y | Y | Y |
| Suitable for user? | Y | Y | Y | Y | Y | Y | Y | Y | Y | Y | Y | Y | Y |
| Single unit purchase price | 3,995 | 1,200 | 3,495 | 3,530 | 3,495 | 1,975 | 2,500 | 3,275 | 2,395 | 1,695 | 1,995 | 3,995 | 2,878 |
| Single unit one year lease (per month) | 200 | 65 | 140 | 157 | 158 | 135 | 244 | 140 | -- | 100 | 100 | 140 | -- |
| APL keycaps available? | Y | Y | Y | Y | Y | Y | Y | N | -- | Y | Y | -- | Y |
| Portable? | N | N | N | Y | Y | Y | N | N | N | Y | N | N | N |
| Printer type | Qume | Thermal Matrix | Qume | Thermal Matrix | Thermal Matrix | Thermal Matrix | Impact Matrix | Qume | Impact Matrix | Thermal Matrix | Impact Matrix | Diablo | Diablo |
| Requires special paper? | N | Y | N | Y | Y | Y | N | N | N | Y | N | N | N |
| Form feeds? | Y | N | Y | N | N | N | Y | Y | Y | N | Y | Y | Y |
| Vertical tabs? | Y | N | Y | N | N | N | Y | Y | Y | N | Y | Y | Y |
| Forms tractor available? | Y | N | Y | N | N | N | Y | Y | Y | N | Y | Y | Y |
| Pin-feed platen available? | Y | N | Y | N | N | N | N | Y | Y | N | Y | Y | Y |
| Friction platen available? | Y | N | Y | N | N | Y | N | Y | N | Y | N | Y | Y |
| Supports X-on X-off protocol? | Y | N | N | N | N | N | N | N | Y | N | Y | N | Y |
| Keeps up with output at highest speed? | N | Y | Y | Y | Y | Y | Y | N | N | Y | N | Y | N |
| Dot Matrix Dimensions | | 5x8 | | 5x7 | 5x7 | 5x7 | 7x7 | | 7x7 | 5x7 | 9x7 | | |

## Table 3—Features of Printing Terminals

| | Anderson Jacobson 510 | Hewlett Packard 2641A | Human Designed Systems Inc., Concept APL | Tektronix 4013 | Tektronix 4014 | Research Inc., Teleray 11 | Research Inc., Teleray 3931 |
|---|---|---|---|---|---|---|---|
| Supports tabs? | Y | Y | Y | N | N | Y | Y |
| Numeric keypad? | Y | Y | Y | N | N | Y | Y |
| Speed range in characters per second | 10-960 | 10-960 | 5-960 | 10-960 | 10-960 | 5-960 | 5-960 |
| Programmable soft keys? | N | Y | Y | N | Y | Y | N |
| EIA accessory jack? | N | Y | Y | Y | Y | Y | Y |
| Powers up with tabs set? | N | N | Y | N | N | N | Y |
| Modular phone connection? | N | N | N | N | N | Y | N |
| Built in modem available? | N | N | N | N | N | N | N |
| Dials access number? | N | N | N | N | N | N | N |
| Pedestal? | N | N | N | N | Y | N | N |
| Side tables? | N | N | N | Y | Y | N | N |
| Maximum printing width | 80 | 80 | 80 | 74 | 133 | 60 | 80 |
| Repeat key? | N | N | Y | N | N | Y | Y |
| Selected repeating keys? | N | N | Y | N | N | N | N |
| All keys repeat? | Y | Y | N | Y | Y | Y | Y |
| Suitable for programmer? | Y | Y | Y | Y | Y | Y | Y |
| Suitable for user? | Y | Y | Y | Y | Y | Y | Y |
| Single unit purchase price | 1,995 | 4,100 | 1,750 | 7,395 | 12,195 | 1,590 | 1,960 |
| Single unit one year lease | 87 | -- | 160 | 444 | 733 | 85 | 60 |
| APL key caps available? | Y | Y | Y | Y | Y | Y | Y |
| Portable? | N | N | N | N | N | N | N |
| Dot matrix dimensions in characters | 7x10 | 9x15 | 7x9 | 7x9 | 7x9 | 8x11 | 5x9 |
| Screen dimensions in characters | 24x80 | 24x80 | 24x80 | 35x74 | 64x133 | 24x80 | 24x80 |
| True overstrike? | Y | N | Y | Y | Y | Y | Y |
| Illegal overstrikes produce what? | last char | out | actual | actual | actual | actual | actual |
| Formatted screen mode? | Y | Y | Y | N | N | Y | N |
| Character color | green | white | white | green | green | white | white |
| Recall things that have gone off screen? | Y | Y | Y | N | Y | N | N |
| Addressable cursor? | Y | Y | Y | Y | Y | Y | N |
| Line block mode with local editing? | Y | Y | Y | N | N | Y | N |
| Detachable keyboard? | N | Y | Y | N | N | Y | N |

- usabilty and portability
- reliability and availability of service.

## 1. Communications Features

Two related factors influence the communications end of *APL* terminals—the speed of transmission and the method of connection to the host computer. Transmission speeds are typically expressed in CPS—characters per second. Terminals may operate at speeds ranging from 10 to 960 CPS; however, terminals operating at speeds over 120 CPS must be "hard-wired" to the host computer; a dial-up telephone line cannot be used.

Terminals using IBM's EBCDIC code can operate at 14.9 or 33.3 CPS; those using the ASCII code can operate at 10, 15, 30, 60, 120, 240, 480, or 960 CPS. Speeds of up to 30 CPS are considered "low" to "standard" for *APL* terminals, and transmission over phone lines is accomplished through a modem like the Bell 103. The 30-CPS speed is the most popular for time sharing terminals and is adequate for most purposes. At this speed, display of a full 8 1/2 by 11 inch page takes less than three minutes (even less time is required if you allow for blank lines and the use of tabs).

At higher speeds, there is no universal modulation standard for transmission over phone lines. For example, at 120 CPS, two popular but incompatible protocols are available: one associated with the Bell 212 modem and one associated with the Vadic 3400 modem. The Bell modem is more prevalent; however, it must be connected directly to the phone line rather than through an acoustic coupler. This limits the portability of the terminal. The two types of modems cannot "talk" to each other, so it is important to check the protocol of the modem chosen to make sure that it is supported by the host computer system.

Some terminals include built-in modems with acoustic couplers for telephone handset coupling or for direct connection to the line. Some direct-connect modems include auto-dialer circuits that remember access numbers and sign-on protocols.

## 2. Entry and Display Features

A number of terminal features center around the entry and display of data at the terminal. A main consideration, then, is the keyboard. Some of the important questions to ask include: "Are *APL* characters printed on the keys, or will I have to look at a chart or paste on *APL* decals? Is the BREAK key in a place where I won't accidentally hit it? Are the BACKSPACE and LINEFEED keys placed conveniently for *APL* editing? Is a 10-key numeric pad available?" (It will be helpful if you'll be entering significant amounts of numeric data.) "Do any of the keys repeat, and, if so, do they repeat using a shift-type REPEAT key or by being held down? Does the terminal have extra, programmable 'soft' keys to recall often-used commands like $)COPY$ or sign-on arguments? If so, are the contents of these keys retained in memory when the terminal is switched off?"

Some primary display considerations include display width, display quality, and support of tabs.

Display width ($\Box PW$) is the number of character columns the terminal can represent. Two standards have evolved from historical accidents—80 characters (from the Hollerith punched card and the standard typed page) and 132 characters (from the IBM 1403 line printer). However, terminals are available that support maximum widths of 64 characters (the IBM 5110 portable computer), 136 characters (Execuport), 158 characters (many daisy-wheel printers, if pitch is set to 12 columns per inch), and even 218 characters (the Texas Instruments 820 in "compressed print" mode).

Obviously, using more columns, more information can be presented on a single page or screen. However, there is a corollary—display formats *designed* for wide terminals look awful when *displayed* on narrow terminals. Long lines that exceed the shorter print width will spill over to the left of the following line, preceded by the six spaces inserted by the *APL* system. This will cause reports to appear somewhat different from the way they were originally designed.

The legibility of the input and output on paper or on the terminal screen is determined by the quality of the display. Printing terminals using Selectric or daisy-wheel mechanisms generally provide good to excellent resolution. Virtually all display terminals and many printing terminals form images by using a matrix of dots. Two factors affect readability: the number of dots used for each character "cell" and the design of the character set. A few dot-matrix representations are excellent (the Hewlett/Packard 2641A has high resolution and distinct characters), and a few are poor (the Texas Instruments 745 and the Decwriter have very small alphabetic characters). Dot matrix printing will serve most users well, but users wanting camera-ready copy should choose Selectric or daisy-wheel mechanisms.

An *APL* terminal's effective display speed can be increased substantially through the use of tabs. As on a typewriter, tab stops are defined as predetermined columns. The *APL* system sends a number of "tab" characters and spaces forward or backward to reach the first nonblank column on a line. Use of this feature can decrease the time required to print tabular reports by 40 to 50 percent. But tabs and backspaces can sometimes cause overflow problems in printing terminals (the terminal may not be able to execute the tab or backspace motion at its rated speed).

3.   Usability and Portability

A number of terminal characteristics fall into a vague category we'll call "usability". For instance, the "feel" of the keyboard to the typist is an important, if somewhat unquantifiable, quality. Another intangible is the quality of the instruction manual. Many calls to support programmers or terminal service people can be avoided if users know how to reset switches or can find answers in the reference manual.

A third intangible feature is the noise a terminal makes. *APL* systems return a "bell" character and beeping noise to signify acceptance of the last input line; can you and your coworkers live with the sounds your terminal makes? Many a terminal has been emasculated (the Xerox 1600-1700 series comes to mind) by a distraught user driven into a frenzy by loud, long beeps.

Terminals are often more useful if they can be moved easily. In the earliest days of *APL*, the desk-sized IBM 1050 and 2741 were the only *APL* terminals. STSC Vice President Allen Rose, then of IBM, had a 2741 sawed in half to make it a "portable" 130 pounds. Similarly, in the early days of STSC, a resourceful manager named Murray Spencer rigged up a pack frame to carry the "lightweight" (60 pounds) Datel terminal.

Today some *APL* terminals are portable in the sense that they can be rolled from room to room (the 150-pound Tektronix 4015 and the 75-pound Anderson/Jacobson 832A, for instance). Others come with a handle or carrying case and weigh about 40 pounds, fitting the "portable" description much like the average television. A few terminals are *truly* portable—in particular, the 16-pound Execuport 4000, the 18-pound CDI 1203 Miniterm, and the 14-pound Texas Instruments 745. These can easily be carried across town to a client or across the country under an airplane seat. However, don't check them as luggage—if you do, you'll likely need to read the next section carefully!

## 4. Reliability and Service

It is inevitable that one day your terminal will break. Furthermore, it will *not* break on a Monday, but on a Friday afternoon. It will not break while you're playing games such as *STARTREK* or *ADVENTURE*, but while you're printing the chairman's monthly report or, even worse, your paycheck. If your terminal is portable, it will break while you're passing through Fargo, North Dakota.

There is little you can do to prevent these failures—consider them acts of God. You can ease the pain by finding a rugged terminal or a responsive service organization or both. In our experience, daisy-wheel printing terminals fail most often (though usually with some prior warning), followed by portable terminals (probably because of rough handling). Display terminals almost never require service.

Check the maintenance options available when you shop for a terminal. Maintenance contracts are available from most manufacturers and are usually a good investment. Many lease agreements require or include purchase of a maintenance contract. Sometimes a friendly vendor will provide "loaner" terminals on an emergency basis to ease the inevitable crisis.

## Features Specific to Printing and Display Terminals

A primary feature of printing terminals is the mechanism used to print images on paper. Some terminals use a mechanism like the IBM Selectric typewriter ball, some use a daisy-wheel printer like that made by Diablo, and some form images through use of a dot matrix. Dot-matrix printers can impact the paper through an inked ribbon, or by applying spots of heat to sensitized paper.

The choice of mechanism affects print quality and terminal operation. Print quality is usually best on Selectric-based or daisy-wheel terminals because characters are formed continuously rather than from several single points. Carbon ribbons can be used to obtain camera-ready copy. The thermal paper used in some dot-matrix printers is quite expensive, and the image may fade in a year or so. On the other hand, a simple flip of a switch will change character sets on a dot-matrix terminal, and there are fewer parts in the print mechanism.

When you're shopping for a printing terminal, check the path of the paper through the machine. Does the paper skew to one side while printing several pages continuously? Is a pinfeed platen (which holds the paper by the holes on either side) available? If you choose a pinfeed platen, can you still use the friction platen to print single sheets of bond paper?

The printhead on some terminals obscures the line currently being printed. This can be bothersome when entering text, but it is particularly frustrating when editing *APL* functions. Manufacturers have come up with several cures for this problem, but unfortunately some of the solutions only cause more problems. Some terminals have a "scroll" feature (Xerox 1700-Diablo 1600), which causes the paper to jump up an inch each time the terminal stops printing for a half-second or so. When another character comes down the line, the paper jumps back to its original position. It's fortunate that this feature is usually defeatable; for a slow typist, its effect is something like that of playing the piano on a crowded bus. On some terminals (Decwriters in particular), the printhead moves *sideways* rather than up. For the typist, this may be an improvement, but for the *APL* programmer it is a nightmare. Insertions and deletions do not occur directly above the position of the printhead, but several spaces to the right. (Or, is it to the left?)

Finally, some printing terminals are plagued by a problem called "buffer overflow", which occurs when a terminal can't keep up with its rated print speed. An overflow condition occurs when text is coming in faster than the terminal can display it, and the terminal does not have sufficient internal storage to hold the incoming text until it catches up. When this happens, the terminal may lose character text, beep loudly, or generally misbehave. Sometimes it won't function at all until you turn it off and allow it to forget the terrible trauma of buffer overflow; of course, this prevents you from signing off normally. Consider what happens when we print a typical report (see Figure 1).

```
                    UNIVERSAL DOOHICKEY, INC.
        PAGE 1                   INVOICE        1 APRIL 1980

               DESCRIPTION       PRICE   QUANTITY      EXT.
                DOOHICKEYS       $9.95           2   $19.90
                  THINGIES       $1.47          10   $14.70
                   DOODADS      $12.98           1   $12.98
              THINGAMABOBS       $6.49          10   $64.90
              ============                      ==   ======
                     TOTAL                      23  $112.48
```

**Figure 1—A Typical Report**

The *APL* system sends the report shown in Figure 1 to the terminal as a stream of characters. There is a character called RETURN which means "move the printhead back to the left margin and advance the paper one line". Doing this takes longer than printing a character like the letter "A". The same is true, to a lesser extent, of BACKSPACE and TAB characters. In our sample report, (assuming that tabs are set), the system may send

[TAB] [TAB] [BACKSPACE] *UNIVERSAL DOOHICKEY, INC.* [RETURN]
*PAGE* 1 [TAB] *INVOICE* [TAB] 1 *APRIL* 1980 [RETURN] [RETURN]

Rather than build terminals capable of executing 30 or 120 RETURNS in a second (as would be required for 30 CPS and 120 CPS terminals without any buffer capability), manufacturers incorporate a small (10- to 150-character) memory to store incoming text. Text so stored is then printed in a first-in, first-out manner. Unfortunately, this buffer sometimes gets entirely full. This is likely to happen when:

- "idle" characters are suppressed
- tabs are in use and there is a large blank space in the middle of output lines
- the text is heavily laced with overstrikes.

A good way to determine whether a particular terminal is prone to buffer overflow is to set tabs and `)TERM NOIDLES`, and then print 15 pages of workspace documentation, particularly function and cross-reference listings. The overstriking and tabbing involved in printing this type of report will exercise the terminal to its fullest. If the printed pages show symptoms such as skipped lines, unaligned tabular columns, and spurious characters, the terminal is prone to buffer overflow, and you will need to slow down its printing speed by inserting idle characters or by not using tabs.

There is greater similarity among *APL* display terminals than among printing terminals. With a single exception, all use television-type displays, storing a screenful of information in internal memory (the Tektronix 4013/4015 terminals use "storage" display tubes to prevent "TV flicker"). There are, however, some differences in the following characteristics:

- screen size
- character quality
- internal memory
- connections to auxiliary devices
- optional transmission modes.

We have already discussed display width and related features and problems. Most display terminals display 24 lines on a screen and 80 characters across each line (a notable exception is the Tektronix 4015, capable of any of the following display sizes: 35 lines by 74 characters, 38 by 81, 58 by 121, or 64 by 133). Warnings mentioned earlier about spillover of wide report lines hold here. Another consideration is the physical screen size. Display tubes in popular terminals range from 5 to 19 inches, measured diagonally. On a five-inch screen, a 64-character width leaves only one sixteenth of an inch per character—late in the day, that may be difficult to read!

Another factor affecting legibility is the quality of the character set. The number of dots per character cell (ranging from 5 by 9 in a Teleray terminal to 9 by 15 in the Hewlett/Packard 2641A) determines the absolute resolution. The choice of patterns to represent characters will vary among manufacturers. There are two basic approaches to displaying *APL* overstrikes on display terminals:

- Display any overstrike by interleaving two "screen memories".
- Maintain an internal overstrike table, displaying the appropriate character when [CHARACTER1], [BACKSPACE], [CHARACTER2] are received.

The first approach (used by Datamedia in its model 1520), allows any overstrike. If, in the future, an *APL* system were to define the overstrike of *O* and *X* as a valid character, the terminal would display *Ø* just like the simplest printer. This is an advantage, but there are also drawbacks: the extra screen memory adds to manufacturing costs, "flicker" is likely to be more noticeable, and the clarity of the pattern of overstruck characters may not be optimal.

However, if a terminal maintains a table of valid overstrikes and displays one character when a valid overstrike sequence is transmitted, a single memory can be used. This is the approach taken by Hewlett/Packard with the 2641A and by Anderson/Jacobson with the 510. When an undefined overstrike sequence is received, the H/P terminal will display *OUT* along the diagonal of the affected cell, and the AJ will display the last character sequence received. One disadvantage in displaying the last character sequence is that "security blots" (such as those displayed for the entry of passwords) are not secure. Consider what happens when you sign on to STSC's *APL∗PLUS* Service. The system overstrikes the three character sequences

```
GHBGSBHSGBSBGBS
M4M4M4M4MNMNMNM
585858HEHEHEHEH
```

to create a security blot. It then backspaces so that the entry of your user number and password

```
)1234567:SECRET
```

will be obscured. If the terminal displays the last character sequence entered, the password *SECRET* will be clearly visible.

Some display terminals have the capacity to store more than a single screenful of information in memory. The ability to recall the previous screen, or several screens, is a valuable option for programmers and those needing to display long reports.

Some display terminals can be connected to devices other than the host computer. There may be a composite video output, suitable for connection to monitors for observation by a number of people. There may be a data connection to a printer or data recorder. On some terminals, the speed of transmission to the printer may be different than that to the host computer. The user may choose to print everything coming down the line, or send a screenful of information to the printer.

When a display terminal is used for text or data entry, optional "line" or "screen" transmission modes can be very useful. In these modes, data can be sent to the host computer one line or one screen at a time, rather than character by character. The benefit is that before the data is transmitted, it may be edited "locally" without any processing from the host. When used with a "protected-fields" feature, a form can be shown on the screen, so that the user can fill in the blanks. Then the data on the screen (without the text of the form) is sent to the host computer.

## Features Specific to Different Types of Use

Different *APL* users use different features of the language, and so are concerned with different terminal features. Consider these four types of *APL* users:

- The casual interactive user—typically signs on for about one half-hour.
- The *APL* programmer—signs on for hours at a time, to develop and test code.
- The data entry operator—transcribes large amounts of information via the keyboard.
- The report printer—produces long reports at the terminal.

Most *APL* users fall into the casual interactive class. Typically, this type of user signs on to the system, enters a few items of data, and prints a one- or two-page report; he may then repeat the cycle. The total elapsed time is 15 to 30 minutes. These users typically are not *APL* experts, nor are they good typists. They place few demands on a terminal, other than that it be reliable and easy to use and that it provide good print quality.

The *APL* programmer typically signs on for several hours at a time to enter, edit, and test *APL* programs. Since the level of interaction with the computer is high, it is important that the programmer find the terminal easy to use. In addition to the fundamental features important to all users, convenience of editing, keyboard touch, and other human-engineering features are important.

The data entry operator will appreciate high transmission speeds and features supporting local editing. After several hours at the terminal, image quality also becomes very important. This type of user may not need a "true" *APL* terminal—if only numbers and normal alphabetic characters are being entered, a terminal with the ASCII character set may be a lower-cost solution.

The user printing very long reports at the terminal will be concerned with print quality, freedom from buffer overflow, and excellent paper tracking. Higher print speeds will be appreciated, as will an end-of-paper alarm.

## Paying for an *APL* Terminal

Once you have evaluated the requirements for a particular application, look at the prices of terminals fitting those requirements. You'll probably find that more features cost more money. You'll also find that terminal prices fall into the following ranges:

- around \$2000 (thermal printers, simple display terminals)
- around \$3000 (daisy-wheel printers)
- around \$4000 (120 CPS printers, feature-packed display terminals).

An important price consideration is not just *initial* cost, but *lifetime* cost; reliability is important, and a terminal for which service isn't available is no bargain at any price.

Furthermore, you needn't buy a terminal in order to have one. Many manufacturers and vendors make lease arrangements available, and a few dealers will even rent terminals on a short-term basis. Rental for a few weeks or months can be an aid during periods of heavy use, or as an extended trial before purchase.

Of the three options, rental is the most expensive. The difference between purchasing and leasing, however, isn't clear-cut. Leasing is advantageous because the owner has an interest in servicing the terminal to keep it in prime condition, and there's likely to be a cheaper, better terminal to lease for your application next year. Ownership can be cheaper, particularly when the tax advantages of depreciation are considered. A typical terminal selling for \$3000 might be available on a one-year lease for \$150 per month, maintenance included. The cost of a three-year loan at 15 percent interest is roughly \$103 per month. When the monthly cost of a maintenance contract (\$20-\$25 per month), is considered, the lease commands a premium of perhaps \$25 per month. This premimum may be worth paying, however, if you're likely to want to replace the terminal before two years are over.

## Conclusion

The wise buyer in the market for an *APL* terminal will compare features and prices, just as he would for any important purchase. By taking some time in advance to determine the needs of the terminal users, the buyer can chart a much easier course through the sometimes bewildering waters of the *APL* terminal market.

*Carl Cheney, currently an applications consultant in STSC's San Francisco office, has been with the company for almost five years. He previously worked for two years at Dallas County Community College and for two years at the University of Texas at Arlington. In 1973 he co-authored, with Harley M. Courtney, a paper titled "An Application of the Binomial Distribution to Sales Planning", which appeared in* The Proceedings of the Fifth International *APL* Users' Conference *(APL Technical Committee, 1973).*

*Cheney attended El Centro College in Dallas, Texas.*

*Scott McAuley joined STSC in 1977 as a marketing representative and is currently an applications consultant in the company's Los Angeles office. Before joining STSC he spent a summer as a junior systems analyst for Sunkist Growers, Inc., and taught APL, accounting, and finance at the UCLA Graduate School of Management.*

*McAuley has a B.A. in economics from the University of California and an M.B.A. in accounting and finance from the UCLA Graduate School of Management.*

# Index

This index references the authors of the papers in this book, along with each occurrence of selected keywords.

*This manual is typeset in 10-point Century Schoolbook and 10-point Video APL and Video **APL** Bold. The text was edited on STSC's **APL*PLUS** System using a photocomposition text editing system developed by James G. Wheeler, a design specialist for STSC. The index was prepared by STSC Vice President Allen J. Rose using the **APL*PLUS** FULLTEXT System.*

*Computerized photocomposition and page make-up were performed by Computer Data Systems, Inc., of Bethesda, Maryland.*